PARTIES AND DEMOCRACY IN THE POST-SOVIET REPUBLICS

Parties and Democracy in the Post-Soviet Republics

THE CASE OF ESTONIA

DAVID ARTER
University of Aberdeen

Dartmouth

Aldershot • Brookfield USA • Singapore • Sydney

Published by
Dartmouth Publishing Company Limited
Gower House
Croft Road
Aldershot
Hants GU11 3HR
England

Dartmouth Publishing Company
Old Post Road
Brookfield
Vermont 05036
USA

British Library Cataloguing in Publication Data
Arter David, 1944–
    Parties and democracy in the post-Soviet republics : the case of Estonia
    1. Democracy – Estonia   2. Political parties – Estonia
    3. Estonia – Politics and government – 1991–
    I. Title
    320.9'4741

Library of Congress Cataloging-in-Publication Data
Arter David.
    Parties and democracy in the post-Soviet republics : the case of
    Estonia / David Arter.
        p. cm.
    Includes bibliographical references and index.
    ISBN 1-85521-466-0
    1. Estonia–Politics and government–1991–   2. Estonia–Politics
and government.   3. Democracy–Estonia.   4. Political parties–
Estonia   5. Post-communism.   I. Title.
JN6615.A58A78   1996
320.947'41–dc20   96–14975
                                                              CIP

ISBN 1 85521 466 0

Typeset by Manton Typesetters, 5–7 Eastfield Road, Louth, Lincolnshire LN11 7AJ, UK.
Printed and bound in Great Britain by Hartnolls Limited, Bodmin, Cornwall

Contents

List of Tables

Preface

In a seminal article in 1990, Richard Katz asked: 'How have parties, their strategies, their roles in elections in particular and European democracy in general changed in response to the challenges of the last quarter of the twentieth century?' Katz's question regarding the adaptive nature and role of parties, while timely, referred only to their evolving *modus operandi* in Western Europe. The present book, however, is concerned with parties and democratisation in the post-Soviet republics. Following an introductory chapter dealing with a number of conceptual issues related to the progression from democratic transition to democratic consolidation, along with the question of party formation and party system development in post-communist Central and Eastern Europe, there is a review of the democratisation process in the major 'European states' of the former USSR. Chapter 2, in other words, concentrates on 'system change' in the 'new' successor states of Ukraine, Belarus and Moldova and 'old' (inter-war) successor states of Latvia, Lithuania and Estonia. Indeed, the primary focus of the volume is on the last-mentioned, Estonia, which re-emerged as one of the smallest states in the New Europe of post-1989, comparable in population size to Slovenia in the former Yugoslavia.

The wholesale (even uncritical) adoption of the Western 'party democracy model' across much of post-communist Europe has contributed to a striking 'legitimacy deficit'; that is, a gulf in attitude between the governors and the grassroots with regard to the role of political parties. Thus in Estonia, as elsewhere, there is, on the one hand, the evidently high level of *constitutional legitimacy* afforded parties – enshrined in the electoral law – along with their *high elite legitimacy*, that is, the belief among strategic decision makers that parties are integral to the policy process and the successful shift to a pluralist Western-style polity. On the other, there is the generally low *popular legitimacy* afforded parties and the widespread public reluctance to recognise them as legitimate instruments of representation. While it seems parties largely control the state – cabinet, parliament and the senior civil service – they have a much weaker toehold in political society and are widely mistrusted and misunderstood by voters both old and (especially) young. Estonia in fact meets all three conditions of an empirically derived *anti-party system* model, exhibiting at once relatively low levels of party voting, electors who attach at best secondary importance to the partisan allegiance of candidates, and numerically significant anti-parties (protest movements) exploiting the underlying popular prejudices against the nascent parties and party system.

A basic premise of this study is that *party building* will materially assist in *society building*, that is in developing regularised and structured patterns of civic involvement in decision making (a 'democratic society') and, by extension, in reversing the accentuated demobilisation and depoliticisation of the citizenry characterising the post-revolutionary period. The main tasks of party building are identified as *depersonalisation* and the generation of an electoral identity distinct from the 'political entrepreneur(s)' whose brainchild the party was; *organisation* and the attraction of a mass membership, coupled with intra-party decision-making structures; and *stabilisation* and the creation of stable voter–party alignments as a corollary of concentration on and seeking to promote the interests of a distinct socioeconomic support base. There have been only two elections since renewed independence – 1992 and 1995 (both analysed in this volume) – but the evidence inclines the author to speculate that, by the time of the third scheduled national poll in 1999, the Estonian party system may well be anchored to discernible cleavage structures and relatively stable configurations of interest-based parties.

This book, then, is a case study of parties and democracy in Estonia set within the broader comparative framework of developments in the post-soviet republics in particular and post-communist Central and Eastern Europe in general. It is based on eight visits to Estonia and its original material derives principally from a series of extended elite interviews undertaken over the two-year period 1993–5. In arranging the interviews I am heavily indebted to Dr Kaja Tael, the Director of the Estonian Institute, her staff at Sakala 3 in Tallinn and, above all, to Krista Kaer who accompanied me for much of my travels and provided me with a uniquely colourful and anecdotal 'Who's Who' guide to Estonian public life. The ten-hour trip from Tallinn to Tartu via Viljandi in Peep's 'car' – vintage Ukrainian – was unforgettable (and in hindsight possessed perhaps a certain allegorical significance)! Spared the ultimate indignity of running out of petrol by a lone Finnish petrol station dispensing the necessary 'two star' juice, we bumped along, effortlessly overtaken by cyclists and buses, and finally arrived in Tartu as night fell. As the lights of the city beckoned, the brakes failed, the windows steamed up and several times we stalled and lay prostrate at the mercy of oncoming vehicles from all directions. Like Estonia under communism, however, we survived to tell the tale and, as the shift to the market spawns more Volvos, Volkswagens and the rest, Peep's jalopy stands (well almost!) as a symbolic reminder of the nation's recent history. Let us hope that Estonians will become as partial to veteran car rallies as the British or at least that they will not unquestioningly pursue a Western-style route to the twenty-first century.

DAVID ARTER
Old Aberdeen, Scotland, August 1995

Acknowledgements

I am grateful to Dr Kaja Tael, the Director, and Krista Kaer of the Estonian Institute, Piret Part of the President's Office and Dr Kersti Unt of the Department of Linguistics, Tartu University, for their practical assistance in facilitating the field work upon which this book is based. I would also like to express my thanks to the following persons who gave generously of their time for interviews: K. Jaak Roosaare MP, Tiina Benno MP, Kalle Kulbok MP, Toivo Jullinen MP, Dr Uku Hänni, Dr Peeter Lorents MP, Professor Raoul Üksvärav MP, Rain Rosimannus, Krista Kilvet MP, Mati Hint MP, Olav Anton MP, Tarmu Tammerk, Dr Erik Terk, Alari Purju, Alla Kallas, Roman Kallas, Agu Laius, Heli Kask, Harri Tiido, Minister Jüri Luik, Raul Mälk, Jarno Laur, Dr Raimo Sule, Dr Rein Ruutsoo, Jaak Allik, Professor Rein Taagepera, Vello Saatpalu MP, Illar Hallaste MP, Minister Lagle Parek, Enn Tarto MP, Andes Mandre, Jüri Toomepuu MP, Tiit Made MP, Ivar Raig MP, Minister Paul-Eerik Rummo, Deputy-Speaker Tunne Kelam, Aleksei Semyonov, Mikhel Pärnoja MP, Ants Erm MP, Tiit Vähi MP, Trivimi Velliste MP, Arvo Kiir MP, Tiit Siinmaa, CSCE Ambassador Klaus Törnudd; Kullo Arjakas, Peet Kask MP, Ants-Enno Lõhmus, Arnold Rüütel, Vaino Väljas, Arvo Sirendi MP, Urmas Sepp, Ene Padrik, Minister Marju Lauristin, Priit Pallum, Alar Olljum, Andrus Saar, Juhan Kivirähk, Jüri Estam and Neeme Kunungas. Professor Michael Waller, Dr Gordon Johnstone and Enn Soorsaar read earlier drafts of this book and I profited considerably from their helpful comments.

Postscript

The only general election in the former Soviet republics since the completion of this volume was the second parliamentary election of the post-communist era in Latvia which took place on 30 September–1 October 1995. It resulted in an increasingly fragmented and polarised assembly. Despite an increase in the electoral threshold from 4–5 per cent in an attempt to enforce mergers of proto-parties, nine parties were returned to the 100-member *Saeima* compared with eight in 1993. As in Estonia six months earlier, moreover, the result represented an anti-government vote. Although no party received more than 18 seats, Latvian Way, the mainstay of the previous coalition, saw its representation more than halved from 36 seats to 17. The left of centre *Saimnieks*, led by the 35-year old former minister of the interior, Ziedonis Cevers, which was only formed in April of the election year, emerged as the leading party with 15.1 per cent and 18 seats. For opponents *Saimnieks*, like Vähi's Coalition Party in Estonia, bore the strong stamp of recycled communist. The second largest grouping, the populist, panacea-peddling and stridently anti-establishment For Latvia, led by Joahims Zigerists, was only founded in November 1994, but boasted the largest membership of 10000. The election results in full are set out below.

The Latvian general election of 30 September–1 October 1995

Party	% Poll	Seats
Saimnieks	15.1	18
Latvian Way	14.6	17
For Latvia	14.9	16
Fatherland & Freedom	11.9	14
Farmers' Union/Christian Democratic Union/Latgale Democratic Party*	6.3	8
Unity Party	7.1	8
LNNK/Greens*	6.3	8
National Harmony	5.6	6
Socialist Party	5.6	5

Source: *The Baltic Independent* 27.10–2.11.1995, p.4.
* = electoral alliance
LNNK = Latvian National Independence Party

On the evidence of the election result, Latvia still appears very much an anti-party system. First, there was the strength of personality voting and the lack of coherent party programmes. The three parties with the best showing – *Saimnieks*, For Latvia and Latvian Way – focused on their campaigns on their leading figures and so, too, did Unity, which surmounted the 5 per cent barrier. Second, anti-party sentiment was particularly strong in the countryside and the anti-party protest movement, For Latvia, emerged Toomepuu-style, as the second largest parliamentary grouping, drawing its main support from the rural poor and pensioners. Like American expatriot Toomepuu, Zigerists is an 'offcomer', born and bred in Germany where he had a history of association with radical rightist fringe groups. Indeed, as a non-Latvian speaker, he was excluded from government by President Guntis Ulmanis. Third, although the turn-out at 71.9 per cent was higher that in Estonia six months earlier, it was generally held to be both low and disappointing. Not surprisingly in view of the heightened polarisation, coalition-building proved a protracted and problematical process. Both Maris Glinbats of Latvian Way and Cevers of *Saimnieks* failed to form cabinets. Ultimately, on 21 December, Andris Škele, a non-partisan businessman, succeeded in forming a 6-party coalition comprising *Sainieks*, Fatherland and Freedom, The Latvian National Independence Party (LNNK), Latvian Way, the Unity Party and the Farmers' Union.

Elsewhere, legislation coming into effect in 1996 consolidated the role of political parties in Estonia (and also Lithuania) whilst also promoting the amalgamation of small parties. In both Estonia and Lithuania a system of state funding to political parties was introduced (in both cases the size of the subvention was made proportionate to the number of parliamentary seats a party held), whilst in Estonia a minimum of 1,000 members was required in order for a party to be able to register for elections. In Estonia the pace of party amalgamation has quickened. On 2 December 1995 the merger of the opposition-based *Isamaa* and Estonian National Independence Party (ERSP) under the name Fatherland Union was finalised, the new party being led by the former minister of economics, Toivo Jürgenson. It seems highly likely that the *Isamaa* splinter group, the Right-Wingers, will before long throw their hand in with the Fatherland Union to create a cohesive opposition party. Furthermore, in February 1996 the former caretaker prime minister, Andres Tarand, instigated a move to merge the miniscule opposition groups, the Social Democrats and Rural Centre (EMKE) as the Moderates (the name of their electoral alliance at the 1992 and 1995 general elections) and this was formalised at the end of April 1996.

Two scandals, leading in turn to the collapse of the Vahi coalition and the dismissal of the head of the armed forces, doubtless confirmed Estonians in their distrust of parties and politicians. On 11 October 1995 the Vahi government collapsed following the revelation that the minister of the interior, Edgar Savisaar, had apparently during the coalition negotiations in March instructed a private security firm to record conversations with other political leaders without their knowledge. Although Vahi returned shortly afterwards at the head of a new cabinet, embracing the Reform Party, whose leader Siim Kallas became foreign secretary, Savisaar announced his withdrawal from politics. No sooner had the dust died down on that scandal that on 3 December 1995 Lieutenant-General Aleksander Einseln was dismissed by President Meri after an acrimonious feud with the defence minister Andrus Öövel. The scandal began when an audit by the ministry of defence revealed mismanagement of funds at the army headquarters and then in a further development a high-ranking officer was arrested by police for allegedly carrying out illegal arms sales. In light of this groundswell of corruption in public office, it was not surprising that Saar poll in November 1995 revealed that 69 per cent of Estonians had no party preference and only a very small proportion of respondents were committed supporters of a political party.

Brooking the trend towards party amalgamations were the events which followed Savisaar's decision to return from political purdah after only two months. Extraordinarily, on 30 March 1996, Savisaar was re-elected Centre Party leader, claiming nearly 80 per cent of the vote (he has remained consistently the most popular politician among the Russian-speaking minority), and this prompted a breakaway 6-member 'Liberal-Centre' faction to form in the *Riigikogu* opposed to the authoritarian management style and personality cult of Savisaar. By 7 April, 40 Centre Party members were reported to have left the party in protest and on 25 May the rebels constituted themselves as a new party, the Development Party, under the leadership of Andra Veidemann. This positioned itself to the right of Savisaar and claimed to direct itself towards small- and medium-sized enterprises together with students. Two events will dominate the political scene in Estonia in autumn 1996: the municipal elections and (indirect) presidential elections (the winner needs 66 *Riigikogu* votes. While Meri is probably narrow favourite to retain his position as head of state, he will face a stiff challenge from Arnold Rüütel who was easily the most popular candidate at the first popular round of presidential voting in 1992 and again at the general election in March 1995. Ironically, in the inevitable horsetrading the rump Savisaar Centre could tilt the balance in Rüütel's favour, although the price may well prove to high for deals to be struck. Savisaar was the only person to refuse an interview to the present author (presumably suspicious of both my motives and questions), but as long as he remains prominent democratic consolidation in Estonia will certainly not lack interest.

1 From Democratic Transition to Democratic Consolidation in Post-Communist Europe

Democracy is the rule of the people. But the [Russian] people are cut off from power. People do not control their own fate. People control nothing. What is our democracy? I have said it many times. This is a false democracy. (Alexander Solzhenitsyn on his return to Russia, May 1994, *Independent on Sunday*, 29 May 1994)

In 1942 the eminent historian Hugh Seton-Watson put the arresting question: 'Is Democracy Possible in Eastern Europe?' and added 'The people may be behind us in some ways, but they are not wild savages to be permanently cowed by lion-tamers, snake-charmers and witch doctors. They are Europeans who have shown their worth in more than one historical crisis.'[1] Seton-Watson's interrogative remains pertinent more than 50 years on, for at least two reasons. First, it is a timely reminder of the lack of a democratic tradition in most of the post-communist successor states – the so-called 'democratic' parties or 'Castle Quintet' in inter-war Czechoslovakia represent a notable exception – and provides a useful antidote to facile Western assumptions of successful democratisation. Second, it points up the fact that from a Western perspective the stakes are high: if democratisation fails in the former Comecon bloc so, too, does the prospect of 'widening' the EU and/or integrating Europe in the fullest sense. Clearly then, there is an urgent need to reduce the 'democratic deficit' between the 'old' and 'new' democracies of the Two Europes, although it is much less clear if and how the West can influence the political processes in Russia and Eastern Europe.

Seton-Watson's prescription for successful democratisation in Eastern Europe was what he called 'education for citizenship': a comprehensive programme of socialisation (presumably through the schools, parties, media and so on). Such a programme remains relevant as a counter to the long years of communist socialisation and the notion of passive citizenship that entailed. However, it is only part of a more complex process. In this chapter it is suggested that, in conceptualising the progression from democratic transition to the achievement of the initial stage of democratic consolidation, three analytically distinct dimensions may be identified in each of which political parties have an important role to play: the three contiguous processes of state-building, nation building and society building. Much of the emphasis in the literature so far has been on state building; that is, the enactment of basic constitutional groundrules, the creation of an institutional framework for the exercise of power, evidence of elite cooperation in coalition formation, the existence of alternation in government and so on. State-building, then, is largely concerned with the definition of institutional structures and the formalisation of systemic procedures for the resolution of conflict in newly sovereign polities.

Yet the need for a complementary 'bottom-up', societal perspective is brought out by the existence of at least two grassroots challenges to the achievement of democratic consolidation, challenges which, incidentally, have been common to both 'Europes' in varying degrees. First, there has been the preponderance of passive citizens, especially among young persons and those under 30. Since the heady revolutionary days of 1989 demobilisation, disengagement, citizen fatigue, political apathy – call it what you will – have become widespread in post-communist Europe. Second, there has existed across the continent a significant, albeit highly volatile, body of anti-party sentiment reflected in recent years in support for the likes of Berlusconi in Italy, Zhirinovsky in the Russian Federation, Le Pen in France, Wachtmeister in Sweden and Toomepuu in Estonia. Indeed, in his study of the emergence of the Czech party system, Michel Klíma observes the way the leading personalities in public life, President Beneš during the First Republic (1918–38) and the Third Republic (1945–8) and President Havel today have embodied a strain of 'anti-party politics'. He adds that 'there dominates a climate in society in which being a member of one of the political parties signifies poor character qualities in a person'![2] It is vital, therefore, to offset the emphasis on 'democratisation from above' (state-building) with an examination of 'democratisation from below' (society-building).

Viewing a 'democratic society' as a *sine qua non*, David Beetham has insisted that a representative democracy not only permits its citizens a much greater level of political activity than the minimum involved in the vote, but also requires it to function effectively.[3] In similar vein, Attila Ágh, analysing the earliest years of the transition to democracy in central Europe, observes that 'to avoid the separation of politics and people, participation is now much more important than in the consolidated [West European] democracies.[4] On the same theme, Paul Lewis, discussing the challenges facing the post-communist region, notes that 'the common denominator has been the implicit struggle to democratise the political culture' and he adds that 'this is likely to provide a central theme of contemporary efforts to establish democracy in Eastern Europe.[5] In evaluating progress towards the development of a democratic culture, moreover, four 'performance indicators', collectively constituting a 'democratic audit', suggested by the Estonian sociologist and politician, Marju Lauristin, appear particularly useful. In somewhat modified form, they are (1) that democratic norms and laws should be known and respected by the majority of people; (2) that there should be tolerance of a variety of conflicting interests and opinions; (3) that there should be the ability to comprehend continuing political processes; and (4) that there should be a willingness and ability to participate in political life.[6] This final indicator is of paramount importance.

Indeed, this chapter largely concentrates on the challenges facing the plethora of proto-parties in Eastern Europe in the task of society-building, that is in the development of a democratic culture and in stimulating patterns of structured civic participation. On Western 'advice', post-communist Europe invested (a little uncritically perhaps) in the standard 'party democracy' model. The new post-communist elites, in short, quickly came to regard it as largely self-evident that parties are the central players, both in the smooth operation of political society and in manning the institutions of government. The Western party democracy 'orthodoxy' has been based on three main premises.

First, parties are viewed as a necessary condition of pluralist democracy and as such their status is properly enshrined in the constitution or constitution-level statute. This view finds its clearest formulation in the 1967 Party Law of the former German Federal Republic which states that: 'Parties are, in constitutional law, a necessary component of the free democratic order ... Parties shall participate in forming the will of the people in all fields of public life.'

Second, parties are charged with specific obligations, the so-called 'input functions', and consequently provide an important link between state and society. By promoting and protecting the interests of voters (interest articulation), by providing information and contributing to opinion-building (socialisation), by presenting a range of policy options (the programmatic function) and affording the possibility of membership status (the organisational function), they permit ordinary citizens at once to participate in, and exercise influence over, public policy decisions. Parties, in short, educate, activate and integrate members of political society.

Third, parties serve as principal agents in the recruitment of elites and as such contribute to resourcing and reinforcing representative democracy and accountable government. Parties provide a career channel for aspiring politicians as well as a stepping-stone to high office, both in government and in opposition. In the last context, it would be argued that parties facilitate periodic alternations in power. In sum, parties select candidates, provide voters with a choice of prospective members of parliament and ultimately contribute the personnel of parliament, cabinet and, possibly too, the central administration.

In the predominantly anti-party cultures of post-communist Europe, however, parties have not been widely regarded as 'a necessary part of the democratic process', to cite from the 1949 *grundgesetz* of the German Federal Republic. Rather, the primary challenge facing parties in the task of society-building in anti-party systems has been to generate a climate in which they are perceived as legitimate (or at least efficient) instruments of representation. Before proceeding to consider the role of parties in the process of democratic consolidation, the briefest note on the nature of the democratic transition in Eastern Europe is in order.

The Features of the Democratic Transition Process in Post-Communist Eastern Europe

In their review of the political science of democratic transition, Dean McSweeney and Clive Tempest conclude that 'there was a distinctively East European route to democracy' and they note that, compared to earlier transitions, democratisation was dependent on the relaxation of foreign control and the opposition of crowds on the streets to the old order.[7] What, then, were the striking features of the transition?

When considering the process itself, a number of points stand out. First, there was the exponential nature of the transition, which combined rapidity with a strongly diffusional or domino-like character. Communist candidates received a pounding in Poland in June 1989 and then, between October and December that year, established leaderships crumbled in the GDR, Bulgaria, Czechoslovakia and, finally, Romania. Even Yugoslavia and Albania, outside Soviet control, were caught up in the revolutionary 'knock-on effect'. Next, the transition was wholly unexpected and was not forecast by social scientists. As Paul Lewis has stated, the collapse of the GDR, the end of normalised Czechoslovakia and the mass uprising against Ceaucescu in Romania constituted 'a sea change quite unforeseen until the tidal wave actually broke'.[8]

Third, the transition to democracy was an overwhelmingly peaceful one, although events in Romania and the Soviet operation in Lithuania in January 1991 represent something of an exception. The oppositionist social movements – Solidarity in Poland, Civic Forum in the Czech Republic, The People Against Violence in Slovakia, Democratic Forum in Hungary, Sajudis in Lithuania, the Popular Fronts in Latvia and Estonia, and so on – moreover were vital both in the non-violent shift of power and in the recruitment of alternative leaders. Finally, and crucially, there was the sheer scale of the transition process in Central and Eastern Europe. This may be described as 'twin-track', in the sense that the post-communist successor states sought to make the simultaneous shift to a competitive polity and competitive economy without a significant tradition of democracy or capitalism. Political change, to be sure, advanced more quickly than economic reform, with the result that the first free elections after the collapse of communism were staged before the privatisation of property had really got under way.

As to the preconditions of democratic transition, the communist economies were struggling and compared increasingly unfavourably with the affluent lifestyle of the Western market systems which were viewed nightly on West German television by the neighbouring East Germans and on Finnish television by the population of Tallinn across the Baltic Sea in Estonia. True, unemployment characterised the West European economies in the late 1980s but, in the case of the Soviet Union and its satellites, there was only a limited outlet for educated persons in the tertiary sector. Latent social strains were the inevitable consequence. Industrial plant, moreover, was badly dated, while the barter trade arrangements which existed between the Comecon states isolated communist Eastern Europe to a degree from the world economy. Moscow's shift to hard currency transactions in January 1990, an attempt to attract strong currencies and foreign investment by diversifying its oil exports, was belated recognition that the communist system could no longer afford to be introspective and, in commercial terms, incestuous.

In their examination of the specific causes of the disintegration of the Soviet empire in Eastern Europe, McSweeney and Tempest, as noted, underline the salience of two factors which, they claim, differentiated democratic transition in that region from earlier transitions. First, they emphasise the role of external factors and the relaxation of foreign control. The behaviour of the Soviet Union, concomitant with the advent of Gorbachev and the abandonment of the Brezhnev doctrine, they contend, meant a loosening of the imperial reins and left the indigenous elites unprotected and exposed. Second, they stress the opposition of crowds on the streets which, it is argued – with the exception of Hungary – was decisive in the breakdown of communist systems in Eastern Europe. Mass revolutionary action, moreover, is seen as an independent force for change, rather than merely a corollary of elite divisions.[9] Von Beyme, however, is unconvinced: the 'velvet revolutions' in Eastern Europe, he claims, were basically the work of intellectuals and their followers in ad hoc demonstrations. Most of society, especially in the provincial towns and countryside, remained apathetic.[10] Rather than taking sides on the question of whether mass opposition was the cause or the effect of elite disunity, Ágh in the article cited earlier, prefers to stress the inefficiency of the established communist leadership, coupled with the fact they would no longer be able to compensate for domestic weakness with the help and support of the Soviet Union.

The Emergence of Party Democracy in Post-Communist Europe

Pursuing the elemental question, 'What were the principal features of the transition from monopolistic communism to pluralist democracy in Eastern Europe?' a little further, at least three compound parts can be identified. First, how long did the process take; that is, what timescale did it cover? Second, what role did the ruling communist party play in the simultaneous shift to a pluralist polity and market economy? Finally, where did the embryonic parties originate?

It is fair to assert that across Eastern Europe there were notable contrasts in the length of the transition to pluralist democracy based on political parties and indeed the role of the ruling Communist Party in that process. For example, in Slovenia the transition was relatively protracted. The 'movement society' of 1982–9, characterised by the interplay of a diverse range of social movements, spawned an agenda – including such basic issues as human rights, equality between the sexes, peace and the environment – which was then adopted by the embryonic political parties in the early 1990s.[11] Other 'slow lane' democratic transitions included Hungary and the Baltic states, the latter throwing up, in 1987–8, ecological and popular front movements whose ostensible rationale was support for Gorbachev's programme of *perestroika*. In contrast, there were 'fast-track' transitions in, *inter alia*, Czechoslovakia and the German Democratic Republic which involved insurgent crowds on the streets demanding immediate political change. In Bulgaria political reform only really began with the fall of the communist leader Todor Zhivkov – after 35 years in post – on 10 November 1989. It was only some months thereafter that the Communist Party's 'leading role' was abolished.

In several of the successor states of the Yugoslav and Soviet federations – Slovenia and Lithuania are cases in point – modernising

Communist Parties assumed a nationalist guise in their search for continued legitimacy, broke with the imperial centres in Moscow and Belgrade and, thereafter, assured (at least) their short-term electoral futures by changing their name. Thus, by 1989, the Slovenian Communist Party, ultimately succumbing to the pressure for sociopolitical change exerted by the 'movement society', came under a reformist leadership which advocated pluralism and decentralisation within the Yugoslav republic. Significantly, on 21 January 1990 Slovene delegates walked out of the fourteenth congress of the Yugoslav League of Communists; the party subsequently assumed the name Party of Democratic Renewal and became the strongest individual party at the first free elections in spring 1990.

Some Communist Parties in the USSR, in contrast, split along ethnic lines and/or over the question of continued membership of the union, with hardline elements supporting counternationalist positions out of fear of the implications for the Russian minority of the achievement of nation-statehood. Within the Communist Party of the Soviet Union itself, there was division between a pro-Gorbachev reformist wing and a conservative wing under Yegor Ligachev. Not all mainstream (as compared to hardline) Communist Parties, moreover, changed their name before the first free elections. In June 1990, less than seven months after the 'velvet Revolution' that had swept communism away, the Czech Communist Party polled just under 14 per cent in the Czech Republic, second only behind Civic Forum, and 16.3 per cent in Slovakia, third behind The Public Against Violence and the Christian Democratic Movement.

Many of the proto-parties of post-communist Europe emerged from fissures in the 'movement society' as a consequence of the fragmentation in the Fronts and Forums that had contested power at the first free democratic elections. Typically, Solidarity in Poland split by July 1990; the Civic Forum in the Czech states did likewise in February 1991. As Vaclav Havel subsequently noted: 'The historical task of Civic Forum was to put an end to totalitarian oppression and open a new space for democracy leading thus, quite naturally, to a rise in political parties of various persuasions.'[12] The Civic Forum itself split into the Civic Democratic Party (ODS), the Civic Democratic Alliance (ODA) and the Civic Movement (OH).

Some of the 'successor parties' aligned themselves with Western party families, as in the case of christian democrats, liberal democrats and social democrats, although the success of the 'historic parties' was often relatively limited. In Bulgaria, to be sure, the communists, rechristened the Socialist Party, won 45.6 per cent and became the largest single party at the parliamentary elections in June 1990. Indeed, earlier the same year they had organised the 'round table' talks which led to the initial democratisation process. After the 1990 general election, the Socialist Party (BSP) contrived cleverly to incorporate the anti-communist Union of Democratic Forces – UDF (a coalition of more than ten proto-parties, established in 1989) into the political system while still controlling the main levers of power. It also engineered an astute tactical compromise by supporting the opposition leader Jelyu Jelev as president. By the third post-communist parliamentary election in December 1994, the BSP (in alliance with the Agrarian Party – Aleksander Stamboliiski and the Ecoglasnost Party), appealing to the 'casualties' of the marketisation process, polled 43.5 per cent to become by far the largest single force, well ahead of the 24 per cent of the UDF.[13] In Poland division in the former ruling Polish United Workers' Party led the strongest splinter group to appropriate the social democracy label with some success. In Hungary, too, the redesignated communists in the guise of the Socialist Party won over 10 per cent of the vote in March–April 1990 and became the third strongest force in Budapest and the areas dominated by heavy industry.

Generally though, the transition to democracy was accompanied by *atomised party systems*: a proliferation of miniscule groupings, most issue-based (that is, glorified pressure groups) rather having pretensions to a cohesive ideology. At the June 1990 elections, The Electoral Grouping of Interest Associations in the Czech Republic sought to represent beekeepers', anglers', animal breeders' and gardeners' clubs, while the Movement for Civic Freedom incorporated a range of causes, among them gay rights and pacifism.[14] The embryonic parties in general had only a very weak popular identity. Their support was often paltry when compared with the social movements that contested the first democratic elections. In Romania in May 1990, the National Salvation Front (renamed communists) under Ion Iliescu polled two-thirds of the parliamentary vote, the ethnic Hungarian Democratic union 7.2 per cent, the urban professional National Liberals under Radu Câmpeanu 6.4 per cent; none of the other 68 'parties' (including an Ecological Movement and Ecological Party, Social Democratic Party and Socialist Democratic Party) competing in the Chamber of Deputies election received more than 3 per cent.[15] A measure of the advance towards democratic consolidation, it is assumed here, is the replacement of atomised party systems with more stable party configurations.

The Analytical Dimensions of Democratic Consolidation

In the consolidation of democracy in Eastern Europe, three parallel, albeit not necessarily complementary, processes may be identified. First, there is the process of state building. As noted, state building involves the generation and formal legitimation (by means of either a popular referendum or the enactment of a provisional assembly) of the constitutional regulations of the newly sovereign polity. By 'newly sovereign' is meant those states regaining independence (the Baltic republics), those acquiring it for, effectively, the first time (Ukraine, Belarus, Slovenia and so on) *and* those satellites freeing themselves from the direct or indirect influence of Moscow (Poland, Hungary and so on). The primary constitutional prescriptions relate to the institutional arrangements and the formal distribution of power within the state, *inter alia* between legislature and executive (whether it is a parliamentary or presidential system), centre and regions (unitary or federal) and so on.

The process of state-building generally covered the period 1989–93. Particular arrangements reflected a trial of strength between the key players, the social movements and embryonic parties, often centred on the validity of reviving either wholly or in part earlier constitutions, although in all the post-communist states republican forms of government were adopted (compare the constitutional monarchies in some of the inter-war successor states). The powers of the head of state were often disputed, notably in the Russian Federation, where the new Yeltsin constitution was approved at the same time as Duma elections in December 1993. Outside Bosnia, the process of state-building was effectively completed by 1994.

Most of the new post-communist systems inevitably emerged as multi-ethnic states, with a Russian-speaking diaspora dispersed through the Baltic (constituting as much as 45 per cent of Latvia's 2.8 million population) and the countries of the Commonwealth of Independent States (CIS); nearly three million ethnic Hungarians spread through Romania, Slovakia, Serbia, Ukraine, Croatia and Slovenia (see Table 1.1); and various frontier or enclave minorities such as the German-speakers in Silesia on the Polish–German border and the Albanians in Kosovo in Serbia complicating the picture. Communist repression had largely held ethnic conflict in check, but the collapse of communism released enormous potential – realised most dramatically in the imbroglio in former Yugoslavia – for ethnic violence. Sporadic ethnic unrest has occurred elsewhere. Hence, although ethnic Magyars cooperated with Romanians in overthrowing the Ceaucescu regime in Romania, ethnic violence broke out in Tirgu Mures in March 1990 when the former communists controlling the state tactically adopted nationalist causes. Ethnic cleavages in (post-communist) new states may be accommodated within the emergent party system. For example, the 7 per cent Hungarians in Romania, largely concentrated in Transylvania, are represented by the Magyar Democratic Union. However, when not contained within the party system, ethnic tensions may spawn secessionist demands.

Table 1.1   The Magyar diaspora in Central Europe

State	Official estimate	Hungarian estimate
Romania	1 600 000	2 000 000
Slovakia	567 000	650 000
Serbia	340 000	400 000
Ukraine	160 000	200 000
Croatia	25 000	40 000
Slovenia	8 500	10 000
Total	2 700 500	3 300 000

Within the republics of the former Soviet Union in particular, the existence of secessionists sentiments, invariably encouraged from Moscow as part of a destabilisation strategy, threatened the territorial arrangements of several of the successor states. The Crimea, home of the Black Sea fleet, which was transferred from the Russian Federation to the Ukraine in 1954 as a gift from Nikita Khrushchev and at present comprising 70 per cent ethnic Russians, is a case in point. In the crippled coalfields of Donetsk and Lugansk the 'unionists' have openly demanded the restoration of Russian as the official language, while at the political level separatist feelings are orchestrated by the Crimean president, Yuri Meshkov, a lawyer and former KGB border guard. In contrast, the remnants of the peninsula's indigenous Tartar population have become increasingly alarmed by the drift towards Moscow. Deported to central Asia by Stalin in the 1940s, over one-quarter of a million Tartars returned with financial assistance from the Ukrainian government in Kiev.[16]

The existence of at least two Ukraines was clearly mirrored in the results of the first round of voting in the March–April 1994 general election. Out of 79 deputies elected at the first round (those who gained an absolute constituency majority), 27 were communists and their allies, principally from the industrialised and pro-Russian east of the country, whereas Kiev and the west returned in the order of 20 market reformers and democratic nationalists, together with a handful of ultra-nationalists.[17] In states like Ukraine and Belarus, the objects of long-term Russification and lacking both a unifying language spoken by a majority of the population and a previous history of independence, with its myths and symbols, a second macro-process has assumed paramount importance in seeking to give a necessary measure of stability to the new state – the process of nation building.

The process of nation building involves creating a sense of national (collective) identity among citizens as a means of seeking the necessary measure of popular allegiance to state arrangements. It usually entails the deployment of suitably unitarian symbols (language, religion, history and so on) as 'resources' capable of mass mobilisation. Attention to nation building is likely to be greatest in those states which lack a previous history of independence (except, perhaps, as a short-lived, wartime puppet regime) and/or an indigenous language spoken by a majority of citizens. Here intensive schooling programmes in the native language have been the norm. Equally, nationalism (a counter-ideology under communism) has formed part of the armoury of the ruling class often directed tactically against one or more ethnic minority. The former Slovakian prime minister Vladimir Meciar's campaign against the Magyar minority in the new state – and his purported belief that Hungary is seeking to recover territory in Slovakia, Romania and Serbia stripped from it by the 1920 Trianon Treaty – was largely designed to bolster a sense of Slovakian nationality.[18]

Economic conditions can, of course, complicate the task of nation-building. By March 1994 the Ukrainian coupon, the *Karbovanets*, launched at parity with the Russian rouble, was worth barely one-twentieth of the Russian currency and, with 85 per cent of the population living below the poverty line, 40 per cent favoured reunification with Russia.

Although the propagation of a strident (Meciar-style) nationalism may well characterise elements within the new political class, nation-building, it is contended here, involves effecting a satisfactory accommodation between dominant and subject nationalities within a state, that is, achieving the necessary degree of *national integration*. In this respect, the process of nation building is far from complete and the problems of national integration, unresolved from the inter-war period, remain to be resolved. Much has revolved around the question of citizenship.

Eastern Europe before 1989 comprised a bloc of one-party states in which the monopolistic or hegemonic Communist or Socialist Party controlled the apparatus of the state, through both its stranglehold on the means of coercion and, more routinely, its vast *nomenklatura* network, and dominated, if it did not entirely emasculate, political society. Elections, though widespread, were 'non-competitive', being designed essentially to legitimize Communist Party control. Against this backdrop, it was not perhaps surprising that, when the 1989 autumn revolutions facilitated competitive elections and the advent of liberal democracy, Eastern Europe was made up of a series of weak political societies. A central challenge of these post-communist states, therefore, has been the *process of society building*.

More than five years on, despite the bestowal of democratic rights and liberal freedoms, political society remains fundamentally weak.

Above all, citizens are generally passive and experience low levels of subjective competence: they feel largely unable to bring influence to bear on the direction of public affairs. Many, indeed, lack trust and confidence in the political system. For example, when, in the Baltic Omnibus survey in November–December 1993, Latvians were asked what they would do in the event of the government considering a measure they perceived to be 'very unjust and harmful', 51.5 per cent replied 'nothing'; 13.5 per cent did not know; only 7.3 per cent claimed they would act through an informal group; and 3.0 per cent said they would make direct contact with the press or political elite. Answers such as 'act through a political party or formal (interest) group' constituted less than 0.5 per cent of the sample.[19] In many ways, the irony of the low subjective competence of citizens in the new democracies of Central and Eastern Europe lies in the fact that people often feel even more politically marginalised than they did under communism. In Slovenia in November 1993, 71.2 per cent of those questioned felt they had no influence over decisions on important social problems, while over 80 per cent saw politics as merely a struggle for power.[20]

Moreover, with the old certainties and simplicities of the communist era gone, citizens in the Central and East European states have tended to find the 'new democratic politics' confusing and even bewildering. In Bill Miller *et al.*'s survey of attitudes in Russia, Ukraine, Hungary, Slovakia and the Czech Republic at the end of 1993, 81 per cent agreed that 'politics is so complicated that I cannot understand what is going on'.[21] Moreover, Gerlach *et al.*'s study in the early 1990s revealed that significant numbers of citizens – 19 per cent in Poland, 18 per cent in Hungary and 9 per cent in Czechoslovakia – believed that 'one party was sufficient'![22] As in Western Europe, *politikverdrossenheit* is widespread. When, in March 1994, 14 Estonian parties met in Tallinn it was significant that one of the agenda items was an exploration of the reasons politicians enjoyed such low prestige among voters.[23]

As noted earlier, the transition to democracy witnessed a plethora of proto-parties. Typically, there were 65 registered parties at the time of the Hungarian parliamentary elections in March–April 1990 and more than 30 other parties and political movements were reported in the press.[24] But in these post-communist systems, parties have largely been unable to bridge the yawning gap between the (predominantly partisan) elites controlling the state and the grass-roots of society, while (apart from the Pensioners' Association and some embryonic trade unions) pressure groups have yet to emerge. In short, the linkage structures remain weak. Partisanship is low by Western standards, parties are widely seen as unrepresentative of public opinion and the nascent multi-party systems are encountering problems of legitimacy.

The average level of partisanship in Miller *et al.*'s five-nation survey was 27 per cent – half that in Britain – whereas 58 per cent complained that 'none of the existing parties represents the interests and views of people like me'. In contrast to 38 per cent of Czech respondents who declared themselves to be 'party supporters', the figure for Ukraine was only 14 per cent. In fact 37 per cent of Ukrainians rejected a multi-party system, something reflected perhaps in the fact that voters in the Western Kiev constituency of Leningradsky at the March 1994 general election (first round ballot) were confronted with a choice of 31 names, only eight of whom declared a party affiliation. The independents included the director of a local car park, a carpenter, an electrician and a woman representing the mothers of fallen soldiers from the Afghan war.[25]

Across Central and Eastern Europe there is a striking contrast between the high levels of mass mobilisation of the revolutionary period and the accentuated demobilisation which has followed it. Approximately one million Lithuanians took part in the 23 August 1989 'Baltic Way' demonstration against the secret articles of the Ribbentrop–Molotov Pact and this included an estimated 60 per cent of all persons with a higher (university-level) education.[26] Yet in her analysis of the 'velvet divorce' between the Czech Republic and Slovakia in January 1993, Karen Henderson notes the passivity (low subjective competence) of citizens when faced with an impending division of a Czechoslovak republic which it was claimed they did not support. She attributes the widespread disillusion and feelings of powerlessness among citizens in large measure to a perception of the interminable elite conflict associated with democratic politics. Popular inexperience of pluralist politics and the protracted process of deliberation and negotiation needed to reconcile conflicting interests, she notes, may have contributed to the onset of 'citizen fatigue'. Put crudely, if the politicians were determined to create two states they should get on with it, as long as this did not involve violence.[27]

In his study of political alienation in the Baltic states – which he observes is especially great in Latvia – Mikhael Rodin attaches much importance to the legacy of communist socialisation, although the high socioeconomic costs of the transition to a market economy can hardly be ignored.[28] However, entrenched patterns of socialisation predating the revolutionary period do not explain another marked feature of the weak post-communist societies of Central and Eastern Europe: the demobilisation of young persons. Typically, in the Duma elections in the Russian Federation in December 1993, twice as many persons aged under 25 abstained or voted against all parties as in the other age groups and in Moscow 60 per cent of young people did not vote. Doubtless this was in part because the salience of politics, previously a means to liberation or, elsewhere in the region, independence, declined and came to be seen as increasingly irrelevant. In part, too, it probably related to the perceived inability of the politicians to deliver a better society (free from crime, violence, poverty and so on). As the 24-year-old Muscovite Jaana Orleanskaya stated: 'At the beginning I believed in some change for the better, but now I want to organise my own life. My faith has disappeared over the last six months and now I have stopped taking any interest in politics. I only believe in my own energy and effort.'[29] During the revolutionary and immediate post-revolutionary period in Central and Eastern Europe, in contrast, the citizenry was in general highly politicised. For example, in a survey conducted in Lithuania in June 1992 – barely nine months after regaining full independence – only 11 per cent of respondents declared themselves not interested in politics.[30]

Even the most cursory review of the evidence would thus suggest that there are three central challenges for society-building in post-communist Europe:

1. creating a heightened sense of subjective competence among citizens and more general trust in the political institutions of the newly sovereign states;
2. developing patterns of collective participation in multiple public organisations – compare the isolation of individuals under communism – and thus the creation of effective linkage networks;
3. promoting a social consensus around the values of liberal democracy.

In this latter connection, there is a widespread assumption in the West of a connection between parties and democratisation in post-communist Europe. As early as 1990, Geoffrey Pridham observed: 'In Eastern Europe it is already clear that political parties are crucial actors in the transitions to liberal democracy from Communist state systems and act as a guarantee of the new political pluralism.'[31] He added that the stage of democratic transitions was complete not simply when a new constitution was enacted, but when the system operated with a popularly elected government. The emergence of embryonic parties has, indeed, been part of a response to strong Western pressure to democratise. It has represented a statement of good intent, so to speak. Equally, the main West European party families have adopted their fraternal fledglings in Eastern Europe and sought to sponsor their development with funding and other forms of 'technical assistance'. For example, there were moves early in 1993 in the European Democratic Union (EDU) to promote the creation of a Conservative Party in Russia – still essentially a nation of clans – but, despite lip-service to the idea from President Yeltsin, nothing came of it.

Clearly, a primary function of parties in post-authoritarian systems is the recruitment of an accountable and, by extension, renewable political elite as an alternative to rule by non-responsible groupings such as the army, church or, indeed, organised criminal associations. The emphasis here is on *the role of parties in state-building*. In other words, the focus is on their participation in constructing the legal framework of the new state by prescribing the basic rules and regulations (constitution making); the recruitment of officials to replace the old *nomenklatura* (elite renewal); and the contribution of the parties to the effective management of the affairs of state in terms of elite cooperation in, *inter alia*, government formation and policy making. There can be no question that the responsible and effective use of power can serve to legitimise democracy. Equally, parties perform a crucial task in organising, mobilising and socialising citizens and, in this way, in internalising democracy at the grassroots. The focus here is on the politics of linkage and *the role of parties in society-building*.

Parties, Party Building and Society-Building

The embryonic party systems of post-communist Europe remain weakly internalised and are generally viewed with much the same degree of mistrust shown towards other political institutions such as the government. Russia exemplifies the point. It was significant that, whereas at the Supreme Soviet elections in the Russian Federation in March 1990, 85 per cent of candidates were Communist Party candidates (some, to be sure, reformist-minded), no less than 60 per cent of candidates at the Duma elections on 12 December 1993 described themselves as 'independents'.[32] Indeed, a party system had signally failed to develop by the last-mentioned date. The only party with a significant membership and broad support base (encompassing the Far East, regions dominated by the military–industrial complex and frontier territories) was Vladimir Zhirinovsky's Liberal Democrats, founded in March 1990, which emerged as the largest single party, with 24 per cent of the electorate. It polled well among servicemen in the Black Sea fleet and Kaliningrad enclave, troops on the Tajik–Afghanistan border and ethnic Russians in Narva in north-east Estonia.[33] In trading off a widespread psychological resentment at Russia's loss of status as a superpower and economic resentment at the efforts of prime minister Yegor Gaidar's 'shock therapy' marketisation programme (one-third of the population lived below the official poverty line), the Liberal Democrats appeared – despite the word 'party' in their title – more an 'anti-party' than a conventional party. Never previously a communist, Zhirinovsky's pronouncements on the return of Russia to its 'natural historic borders' – annexing parts of

Finland, Poland, Ukraine and even Alaska – were too extreme even for the National Salvation Front.[34]

Across Central and Eastern Europe, the notion of party was, of course, widely associated with *the party* – the ruling Communist Party and the elitist bastion of privilege it represented – and, accordingly, was viewed with suspicion by ordinary citizens. As Frances Millard has noted, at the 1990 local elections in Poland the 'non-party' independent label was used as a way of disguising party allegiance, since this was seen in some areas as an obstacle to success.[35] The revolutionary social movements, of course, went under the name of 'Fronts', 'Forums' and so on, but these fragmented relatively quickly. By July 1990, as noted, Solidarity in Poland (which was founded in August 1980) had split, torn apart by a combination of personal ambition and ideological division. As in the case of the Popular Front in Estonia, many of its parliamentarians were also members of the nascent political parties. Moreover, a deep rift was created when the Centrum faction backed Lech Walesa for president, while another internal grouping, ROAD, the Citizens Movement for Democratic Action (which had emerged in July 1990) favoured the prime minister, Tadeusz Mazowiecki.

Significantly, though, a number of the 'successor parties' emerging from the factionalisation and fragmentation of the 'movement societies' avoided the international loan word 'party' in their designation. For instance, when the Hungarian Democratic Forum (MDF) which originated in a meeting at Lakitelep on 27 September 1987 – organised by opposition intellectuals, including Imre Pozsgay, at the home of Sandos Lezsek – became a party (rather than political–intellectual movement) in June 1989, it retained its original name.[36] The inaugural meeting in autumn 1987 consisted of populist writers, intellectuals and members of the reform wing of the Communist Party, most prominently Pozsgay, all of whom emphasised the uniqueness of the Hungarian past and entertained the possibility of a 'third way'. By 1989, when the party was formed, christian democratic and liberal influences were also in evidence. Prior to the 1990 election, however, the leadership of the Hungarian Democratic Forum distanced itself from 'third wayism' and the reform communists. Throughout this period, Pozsgay sought to deploy the MDF to promote the views of the Communist Party's reform wing, while for the literati the association with the reformist communists, especially Pozsgay, provided legitimacy and reduced the likelihood of harassment.[37]

The embryonic party systems of post-communist Europe also contained parties of 'irresponsible opposition', peddling simplistic solutions to the complex problems thrown up by rapid socioeconomic transition. In addition to Zhirinovsky's Liberal Democrats in the Russian Federation, other populist and radical nationalist groups emerged across the region – as much social movement as conventional party – seeking to exploit the potent electoral mix of economic misfortune and political discontent by presenting themselves as opposed to the new party establishment. Thus, in Poland, Andrzej Lepper's Self-Defence (*Samoobrona*) exhorted the losers from the marketisation process, the 'working people, impoverished, exploited and injured' to defend themselves and, in a style reminiscent of Henri Dorgères in the French Third Republic in the 1930s, employed direct action (including blockading major roads with convoys of lorries and tractors) to assert the case for cheap investment credits and the central direction of agriculture. Lepper also canvassed against a dependence on the West from where, he insisted, Poland had received 'only beer kiosks, sex shops and porno films'.[38]

It was a measure of the weak popular allegiance towards, and impatience with, the new party establishment (as well as a reaction against the social costs of modernisation) that reformist communists had gained power in Poland and Lithuania by 1992–3. Indeed, it may be appropriate to describe a shift across Central and Eastern Europe from one-party to anti-party systems. The challenge of the pro-system parties in an anti-party system is to work to create a political culture in which parties are accepted as legitimate instruments of representation and interest articulation. The assumption is that the better parties are able to perform their classical input functions, that is, the more effective the party-building process, the greater their contribution to society-building and the creation of a culture of civic participation.

As an ideal type, an *anti-party system* may be defined by reference to three key conditions:

1. that partisan allegiance provides the basis of candidate choice for only a minority of active voters at general elections. Put another way, for more than half of those going to the polls, the party affiliation of candidates is of (at best) secondary importance in determining how they cast their vote;
2. that non-voting describes the electoral behaviour of at least one-third of the electorate: in short, turnout should be 66 per cent or below;
3. that there exists an 'anti-party' or 'anti-parties', diametrically opposed to the agenda and style of the other fledgling parties.

As in Western Europe, it is not possible to give a strict definition of an anti-party in Eastern Europe. A number of features, however, may contribute to identifying the genus. First, in common with its West European counterpart, an anti-party in post-communist Europe seeks to trade off the deep mistrust, cynicism and lack of confidence in parties and politicians, together with the low levels of subjective competence experienced by voters. It thus presents itself as diametrically different in style from the other parties, may well have movemental characteristics and will be society-oriented rather than state-centred. Second, the East European anti-party will be implicitly or explicitly opposed to the old elites – with their past in the clientelistic culture of communism – currently leading the new parties. Anti-parties offer 'new blood', a 'clean licence' and 'national cleansing'. Third, anti-parties will tend to peddle simplistic, at times draconian solutions to complex problems. They will carry little ideological baggage, lack fraternal groupings in the West and have very low coalition potential.

A low level of partisanship in determining voter choice and, by extension, a cultural predisposition against political parties may be regarded as the distinctive feature of an anti-party system although, while a necessary condition, it is not a sufficient condition of one. Electoral abstentionism or support for the 'sleeping party' is also a relevant dimension, as too is the presence of one or more anti-parties.

Interestingly, in noting its prevalence across Central and Eastern Europe, Danica Fink-Hafner has distinguished between old and new anti-party feeling. Anti-party sentiment, in the sense of criticism of the system and the ruling Communist Party, was an element in old regime politics. However, new anti-party sentiment, at least in Slovenia, she notes, derives from a sense among the people that the party elites do not care sufficiently about the basic living conditions and prospects of ordinary citizens. Furthermore, the new party elites still fight over ideological and historical issues and have not recognised the need for developing a policy orientation.[39]

A central assumption in this study is that the anti-party system is a transitional, developmental stage between a one-party system and the emergence of institutionalised multipartism. It occurs on a time spectrum between 'democratic transition' and 'democratic consolidation' and raises the central question of the interrelationship between the development of parties and the development of democracy. Clearly, during periods of accelerated social and economic transition, with the attendant likelihood of an increase in conflict intensity, parties serve as an important link between state and society – an antidote to non-conventional political behaviour – and as an agency in promoting a stable relationship between governors and governed. They are, in short, central to democratic consolidation.

Post-communist Europe: Party Systems without Cleavage Structures

When considering the contribution of parties to democratisation, it is important to distinguish the process of *party-formation* – the cycle (variable in length) from conception to creation – and the process of *party-building* – the cycle from inception to institutionalisation. Party formation, it is contended here, is bound up with the period of democratic transition, whereas party-building is associated with the stage of democratic consolidation. The formation of political parties in post-communist Europe have been the subject of several research projects which have concentrated on the Czech Republic, Slovenia, Hungary and Poland, leaving the Baltic states and Estonia (the main focus of this book) untouched.[40] In any event, it is suggested here that party formation, which embraces the span from the birth of the idea to the birth of the party, can be subdivided into three analytically distinct stages (although, in practice, a measure of conflation is quite possible).

First, there is the *origination* of the party. The relevant question here is: how and in what circumstances was the idea of the party conceived? Was it the result of a personal initiative, an organisational venture or something else? Next, there is the period of *gestation* of the notion of the party. The relevant issues here concern the germination and development of the seeds of the idea, the procedures for advancing it, the mobilising and coordinating of a body of activists and so on. Finally, there is the *foundation* of the party. This involves consideration of when and where it was created and for what purpose.

Party-building, the secondary stage in the mutation of political parties, has remained a surprisingly neglected field in West European politics. Of course there have been a few case studies. Robert Harmel and Lars Svåsand have analysed the phenomenon in relation to the *entrepreneurial issue party* – a party formed, not from a social movement, but rather by one person who does not hold a position in the government. Concentrating on the Progress Parties in Denmark and Norway, created by Mogens Glistrup and Anders Lange, respectively, they conclude that the process of institutionalisation appeared complete when, having identified and communicated their message to voters and developed an organisation, the parties stabilised themselves on the political spectrum and achieved the threshold of coalition potential, that is 'relevance' in Sartori's terms.[41]

Very few studies bearing (even indirectly) on party-building in a post-communist state have appeared, not least perhaps because the process remains in its infancy. Stephen Silva's analysis of the Social Democratic Party (SPD) in eastern Germany (the former German Democratic Republic) is, however, illuminating. In it he identifies the major structural constraints placing the SPD at a long-term disadvantage in the five new east German *länder* and creating what he terms as 'eastern deficit' or *Ostgefälle* in the party. One of these is the legacy of the long period of Socialist (SED) rule and although the SPD constitutes an extreme case, all the political parties in eastern Germany, he concludes, are experiencing difficulty in attracting and retaining members.[42] Despite the lack of a literature upon which to draw, the need for a generalised model of party-building in post-communist systems is suggested by the existence of at least three common denominators:

1. all the parties are effectively starting from scratch and have originated in the last five years;
2. all seek to institutionalise themselves in weak civil societies, often with little or no pre-communist tradition of democracy and pluralist party politics;
3. all operate in (at least relatively) poor countries struggling to make the shift to a competitive market economy. It cannot be doubted that the extent of the success of the economic reform programmes will have a bearing on the perceived legitimacy of the democratic process and the success of party-building.

With the above in mind, three stages in an empirically derived model of party-building – that is, the institutionalisation of parties in Eastern Europe – can be delineated.

First, there is *depersonalisation*, that is the functional imperative to develop and communicate a message, and thus an identity, distinct from the 'notable(s)' founding the party and with whom it has become largely synonymous. This will almost certainly entail the *ex post facto* generation of programmes and policies informed by a common set of principles and relevant to the needs of one or more selected social constituencies. It may also involve a change of party name and/or leadership.

Second, there is *organisation*, that is promoting the party as a voluntary membership organisation, with rules and structures relating to the participation and influence of members in decision making. In anti-party systems with low living standards, even a nominal levy could, of course, act as a deterrent and a high voter–member ratio may be unrealistic in anything less than the medium term. Nonetheless, incentives in attracting a core of active members (party 'militants') might include the possibility of nomination of candidates in local or national elections; participation in the selection of candidates and party decision making; and the prospect of benefiting from other types of party patronage. Still, it seems highly likely that the East European parties will develop as governing organisations – based on their representatives holding office in government or the national parliament – far more (quickly) than as voluntary membership organisations.[43]

Finally, there is the *stabilisation* phase, that is the development of a stable and coherent social support base which in turn contributes to the emergence of regularised patterns of partisan alignment. In a wider sense, the formation of entrenched configurations of partisan allegiance may be considered an important indicator of progress from the stage of democratic transition to democratic consolidation. Particularly salient, it is held, is the incidence of *sectional parties* representing distinct socioeconomic clienteles, in contrast to parties grouped around the nationalist issue and questions linked to regime building. As the former Estonian Communist Party's ideological secretary, Mikk Titma, noted pertinently: 'These will surely be the last elections [1992] in which politicians can make headway by attempting to mobilise the "nation" as a whole on the basis of anti-communist, pro-independence slogans. From now on, it will be necessary to define one's political appeal more closely and to be linked to particular interest groups or social classes.'[44]

Implicit support for the need for progression along the lines of the aforementioned party-building model could be gained from Viktor Davidkin's critique of Yegor Gaidar's Russia's Democratic Choice – a merger of two existing proto-parties – founded in June 1994.[45] Concerned that a personality party was being created, Davidkin argued that three fundamental questions were in need of resolution: (1) would the new party be based on personality or ideology (the challenge of depersonalisation); (2) would the new party create a national network of local branches (the challenge of organisation); (3) which section(s) of society should the new party aim to win over (the challenge of stabilisation, namely building stable bases of partisan allegiance)?

One such class party has already begun to reassert itself on the East European stage: the agrarian party. Thus a Peasants' Party has emerged in Croatia, boasting the same regional support strongholds north-east of Zagreb as between the wars when, under the leadership of Stefan Radíc, it contested the Serbian domination of the new Yugoslavia. In Latvia, the Agrarian Party, although small compared with the Latvian Way, is at present a member of the governing coalition. In Estonia there are no less than three agrarian parties – one in government, one in opposition and one outside parliament altogether. Other sectional parties will doubtless emerge as voting becomes more instrumental and less expressive and as the social stratification diversifies under the impact of marketisation. Herbert Kitschelt, at least, is confident that 'the occupational model of political choice should gain some importance in explaining voting patterns and party alignments in subsequent [East European] elections'.[46]

Notes

1   Hugh Seton-Watson, *Eastern Europe Between the Wars 1918–1941* (Westview: Boulder–London, 1986), pp.264–7.
2   Michel Klíma, 'The Emergence of the Czech Party System', paper given at a conference on 'Party Politics in the Year 2000', University of Manchester, 13–15 January 1995, p.8.
3   David Beetham, 'Liberal Democracy and the Limits of Democratisation', in David Held (ed.), *Prospects for Democracy*, Special Issue of *Political Studies*, **XL**, 1992, pp.40–53.
4   Attila Ágh, 'The Transition to Democracy in Central Europe: A Comparative View', *Journal of Public Policy*, **11**, (2), 1991, pp.131–51.
5   Paul G. Lewis, 'Democratisation in Eastern Europe', *Coexistence*, **27**, 1990, pp. 245–67.
6   Svennik Høyer, Epp Lauk and Peeter Vihalemm, *Towards a Civic Society: The Baltic Media's Long Road To Freedom* (Nota Baltica: Tarta, 1993), p.273.
7   Dean McSweeney and Clive Tempest, 'The Political Science of Democratic Transition in Eastern Europe', *Political Studies*, **XLI**, 1993, pp.408–19.
8   Lewis, 'Democratisation', p.246.
9   McSweeney and Tempest, 'Political Science', pp.412–19.
10 Klaus von Beyme, *Transition to Democracy in Eastern Europe* (Macmillan: London, 1996).
11 Danica Fink–Hafner, 'Political Modernization in Slovenia in the 1980s and the early 1990s,' *The Journal of Communist Studies*, **8** (4), 1992, pp.210–26.
12 Vaclav Havel 'Why the Forum Had to Go', *The Guardian*, 17 November 1994.
13 Georgi Karasimeonov, 'The Parliamentary Elections of 1994 and the Development of the Bulgarian Party System', paper given at a conference on 'Party Politics in the Year 2000', University of Manchester, 13–15 January 1995, p.10.
14 Gordon Wightman, 'The June 1990 elections in Czechoslovakia: A Plebiscite for Democracy', *Representation*, **29**, (108), 1990, pp.18–22.
15 Dennis Deletant, 'The Romanian Elections of May 1990', *Representation*, **29**, (108), 1990, pp.23–6.
16 'Crimea tries to turn the clock back', *Independent on Sunday*, 27 March 1994; 'Crimea tiptoes out of Kiev's reach', *The Guardian*, 26 March 1994.
17 'Ukrainians have another flutter at the polls', *The Guardian*, 11 April 1994.
18 'The threat here is the temptation to return to a 'Great Hungary' supported by Budapest, as well as by Hungarian parties in Slovakia', Meciar stated in September 1993; 'A tragedy waiting to happen', *Independent on Sunday*, 28 November 1993.
19 Mikhael Rodin, 'Political Trust in Baltic States', paper presented at the Political Studies Association Annual Conference, Swansea, 29–31 March 1994.
20 Danica Fink-Hafner, 'Anti-Party Sentiment in a Context of Democratic Transition. Slovenia in Comparison to other Post-Socialist Countries', European Consortium of Political Research, Madrid, 17–22 April 1994.
21 Bill Miller, Stephen White, Paul Heywood and Matthew Wyman, 'Democratic, Market and Nationalist Values in Russia and East Europe: December 1993', paper presented at the Political Studies Association Annual Conference, Swansea, 29–31 March 1994.
22 P. Gerlach *et al.* (eds), *Regimewechsel, Demokratisierung und politische Kultur in Ost-Mitteleuropa* (Böhlau: Vienna, 1992).
23 'Multi-party summit probes co-operation', *The Baltic Independent*, 1–7 April 1994.

24 Nigel Swain, 'Hungary's New Political Parties', *Lorton Paper 5*, Lorton House, 1991, p.4.
25 'Ukrainian voting leaves political deadlock intact', *The Guardian*, 30 March 1994.
26 Vladas Gaidys and Danute Tureikyte, 'Political Preferences in Lithuania, 1989–1992', *Emor*, **3**, (3), 1992, pp.19–22.
27 Karen Henderson, 'Divisive Political Agendas: the Case of Czechoslovakia', in Patrick Dunleavy and Jeoffrey Stanyer (eds), *Contemporary Political Studies 1994* (Political Studies Association of the United Kingdom: Exeter, 1994), pp.407–19.
28 Rodin, 'Political Trust', p.5.
29 'Farewell Uncle Vanya', *The Guardian Weekend*, 2 April 1994.
30 Gaidys and Tureikyte, 'Political Preferences in Lithuania', p.21.
31 Geoffrey Pridham, 'Political Actors, Linkages and Interactions: Democratic Consolidation in Southern Europe', *West European Politics*, **13**, (4), 1990, p.105.
32 'Apatia laimentaa vaaleja Venäjällä', *Helsingin Sanomat*, 3 March 1990; 'Neuvostokansa kävi uurnille', *Helsingin Sanomat*, 19 March 1990.
33 'The bitter end of empire', *The Guardian*, 14 December 1993; 'A dream ticket for disgruntled army', *The Guardian*, 15 December 1993.
34 Zhirinovsky was a prominent figure in the 'Marches of the Hungry Queues' which protested against food shortages in late 1991. Peter Lentini, 'Political Parties and Movements in the Commonwealth of Independent States', *Lorton Paper 7*, Lorton House, 1992, p.11.
35 Frances Millard, 'Poland: A Party System in Transition', *Lorton Paper 6*, Lorton House, 1991, p.13.
36 Swain, 'Hungary's New Political Parties', p.11.
37 I am grateful to Dr Gordon Johnstone of Leeds Metropolitan University for background information on the formation of the MDF.
38 Frances Millard, 'Nationalism in Poland, 1989–93', paper presented at a conference on 'Integration and Disintegration in Contemporary Europe', Gregynog Conference Centre, Central Wales, 28 October 1993. At the September 1993 general election, Self-Defence polled 2.8 per cent of the vote.
39 Fink-Hafner, 'Anti-Party Sentiment', p.7.
40 Gordon Wightman, *Party Formation in East-Central Europe* (Edward Elgar: Aldershot, 1995); Michael Waller, 'From Mobilising Dissent to Aggregating Interests in Eastern Europe', *The Journal of Communist Studies*, **8**, (1), 1992; Paul Lewis, 'Democracy and its Future in Eastern Europe', in David Held (ed.), *Prospects for Democracy*, (Polity: Oxford, 1992).
41 Robert Harmel and Lars Svåsand, 'Party Leadership and Party Institutionalisation: Three Phases of Development', *West European Politics*, **16**, (2), 1993, pp. 67–88.
42 Stephen J. Silva, 'The SPD in Eastern Germany after Unification', *West European Politics*, **16**, (2), 1993, pp.24–48.
43 Richard S. Katz and Peter Mair, 'The Cross-National Study of Party Organizations', in Katz and Mair (eds), *Party Organizations: A Data Handbook on Party Organizations in Western Democracies 1960–1990* (Sage: London–Newbury Park–New Delhi, 1992), pp.4–6.
44 Mikk Titma, 'Estonia: Right Turn?', *East European Reporter*, **5/6**, 1992, pp.81–2. See also Indrek Kannik, 'A View from the Fatherland', *East European Reporter*, 5 May 1992, pp.77–8.
45 Viktor Davidkin, 'New name, same old idea', *The Guardian* 16 June 1994.
46 Herbert Kitschelt, 'The Formation of Party Systems in East Central Europe', *Politics and Society*, **20**, (1), 1992, pp.7–50, especially p.27.

2 System Change in the Former Soviet Republics

The upheavals of 1989–91 did not represent revolutionary changes, but rather the culmination of a long-term process of collapse ... They resulted not in a transition from communist totalitarianism to Western-style capitalist democracy, but merely in a redistribution of power and privileges within already existing ruling groups. (Bill Lomax, 'Impediments to Democratization in East-Central Europe', in Gordon Wightman (ed.), *Party Formation in East-Central Europe* (Edward Elgar: Aldershot, 1995), p. 188)

Impediments to Democratisation

Arguing that across Central and Eastern Europe there is a conspicuous absence of what are widely regarded as the basic prerequisites of the successful transition to capitalist democracy, and highlighting the concomitant risk of the emergence of a 'new authoritarianism', Bill Lomax has identified three possible impediments to democratisation in the region. First, he notes that, in several states, leadership renewal has been at best partial and a section of the old communist elite has remained in power. Indeed, the upheavals of 1989–91, he insists, resulted not in a shift from communist totalitarianism to Western-style capitalist democracy, but simply in a redistribution of power and privileges among already existing groups.[1] In particular, Lomax emphasises how, in the case of Hungary, a democratic bourgeoisie – widely viewed as necessary underpinning to liberal democracy – has not formed, but that instead there has been the transformation of a ruling group of old party bureaucrats and state managers whose power was formerly based on political domination into one based on economic domination. In the words of Judit Kiss: 'Privatization is often just a pseudonym to mark processes that have nothing to do with it or even jeopardise it.'[2]

Second, Lomax contends that, contrary to the Western wisdom, which sees parties acting as important channels of communication between governors and governed, the East European parties are not performing their linkage function and are thus not reinforcing the 'by' element in Abraham Lincoln's classical formulation of democracy. More seriously, it is argued that, because of their 'tribal' character (rooted in friendship networks), ideological self-identifications bound up with broad emotive concepts (such as nation, race and religion) rather than particularist interests, and their general lack of specific policy programmes, parties are estranged from the people. Personality- rather than programme-based, elitist and intellectual rather than mass-mobilising, 'clan-like' rather than social cleavage-based parties, Lomax concludes, operate in a way that contributes to preserving, rather than bridging, the gap between political elites and society.

Finally, he argues that, as former dissidents have come to constitute an element of the new political class in Central and Eastern Europe, their earlier commitment to the establishment of civil society has given way to an almost exclusive involvement in the realm of party politics. Fearing that a frustrated people might turn against the democratic system in which they are stakeholders, the former dissidents seek to demobilise the very forces that undermined communist rule.

Throughout Lomax is legitimately concerned to challenge assumptions about the likely success of democratisation in post-communist Europe and to question the nature and direction of the transition process. He views the very notion of transition as misleading, claiming that the upheavals of 1989–91 did not represent revolutionary changes but, rather, were the culmination of a long-term process of disintegration. He is particularly critical of the inherent elitism of intellectual attitudes, but ultimately takes comfort in the possibility of a radical popular reaction to a 'new authoritarianism' which might seek to diminish the recently acquired democratic rights of citizens.

Inferred in Lomax's analysis are three points, touched on at various intervals already in this volume, which will inform our overview of the course of democratisation in the post-Soviet republics. First, there is the distinction between power structures (as prescribed by law) and the real distribution of power, since it is clear that constitutional modernisation does not necessarily entail radical elite renewal or, indeed, guarantee the desired distribution of power. Second, the implicit thrust of Lomax's argument is that the introduction of a Western 'party democracy model' does not *ipso facto* promote a democratic society. Parties may control the organs of state but, because of their highly elitist character, have only a weak toehold in political society. Finally, the post-communist political class (both the old and more particularly new elements) may perceive a potential contradiction between the need for institutionalising the governmental system (state-building) and promoting the high level of popular participation (society-building) that may threaten the success of democratic transition. The depoliticisation and demobilisation of mass publics – compare the active popular involvement of the 'revolutionary days' – are viewed as a *sine qua non* of effective political management (government), at least in the short to medium term.

The widespread popular anti-party sentiment should also be recalled. Hostility to parties was prevalent among political activists in the first stages of post-communist rule although, as Gordon Wightman has noted, Václac Klaus in the Czech Republic was an exception among new politicians in not sharing the assumption that animosity towards parties was widespread among the electorate.[3] In his Czech perspective on the impediments to the development of democratic politics, however, Zdenek Zboril notes that anti-party prejudice significally predated the advent of communist rule: 'Experience even before 1948 had predisposed the citizens of Czechoslovakia to be wary of political parties', Zboril observes. 'Most had been tainted in popular eyes by their behaviour at the time of the Munich Agreement in 1938 when the "treason" of Czechoslovakia's Western allies found its counterpart on the domestic scene in the passivity of the parties and their inability to overcome their particular interests and find a joint solution to the crisis Munich had created for the Czechoslovak state.'[4]

The European 'successor states' that emerged between the abortive anti-Gorbachev coup on 20 August 1991 and the disintegration of the Soviet Union in December the same year can be divided into two groupings. Ukraine, Belarus and Moldova had virtually no previous history of independence and the achievement of sovereignty did not usher in early parliamentary elections to sweep away the old communist guard. Rather, the former communist-controlled assemblies elected a head of state who proceeded to dominate the political stage, often in harness with the old party *nomenklatura*. Thus, in Belarus, Stanislav Shuskevitsch, a university professor and prominent human rights campaigner, who came to the fore in the aftermath of the 1986 Chernobyl disaster, was elected chair of the Supreme Soviet in September 1991; in Ukraine, the former Communist Party secretary, Leonid Kravchuk, was elected on 1 December 1991; and in Moldova, Mircea Snegur, former deputy leader of the Communist Party, was elected unopposed on 8 December 1991. In all three cases, the frailty of parliamentary democracy to date has been reflected in the fact that none is a full member of the Council of Europe, although Ukraine looks likely to become one in relatively short order. Economically, the 'new' successor states of Belarus, Ukraine and Moldova are closely linked with the Russian Federation and the Common-wealth of Independent States (CIS), although under Leonid Kuchma (who replaced Kravchuk in July 1994) Ukraine has adopted a more Western outlook and economic management style. Belarus, a full CIS member, has closest economic ties to Moscow. It already has a cus-toms union with the Russian Federation even if a proposed currency union proved still-born when Russia refused to deal in Belarus rou-bles, the value of which halved between their introduction in 1993 and 1995. Moldova joined the CIS in April 1994 but does not partici-pate in any of its military structures and has in fact acceded to NATO's 'Partnership for Peace'. Ukraine is only an associate mem-ber of the CIS and in summer 1995 negotiated a temporary trade relations agreement with the European Union (EU), although this was made contingent on the promised closure of the Chernobyl power plant.

The Baltic republics of Latvia, Lithuania and Estonia, in contrast, were inter-war ('old') successor states, spawned by the collapse of the Czarist Romanov Empire and which, following the defeat of the hardline Moscow coup attempt, were widely viewed in the West as having a legal (or at least strong moral) right to independence and also profited from the support of the emergent Russian leader, Boris Yeltsin. They possessed at the point of renewed independence a lim-ited but not insignificant tradition of pluralist democracy and party politics, a liberal record of granting cultural autonomy to national minorities and an inter-war history of strong commercial links with the West. In the four years of independence, moreover, there has been substantial progress towards reintegrating the Baltic states into Western Europe. All three are members of the Council of Europe, Latvia being the last Baltic state to join the 34-member organisation in February 1995. All three are members of NATO's 'Partnership for Peace' and contribute a Baltic Peacekeeping Battalion (Baltbat) – backed by US subsidies – stationed at Adazi in Latvia. Moreover, all three have concluded association agreements with the EU – uniquely in the Estonian case involving no transitional period – and these were ratified by the EU member parliament over 1995–6. The Baltic states, which have reached agreement on a visa-free Baltic region, are also engaged in free-trade talks with the four remaining EFTA states of Norway, Iceland, Switzerland and Liechtenstein.

The aim of the present chapter is briefly to review the progress towards democratisation in the former European republics of the Soviet Union, using the analytical framework presented in Chapter 1. In this way it is hoped to set the Estonian experience of democratic transition in a wider comparative perspective. Before concentrating on the politics of transition, however, a background note on the economics of change in post-communist Europe is in order. Thus, whilst the six Central European states of Poland, the Czech Republic, Slovakia, Hungary, Romania and Bulgaria have EU 'association agreements' (as, we have noted, do the three Baltic republics), the CIS '12' are generally ailing. Only a few of them have reformed their currencies and most are havens for fixed exchange rates.

In 1990 the post-communist states suffered a collapse in output on a scale with which there had been nothing comparable in peacetime Europe since the recession of the 1930s. Following the trauma, Poland, the Czech Republic, Slovakia, Hungary, Romania and Bulgaria have gradually got their economies back on a growth course, although in none of the 'six' is the national product at the same level as before 1989–90. Their recovery is also very closely tied to exports, since investments and the financial system are too weak to sustain growth. Nonetheless, Poland recorded economic growth as early as 1992 and three years later GDP was in the order of 90 per cent of its 1989 level. According to the Hungarian economist Janos Gacs, the firmest basis for growth is in the Czech Republic, whereas in Hungary serious exchange and trade deficits will slow things down. In Romania and Bulgaria the collapse was the deepest and economic revival remains very fragile. Whilst the economic situation varies from one country to the next and a common prescription is clearly not appropriate, the aforementioned six differ dramatically from the European CIS republics of Russia, Ukraine and Belarus, where national output dropped again in 1994 and where there are no signs of recovery.[5]

Democratisation in the European States of the Former Soviet Union

In seeking to make a rudimentary appraisal of the progress made by the European states of the former Soviet Union towards democratisation, it is proposed to apply the three analytical dimensions of the post-communist transition process set out earlier. A condition of democratic transition, it was argued, is the successful completion of state-building, that is the formulation and legitimation of a body of pluralist groundrules describing institutional arrangements and prescribing the formal distribution of power in the newly sovereign polity. Any attempt quantatively to evaluate progress in state building is fraught with difficulty, but two broad questions seem pertinent to any assessment:

1   When was the new constitution enacted and how (that is, by a vote of the legislative assembly and/or referendum)? There is an obvious rider: has the constitution become the object of broadgauge elite agreement or does it remain a contentious issue?

2   How many national elections have there been since the achievement of independence and how open and free have they been? In
other words, is there at least tentative evidence of parliamentary
democracy at work or have parties and interest groups been
stifled and prevented from organising and campaigning freely?

Nation-building, which is closely allied to state-building, involves
generating a sense of national identity among the population in the
minimal sense at least of a broad measure of civic allegiance to the
outward symbols of the nation-state: its language, territory, emblems,
tradition and so on. While the existence of such a sense of 'belonging' may be difficult to prove, four questions might reasonably be
said to provide an analytical framework:

1   Is there a native language used by the majority of the people
which is also the official language of the state?
2   Conversely, have there been attempts to revivify the indigenous
language and make it available to citizens through intensive study
programmes – a type of obligatory vernacularisation?
3   How effectively are any ethnic cleavages accommodated by the
constitution and nascent party system?
4   Are there any ethnic minority groupings seeking to secede and
belong to another state?

The process of society-building and the emergence of structural
patterns of popular involvement in decision making is bound up
with the stage of democratic consolidation. The measurement of the
democratic character of political society (culture) is inevitably multi-
faceted and complex, but for the purposes of this brief review two
questions will suffice:[6] What has been the turnout at general elections since independence, and has the trend been up or down?

Ukraine: a State, Yes, but a Nation?

In August 1991 Ukraine became the largest state in Europe in terms
of its surface area, and with 52 million inhabitants (approximately
the same as in France) it boasted the fourth largest population. Ukraine
declared its independence in 1918 following the overthrow of Czarist
absolutism in Russia and the subsequent Bolshevik revolution in St
Petersburg, but when Russia made peace with Germany at the Treaty
of Brest-Litovsk in March 1918 the latter viewed Ukraine as a client
state. It was particularly attractive to the Germans as a granary for
Central Europe. Between 1918 and 1919 a series of nominally independent Ukrainian governments were formed, although, as the Ger-

man General Max Hoffman wrote: 'The difficulty in the Ukraine is simply that the central *Rada* [administration] has only our rifles behind it.'[7] When the Paris Peace Conference convened in January 1919 the outcome of the Russian civil war left the future of Ukraine in the balance, but in 1921 it was annexed by the Bolsheviks.

The first stage in the renewed transition to independence in Ukraine was modelled on Baltic practice and saw former dissidents in Galicia pressing for the creation of a popular front in support of *perestroika*. Some 15 months after the formation of mass opposition movements in Estonia, Latvia and Lithuania, on 8 September 1989, *Rukh* or the 'Popular Movement for Restructuring' (Rukh means 'movement' in Ukrainian) held its inaugural congress in the capital, Kiev, and its role in activating nationalist opposition warrants emphasis.[8] With a population of 5.4 million (over half that of the entire Western Ukraine), Galicia, the stronghold of Rukh, was in fact reminiscent of the Baltic republics – except that, as Russians made up only 5 per cent of the West Ukrainian population, there was no place for the counter-nationalist Interfront. The Interfronts were hardline, reactionary organisations, led by local figures but orchestrated from Moscow, which sought to defend the privileged position of Russian ethnic minorities across the Soviet republics. Galicia formed part of the Austrian partition of the Dual Monarchy before 1918 and, subsequently incorporated into Poland, it escaped the devastation of Stalinist rule. When the Soviets occupied the area after the Second World War, they confronted a militant nationalist movement which embraced ordinary people right down to the last village. Not surprisingly, therefore, the nationalist movement revived in Galicia under *glasnost* and spread to other areas of Western Ukraine, particularly Volhynia.[9] Significantly, two weeks after the official launch of Rukh, Gorbachev flew to Kiev to oversee the removal of the ardent Brezhnevist Volodymyr Ivashko, an uninspiring but conciliatory apparatchik.

Also inspired by Baltic developments and in particular the 'Baltic Way' which stretched from Tallinn to Vilnius in protest against the fiftieth anniversary of the notorious Molotov–Ribbentrop pact on 23 August 1989, the initial surge in the mass mobilisation of nationalist opposition achieved by Rukh over the first half of 1990 involved crowds on the streets in impressive numbers. Thus, on 22 January 1990, almost one million people formed a human chain from Kiev to Lviv to mark Ukraine's declaration of independence in 1918 and when, on 16 July 1990, the Supreme Soviet was virtually unanimous in issuing a Declaration of Sovereignty (there were similar declarations in the Baltic republics between November 1988 and July 1989) thousands thronged parliament as it debated the declaration. In this first phase of the independence struggle, Rukh's role was crucial and its support extensive. Despite widespread fraud, the Rukh-led electoral bloc gained one-quarter of the parliamentary seats at the March 1990 Supreme Soviet elections and Rukh's membership rose to over half a million. There were other unofficial opposition groups such as the Ukrainian Language Society, *Zelenyi svit* ('Green World') and Memorial, which also gained in strength. This Rukh-led phase of popular mobilisation culminated on 22 July 1990 in Ivashko's resignation and his replacement by Leonid Kravchuk as head of Ukraine's Supreme Soviet (parliament). At the same time, Stanislav Hurenko became First Secretary of the Ukrainian Communist Party.

The previous month, a Soviet economic blockade imposed by Gorbachev had obliged the Lithuanians to accept in principle a moratorium on their declaration of full independence on 11 March 1990 and a series of fruitless talks began. Indeed, taking their lead from Moscow's increasingly menacing stance towards the Baltics, Kravchuk (who emerged as the only person capable of coping with Rukh in public debate) and Hurenko set out to undermine the achievements of the Ukrainian nationalist movement. Demonstrations in the vicinity of parliament were banned; troops were massed outside the capital city; the opposition's (previously highly effective) use of radio and television was restricted; administrative obstacles were placed in the path of the democratically controlled regional and local soviets; and the radical nationalist deputy Stepan Khmara was arrested in an act of unashamed provocation. As Bohdan Krawchenko has observed: 'This conservative backlash poured cold water on the euphoria over the adoption of Ukraine's declaration of sovereignty.'[10]

The second stage in the transition to independence in Ukraine (there was no immediate parallel in the Baltics) was the counter-mobilisation against the rearguard action of Kravchuk and Hurenko which was led by the students. In the early days of October 1990, a small group of students went on hunger strike and camped in October Revolution Square in Kiev. They were quickly joined by hundreds of others who turned the square into a 'miniature Woodstock'.[11] Universities and other higher education institutions went on strike, an all-Ukrainian student strike committee was formed and on 16 October about 150 000 marched on parliament, with naval cadets at the head of the procession and over one thousand Afghan veterans serving as marshals. When, on 18 October, a large column of workers from Kiev's biggest factory descended on parliament in support of the students, the government caved in. The chairman of the Council of Ministers (prime minister), Vitalis Masol, was forced to resign and it was made a strict condition of adhering to Gorbachev's new 'Union Accord' that there be prior passage of a constitution enshrining Ukraine's sovereignty.

The third and final stage of the transition process came in the wake of the abortive anti-Gorbachev putsch in Moscow in August 1991.

For the first two days of the coup Kravchuk seemed reluctant to condemn the Emergency Committee. However, as soon as it became unequivocally clear that the hardliners were doomed, he supported a declaration of independence, passed by the Ukrainian parliament on 24 August, and then made the 'implementation' of independence contingent on ratification in a popular referendum. It was duly sanctioned by over 90 per cent of voters in December 1991 and the referendum coincided with the first presidential election, at which Kravchuk gained 61 per cent of the vote.

Ultimately, it cannot be doubted that, as one expert has noted, 'the drive for statehood was motivated by a profound realization of just how mismanaged and ravaged Ukraine's economy had been at the hands of Moscow'.[12] Until 1990, 95 per cent of the Ukrainian economy was controlled by Moscow, which in turn was responsible for more than 90 per cent of what was produced in Ukraine. Under one-quarter of Ukraine's income remained in the republic, the rest being repatriated by the centre. Consequently, the shift from the colonised command economy to a pluralist market economy represented a big leap and one accompanied by the same collapse in industrial production that attended the economic transition in the Central and East European successor states. Unlike the experience of the so-called Visegrad bloc of Poland, Hungary and the Czech Republic, however, few signs of economic recovery have yet been apparent. Indeed, it warrants emphasis that the embryonic post-independence political system has operated under enormous economic strain and the more Ukraine has declined economically, the greater the pressures for re-integration into the Russian-led CIS have become.

The economic picture in Ukraine since 1991 has been uniformly bleak. True, the following year, parliament made provision for the privatisation of housing and small firms and also facilitated the repatriation of profits by foreign investors. But the mood of crisis deepened as production fell and living standards plunged, while by November 1992 inflation was running at 30 per cent per month. The following year brought no improvement: between January and September 1993, industrial production fell 21 per cent year-on-year; the central planning system collapsed; there were strikes and a chronic shortage of supplies; and over the year as a whole inflation rose at 2 per cent daily. It all meant that homes were inadequately heated and most people could barely afford to feed and clothe themselves. In 1994 industrial production was down a further 30 per cent year-on-year, the value of the *karbovanets* depreciated more than threefold – from 30 000 to the US dollar to over 100 000 by the end of the year – and the trade deficit grew (largely because of energy imports from Russia). Following a comprehensive economic reform plan, the International Monetary Fund (IMF) agreed a 360 million dollar loan, but in April 1995 the credit package was postponed pending the enactment of the 1995 budget.

In briefly considering the process of state-building since independence, it needs emphasis that Ukraine emerged de facto as a president-dominant system which has been characterised by intermittently high levels of conflict between the executive and legislature. The first president, Kravchuk, having opposed the democratic and nationalist movements in autumn 1990, used the communist-controlled assembly (Supreme Soviet elected in March 1990) to acquire sweeping powers and most of the local officials he appointed were members of the former *nomenklatura*. The old communist government under Vitold Fokin was also retained in office. Even so, conflict between president and parliament was manifest on several occasions, notably in November 1993 when the assembly voted to postpone Kravchuk's undertaking (of the previous year) to transform Ukraine into a non-nuclear power. It argued that such a move should be made conditional on foreign financial aid and security guarantees.

The gravity of the economic crisis led in October 1992 to the replacement of Fokin by Leonid Kuchma (formerly director of one of the Soviet Union's largest missile factories) and parliament granted him extraordinary powers to reform the economy. However, Kuchma proceeded to resign in September 1993 when parliament nonetheless frustrated his moderate reform programme based on an attempt to impose a measure of regulation rather than simply privatising the major sectors of the economy. Against this backdrop of increased governmental instability and a fractious legislature, the political continuity afforded by the presidential office assumed greater importance, while the president's role as a policy initiator was also enhanced.

Since his defeat of Kravchuk in the second round of the presidential elections on 10 July 1994 (Kravchuk was the best-supported candidate in the first round, with 37.7 per cent), Kuchma, like his predecessor, has been the dominant politician in Ukraine, albeit pursuing a more westward foreign and commercial policy orientation, along with a more regulated reform of the economy. Ironically, during the presidential election campaign, Kuchma emphasised the need for closer economic ties with Russia which he justified in terms of saving the Ukrainian economy and thereby the state itself. However, in October 1994 he announced (and parliament approved) a comprehensive reform programme (commended by the IMF) which included the reduction of subsidies, the lifting of price controls, lowering taxes, promoting privatisation in industry and agriculture and reforming the currency and banking systems. But conflict between the legislative and executive arms of government persisted. When Kuchma fixed a referendum for 28 June 1995 in an ostensible attempt to ease the deadlock, this fell foul of parliament. On 1 June the assembly voted by 252 votes to nine to veto the presidential decree, insisting the whole manoeuvre was simply a presidential device to acquire more power.

Legislative renewal did not take place in Ukraine until March 1994, well after the first general elections in the Baltic states, and this meant that, for the first three years of independence, the legislature was the Supreme Soviet elected in March 1990. Put another way, there has been only one general election in the post-communist period and it was conceded only reluctantly when the old assembly was faced with an outbreak of mass unrest. The coalminers and industrial workers in the Donbass region of Eastern Ukraine went on strike in spring 1993, forcing Kravchuk to issue a decree fixing a referendum for September 1993 to test confidence in both parliament and president. Clearly, Ukraine's political institutions suffered from very low levels of popular legitimacy, something confirmed by Yuri Boldyrev, a former mine electrician and strike organiser who became deputy to the mayor of Donetsk, the Russian-speaking coal 'capital'. According to Boldyrev: 'Ukraine is dead ... the parliament are idiots, the government are idiots, the president is an idiot.'[13] Certainly when public reaction to a short-lived agreement with Russia over nuclear weapons and the Black Sea fleet proved hostile, parliament cancelled the referendum and instead set parliamentary elections for March 1994 and a presidential election for June 1994. The first post-communist general election in Ukraine, in short, was a concession to a public opinion inflamed by economic distress and increasingly disillusioned with the prospects of any improvement. As Sarah Birch noted, commenting on the parliamentary and presidential elections of 1994: 'For a significant portion of the electorate, faith in an independent state as a guarantor of the well-being of Ukraine and nation-building as a priority are on the wane.'[14] On the other hand, Ukraine can boast alternation in the presidential office and government and at least one renewal of parliament since achieving independence in 1991.

Turning to the aforementioned question of nation-building, Ukraine emerged as a multi-ethnic state in which its 73 per cent Ukrainian population was concentrated in the more agrarian West and 22 per cent Russian in the industrial East, although ethnic Ukrainians formed a majority in all the country's provinces except the Crimea. As in the Baltic states, the indigenous language and culture had been suppressed under Soviet rule. A survey of the parents of first-form pupils in Kiev in 1988 revealed that only 16.5 per cent of respondents used Ukrainian at home and only 4.7 per cent spoke it at work.[15] In the 1988–9 school year, only 47.5 per cent of children studied in Ukrainian-language schools and in most of the large cities of the Donbass and also southern Ukraine there was not a single native-language school. In higher education, too, the language of the ethnic Ukrainian majority was used only a minority of the time. In 1987 only 14 per cent of lectures at Kiev University were delivered in Ukrainian. Centuries of Russification took an inevitable toll and in the late 1980s books in Ukrainian constituted only about 20 per cent of all published volumes. As the nationalist Ryszard Kapuścínski observed: 'The average Ukrainian is not even familiar with the names of the greatest Ukrainian writers of the twentieth century, Mikola Khvileva and Vladimir Vinnitchenko.'[16]

The transition to independence brought with it a concern to elevate Ukrainian to dominant-language status and to rediscover Ukrainian history and culture. In November 1989 Ukrainian was recognised as the official state language, although the Masol government stalled on implementing the new law. Under Kravchuk, however, there was a vigorous Ukrainianisation programme in schools and colleges and Ukrainian-language publications were actively encouraged. Ukraine also moved quickly to create its own armed forces and more than half a million soldiers took an oath of allegiance to the new nation-state. The results of the Ukrainianisation programme were not an unequivocal success, however, and there is evidence of resistance from the Russian and Russified segments of the population. By 1993 Ukrainian-language newspapers were unavailable in large areas of Ukraine and schools remained Russified.

Noting the virtual absence of interethnic conflict in Ukraine, Krawchenko has pointed to the way the social structure during the transitional period mitigated against the formation of the type of reactionary Interfronts that characterised the Baltic region. The working class in pre-independent Ukraine was Ukrainian, he observes, and accordingly Russian hardliners could not deploy populist demagogy to provoke a mass backlash against the intelligentsia leading the nationalist movement.[17] In the independence period, however, Moscow has been able to fan separatist sentiment in the Crimea. For example, the separatist cause was materially assisted when the Russian Duma (elected in 1990) negated the transference in 1954 of the Crimea from Russia to Ukraine and called for negotiations over the peninsula's future. The town of Odessa, with a heterogeneous mix of Russians, Ukrainians, Greeks and Jews, also demanded to be a free zone. As the economic privations experienced by ordinary people have worked to undermine the effects of Ukrainianisation and vitiate the nation-building process, Crimean separatism has continued undiminished.

Indeed, threats and counterthreats have abounded. At the end of March 1995, the Ukrainian parliament, *Verkhovna Rada*, annulled Crimea's constitution and abolished its presidency. President Kuchma in fact threatened to dissolve the region's legislature in response to threats from Crimean deputies to hold a referendum on reunification with Russia during the 29 April municipal elections. Ukrainian parliamentarians also voted to launch criminal proceedings against Crimean president Yuri Meshkov for promoting secession from the Ukraine. The following month, 35 of Crimea's 98 members of parliament – including the native Tartars (see Chapter 1, pp. 10–11) and several independents – wrote to Kiev supporting Kuchma's threat to dissolve the Crimean legislature.

Any assessment of society-building in Ukraine, that is analysis of the extent of the emergence of a 'democratic society', however rudimentary, must begin with the strength of nationalist opposition and the high levels of mass mobilisation exhibited in Galicia during the transition to independence. Galicia was the bedrock of popular nationalist sentiment. It was not surprising, therefore, that at the Supreme Soviet elections of March 1990 democratic opposition candidates won 43 of the 47 Galician seats.[18] In connection with Gorbachev's pan-Soviet referendum on the future of the union on 17 March 1991, moreover, the three Galician *oblasts* organised an extra question asking voters whether or not they wanted Ukraine to be an independent state. Almost 90 per cent answered in favour. Western Ukraine also provided a valuable organisational input into the nationalist movement in Eastern Ukraine and Galicia regularly provided support for demonstrations in that region.

Yet in contrast to the mass political involvement of the transitional period (witness among other things the human chain on 22 January 1990 to mark the first Ukrainian declaration of independence in 1918) demobilisation and depoliticisation characterised the immediate post-independence period and were particularly pronounced among young people. To compound matters, Rukh split early in 1992 between pro-Kravchuk elements and those favouring transforming the opposition movement into a political party. Protoparties predated independence, but the party system has remained very weak. Thus, commenting on the Ukrainian multi-party system on the eve of the 1994 general election, Taras Kuzio noted: 'Parties formed around a particular leader. They have failed to establish themselves in rural areas or small towns and what can be called civil society exists only in Western Ukraine and Kiev. Parties are still relatively weak with limited appeal to the public (who are suspicious of the word "party"), to young people in particular and to a meagre press.'[19] Only in Galicia, he adds, do parties have branches at the local level and very few parties have targetted social constituencies. The exceptions, he concludes, are the Peasant Democratic Party (bourgeoisie) and the Liberal Democratic Party of Ukraine and Party of Democratic Revival of Ukraine (entrepreneurs/ new business).[20]

In view of the weak nature of the party system and the strength of anti-party sentiment, electoral participation at the first post-communist general election in Ukraine in March–April 1994 was relatively high. While in the first round on 27–8 March only 49 out of a full complement of 490 deputies were elected, turnout was better than expected. It was highest in Western Ukraine, surprisingly good (60.8 per cent) in Crimea – given that the Crimean president Meshkov had called for a boycott – but only 56 per cent in the capital, Kiev. Sarah Birch has suggested that Kravchuk's prediction that a low turnout would invalidate many electoral contests, and that the elections would fail to produce the minimum of 301 deputies necessary to make the new parliament quorate, may well have motivated voters to go to the polls.[21] Only half of those parliamentarians elected in the first round were officially recognised representatives of political parties. The second round succeeded in filling a further 287 seats, so that by mid-April 336 out of 490 deputies had been elected. Turnout was again relatively high, with a national average of 66.9 per cent. Communists and Socialists together made up the largest bloc in the new Ukrainian parliament. At the presidential election two months later, turnout was just over 70 per cent in both rounds, Kuchma winning 52.1 per cent to Kravchuk's 45.5 per cent in the second.[22] The figures, of course, point up the limitations of using electoral participation as the sole indicator of the extent to which political society has been democratised.

Belarus: Neither a Nation nor (Soon) a State?

Belarus is a country of ten million people, situated between Poland and Russia, and its capital Minsk, where the CIS was founded in December 1991, boasts a population of 1.6 million. As a new state it had a history of independence that was even shorter than that of Ukraine. Following the proclamation of the Belarusan Democratic Republic on 25 March 1918, the briefest period of autonomy was ended ingloriously by a Polish invasion the following year. There can be no doubt, moreover, that as Urban and Zaprudnik note: 'The great majority of Belarusans [who lived] on the land had little or no notion of national identity, much less national independence.'[23] During the inter-war period, the Belarusan lands were divided (by the Treaty of Riga in 1921) between Poland and Soviet Russia. In the 'western territories' there was a brutal policy of Polonisation against the 3.5 million Belarusans under Polish sovereignty. The five million under Soviet rule were incorporated into the Belarusan Soviet Socialist Republic (BSSR) that was founded on 1 January 1919. In contrast to the Polish 'partition', the BSSR prospered in the 1920s as Moscow encouraged the revival and development of national cultures and it was significant that a Belarusan State University (the first on Belarusan soil) was set up in Minsk. The repression of the 1930s, however, reversed the gains of the previous decade and drove nationalist expressions underground.[24] The 'western territories' were incorporated into the BSSR by the secret protocols of the Molotov–Ribbentrop pact, although in the post-Stalin period the BSSR's political elites enjoyed relative autonomy from Moscow. On a socioeconomic note, industrialisation and the attendant urbanisation processes affected Belarus relatively belatedly and it was only in the 1980s that a sizeable and educated town-based population – potentially receptive to nationalist ideas – emerged.[25]

When viewing the process of transition to renewed independence in Belarus (the name 'Belarus' was officially adopted on 19 September 1991) in a comparative perspective, several points warrant emphasis. First, as elsewhere, the Belarus nationalist movement was led by intellectuals – writers, artists, scientists, journalists and so on – and, like their Ukrainian counterparts, they were inspired by developments in the Baltic region. Moreover, as in Estonia and Latvia in particular, relatively educated young people were notably active in working to preserve and promote the language and historical memory of the nation. By January 1989, in fact, the youth movement was demanding an independent Belarus.

Second, as in the Baltic republics and Ukraine, the Belarus Popular Front (BPF), which emerged in October 1988, spearheaded the democratic opposition movement and, by the time of the Supreme Soviet elections in March 1990, claimed a membership in excess of 100 000. It was not able, however, to attain the scale of mass mobilisation of Galicia and the Baltics and the response in the rural districts was particularly poor. Even the 40 000 BPF supporters that gathered in the Minsk Dynamo stadium on 19 February 1989 (as part of its Supreme Soviet election campaign) was relatively small beer when compared with the quarter of a million Estonians that massed in the Song Stadium in Tallinn in September 1988.

Third, in Belarus, the nationalist opposition met with much greater opposition from the Brezhnevist elements controlling the party state than elsewhere. Significantly, the Communist Party of Belarus was alone among the republic-level Communist Parties in forbidding its members from joining the Popular Front and when the BPF was formally inaugurated in June 1989 it was not in Minsk, but the Lithuanian capital Vilnius! Unlike the Baltic republics, moreover, the Belarus Communist Party did not split into nationalist–reformist and hardline pro-Moscow wings and when, early in 1990, the youth movement *Komsomol* broke with the authorities to found Democratic Consent, designed to foster dialogue between the nationalist opposition and those elements in the party committed to *perestroika*, its call fell on deaf ears.

Finally, as in the Baltics and Ukraine, a language law in January 1990 (establishing Belarussian as the official state language) was followed by a Declaration of Sovereignty (27 July 1990), more comprehensive in its scope than elsewhere but, significantly, the BPF never came out for full independence and always favoured state sovereignty within the framework of a CIS-style arrangement. In short, it is even less clear than in Ukraine and the Baltic republics that Belarus would have become fully independent without the catalyst of the abortive coup in Moscow on 19 August 1991.

In analysing the rise of an opposition movement in Belarus during the Gorbachev era, Urban and Zaprudnik identify three main factors. First, there was concern about a steady decline in the use of the native tongue as the primary language for the 77.8 per cent ethnic Belarussians in the BSSR. Accordingly, on 15 December 1986, 28 Belarusan intellectuals addressed a petition to Gorbachev (it was also signed by several rank-and-file workers and subsequently endorsed by the BSSR's Writer's Union) in which it was observed that since 'language is the soul of the nation' action was urgently required (from the CPSU First Secretary) 'to save the Belarus people from spiritual extinction'.[26]

Second, there was a sense of outrage at the discovery of Soviet atrocities committed against the Belarus people between 1937 and 1941, particularly the massacres at Kurapaty. An organisation known as Martyrology of Belarus, led by Vasil Bykaŭ, was set up in October 1988 following revelations of Soviet genocide and the location of over 500 mass graves (with the remains of an estimated 300 000 innocent victims) in the Kurapaty wood near Minsk.[27] At its inaugural meeting Martyrology also established the Belarus Popular Front with the archeologist Zianon Pazniak, who had discovered the mass executions at Kurapaty, as its president. The BPF's first act, a demonstration drawing 10 000 people on 30 October 1988, which revived the national custom of *Dziady* (remembrance of the dead) and coincided with the Soviet Union's 'Day of Remembrance' for the victims of Stalinist terror, was forcibly dispersed by the police.[28]

Finally, there was protest at the ruin wrought by the Chernobyl disaster and the callous attitude of the authorities to the aftermath. About 70 per cent of the Chernobyl fallout had settled on two-fifths of the territory of the BSSR and directly threatened the lives of about 2.2 million people, but the Republic's officials took little action except seeking to suppress the truth.

The BPF's rally in the Minsk Dynamo stadium on 19 February 1989 marked a turning-point in the struggle between the nationalist movement and communist authorities and, although the Supreme Soviet elections the following month were less than free and the assembly remained communist-dominated, the largest bloc comprised intellectuals and technocrats, many of whom were sympathetic to the BPF. Indeed, the Declaration of State Sovereignty was the result of a compromise between the chair of the Supreme Soviet, N.I. Dzemiantsei, and the deputy-chair and BPF candidate, S.S. Shuskevitsch. It went beyond the primacy of Belarus law on Belarus territory to include ownership of all economic and natural resources, as well as an announcement that the BSSR was to be a neutral and nuclear-free state.

Like Ukraine, Belarus has developed as a president-dominant system in which Alyaksandr Lukashenko, the head of state since June 1994, has deployed the referendum as a personal agenda-setting instrument with which to work towards the reintegration of Belarus and the Russian Federation. Thus, in a referendum in May 1995, 77.6 per cent of voters gave the president powers to dissolve parliament if it violated the constitution. Significantly, moreover, 82.4 per cent backed Lukashenko – the only member of parliament to vote against independence in 1991 – in seeking closer economic ties with Russia. Indeed, Lukashenko organised four referenda on 14 May 1995 in order to back his concern to shift Belarus away from neutrality towards his desired *Ostpolitik*. He told his supporters (and the media): 'Slav unity is the most important issue in our lives. I'm sure people will vote in favour. If the people call for it, we will also have a political union even closer than the Soviet Union was. For the moment I am talking about economic union.'[29] The new constitution was not adopted until March 1994 and three months later Lukashenko, a former *Kolkhoz* boss, received 80 per cent of the vote in the second round run-off ballot to defeat the strong favourite, Vyacheslav Kebich. As a political outsider, Lukashenko was committed to rooting out corruption and reversing price increases.

Legislative renewal was belated in Belarus since the election to the first post-Soviet parliament did not take place until May 1995 and the evidence suggests it was in any event far from free. Certainly, the small nationalist opposition complained that they had no access to the media after Lukashenko banned candidates from television. It appears too that 19 nationalist parliamentarians who staged a sit-down strike in protest against the referendum on economic integration with Russia were, on 13 April 1995, forcibly removed from the assembly building by the presidential guard. In response, five Lithuanians sent a protest note to the Belarussian ambassador in Vilnius complaining at the mistreatment of their Belarussian colleagues.[30]

The legitimacy of the parliament (Supreme Soviet) elected in 1990 was challenged by the BPF and its leader Zianon Paznyak, and in March 1992 it organised a grassroots petition which managed to collect the 400 000 signatures necessary to force a referendum on the question of staging a general election. However, this was blocked by parliament in October the same year. Though a general election was finally held on 14 May 1995, in conjunction with the four presidential referenda, the future of parliamentary democracy in Belarus looks in grave doubt. Thus Lukashenko, who after the referenda claimed it was unnecessary to stage further parliamentary elections, issued a decree during the campaign debarring candidates from appearing on television – a response to what he described contemptuously as 'party agitation'.[31] Lukashenko's actions met with the disapproval of the Council of Europe which reported that Belarus did not conform to its membership standards. The Council stated that the elections had not conformed to acceptable norms because the candidates did not receive adequate funding or presentation time in the media.[32] Not only has there been only one general election since independence, but there has been minimal elite turnover in the political executive. There is not a single young generation reformer in the government, but rather the same bureaucrats as ten years ago.

If the Belarus nationalist movement has been relatively weak and suppressed, Lukashenko has nonetheless engaged in an active 'de-nationalisation programme' designed to thwart the nation-building efforts of his predecessor. At the May 1995 referendum, 83.1 per cent voted for Russian to be elevated to the status of an official language alongside Belarusian. Furthermore, in another of the referenda, 75.7 per cent were in favour of a return to the symbols of the Soviet period, the red flag, for example, albeit without the hammer and sickle and rhetoric about the workers of the world uniting. Both outcomes reflect the relatively weak sense of nationality among Belarusians. It is often said that Belarusians are not quite Russians and not quite Ukrainians. In fact, Belarus has distanced itself from the market-economic and democratic ambitions of its near neighbours. It fared relatively well during Soviet times and seems to yearn for a return to the past. Above all, it seeks to benefit from Russian raw material and energy resources which its massive machine and paper industries need. During the Soviet era, Belarus was completely lacking in raw materials and there was a strict command economy; nowadays, energy is imported from Russia by special arrangement at below market prices. In Lukashenko's perception, the case for political nationalism is vitiated by the imperative of economic integration with the Russian Federation.

The former communist elite has held power and the opposition nationalist parties have been hounded by the president and old guard. It was significant that of those (under 50 per cent of delegates) elected in May 1995, about half were communists or their allies in the Agrarian Party. Although Lukashenko opposed the 14 May 1995 general election and made a point of not voting, the 50 per cent turnout necessary for the poll to be valid was achieved and 64.5 per cent participated in the first ballot. However, only 20 out of 260 delegates were elected outright, having gained an absolute majority, and a run-off ballot was scheduled for two weeks later. In the second round only 120 out of 260 seats were filled, largely because turnout fell below the required 50 per cent.[33] Accordingly, Lukashenko was placed in the invidious position of having to decide whether to hold new elections or to change the electoral law retroactively, since according to the election statute two-thirds of members had to be elected before parliament could legally function. Lukashenko appealed to the outgoing Belarusian parliament to reduce its quorum rules to two-fifths so that the new assembly could convene. However, the old legislature failed in two separate votes to reach a decision on transferring power to its successor and instead decided to hold 'top-up' by-elections in November. All this doubtless confirmed Lukashenko in the view that parliamentary democracy was complicated and inefficient when compared with the simplicities of presidential rule by referendum. Certainly, voter apathy has helped to bolster presidential authority and, at the 11 June 1995 local elections, turnout fell below the required 50 per cent.

An economic postscript. In 1994 Belarus and Russia negotiated on a common currency but, although an agreement was close, it foundered when reformists in Russia pointed out that it would be very expensive and could destroy Russia's fiscal policy. Belarus has not succeeded in controlling inflation (2200 per cent in 1994 when GDP dropped 21 per cent) or in freeing prices. Consequently, in March 1995, the IMF refused to grant it a 250 million dollar loan. Privatisation has proceeded very slowly and 90 per cent of economic activity is still in the hands of the state. A customs union has been agreed between Russia, Belarus and Kazakhstan.

Moldova: A 'Ménage à Trois' or the 'Eternal Triangle'?

Moldova, the former Soviet republic of Moldavia, which is wedged between Romania and Ukraine, was constructed out of the ethnic Romanian bulk of Bessarabia in 1940 and at present has a population of 4.4 million. 676 000 people are resident in the capital city of Chisinau. On 29 August 1991, Alexandru Mosanu, speaker of the 'national' parliament, proclaimed Moldovan independence, repudiated the Molotov–Ribbentrop pact, urged democratic legitimacy as the basis for statehood, called on the United Nations to accept Moldova as a full member and asked the governments of the world to recognise its independence. Unlike Ukraine and Belarus (with four years and nine months, respectively) and, of course, the Baltic republics (during the inter-war period), Moldova, at the time of its forcible incorporation into the USSR in 1940, had never existed as an independent state. Rather, it had formed part of Romania and, as Daria Fane comments: 'For many Moldavians, the goal of independence was reunification with Romania.'[34]

The transition to independence in Moldova mirrored the major developments in the other European Soviet republics, including on 23 June 1990, a Declaration of Sovereignty. Crucially, however, on 31 August 1989, Moldova became the first Soviet republic to pass a language law instating the language of the indigenous people as the official language, reclaiming the Latin script (Stalin had introduced the Cyrillic alphabet and injected a range of Russian loan words) and formally proclaiming that the Moldavian and Romanian languages were one in the same. Despite a compromise formula which stipulated that Russian would be the language of interethnic communication, strikes at Russian factories continued for about a month. The language law was a turning-point in the transition to independence, while also polarising relations between the numerically dominant Moldova population and the various 'subject' minorities, particularly the Russian.

Unlike the Popular Fronts in the Baltic republics and Ukraine, the Moldovan Popular Front (MPF) and leaders such as Mircea Druc advocated reunification with Romania rather than independence as such. The achievement of Moldovan independence in short was a stepping-stone – a means rather than an end. Thus the MPF's opposition to the 8 December 1991 presidential elections, overtly at least, was that the ballot would institutionalise the leader of a state that implicitly acknowledged the consequences of the Molotov–Ribbentrop pact. Earlier, on 27 June 1990, the MPF had organised a human chain to mark the fiftieth anniversary of the Red Army's entry into Bessarabia and North Bukovina. It called for the annulment of the decision of 2 August 1940 handing over a slice of Bessarabia to Ukraine. But it was the promotion of Moldavian that was the MPF's motor force and on 27 August 1989 hundreds of thousands of people – predominantly Moldavians – packed a Front rally in support of the language law. In a separate rally nearby an estimated 2000 members of the Russian 'counternationalist' group *Yedinstvo* ('Unity') – a Baltic-style Intermovement – protested against the law. According to one of its leaders, Vladimir Solonar, *Yedinstvo* grew out of the realisation that the non-Moldovan ethnic groups had to press their own interests, in particular parity between Russian and Moldovan as official languages.[35] Incidentally, the 'unionist' cause was given an extra fillip when Moldovan national television started broadcasting Romanian television on 14 October 1990.[36]

The rise of the MPF and the passions aroused by the language issue challenged and ultimately divided the ruling Communist Party in Moldova. Under Petr Luchinski, who replaced Semen Grossu as

First Secretary of the Moldavian CPSU on 16 November 1989, a more 'nationalist' strategy was pursued and something of a rapprochement with the MPF effected. Under him, the ruling party accepted the provisions of the August 1989 language law, including the shift to Latin script, and condoned the Moldavian flag and other outward symbols of Moldavian nationalism. Despite Luchinski's conciliatory, indeed concessionary stance, the Moldavian Communist Party declined as an organisation and it was reported that, during 1990, 13 per cent of its membership left the party. On 4 February 1991 Luchinski was replaced by Grigori Yeremei who, in contrast, came increasingly to be perceived as an apologist for Moscow, especially in respect of his support for Gorbachev's planned referendum on the future of the Union on 17 March 1991. Indeed, at this stage, about one year after the Estonian and Latvian parties, the Moldavian Communist Party split along essentially ethnic lines. A nationalist Independent Moldavian Communist Party was founded on 8 April 1991 by a democratic faction called Democratic Platform and broke with the CPSU, whereas the rump Moldavian Communist Party, which increasingly drew on Russians and Russified minorities, remained loyal to Moscow.

The nascent Moldova, then, was riven by centrifugal forces which severely complicated both the state- and nation-building processes. For example, the legitimacy of the presidential elections of 8 December 1991 was sorely challenged by twin counternationalist movements, on the one hand, and a Popular Front boycott, on the other. Thus the Gagauz Republic (which proclaimed its autonomy in November 1989) and Dnestr republic (independent since 2 September 1990), which stated they would not participate, held their own presidential elections a week earlier, on 1 December. The two secessionist republics had organised their own Union referenda on 17 March 1991 despite the Moldavian Supreme Soviet's decision on 19 February not to stage the Gorbachev referendum. The MPF, moreover, declared the elections illegal and the Democratic Youth Party, which claimed 100 000 supporters, joined the Front in the boycott. The Front organised rallies against Mircea Snegur, the existing head of state, and an estimated 10 000 people united on 3 November under the slogan 'No to Presidential Elections in Moldova'. Initially, the MPF wanted to run Mircea Druc, but he was eliminated when the presidential electoral law excluded as candidates those who had not been permanently resident in Moldavia during the previous ten years. Consequently, the MPF decided not to take part in the election.

Summing up, there was from the outset a three-pronged challenge to the territorial sovereignty of the new state and, in view of the strength of this anti-system (separatist) sentiment, its survival has been as remarkable as the progress it has made towards a market economy. First, the embryonic state was confronted by groups, most notably the MPF, which favoured union with Romania and sought to restore such visible symbols of its western neighbour as the Romanian flag. Next, the ethnic Slavs in Transdnestria proclaimed independence in 1991 and, backed by the former Soviet Fourteenth Army, took control of one Transdnestrian town after another during the early part of 1992. Although situated at the industrial centre of the Moldovan state, Transdnestria is a peripheral strip of land flanking Ukraine on the east bank of the Dniester river. Finally, the christian Turkic-speaking population in the self-proclaimed Gagauz Republic in the south-west, like Transdnestria, ultimately wanted unification with the Russian Federation. Significantly, President Snegur, faced with what amounted to civil war in the east of the country, was forced to declare a state of emergency throughout Moldova in March 1992. In short, the territorial foundations of the new state seemed extremely shaky and the edifice that was Moldova was threatened with at least partial collapse.

Even more so than in Ukraine and Belarus, the Moldovan political system since 1991 has been completely dominated by a single individual, Snegur, previously a leading communist official, who became closely associated with the Moldovan independence movement. Snegur, the incumbent head of state, as mentioned, won the December 1991 presidential elections unopposed, with 98 per cent of the vote, when the MPF boycotted the election; his pro-independence Agrarian Party gained a majority of seats in the first post-communist general election in February 1994 on a strong programme of political pluralism and market economic reform; and, unlike the first heads of state, Kravchuk in Ukraine and Shuskevitsch in Belarus (both deposed), Snegur has survived in office throughout the independence period. His ability to act on the Transdnestria situation and to deal with the Russian president Boris Yeltsin has been crucial to maintaining his position. Thus, in April 1994, Snegur initiated talks, with the assistance of mediators from Russia and the Conference (now Organisation) on Security and Co-operation in Europe (OSCE), and in October that year Russia and Moldova agreed to a phased withdrawal over three years of the Fourteenth Army, despite vehement objections from its commander, Aleksandr Lebed, and local Russians.

The intensity of ethnic conflict in the newly-independent Moldova contributed to an institutional paralysis and the debilitation of parliament in particular, enormously complicated the task of enacting the basic political groundrules of the new state. Thus, faced by a boycott of Transdnestria delegates, orchestrated by the secessionist leader, Igor Smirnov, and opposition from the MPF, the national parliament in 1993 failed to command the necessary majority to adopt a new constitution. It was only the election as speaker of Petr Luchinski, the former First Secretary of the Moldavian CPSU, who enjoyed considerable authority as a strong but reform-minded politician, which materially assisted in the resolution of matters and, backed by Snegur, a new constitution, enshrining autonomy from Transdnestria, was enacted in July 1994.

The frailties of parliament were further exposed when Moscow, in return for agreement on the phased withdrawal of the Fourteenth Army, pressed Moldova to join the CIS. The absence of East Bank delegates gave the MPF sufficient numerical strength to block parliamentary approval. Enough delegates then walked out to enforce recourse to the electorate. The first post-communist general election, in short, may be regarded as something of a last resort when ethnic rivalries completely hamstrung a national assembly whose composition dated back to the Soviet era.

The multi-ethnic character of Moldova has rendered the task of nation-building, that is, the creation of an overarching Moldovan identity, even more difficult than state-building. In other words, if the legitimacy of the state can be enhanced, and ethnic minorities integrated in principle by means of a federal or quasi-federal constitution, creating loyalties that transcend subcultural allegiances appears extremely problematical. Despite Sovietisation, the majority of the Moldovan population (65 per cent) is Romanian-speaking and, in view of the resounding victory at the February 1994 general election for those candidates favouring independence over unification with Romania or closer ties with Russia, it may reasonably be surmised that this majority is more or less reconciled to being Moldovan citizens. This cannot be said of Transdnestria where, despite the regional autonomy built into the July 1994 constitution, separatist pressure has been maintained.[37] Nearly 54 per cent of the Transdnestrian population of 730 000 is Slavic, roughly equally divided between Russians and Ukrainians, both of whom enjoyed privileges under the Soviet regime, compared with 40 per cent Moldovan, and in March 1995 a referendum instigated by pro-Russian leaders was held on whether the Fourteenth Army should remain in the region 'as a guarantor of peace and stability'. In a reportedly high (but unspecified turnout) 94 per cent favoured the continued presence of the Fourteenth Army. Separatist sentiment still appears strong.

Turning our attention from the 'new' European successor states of the former Soviet Union to the 'old' successor states of the inter-war period, it is worth emphasising that the three Baltic republics of Latvia, Lithuania and (the main focus of this volume) Estonia, like Ukraine, Belarus and Moldova, (re)gained independence in the immediate wake of the failed anti-Gorbachev coup in August 1991. In these small states, with a combined population of about eight million, the legacy of Soviet rule was immediately apparent in the form of 145 000 Red Army troops, widely regarded as the strong arm of the 'occupying power', and various nuclear installations (for example, at Skrunda and Paldiski) that would need dismantling. There were also over one million ethnic Russian civilians in Latvia and about half a million in Estonia, a large majority of them workers brought in under the Soviet regime to staff the factories and dilute nationalist sentiments among the Balts. Not surprisingly, the CPSU was banned in all three Baltic states directly after the August 1991 coup attempt, although some of its members continued to play a prominent role in local Russian-language political circles in Latvia and Estonia. Across the region, moreover, laws were quickly adopted banning former KGB agents from standing for parliament and high office.

Despite important differences (to be delineated shortly), there were several common denominators in the independence process in the three Baltic states. First, the independence movements were preceded by openly pro-independence groups emanating from associations of dissidents. There was significant transnational cooperation between Baltic dissidents and their first joint document appeared as early as 1969. Ten years later, an appeal to the United Nations on 23 August 1979 – the fortieth anniversary of the Molotov–Ribbentrop pact – in which the illegal Soviet occupation was roundly denounced, was signed by 45 Baltic dissidents, 36 of them Lithuanians.[38]

Second, the mainstay of the nationalist opposition comprised popular movements formed in 1988 (Popular Fronts in Estonia and Latvia and Sajûdis in Lithuania) ostensibly set up in support of Gorbachev's reformist programme of *perestroika* and boasting a highly heterogeneous support base, including some (albeit not many) ethnic Russians. In all three states, the Popular Fronts were initiated by men like Jánis Peters (secretary of the Latvian Writer's Union and later ambassador to Moscow), liberal intellectuals from the cultural elites (Communist Party members by necessity), along with junior members of the communist establishment, although mostly from the state rather than party.[39] The toleration, possibly even support, extended at the outset to these movements by reformist sections of the Moscow leadership and the KGB resulted from their being viewed as allies against the hardliners in the CPSU.[40]

In addition to the Popular Fronts, radical nationalist opposition centred on the citizens' committee movements which in 1990 elected a Congress of Estonia and Congress of Latvia (voters comprised only those who were citizens of the inter-war republics and their descendants). The Congresses viewed the Supreme Soviets, controlled from spring 1990 by the Popular Fronts, as 'institutions of foreign occupation' and relations between the Fronts and citizen committee movements were strained for long periods. Unlike the case of Latvia and Estonia, the nationality issue did not bulk large in the thinking of ordinary Lithuanians, who did not view the small Russian and Polish minorities as a great threat. This would probably explain in large part why in 1992 Lithuania swung to the left – and Algirdas Brazauskas' Democratic Labour Party (formerly Communists) became easily the largest party – whilst, in the shape of victories for *Isamaa* (Fatherland) and Latvian Way, Estonia and Latvia shifted to the centre-right.

In all three Baltic states, the independence process witnessed a very high level of mass mobilisation. This found most notable expression in the 'Baltic Way' demonstration on 23 August 1989 when two million Balts – two-fifths of the entire native population of the region – formed a continuous 370-mile human chain from Vilnius through Riga to Tallinn to demand independence. Inevitably, the publication of the truth of the Molotov–Ribbentrop pact in 1989 and the manner in which the Balts came to be annexed in 1940 came as a considerable shock. It is worth noting, too, that the Baltic Way predated the 'crowds on the streets' that were a hallmark of the autumn revolutions in Central and Eastern Europe.

In both Estonia and Lithuania in April 1990 attempts were made to transform the Popular Front and Sajûdis from umbrella organisations into disciplined parties, but both endeavours foundered, in part for ideological reasons, but mainly because they were associated with the personal ambitions of their leaders, Vytautas Landsbergis and Edgar Savisaar.[41] In other words, personality conflicts at the leadership level within the Baltic popular opposition movements led to their fragmentation and the formation of proto-parties well before the final recovery of independence.

Lithuania: The Confrontational Course to Independence

Lithuania, which borders Belarus, Latvia, the Russian enclave of Kaliningrad and Poland, has a population of about 3.7 million people, 592 000 of them living in the capital Vilnius. Ethnically, it is the most homogeneous of all the Baltic states; indeed, after Armenia it was the most homogeneous of all the Soviet republics. About 80 per cent of the population are Lithuanians, compared with 7.0 per cent Poles and 9.4 per cent Russians. The Poles are predominantly peasants, concentrated in the eastern area surrounding Vilnius which was occupied by Poland in the inter-war period. The Russians, in contrast, are geographically dispersed across Lithuania, with just over one-third speaking reasonable Lithuanian. Predominantly Catholic (embracing catholicism in the fourteenth century, the Lithuanians were the last people in Europe to become Christian) the church in Lithuania played a prominent role in the dissident movement. For example, in 1972 the underground *Chronicle of the Catholic Church* documented the government's illegal anti-Catholic campaign, while the Catholic human rights movement had extensive popular support. In the early 1970s over 50 000 Lithuanians signed a petition protesting at the government's religious persecution. The Catholic church later identified closely with cultural nationalism and Landsbergis' vision of a 'Lithuanian Lithuania', itself reminiscent of de Valera's dream of an Irish Ireland gnawed at as little as possible by the worm of civilisation, especially the British.

As in the other two Baltic states, a history of individual dissidence stretched back to the late 1960s and included people such as Antanas Terleckas and Viktoras Petkas, who were imprisoned for anti-Soviet activities. In 1978 they formed the *Lithuanian Freedom League* (Lietuvås Laisves Lyga) although this did not surface until a decade later. Significantly, the Freedom League, unlike the popular front movement Sajûdis, but in common with the Estonian and Latvian 'citizens committees', boycotted the Supreme Soviet elections in March 1990. Petkas was also involved in a Helsinki Watch group in the late 1970s.[42]

As in Estonia and Latvia, ecological protest provided a manifest rationale and a convenient umbrella for the emergent nationalist movement that was spawned by the changed climate of *glasnost* and *perestroika*. Certainly, Moscow's plans to develop Lithuania's hazardous chemicals industry was a factor contributing to the formation of Sajûdis in June 1988, although the main outrage focused on a proposed fourth reactor at the Ignalina nuclear power plant – the biggest in the western part of the Soviet Union – opposition to which was swelled by the Chernobyl disaster in April 1986. Landsbergis was elected chairman of the Sajûdis Council in November 1988 and at the March 1990 Supreme Soviet elections he and Sajûdis won a clear victory on a platform of complete independence.

Lithuania's Declaration of Independence on 11 March 1990 – less than two years after the demonstrations for an Estonian Popular Front triggered the whole revolutionary course in the Baltic – brought Lithuania into direct conflict with the Kremlin. Earlier, in January that year, Gorbachev had paid a dramatic visit to Vilnius in an (unavailing) attempt to prevent the Lithuanian Communist Party (the first in the Baltic region) from proceeding with its decision to separate from the CPSU. Lithuania's showdown with Moscow suddenly became a focus of Western media attention and was viewed with a mixture of interest and apprehension by Tallinn and Riga. Within days of the declaration of independence, both Gorbachev and the Congress of People's Deputies in Moscow demanded its annulment. This was followed by direct pressure and the seizure by Soviet paratroops of Lithuanian deserters from the Soviet army who were housed in a psychiatric clinic near Vilnius under the 'protection' of the Red Cross flag.[43] Thereafter, there was the possession, initially by Soviet Interior Ministry troops, of buildings in Vilnius owned by the CPSU but by then under the control of the majority 'nationalist' wing of the party led by Algirdas Brazauskas. A sustained oil blockade imposed by Gorbachev obliged a fundamental reappraisal in Vilnius and on 23 June 1990 the Supreme Soviet approved what amounted to an embargo on the implementation of the declaration of independence (though the declaration itself was not rescinded).

When the Lithuanian government raised food prices by an average 32 per cent on 7 January 1991 and a crowd of Poles and Russians gathered to demand the resignation of the government and parliament (Supreme Soviet) – the Prunskiene administration did in fact resign and the price increases were cancelled – the situation was clearly one that could be exploited by Moscow and so the second act of the Lithuanian independence conflict began. Four people were injured when, on 11 January, paratroopers stormed the Press House in Vilnius and Lithuanian Defence Department buildings in several cities were occupied. When Landsbergis, who in March 1990 had been elected chair of the Supreme Council and de facto head of state, sought to contact Gorbachev, the Soviet president declined to speak to him.[44] Finally, 14 Lithuanians were killed on the night of 13 January when a crowd tried to defend the TV tower and TV station against Russian paratroops in armoured vehicles. The whole dramatic and bloody episode, widely reported in the West, elevated the status of Landsbergis and the Lithuanian independence cause and led to a storm of protest, not only in the USA and Western Europe, but in Russia itself.

The achievement of independence in August 1991 was followed by a political battle over the form the new constitution should take, with Landsbergis seeking (ultimately unsuccessfully) to create a French-style executive presidency. Yet if the state-building process was characterised by high levels of elite conflict, the population as a whole appeared largely uninterested and a referendum on the presidential question on 23 May 1992 failed to produce a sufficiently high turnout to meet the requirements of Lithuanian law. In his concern to create an executive presidency, to be sure, Landsbergis' rhetoric became increasingly extremist as he endeavoured to argue that parliament had betrayed the nation and that it was Sajûdis that now represented the national will.[45] It was certainly Sajûdis which organised the necessary signatures to stage the aforementioned referendum on the presidential question. In the event, turnout was only 57.5 per cent and this meant that, although 69.4 per cent approved a strong presidency and only 25.6 per cent opposed it (5 per cent cast invalid ballots), the result was well short of the 51 per cent of all eligible voters required by Lithuanian law. Ultimately, the new constitution, enacted on 1992, provided for a government responsible to parliament, but with stronger presidential powers than those in Estonia. The president was vested with the right to propose to parliament candidates for a range of offices – the commander of the army and security service, state controller, chairman of the State Bank, senior judges and so on – without having to ask the advice of the prime minister. But the head of state could only appoint or dismiss ministers at the recommendation of the prime minister.[46]

At the first post-communist presidential elections on 14 February 1993, Brazauskas won 60 per cent of the vote against 38 per cent for Stasys Lozaraitis, the Ambassador to Washington, who was supported by Sajûdis. Brazauskas had become Lithuanian Communist Party secretary on 20 October 1988 and little more than a year later was at the helm when his party became the first in the Baltic region to break with the CPSU (subsequently renaming itself the Democratic Labour Party – LDDP). However, the month of his appointment as party secretary, Brazauskas, under intense pressure from Moscow, blocked a declaration of sovereignty similar to that already passed by the Estonian Supreme Soviet (it did not come about until 18 May 1989) and, accordingly, Brazauskas' reputation was badly dented among Lithuanian nationalists. His position revived when, like Arnold Rüütel in Estonia and Anatolijs Gorbunovs in Latvia, he evaded responsibility for government between 1990 and 1992 (compare the case of Landsbergis, who bore the attendant unpopularity) and then picked up popular support as the plain-speaking LDDP leader who triumphed at the parliamentary elections of October 1992.[47] Brazauskas has dominated Lithuanian politics since his elevation to head of state in February 1993.

Nation-building, or more specifically, the protection and promotion of the national culture, was the dominant theme of the political right (Sajûdis) at the first post-communist general election in Lithuania in October 1992, although in view of the ethnic composition of the newly independent state it was not perhaps surprising that the nationality issue had less electoral significance than in Latvia and Estonia. For Sajûdis, the threat to the nation came from communists and the communist past and accusations of KGB involvement were prominent throughout the campaign. A Sajûdis poster read: 'The deputies, like the whole country, are divided into two groups – communists and anti-communists. The communists have rebaptised themselves with many names: LDDP, Liberals, Social Democrats, Centrists and Moderates.'[48] Almost all the proto-parties and groupings, it was inferred, contained crypto-communists, the exception being Sajûdis. In the event, the nationality issue proved of secondary importance and it was the sharp decline in living standards that cooked Sajûdis' electoral goose. The Sajûdis-led government tried to prepare for winter by saving on fuel and by October most households were limited to two days' hot water weekly.[49] Brazauskas was also able to make much political capital by opposing enforced decollectivisation and he tied his arguments very closely to the condition of the farmers. Like Rüütel in Estonia, he became the man of the rural people.

If the level of electoral participation is used as a very crude indicator of the democratic nature of society, and by extension the progress made in society-building, Lithuania in 1992 ranked broadly alongside Estonia. In the first round in the first post-communist general election in October 1992, 72 per cent turned out to vote, although by the second round this had fallen to 60 per cent. The average was only fractionally lower than the 67 per cent of Estonians that took part in their general election the previous month. True, by the local elections of 25 March 1995, turnout had slumped to 43 per cent and the opposition-based Homeland Union (previously Sajûdis), led by Landsbergis and Gediminas Vagnorius, profiting from its core, loyalist support, won 29.1 per cent of the vote. Brazauskas' ruling LDDP, in contrast, clearly affected by the low turnout, managed only 19.9 per cent of the vote.[50]

Of particular relevance to the 'parties and democratisation' theme of the present volume, and sharing the author's assumption that a strong party system is a necessary condition of *democratic consolidation*, is Terry D. Clark's work on the *Seimas* poll of October 1992.[51] Clark's case-study comes to the optimistic conclusion that 'the Lithuanian elections demonstrate the progress of the process of democratic consolidation in the republic'.[52] This assertion is based on three analytical variables: the extent of party fragmentation, the numerical strength of extremist (anti-system) parties and the nature of party–social group linkages. On the first-mentioned, Clark notes that 17 parties and electoral alliances contested the 1992 general election. However, although 11 parties and political movements eventually won seats in the Seimas, only five – the LDDP, Sajûdis, the Christian Democrats and their allies, Social Democrats and the Union of Poles – won proportional representation (PR) list seats (there were 70 of these in all) and this quintet ultimately controlled 124 of the total of 141 Seimas deputies (71 were allocated on a single-member, double-ballot basis). Setting aside the Union of Poles, which capitalised on the lower 2 per cent threshold for ethnic minority parties, Clark speaks of a 'four-party system': four 'relevant' parties in the sense of parties able to influence legislative outcomes.[53] Despite the low 2 per cent barrier for ethnic groupings, in contrast to 5 per cent for other parties, none of the Russian minority parties gained representation and it appears that the Russian population largely came down on the side of the overwhelming winner, Brazauskas' LDDP.

Second, in stressing the absence of extremist parties in parliament, Clark dismisses the possibility that the LDDP could be viewed as an extremist, anti-democratic party. He notes that the LDDP was the first CPSU affiliate to leave the party in December 1989 and then supported the republic's drive for independence. It also urged the withdrawal of Russian troops from Lithuania.

Finally, on the question of party–group linkages, Clark points to the way the political Left – defined as the LDDP, Social Democrats and Union of Poles – won overwhelmingly in the rural areas, whereas the political Right (Sajûdis and Christian Democrats) did best in the towns. He adds 'The primary factor which appears to account for peasant support for the left and in particular the LDDP is the parties' opposition to the land privatization programme which has impoverished the rural population and undermined their pre-independence social benefits.'[54]

Clark's is a systematic and superficially persuasive analysis which implies, if it does not explicitly state, that Lithuania has emerged as a 'moderate multi-party system', in Sartori's terms. There is a fundamental bipolarity and at least the possibility of alternation and a shift to the political right. On two points, however, a stronger 'grassroots perspective' on the embryonic parties would have been valuable. First, Clark does not present evidence on the strength of 'party' versus 'personality' voting, the latter being clearly encouraged in the 71 single-member constituencies. Can a party system be regarded as strong, as it is considered in Lithuania, if party identification is weak? Second, in the absence of explicitly interest-specific (class) parties, along the lines of the Agrarian Party in Latvia and Rural Centre Party in Estonia, a discussion of the electoral strategies (if any) of the parties would have been helpful. Did the parties actively concentrate on particular constituencies – were they, for example, *for* the peasants as well as being *of* the peasants? Finally, Clark's assumption that ethnic parties tend to hold back the integration of national minorities, that the failure of the Russian parties to gain representation could be viewed in a positive light, seems at least open to question. The denominational Christian Democratic Party has been distinctive in the Baltic region in the strength of its support and is one of the few numerically significant groupings to be expressly grounded in a mainstream West European party ideology. Several of the issues raised above will be considered in the Estonian case later in this volume.

Latvia: the Baltic Back Marker in the Independence Process

Latvia, which borders Lithuania, Estonia, Belarus and Russia, has a population of 2.7 million, 34 per cent or 917 000 people based in the capital city, Riga. Although native Latvians number 52 per cent of the total population, they constitute a numerical minority in Latvia's seven largest cities where Russians, Belarusians and Ukrainians make up the lion's share of the non-native majority. Until the advent of Gorbachev there was extensive Russification, especially of the Latvian education system, and this represented a case of what Nils Muizneks has described as 'asymmetric bilingualism'.[55] For example, Latvian-language schools required four to six hours of Russian language tuition weekly whereas Russian-language schools required only two hours of Latvian per week. Latvian 'sixth-formers' were also obliged to take a final examination in Russian, but their Russian contemporaries were exempt from a comparable test in Latvian. Doctoral dissertations, moreover, had to be translated into Russian before they could be accepted. The difference in linguistic proficiency was marked. In the 1989 census only 21.1 per cent of Russians claimed a knowledge of Latvian while 65.7 per cent of all Latvians claimed knowledge of Russian (97.4 per cent, however, regarded Latvian as their native language).

On a related political note, a primary factor in Latvia's generally slower progress towards independence than her Baltic neighbours lay in the fact that more than half the Latvian Communist Party (LCP) members were Russians. On 1 January 1989, Latvians accounted for only 39.7 per cent of party members and candidates compared with the Russian share of 43.1 per cent and a section of the Latvian total comprised *latovichi*, Soviet-born or Soviet-educated Russified Latvians (who usually spoke little or no Latvian) and who were 'imported' after the Second World War to fill the leading positions in society.[56] In the context of the ethnic composition of the LCP, it is hardly surprising that, while in December 1989 and March 1990, respectively, the Lithuanian and Estonian Communist Parties voted to break with the CPSU, a majority of the Latvian party in April 1990 remained loyal to Moscow.

If Estonia was the first Baltic state to issue a declaration of sovereignty, in November 1988, (Latvia was the last, on 28 July 1989) and Lithuania was the first to declare full independence, in March 1990, Latvia witnessed the first patriotic demonstrations in the Baltic region when the 'Helsinki-86' group organised a demonstration at the Freedom Monument in Riga to mark the anniversary of the Stalinist deportations of 1941.[57] Further demonstrations followed in short order on the anniversary of the Molotov–Ribbentrop pact on 23 August and again on 18 November, the date of Latvia's first declaration of independence.

Prior to the emergence of a popular front, modelled on Estonian lines in June 1988, three strands of (partially overlapping) regime opposition in Latvia can be identified. The first, ecological protest,

was not expressly nationalist in character, but saw the mass mobilisation of opposition to a proposed hydroelectric dam on the river
Daugava. Criticism by the journalist Dainis Ivans (later president of
the Popular Front) and writer Arturs Snips in a popular Latvian
cultural weekly in mid-October 1986 led to over 30 000 letters of
objection from all the nationalities in Latvia and, ultimately, in summer 1987, to the cancellation of the project. Facilitated by *perestroika*
and stimulated by Chernobyl, the environmental movement embraced
a range of activists and generally contributed to a heightened sense
of subjective competence among the population as a whole, a feeling
that meaningful influence could (just!) be exerted on decision making.

The second element in the opposition movement, the Environment
Protection Club (VAK), like the National Heritage Society in Estonia,
was an umbrella for several groups, all of which focused on reviving
the historical memory of the nation. Comprising an assortment of
mainly young people, these groups had been active from 1983 repair-
ing old churches and monuments. VAK was a radical nationalist
organisation which was committed to working for democratisation
and full independence. Some of its most radical members formed
Latvia's National Independence Movement (LNNK) in late June 1988
and were closely involved in the 'citizens' movement' of summer
1989.

Finally, the dissident-based 'Helsinki-86' was formed in July 1986
by three Latvian workers in Liepāja, possessed only a small membership and, though severely repressed, wrote letters of complaint to the
authorities and appeals to the West. It was denied access to the
media, but through its *samizdat* it argued for the elevation of Latvian
to the status of official language, an end to non-native immigration
and, ultimately, called for the restoration of Latvian independence
and adherence to international covenants on human rights. Although,
following the non-violent demonstrations of 1987, several of its organisers were detained and a number of its activists exiled to the
West, 'Helsinki-86' mobilised thousands of ordinary Latvians and
was crucial in setting a nationalist agenda. It had successfully defied
the system.

Much as in Estonia, the Latvian Popular Front originated in concept at an extended plenary of the Writer's Union on 1–2 June 1988
devoted to the 'Urgent Problems of Soviet Latvian Culture on the
Eve of the Nineteenth CPSU Conference'.[58] At a highly charged (and
televised) session Mavriks Vulfsons, a veteran political commentator,
openly described the events of 1940 as an 'occupation', not a 'socialist revolution'; several speakers criticised the LCP leadership as inca-
pable of meeting the challenges of the day; and a resolution was
passed demanding decentralisation and 'sovereignty' (in the econ-

omic, defence and cultural spheres, including the creation of a republican citizenship). There were also demands for a halt to censorship, the separation of the legislative and executive branches of government and the appointment to leading positions of non-party members. A group led by the journalist Viktor Avotins circulated a document arguing the need for a 'democratic popular front' in Latvia. The LCP chief, Boris Pugo, strategically modified his hardline stance towards the notion by August, but when, by the end of September, the Front could boast over 80 000 members, Pugo was 'promoted' to lead the Party Control Commission in Moscow. Janis Vagris became the LCP First Secretary and Anatolijs Gorbunovs became chair of the Supreme Soviet. Launched officially on 8–9 October 1988, the Latvian Popular Front initially demanded 'sovereignty' within the Soviet Union. Hard on the heels of the LNNK Congress, it came out for full independence on 31 May 1989.

The Latvian Popular Front survived as a movement and a parliamentary grouping longer than elsewhere in the region. Like Sajûdis, however, it suffered from conflict between the communist and ex-communist moderates, on the one hand, and the more radical nationalists, on the other. Before independence, the Popular Front had, publicly at least, taken a conciliatory line towards the Russians. Afterwards, however, the movement swung sharply in a nationalist direction and at its Congress in November 1991 the Popular Front adopted a set of slogans which were basically indistinguishable from those of the radical nationalists.[59] On 4 May 1990, the Front-dominated Latvian Supreme Council (government) declared null and void the Soviet annexation and established a transitional period leading to de facto independence. By the June 1993 election the Popular Front was disintegrating.

As in Estonia, radical opposition to the Popular Front was channelled through the 'citizens committees' which in May 1990 organised elections to a Latvian Congress. A split in the radical nationalist camp became quickly evident, however, and as a result of their intractable opposition to the Supreme Soviet and Popular Front, the 'extreme radicals' split from the main radical nationalist group, the LNNK, which had cooperated with the Popular Front and indeed participated in the organisation in 1990. Accordingly, unlike the Estonia Congress which remained a 'broad church' for nationalist opposition, its Latvian counterpart had by 1991–2 become dominated by extreme radical nationalists, such as Māris Grínblats and Višvaldis Brinkmanis, whose statements threatened war with Russia and alarmed the electorate.[60]

Unlike Estonia and Lithuania, Latvia held elections without agreement having been reached on either a new constitution or a naturalisation law, that is before the process of state-building was formally complete. Progress towards a new constitution was retarded in Latvia, compared with the other Baltic states, in large part because of the size of the Russian minority. Indeed, more generally, the numerous Russian representatives in the Supreme Soviet made it difficult to generate stable alliances of deputies behind particular reforms. Another crucial factor in the delay in enacting a new Latvian constitution lay in the inability of the Latvian deputies to resolve the thorny issue of citizenship. This prompted the de facto head of state, Gorbunovs, in March 1992, to propose that only citizens of the pre-1940 Latvia be allowed to vote in a planned referendum on citizenship. Finally, in June 1994, the Latvian parliament passed a citizenship law which included a controversial quota system for the naturalisation of new citizens. However, in the face of adverse Western reaction, and in response to an appeal from President Ulmanis, parliament subsequently modified the law and, while this was approved by the Council of Europe, Moscow continued to voice objections. In its present form, candidates for citizenship must have been born in Latvia (after the year 2000 a three-year residency requirement will apply) and must also pass tests on language and history as well as swearing an oath of allegiance.[61]

Attempts to 'nationalise' (to 'Latvianize') the political executive preceded the achievement of independence – a law in 1989 required state officials to be bilingual – and the attainment of independence brought a concerted programme designed to promote the national language, culture and, by extension, national identity of the Latvian people. In March 1992 a language law was adopted which, while acknowledging the right of minorities to use their mother tongue, guaranteed an education only in Latvian. The Ministry of Education also instigated increased Latvian language teaching in Russian schools. Public symbolism was also made predominantly Latvian. For example, the Moscow District of Riga was renamed Latgale, despite the fact that Moscow Suburb (*Moskauer Vorstadt*) is its historic name. All over the centre of the capital, street signs in Russian were removed.[62] True, the introduction of a Latvian rouble (as a temporary measure) was necessitated by a severe currency shortage rather than nationalist concerns (it was not backed by hard currency and created financial confusion) and it was October 1993 before the introduction of a permanent currency, the *lats*, was completed. The strong emphasis given to nation-building by the post-independence governments did nothing, of course, to facilitate the integration of the non-Latvian minorities and although resentments did not spill over in public, Moscow exploited the situation to claim further evidence of discrimination against the Russian diaspora in the Baltic.

The first post-communist election in Latvia was held on 5–6 June 1993, with 23 parties submitting lists and eight exceeding the 4 per cent threshold required for seats in the *Saeima*. These eight parties received a combined 89 per cent of the popular vote.[63] The election was won by Latvian Way, a mix of 'both radicals and moderates from the Popular Front, moderate Latvian émigrés under the leader of the World Federation of Free Latvians, Guars Meierovics, and former members of the Communist establishment'.[64] It won 32.2 per cent compared with 13.4 per cent for the LNNK, led by Eduards Berklavs, 10.6 per cent for the Agrarian Party, 5.0 per cent for the Christian Democrats and 4.8 per cent for the Democratic Centre. All five of these parties favoured making the franchise available to non-Latvians subject to residence, language and loyalty requirements. Latvian Way for its part was far less cohesive than its nearest equivalent, *Isamaa*, in Estonia and victory was predicated on the acquisition of Gorbunovs, by far the most popular politician in Latvia. The Popular Front under Ivars Godmanis, in contrast (with 2.6 per cent) failed to muster the 4 per cent necessary to qualify for representation in parliament. Three of the successful parliamentary parties had views on the citizenship issue which fell outside the consensus. 'For Fatherland and Freedom' which polled 5.4 per cent, advocated a 'Latvia for Latvians' approach and was suspicious of anything but the most carefully controlled extension of citizenship. The Concord Party, in contrast, with 12 per cent support, promoted the extension of citizenship to all non-military personnel and the need for long-term economic links with Russia. Finally, the Equality Party, which managed 5.8 per cent, argued for equal status for ethnic Russians as long as they had been resident in Latvia on 4 May 1990, when the Supreme Council had declared de jure independence.

In a not insignificant sense, the 'democratic access' of Latvians was more restricted than for Estonians and Lithuanians in that the first post-communist head of state was not directly elected by the people. Guntis Ulmanis was nominated by parliament. Ironically, it is the Agrarian Party that now strongly favours a referendum on the question of staging popular presidential elections.

Estonia

The restoration of independence in August 1991 meant that Estonia became one of the smallest states in the 'New Europe', with a population of only one and a half million, making it broadly similar in size to that of Slovenia. Unlike the latter, however, it re-emerged a multiethnic state: approximately 900 000 people are Estonians and 600 000 non-Estonians, mainly Russians. Post-communist Estonia, in short, lost the cultural homogeneity of the inter-war republic and faced the challenge of integrating its national minorities. Since the bulk of the rest of this volume will focus on the question of parties and democratisation in Estonia in the period before and after the recovery of independence, only a few general introductory remarks on the politico-economic progress made since 1991 will be essayed.

On the political stage, Estonia quickly succeeded in reitegrating itself into the international community. It was admitted to the CSCE on 10 September 1991, the UN in 1992 and became a member of the Council of Europe on 14 May 1993. Moreover, exactly one week after Lithuania's formal approach to NATO on 4 January 1994, the *Riigikogu* (parliament) voted decisively in favour of preparing a draft law on an application for NATO membership. It also approved Estonian involvement in NATO's 'Partnership for Peace' (PFP) initiative. On 9 May 1994 Estonia, the two other Baltic states (and Poland, Hungary, the Czech Republic, Slovakia, Romania and Bulgaria) became 'associate partners' in the Western European Union (WEU), with the concomitant option (going further than the PFP) of participating in joint WEU operations. Finally, in spring 1995 Estonia concluded an 'association agreement' with the EU which, uniquely, involved no transitional period.

Economically, Estonia had made giant strides forward, prompting reference in some Western circles to an Estonian 'economic miracle'. It became the first country in the former Soviet Union to break out of the rouble zone and on 20 June 1992 introduced its own currency, the *kroon*, which has been tightly linked to the *Deutschmark*. A strict monetary policy and a highly liberal trade strategy, eschewing customs protection, brought plaudits from the International Monetary Fund (IMF), World Bank and the European Bank for Reconstruction and Development.

Two distinctive constitutional strictures have symptomised the supreme importance attached to economic rectitude: a balanced budget is a constitutional requirement and a currency devaluation is not permitted by law. Initially, the fact that the *kroon* was undervalued created a stable and conducive economic environment. But, in the context of the post-communist Central and East European systems, the unique feature in the Estonian approach was the introduction of a Currency Board system along the lines of Hong Kong. Fully backed by gold (deposited in other countries and international clearing banks before the Second World War and returned to Estonia after independence was regained) and foreign currency reserves, the money supply is totally indigenous and regulated by market forces (increased assets would increase the money supply) and the government cannot directly influence it.

Despite a range of social and economic problems – such as high unemployment, especially in the south, high levels of crime and the slow pace of the restitution of land to its previous owners – the transition to a pluralist polity has largely been achieved. A new constitution was approved at a referendum in June 1992; a general election the following September returned the first post-Soviet *Riigikogu*; and a right-wing coalition comprising the Estonian National Independence Party, Rural Centre Party and Social Democrats (strong advocates of privatisation) and dominated by the *Isamaa* (Fatherland) assumed office. True, there have been routine teething troubles in the form of political scandals, ministerial resignations and, indeed, sackings. By April 1994 the popularity of the governing coalition had fallen below the 5 per cent vote threshold required for representation in parliament. But it was not until January 1994 that Estonia experienced a full-blown constitutional crisis. The president, Lennart Meri, initially refused to confirm four new ministerial appointments which formed part of a cabinet reshuffle. Although he did ultimately ratify the posts, Meri's venomous attack on Mart Laar, the prime minister, in the *Riigikogu* did nothing to enhance the office of either president or prime minister.

The standing of the latter plummeted further when, on 2 September 1994, Laar and the president of the Bank of Estonia, Siim Kallas, revealed that 2.3 billion Soviet roubles, withdrawn as the Estonian *kroon* was introduced, had been sold for 1.9 million US dollars in late 1992 and early 1993. Laar admitted he had deliberately withheld information on the sale earlier, fearing that it might jeopardise the withdrawal of Russian troops from Estonia.[65] On 6 September Laar's coalition partners demanded his resignation and on 20 September the minister of social affairs, Marju Lauristin (Social Democrats), resigned, referring to an 'ethical crisis in government'.[66] Laar's own party, *Isamaa*, did not demand his resignation, but on 26 September he lost a vote of no confidence in the *Riigikogu* by 60 votes to 27 (with one abstention) and was forced to step down. He was replaced as a caretaker prime minister – until the March 1995 general election – by Andres Tarand. The second post-independence general election saw Estonia shift to the left or at least left-centre (the highly arbitrary nature of the party political spectrum is discussed later). Tiit Vähi (briefly prime minister in 1992) led a coalition comprising his Coalition Party (named after the right-wing Finnish party of the same name), the Rural People's Party created by Arnold Rüütel, the former president of the Estonian Soviet Socialist Republic (ESSR), barely six months before the election, and the Centre Party, led by the former Popular Front leader, Edgar Savisaar. The election is discussed in detail later in this volume.

There are only three references to political parties in the 1992 Estonian constitution. Article 30 states that the law may restrict the right of some categories of civil servants to join political parties; article 48 stipulates that only Estonian citizens may be members of political parties and that those parties whose aims and/or activities are 'directed towards the violent change of the constitution' shall be prohibited; article 84 posits the *pouvoir neutre* principle in insisting that, upon assuming office, the President of the Republic shall suspend his or her membership of a political party.

Despite the paucity of the constitutional recognition afforded them, Estonia may, paradoxically, already be considered a party democracy in the sense that the infant parties have been nationalised and form an extended arm of the state. Inter-party cooperation facilitated a new constitution; parties have monopolised government and predominated in parliament – there have been no independents in the various cabinets albeit there have been several in the *Riigikogu*; and the dominant coalition party, *Isamaa*, before it fractured in the summer of 1994, had been engaged in party-politicising public appointments. Admittedly, there have not been the Petkā practices – the broad-gauge cooperation across the political spectrum – that gave rise to cabinets of all the major parties in inter-war Czechoslovakia. Government–opposition relations in fact have been generally adversarial in the British two-party mould, although the new Vähi coalition was given a 100-day 'honeymoon' by the opposition before hostilities commenced in earnest. But Estonia is a party democracy in which the position of parties is ensconced by law, particularly the May 1994 enactment on party funding.

There remains, nonetheless, a striking discrepancy between the constitutional and popular legitimacy afforded political parties. This 'legitimacy deficit' has meant that, while parties are, and perceive themselves to be, central to the policy-making process, they have only a weak toehold in political society. Parties thus face a stern challenge in seeking to gain acceptance as legitimate and efficient instruments of representation and, by extension, agencies in the socialisation, mobilisation and organisation of voters.

Conclusion

The aim of this contextual chapter has been to undertake a 'whistlestop' review of the transition process, that is, of system change, in the European 'successor states' of the former Soviet Union, bearing in mind Lomax's implicit challenge to assumptions of successful democratisation in Central and Eastern Europe set out at the beginning. In a number of ways, the post-Soviet republics readily lend themselves to comparative analysis. Thus, with the notable exception of Ukraine, all are relatively small states, ranging from ten million in Belarus to one and a half million in Estonia, and all gained independence (virtually had independence thrust upon them) as a result of the failure of the anti-Gorbachev coup in August 1991. In the cases of Ukraine, Belarus and Moldova, the new states had no or virtually no previous history of independence, while apart from Estonia and Latvia none had a tradition of pluralist party politics. The direction of state-building, however, differed quite markedly in the new and old successor states in respect of the basic constitutional groundrules, the extent of elite cooperation and the degree to which there has been an alternation in power.

In Ukraine, Belarus and Moldova, constitutional modernisation was retarded (new forms of government were not enacted until 1994) and a dominant head of state worked in tandem with, as well as often in the teeth of, opposition from communist-dominated Supreme Soviets (parliaments) deriving from 1990. Independence, in short, did not betoken a shift to the principle of parliamentary democracy; rather, the new post-Soviet republics emerged as essentially president-dominant systems characterised by intermittently high levels of conflict between the legislative and executive arms of government. It was significant that presidential elections preceded parliamentary elections in all three and that legislative renewal was belated (general elections were not held in Moldova until February 1994, in Ukraine until March 1994 and in Belarus until May 1995) and then recourse to the polls was conceded only in the face of popular protest. Parliamentary elections were thus essentially last resorts rather than first options. There has, to be sure, been alternation in the presidential office in Ukraine and Belarus, though not in Moldova, and governments have also changed hands. But if Pridham's assertion that the process of democratic transition is complete only when the political system operates with a popularly elected government is applied in the 'new' successor states, it is clearly premature to speak of the successful completion of democratic transition. The future of parliamentary democracy looks in gravest doubt, perhaps in Belarus, where Lukashenko is openly opposed to general elections and where the May 1995 campaign was far from free and nationalist opposition deputies were harassed.

On the subject of nationalism, it might be surmised that nation building would be of paramount functional importance in new states which, as Soviet republics, experienced periods of intense Russification (the systematic reduction of their native languages) and, as independent states, encountered the centrifugal forces of ethnic separatism (*inter alia* in Crimea, Transdnestria and Gagauz). The Popular Front movements, especially in Belarus, it will be recalled, emphasised the protection of the indigenous language as the soul of the nation. If the earlier case for a multidimensional approach to an analysis of democratisation remains as strong as ever, the reality is that in Ukraine economic strains have to a degree jeopardised the achievements of Kravchuk's vigorous Ukrainianisation programme, while in Moldova the situation facing Snegur was complicated by the fact that Moldovan is effectively the same language as Romanian and the Moldavian Popular Front sought reintegration into the 'mother country'. Exceptionally in Belarus, Lukashenko is apparently engaged in a 'denationalisation' programme, supporting pro-Russian sentiments and the notion of Slav unity as a means of undermining nation-statehood.

The road to 'democratisation from below', that is building a democratic society – an integral component of democratic consolidation, it was argued – remains long and hard. Thus outside Galicia, civil society in Ukraine remains weak and the legitimacy of the political system low. Survey evidence indicates, moreover, that about two-fifths of Ukrainians reject a multi-party system and, apart from fitful strike activity in the Donbass, demobilisation and depoliticisation have been prevalent, especially among previously active young people. The same is broadly true in Moldova and Belarus where low turnout at the 1995 general election meant that a quorate assembly could not be constituted.

State-building took a different course in the 'old' successor states in the Baltic. They emerged as essentially parliamentary systems in which governments have been recruited from and in turn responsible to popularly elected assemblies: the 100-seat *Riigikogu*, 101-seat *Saeima* and 141-seat *Seimas*, respectively. General elections were staged much earlier in the Baltics – in September 1992 in Estonia, October 1992 in Lithuania and June 1993 in Latvia – than in Ukraine, Belarus and Moldova; they were not concessions to appease a discontented populace (although there was discontent in evidence); and, unlike the experience of the 'new' successor republics, turnout, although relatively modest, has ensured that there have been no problems in constituting a quorate assembly. The parliamentary basis of constitutional arrangements in the Baltics has been reflected in the fact that the assembly is charged with nominating the head of state in Estonia (the first direct round in the September 1992 election excepted) and Latvia, and that Landsbergis' proposal to create a strong executive presidency in Lithuania was defeated in May 1992. This is not to say that presidents Meri (Estonia), Ulmanis (Latvia) and Brazauskas (Lithuania) have been merely symbolic figureheads or that there have not been frictions between the heads of stage and assemblies over matters of constitutional interpretation. But there has not been the presidential presumption against, and suspicion of, parliamentary democracy of Lukashenko or the deep-seated legislative–executive conflict of Ukraine. Moreover, as in several of the Visegrad states, a second post-independence general election has been held in Estonia (March 1995) and Latvia (October 1995).

In Estonia and Latvia, nation (re)building, as the controversial issue of citizenship demonstrated, involved a conspicuous inversion of power relationships, with the ethnic Russian minorities displaced by the indigenous majority population as the 'dominant nationality' (in Stein Rokkan's terms). Even in the relatively homegeneous Lithuania, the political right promoted a vigorous programme of cultural nationalism. The first general elections in Estonia and Latvia in particular centred on the 'national question', as opposed to economic issues, and the success of the Right was in large part due to its nationalist, that is anti-communist stance. Elements of the radical Right have favoured repatriation and eschewed the national integration of ethnic minorities.

Although it would be wrong to exaggerate the differences between the new and old Soviet successor republics, the incidence of regular and free elections, alternation in government, the enactment of citizenship legislation and the representation of ethnic parties (in Lithuania and Estonia) would all indicate a successful democratic transition in the Baltic. In Estonia and Lithuania, though not Latvia, moreover, party laws have vested political parties with a central role in the democratisation process. However, the Baltic party systems have not yet stabilised, party identification remains generally weak, cleavage structures are still relatively undeveloped and there is evidence of significant levels of demobilisation and depoliticisation among the people at large. In short, parties face some stiff challenges on the road to democratic consolidation.

Notes

1 Bill Lomax, 'Impediments to Democratization in East-Central Europe', in Gordon Wightman (ed.), *Party Formation in East-Central Europe* (Edward Elgar: Aldershot, 1995), p.180.
2 Ibid., p.183.
3 Gordon Wightman, 'Conclusions', in Wightman, *Party Formation*, p.248.
4 Zdenek Zboril, 'Impediments to the Development of Democratic Politics: a Czech Perspective', in Wightman, *Party Formation*, pp.202–216, especially p.203.
5 'Itä-Euroopan kasvu on haurasta', *Helsingin Sanomat*, 15 May 1995.
6 See David Arter, 'Beetham's 1, 9, 18, 27 and 30 or Will Finland be a "net democratic contributor" to the European Union?', in Joni Lovenduski and Jeffrey Stanyer (eds), *Contemporary Political Studies 1995*, Volume Two (Political Studies Association of the United Kingdom: Exeter, 1995), pp.799–807.
7 David Arter, *The Politics of European Integration in the Twentieth Century* (Dartmouth: Aldershot, 1993), p.16.
8 Bohdan Krawchenko, 'Ukraine: the politics of independence', in Ian Bremmer

and Ray Taras (eds), *Nations and Politics in the Soviet Successor States* (Cambridge University Press: New York, 1994), p.75.

9   Ibid., p.80.
10 Ibid., pp.77–8.
11 Ibid., p.78.
12 Ibid., p.87.
13 'Not so quiet on the western front', *The Guardian*, 18–19 December 1993.
14 Sarah Birch, 'The Ukrainian Parliamentary and Presidential Elections of 1994', *Electoral Studies*, **14**, (1), 1995, pp.93–99, especially p.99. See also Wilson and Bilous, 'Political parties in Ukraine', *Soviet Studies*, **4**, 1993, pp.693–701.
15 Krawchenko, 'Ukraine', p.85.
16 Arter, *The Politics of European Integration*, p.244.
17 Krawchenko, 'Ukraine', p. 86.
18 Ibid., p.80.
19 Taras Kuzio, 'The Multi-Party System in Ukraine on the Eve of Elections: Identity Problems, Conflicts and Solutions', *Government and Opposition*, **29**, (1), 1994, pp.109–27, especially p.110. See also Alexander J Motyl, *Dilemma of Independence. Ukraine After Totalitarianism* (Council on Foreign Relations: New York, 1993).
20 Kuzio, 'The Multi-Party System', p.120.
21 Birch, 'The Ukrainian Elections of 1994', pp.95–6.
22 Under Kuchma Ukraine has been active in forging the international links necessary to revitalise the economy and by extension protect its statehood. In April 1995 Ukraine signed a military cooperation agreement with China – Ukraine's largest trading partner after Russia – and the same month agreed to close down the Chernobyl nuclear power station by the year 2000, subject to receiving additional Western aid. Conversely, a temporary trade relations agreement with the EU in June 1995 was made contingent on Ukraine's promise to close Chernobyl down: 'Yhdysvallat ylisti Ukrainan päätöstä luopua ydinaseista', *Helsingin Sanomat*, 12 May 1995.
23 Michael Urban and Jan Zaprudnik, 'Belarus: a long road to nationhood', in Bremmer and Taras, *Nations and Politics*, p.105.
24 Ibid., p.106.
25 Ibid., p.108.
26 Ibid., p.109.
27 Ibid., p.110–11.
28 Ibid., p.111.
29. 'Belarusians overwhelmingly approve economic integration with Russia', *The Baltic Independent*, 19–25 May 1995.
30 'Outrage over attack in Belarusian parliament', *The Baltic Independent*, 21–7 April 1995.
31 'Valko-Venäjä hakee tulevaisuutta menneestä', *Aamulehti*, 24 May 1995.
32 'Valko-Venäjän vaaleissa ei saatu uutta parlamenttia', *Helsingin Sanomat*, 30 May 1995.
33 'Belarus votes for a return to Soviet era', *The Scotsman*, 15 May 1995; 'Valko-Venäjän parlamenttivaalit jäävät kansanäänestysten varjoon', *Helsingin Sanomat*, 14 May 1995; 'Valkovenäläiset kannattivat tiivimpiä suhteita Venäjään', *Helsingin Sanomat*, 16 May 1995.
34 Daria Fane, 'Moldova: breaking loose from Moscow', in Bremmer and Taras, *Nations and Politics*, pp. 121–53, especially p.121.
35 Ibid., pp.135–8.
36 Ibid., p.130.
37 Stephen Iwan Griffiths, *Nationalism and Ethnic Conflict* (Oxford University Press: Oxford, 1993), pp.81–5.

38 Anatole Lieven, *The Baltic Revolution: Estonia, Latvia, Lithuania and the Path to Independence* (Yale University: New Haven–London, 1993), p.105.
39 Ibid., p.293.
40 Ibid., p.223.
41 Ibid., p.256.
42 Richard Krikus, 'Lithuania: nationalism in the modern era', in Bremmer and Taras, *Nations and Politics*, pp.157–81, especially p.167.
43 Lieven, *The Baltic Revolution*, p.239.
44 Ibid., p.250.
45 Ibid., p.260.
46 Ibid., p.265.
47 Ibid., p.255.
48 Ibid., p.267.
49 Ibid., p.267. Heating was switched on only in mid-October, two weeks later than usual, and then restricted to 13 degrees centigrade.
50 Virgis Valentinavicius, 'Lithuania shifts right – on a local scale', *The Baltic Independent*, 31 March–6 April 1995.
51 Terry D. Clark, 'The Lithuanian Political Party System: A Case Study of Democratic Consolidation', *East European Politics and Societies*, 9, (1), 1995, pp.41–61.
52 Ibid., p.45.
53 Ibid., p.51.
54 Ibid., p.56.
55 Nils Muizneks, 'Latvia: origins, evolution and triumph', in Bremmer and Taras, *Nations and Politics*, p.188.
56 Ibid., p.185, 187.
57 Lieven, *The Baltic Revolution*, p.221.
58 Muizneks, 'Latvia', pp.192–4.
59 Lieven, *The Baltic Revolution*, p.298.
60 Ibid., p.291.
61 'Naturalisation department to pass first new citizens', *The Baltic Independent*, 7–13 July 1995.
62 Lieven, *The Baltic Revolution*, p.313.
63 Philip John Davies and Andrejs Valdis Ozolins, 'The Latvian Parliamentary Election of 1993', *Electoral Studies*, 13, (1), 1994, pp.83–6.
64 Lieven, *The Baltic Revolution*, p.301.
65 Although the official statement did not disclose the identity of the buyers or mediators, the money was in all likelihood sold to Chechenya and the middlemen were almost certainly Estonian businessmen with close contacts with the government. Certainly, the leading opposition Coalition Party claimed to have received information from 'government circles' that the roubles had been delivered to Chechenya.
66 'Rouble scandal set to unseat PM', *The Baltic Independent*, 9–15 September 1994; 'Parliament set to oust PM', *The Baltic Independent*, 23–9 September 1994.

3 Parties and Democracy in the Estonian First Republic

The inter-war Estonian republic was a successor state of the czarist Romanov empire. It became an active member of the League of Nations, enacted a liberal law on Cultural Autonomy in 1925, and possessed in the 15 June 1920 constitution one of the most democratic documents in contemporary Europe. Perhaps it was too democratic since, in allowing the outcomes of referenda initiated by the people to override – where they clashed with – the decisions of the national assembly, the *Riigikogu*, it provided a mechanism which extremists could (and did) use to discredit and undermine the structures of representative democracy. In any event, when the impact of recession was superimposed on a new state experiencing the familiar teething troubles of building durable cabinets, the strain became too much and in 1934 pluralist democracy gave way to an authoritarian regime under the presidency of Konstantin Päts.

Nonetheless, as Toivo U. Raun has noted, Estonian authoritarianism in the 1930s was one of the mildest in Eastern Europe. No one was executed on political grounds and virtually all political prisoners were freed in 1938. Moreover, there was possibly a swing back towards greater political participation in the final years of independence.[1]

Civil Society in Estonia on the Threshold of Independence

At the point of achieving independence in February 1918, Estonia was a relatively modernised civil society. First, in contrast to Lithuania, where almost one-third of the population was illiterate at the time of the establishment of the inter-war republic, the Estonian people were highly literate.[2] By the end of the nineteenth century, the ability to read in people over the age of ten was virtually 100 per cent, while between 1881 and 1922 the ability to write rose appreciably, from approximately 40 per cent (for people over 14) to over 90 per cent (for those over ten years).[3] The latter figure would have been higher still had the newly-acquired Petserimaa (or Setumaa) on the south-eastern border with Soviet Russia, and part of Pskov province under czarism, been excluded. The establishment of an Estonian-language education system, moreover, signalled the beginning of a new era in Estonian culture. Estonia was also one of the most homogeneous of the successor states of the New Europe of the inter-war years. Approximately 88 per cent of its 1.1 million citizens was made up of Estonians – the largest ethnic minority, numbering 8.2 per cent of the population, comprised Russians – with 78 per cent of them being Lutheran (as opposed to 19 who belonged to the Russian Orthodox church).

Second, at the time of gaining independence, a small native middle class existed and this developed rapidly during the inter-war period. In the countryside, a land reform programme promoted by the leftist-controlled Constituent Assembly and the Labour cabinet of Otto Strandmann in October 1919, which was designed as a measure of social engineering, served to displace the Baltic Germans from their position of historic dominance (in 1918 they owned an estimated 58 per cent of rural land) and created a new stratum of family-sized Estonian farms. Indeed, as a result of the agrarian reform programme, the number of landholdings rose by about two and a half times compared with the number in 1919. The realisation of statehood also swelled the ranks of the nascent urban middle class by creating a mass of positions for native Estonians in the government, military, education, professions, Lutheran church and in the private sectors of the economy.

Third, there existed a range of secondary organisations ranging from youth clubs to trade unions and agricultural societies. The latter, for example, were advocated by C.R. Jakobson in the mid-nineteenth century and by Jaan Tônisson thereafter and were anchored in those farmers in southern Estonia who managed to break clear of the Baltic–German manor-owners and acquire their own holdings. The agricultural societies provided an organisational infrastructure for the Rural League (*Eesti maarahva liit*) which emerged in spring 1917, gained 22 per cent of the vote in the election for the Estonian Provincial Assembly (*Maapäev*) on 7–8 July that year (see Table 3.1) and became the largest single grouping in that body.

Finally, a number of embryonic political parties were already in existence at the time of the achievement of independence. The first Estonian parties were in fact formed as a by-product of Czar Nicholas II's October 1905 manifesto, when the 'nation' was granted representation in the Russian Duma. Estonia was allocated five delegates to

Table 3.1 Estonia: the road to independence

4 March 1917 Following the collapse of czarism, a meeting in Tartu of leading Estonian politicians demands a separate Estonian administration.

12 March 1917 The Russian provisional government provides for Estonian regional autonomy within the Russian confederation with a High Commissioner (appointed by Russia) assisted by an Estonian Provincial Assembly (*Maapäev*).

7–8 July 1917 Elections commence to the 62-member Provincial Assembly. The Rural League emerges as the largest group. However, nearly a half of all delegates comprise socialists (of various types).

28 November 1917 Following the disintegration of the Russian provisional government, the Provincial Assembly declares itself the highest authority in Estonia.

January 1918 Elections to a Constituent Assembly (originally favoured by the Bolsheviks) are cancelled when, after two-thirds of the vote have been counted, it becomes clear that the Communists could not win.

24 February 1918 In defiance of the nominal control of the Bolsheviks, the Emergency Committee of the Provisional Assembly proclaims Estonian independence and sets up a provisional government.

February–11 November 1918 German occupation of Tallinn. Occupying Germans and German Balts plan to make Estonia part of the German crown. The majority of Bolsheviks return to Russia; the provisional government remains underground.

22 November 1918 Following the First World War armistice, the communists seek to seize power in Estonia, set up a 'counter-government', the Estonian Working People's Commune (*Eesti töörahva kommuun*) in Narva and claims about half Estonia before being forced to retreat by January 1919.

5–7 April 1919 Elections to a Constituent Assembly. Social Democrats win over one-third of all delegates, provide the president, August Rei, and quickly embark on a radical land reform programme. (The communists have not taken part in the elections.)

23 April 1919 The Constituent Assembly confirms the proclamation of independence by the Emergency Committee.

2 February 1920 Peace of Tartu. Estonia becomes the first successor state whose sovereignty is legally recognized by Soviet Russia.

15 June 1920 Enactment of the first Estonian constitution. A 100-member parliament (*Riigikogu*) to be elected every three years; liberal provisions for popular initiatives and no independent executive.

the First and Second Dumas in 1906–7 and these were shared by the Radicals of Konstantin Päts, Tônisson's Progressive National Democrats and Peeter Speek's Social Democrats. Personal networks, often centred around newspapers – Tônisson's *Postimees* in Tartu or Päts' *Teataja* in Tallinn, for example – together with various university clubs and professional societies were of strategic significance in the organisation of the first parties.[4] Moreover, although the first Estonian parties were clearly affiliated to fraternal groupings in Russia, all except the Communists broke with their Russian counterparts over the issue of national rights.

The Party System and Cleavage Structures

Estonia in many ways typified the teething troubles experienced by European states (both old and new) following the completion of mass democracy after the First World War.[5] The Estonian constitution enfranchised men and women over the age of 20 and deployed a PR system to elect a 100-member *Riigikogu* for a three-year term. Crucially, the new form of government created an assembly-dominant system: there was no independent executive, the *riigivanem*, the prime minister (literally 'state elder') was selected by parliament and the 'checks and balances' mainly consisted of a liberal popular initiative provision (25 000 voters could initiate legislative proposals). There was thus no executive figure empowered to mediate in the process of coalition-building and/or charged with working to resolve cabinet crises – government maintenance – as and when they cropped up.

Moreover, despite the cultural homogeneity of the Estonian state, there was a proliferation of political parties closely associated with their leading personalities (such as Päts, Tônisson and Rei). This contributed to familiar problems of cabinet instability. Encouraged by a PR list voting system, which, in practice, treated the country as a single constituency, there were, for instance, 14 parties represented in the 1923–6 Riigikogu (no less than 26 had contested the elections in 1923), while between April 1919 and the coup of 12 March 1934 there were 21 cabinets with an average lifespan of eight months. Table 3.2 sets out the distribution of Riigikogu seats following the five general elections held between 1920 and 1932. True, notwithstanding the absolute number of parliamentary parties, three groupings – the Socialists, Centrists and Agrarians – held between 83 and 90 per cent of the Riigikogu seats during this period. There was also a comfortable majority throughout for the non-socialist parties. But the high levels of government instability made it easy for the quasi-fascist Central League of the Veterans of the Wars of Independence (*Vabadussôjalaste*

Table 3.2   The distribution of *Riigikogu* seats by political party, 1920–32

	1920	1923	1926	1929	1932
Left					
Communists	5	10	6	6	5
Independent Socialists	11	5	—	—	—
Social Democrats	18	15	—	—	—
Socialist Workers	—	—	24	25	22
Centre					
Labour	22	12	13	10	—
National Democrats	10	8	8	9	—
Homesteaders	—	4	14	14	—
Others	—	6	—	—	—
National Centre	—	—	—	—	23
Right					
Christian Democrats	7	8	5	4	—
Farmers'	21	23	23	24	—
United Agrarians	—	—	—	—	42
Landlords	1	2	2	3	—
National minorities	5	7	5	5	8
Total	100	100	100	100	100

Keskliit), which was founded in 1929, to discredit the political system and inveigh against the 1920 constitution, especially when the slump placed an extra load on institutional arrangements and made it difficult for democracy to deliver the economic goods.

The amalgamation of the parliamentary parties into three broad umbrella groups might have been expected in some measure to facilitate a greater longevity of cabinets. In 1925 the Social Democrats and Independent Socialists joined forces as the Estonian Socialist Workers' Party (*Eesti Sotsialistlik Tööliste Partei*) under August Rei, the former President of the Constituent Assembly. The National Democrats, Labour, Christian Democrats and Landlords fused in 1931–2 to form the National Centre Party (*Rahvuslik Keskerakond*) under Jaan Tônisson. Finally, in 1932 the Farmers' Party and Homesteaders combined as the United Agrarians (*Põllumeestekogude ja Põllumeeste*) led by Konstantin Päts. However, although the merged units commanded 87 per cent of the Riigikogu seats in 1932, cabinets remained short-lived and between mid-1932 and October 1933 there were no less than four of them.

When viewing the nascent Estonian party system from a cleavage structure perspective, it is clear that *nationalism versus communism* was the primary conflict dimension in the early independence years and constituted a valence issue in uniting the pro-system forces across the board. The communists were never formally proscribed, but even before the failed coup attempt on 1 December 1924 they participated in elections in the guise of various front organisations. Their best performance, ten Riigikogu seats, was achieved in 1923 as the United Front of Working People (*Töörahva ühine väerind*), when there was economic distress and rising unemployment, and in the municipal elections the same year they polled 35–6 per cent in Tallinn, Narva and Pärnu. Between 1926 and 1932 the communist fronts won between five to six parliamentary seats, but by the end of the first decade of independence the communist threat had receded. At the beginning of the 1930s the communists' position was so weak that their Central Committee was obliged to operate from the Scandinavian countries.

The nationalist question, then, was initially the paramount cleavage in the party politics of inter-war Estonia, as it was following the restoration of independence in 1991. Indeed, following the failed coup, a government of national unity, comprising all the main parties, including for the first time the Social Democrats, was formed, with the National Democrat, Jüri Jaakson as *riigivanem*. It was not insignificant, moreover, that Päts' bloodless coup in 1934 and the authoritarian regime that followed it were legitimised by reference to 'national salvation', and the Fatherland League (*Isamaa liit*) he created – based on his following in the Farmers' Party – was the only party not to be outlawed.

By the time that Estonia was hit by the worst effects of global recession in 1932–3, however, three broad-based party groupings had emerged, based on two essentially class-based cleavages. First, there was the *town versus the country* (the clash of consumer and producer interests) which spawned a single rural party, the United Agrarians, and the predominantly urban National Centre Party. Second, there was the conflict between *workers* and *owners* which gave rise to the Socialist Workers' Party.

The *United Agrarians* were the largest party in 1932, with 42 Riigikogu seats. They embraced the Päts' Farmers' Party– until 1921 known as the Estonian Rural League – which was the most conservative of the democratic parties and even incorporated urban upper-class elements, and the Homesteaders (*Asunikkude partei*), a liberal splinter of the Farmers' Party, which assumed the name 'Homesteaders' in 1925. The Homesteaders were comparable to the Scandinavian agrarian parties in recruiting the bulk of their support from the newly independent small and medium-sized farm proprietors. They polled 14 per cent of the poll at the general elections of 1926 and 1929.

The United Agrarians thus represented a merger between the older established farmers, particularly in southern Estonia, who owned their land before independence, and the newly-created farmsteaders born of the land reform programme which, incidentally, was effectively completed by 1926, when it had created holdings with an average of 23 hectares of agricultural land. In 1932, 95 per cent of the United Agrarians' vote derived from the countryside and this accounted for 59 per cent of the total rural vote. It bears emphasis that, at the time of the onset of recession, Estonia was still essentially a farming nation with about 47 per cent of the economically active population engaged in agriculture (compared with 23 per cent in industry).[6]

The *Socialist Workers' Party* was the largest Riigikogu party following the 1926 and 1929 general elections, gaining 24 and 25 seats, respectively, but in 1932 the figure dropped to 22. Despite being consistently one of the three largest parties, the Socialist Workers participated in only four coalitions before October 1932 and held the *riigivanem's* post only once between 1928 and 1929. They did, to be sure, play a generally responsible role as the leading opposition party and progressed by fielding Russian candidates in the predominantly Russian-speaking areas at the 1929 general election.

The Socialist Workers' Party pivoted on a rural–urban working-class axis. In 1932, 54 per cent of its total vote came from the countryside, mostly from agricultural labourers (although, according to the 1934 census, there had been a fourfold reduction in the size of the landless rural population since the late czarist era), while 39 per cent derived from the towns. The 'middle-class socialists' were concentrated in the Labour Party (*Eesti Tööerakonna*).

The National Centre Party, with 23 seats in 1932, was predominantly an urban middle-class party although, by embracing groups as disparate as Christians, socialists and the pro-capitalist landlords, it inevitably lacked a clear ideological focus. Virtually two-thirds (62 per cent) of its vote in 1932 was drawn from towns and cities, while over two-fifths (43 per cent) of urban residents voted for it.

Even the rationalisation of the atomised party system into three broad blocs did not conduce towards heightened inter-elite cooperation. Thus, in May 1933, the Farmers' Party withdrew from the United Agrarians, leaving the Homesteaders to remain critical of their leader Päts both before and after the seizure of power in 1934. At critical junctures, notably when recession was at its worst, the political parties were unable to deliver political stability. None of the three blocs comprised a Riigikogu majority in its own right and the absence of a catch-all party to achieve the necessary measure of compromise between competing interests meant that disagreements over economic questions (the clash of class interests) led to the collapse of numerous cabinets. Tönu Parming in particular has stressed the failure of the party leaders to act as crisis mediators during the depths of the recession and the way, in consequence, that the urban middle class sought political stability outside the sphere of pluralist democracy – in the extraparliamentary Veterans' League.[7]

In addition to the mainstream parties, Estonia's liberal laws on cultural pluralism permitted the presence in the Riigikogu of several ethnic minority parties. Their primary goal was the protection of cultural autonomy, especially through the promotion of teaching in the relevant minority language (article 2, paragraph 12 of the 1920 constitution, for example, gave ethnic minorities a right to education in their mother tongue in those local government areas where a majority of inhabitants were not Estonian). None of the ethnic nationalist parties – based on the Russian, German, Swedish and Jewish minorities – participated in government. Collectively, however, they obtained between 3.3 per cent and 6.7 per cent of the parliamentary seats and by cooperating gained places on the key parliamentary committees.

Both the ethnic and the Estonian parties had their own press. There were nine newspapers and magazines in languages other than Estonian and about 440 newspapers and 500 magazines published in Estonian between the wars. As Epp Lauk and Tiina Kaalep have observed, the 1920s could be characterised as the years of 'party journalism', in so far as all the major parties had their regular standard-bearers, including such influential dailies as *Vaba Maa* (Labour) – this was the name adopted by the Estonian Popular Front organ in 1988 – and *Postimees* (Centre).[8]

Finally, the party system, or at least several of the parties – among others, the Farmers' Party, Homesteaders and Socialists – continued to operate in exile in Sweden after the Soviet occupation and incorporation of Estonia as the sixteenth socialist republic of the USSR on 25 August 1940.

In reviewing the democratic experience of the Estonian First Republic (a short chronology of events is set out in Table 3.3), a number of observations and complementary questions are in order. First, the process of state-building produced, in the shape of the 1920 constitution, what Rein Taagepera has described as 'ultrademocracy'.[9] Indeed, the institutional distribution of power prescribed in the 1920 document and, in particular, the way it militated towards a completely dominant national assembly at the expense of an independent executive, contributed to, if it did not exactly cause, the high levels of government instability. The result was that the issue of constitutional reform was on the political agenda *before* the rise of the Veterans' League. In any

Table 3.3 Estonian democracy between the wars: a chronology of the main events

1919	(October) Otto Strandmann's Labour cabinet embarks on an extensive land reform programme.
1920	(15 June) Enactment of an 'ultrademocratic' constitution.
1922	Estonian trade with Russia 25 per cent of its total trade (3 per cent in 1935).
	Estonia becomes a member of the League of Nations.
1923	Estonian–Latvian Defence Alliance.
	No less than 14 parties elected to the Riigikogu following the second post-war election.
1924	(1 December) Attempted communist coup in Tallinn fails.
1925	Highly liberal Cultural Autonomy Law enacted.
1926	Land reform programme effectively completed.
1928	Estonia reverts from Finnish-style 'mark' to the 'kroon' as the national currency unit.
1930	Rise of Peasants' Movement in southern Estonia modelled on the Finnish Lapua movement.
1932	Estonia signs a non-aggression agreement with the Soviet Union.
1932–3	Estonia hit by the worst effects of global recession.
1933	(October) Strong president-dominant constitution proposed by the Veterans' League supported by 73 per cent of voters in a referendum.
1934	Baltic Entente between Estonia, Latvia and Lithuania.
	(March) Konstantin Päts introduces martial law and the proscription of political parties.
	(November) Failure of the Veterans' League's attempted coup.
1934–8	Päts rules by decree.
1938	Amnesty to all political prisoners.

event, by 1934 the state had shifted from ultrademocracy to authoritarianism. Although the pluralist interlude in Estonia lasted more than twice the length of liberal democracy in Poland or Lithuania between the wars, it was nonetheless very brief – less than a decade and a half in all – and in the space of five parliamentary elections there was scarcely time for a democratic tradition to develop. There was, moreover, conflict between direct democracy (based on the popular initiative) and representative democracy centred on the Riigikogu, with the generous referendum provisions bound up with the former serving to discredit and finally to undermine the latter.

Second, the process of nation-building in Estonia involved promoting the previously suppressed Estonian language and culture. Thus education became available in Estonian at all levels, Tartu University adopted Estonian as its language of tuition, an Estonian Academy of Sciences was created, and international classics were translated into Estonian.[10] Equally, the liberal legislative framework created in 1925 facilitated relatively high levels of national integration: the ethnic minorities, particularly Germans and Jews, participated extensively in the economy and, via the minority language parties in the Riigikogu, they were also engaged in the political life of the First Republic before 1934.[11] In the inter-war context, in short, ethnic relations in Estonia were good and the only conspicuously non-integrated group comprised the poorly-educated Russian-speaking peasants along the eastern borders. Furthermore, the process of nation-building was not materially affected by the transition to an authoritarian state under Päts.

Third, the fact that there was a multiplicity of parties, several of which, as noted, continued to operate in exile after the Stalinist annexation in 1940, prompts the question, did a party tradition develop between the wars? Alternatively, did the strength of anti-party sentiment, rooted in a perception of weak cabinet government and exacerbated by economic recession, preclude such a possibility? Further, since parties are normally regarded as an integral part of civil society, Päts' ban on their activities and the contiguous censorship of the party press in 1934 plainly served to frustrate the process of society-building. Was it possible that in 1934, therefore, Estonia shifted from being an anti-party to becoming a one-party authoritarian system in the reverse of the way the newly independent Estonia in the 1990s may be argued to have progressed from 50 years of one-party (communist) rule to assuming some of the main features of an anti-party system?

The Estonian First Republic: an Anti-party System?

In the light of the collapse of liberal democracy in 1934, then, it is worth concluding our discussion of parties and democracy in inter-war Estonia with reference to the anti-party system model delineated in Chapter 1 and applied more fully to the post-independent Estonian party system of post-1991 in Chapters 8 and 9. Three questions are crucial: what was the extent of partisan identification between the wars; what was the extent of partisan/non-partisan voting in inter-war Estonia; and were there numerically significant anti-parties or a body of anti-party sentiment in the post-czarist successor state? Only brief answers will be essayed.

As regards the first question, there are, of course, no survey data with which to gauge the extent or nature of party identification, although a *prima facie* case for predominantly rational–instrumental patterns of voting behaviour might reasonably be deduced from the existence of class parties and the evidence of a relatively high degree of political cohesion among the main sectional interests in society. As mentioned earlier, by the early 1930s three out of five rural voters backed the United Agrarians, virtually all of their support deriving from the countryside. Equally, if membership of a party is construed as a measure of a high level of partisan identification, Estonian levels were modest. Party organisation in Estonia between the wars, in short, remained generally weak. The best organised for some time was the Estonian Communist Party which, in 1920, had about 700 members, rising to about 2000 on the eve of the unsuccessful coup in 1924 and declining sharply thereafter.

True, mergers such as the National Centre Party were relatively broadly constituted: the NCP had both a Woman's Organisation and a Youth Organisation, while in 1932 there were 46 local party branches alone in its southern district organisation based in Tartu. In April 1932 58 members attended an evening function of the Tartu district party and there were more for the visit of the party leader Jaan Tônisson.[12] But data on the other parties are patchy and there is no file at all in the state archives on the United Agrarians, making conclusions about party membership and organisation inevitably hazardous. What might safely be posited, however, is that, although the inter-war republic boasted a more developed party system than Estonia in the mid-1990s inasmuch as it was based on interest cleavages and relatively cohesive party programmes, it did not yield a party tradition in the sense of parties as mass membership organisations. Furthermore, parties tended to operate in a vacuum and, unlike the situation in Finland, there were no real links between parties and party-based cultural organisations (sports associations, youth clubs and so on).[13]

As to the extent of partisan/non-partisan voting, statistics on national turnout at the five general elections between 1920 and 1934 simply do not exist. All that can safely be stated is that turnout in the countryside in the early elections was low – approximately 30 per cent for the Provincial Assembly in July 1917 – and that, in contrast, at the third and successful constitutional reform referendum prompted by Veterans' League signatures in October 1933, turnout was unusually high, at about 56 per cent. It is a fair surmise that over the five Riigikogu elections between 1920 and 1934 about one in two eligible persons was a 'sofa voter'.

Anti-partism, grounded in the popular association of parties with government instability and ineffectual parliamentarism, although increasing, was largely confined to small extremist groupings during the 1920s. In 1923, for example, an Ex-Serviceman's Party, exploiting the disenchantment of demobilised soldiers, succeeded in gaining a single Riigikogu seat. By 1930 and the advent of recession, however, anti-party protest was apparently becoming far more widespread. In 1930 a (largely) southern Estonian peasants' movement, modelled to a degree on the Finnish Lapua movement (*Lapuan liike*), sprang into being, articulating discontent with the system of 'parliamentary absolutism'. It planned a march on Tallinn and the organisation of a petition demanding a reduction in the number of Riigikogu members and, indeed, in their salaries.[14] But it was the escalating support for the Veterans' League in the early 1930s which constituted the clearest case for mass disaffection with parties and parliamentary democracy. As one writer has noted: 'The Veterans appeared to be especially successful in mounting a kind of populist attack on alleged corruption and nepotism among the political parties in power.'[15] It also peddled the type of corporatist solutions later taken up by Päts following the proscription of political parties in March 1935.

At its 1932 Congress, a fiery young lawyer, Artur Sirk, propelled the Veterans' League into politics and, by establishing a nationwide organisational network and recruiting non-veterans into its ranks, the party saw its numbers swell. A curious hybrid, part popular movement, part paramilitary organisation (with parading and, in some cases, full uniforms), the Veterans' League, above all, demanded a strong executive constitution. Accordingly, in November 1932 it submitted the draft of a revised form of government to parliament so that it could be put to a referendum vote. To achieve that end, the Veterans had collected nearly 56 000 signatures by the end of January 1933, but the following month, in something of a pre-emptive strike, the Riigikogu put its own constitutional draft to the people. This, and a later version, in turn, were defeated when the Veterans and Socialists combined to oppose them. Finally, on 14–16 October 1933, the Veterans' League won an absolute majority in the local elections in several of Estonia's large urban centres and, ironically, it was using the powers vested in the Acting Chief Executive under the Veterans' constitution that, in April 1934, Päts ordered the permanent closure of the League's organisation. In so far as the rise of the Veterans' League embodied a diffuse anti-partism, moreover, it seems to have been concentrated on the urban middle class, since it was they who were hardest hit by recession.

In considering the Veterans' League as a fascist movement, Andres Kasekamp brings out its struggle against Marxism and the paramount importance it attached to a law proscribing the Socialists. Of more immediate interest, however, is his general conclusion: the Veterans' League 'did not attack one particular party, but parties in general'; it advocated 'democracy without parties'.[16]

Democracy based on parties ended in Estonia in 1935. True, nobody was executed during Päts' authoritarianism and there was an amnesty for political prisoners (Veterans, Communists and so on) in 1938. But this so-called 'Era of Silence' never witnessed the restoration of parties; the 1938 constitution was presidential in character; and parliament was replaced by corporatist bodies with (nominally at least) consultative powers. Whether Päts ultimately planned to relinquish his hold on what his prime minister termed 'guided democracy' – as is sometimes suggested – must remain an open question. The fact was that Stalin delivered a pre-emptive strike.

Notes

1   Toivo Raun, *Estonia and the Estonians* (Hoover: Stanford, California, 1991), p. 241.

2   Anatol Lieven, *The Baltic Revolution: Estonia, Latvia, Lithuania and the Path to Independence* (Yale University: New Haven–London, 1993), p.64.

3   Ibid., p.133. See also Kärt Jänes (ed.), *Tundmatu Eesti Vabariik* (Jaan Tônissoni Instituut: Tallinn, 1993).

4   Eduard Laaman, *Erakonnad Eestis. Sissejuhatus Poliitikasse IV* (Eesti Kirjanduse Seltsi kirjastus: Tartu, 1934), pp.15–21.

5   Stanley Vardys, 'Democracy in the Baltic States 1918–1934: The Stage and the Actors', *Journal of Baltic Studies*, X, (4), 1979, pp.320–36. See also Georg von Rauch, *The Baltic States: Estonia, Latvia, Lithuania, The Years of Independence, 1917–1940* (Hurst: London, 1974).

6   Tônu Parming, *The Collapse of Liberal Democracy and the Rise of Authoritarianism in Estonia* (Sage: London–Beverly Hills, 1975), pp.18–20.

7   Ibid., pp.63–70.

8   Epp Lauk and Tiina Kaalep, 'Journalism in the Republic of Estonia during the 1920s and 1930s', in Svennik Høyer, Epp Lauk and Peeter Vihalemm (eds), *Towards a Civic Society. The Baltic Media's Long Road to Freedom*, (Nota Baltica: Tartu, 1993), pp.119–141, especially pp.128–30.

9   Rein Taagepera, *Estonia. Return to Independence* (Westview: Boulder–San Francisco–Oxford, 1993), p.53.

10 Ibid., p.52.

11 Ibid., p.51.

12 Jaan Tônisson, 'Üldine kitsukus ja Rahvuslik Politika 1932', *Eesti Rahvuslik Keskerakond*, Eesti Riigiarhiv (party file in the State Archive in Tallinn).

13 I am grateful to Rein Ruutsoo for bringing out this comparison.

14 Vincent E. McHale, 'Historical Estonia, 1917–1940', in Vincent E. McHale and Sharon Skowronski (eds), *Political Parties of Europe* (Greenwood: Westport, Connecticut–London, 1973), p.394. See also The Information Department of the Royal Institute of International Affairs, *The Baltic States: A Survey of the Political and Economic Structure and the Foreign Relations of Estonia, Latvia and Lithuania* (Greenwood: Westport, Connecticut, 1970), p.48.

15 Ibid., p.395.

16 Andres Kasekamp, 'The Estonian Veterans' League: A Fascist Movement?', *Journal of Baltic Studies*, XXIV, (3), 1993, pp.263–4.

4 The Estonian Soviet Socialist Republic: from Regime Resistance to the Reconstruction of Civil Society, 1945–87

Broadly speaking, the aim of imperial rule in Estonia after the Second World War was the Sovietisation of the state, the elimination of private property and the destruction of civil society. True, the management techniques varied from Stalinist-style terror, or its credible threat, in the late 1940s and 1950s to the less severely punitive, but equally suffocating KGB-run monitorialism (interrogations, admonitions and minor sanctions) of the later Brezhnev years. Throughout the Estonian Soviet Socialist Republic (ESSR), however, there was a basic validity in the maxim articulated by the ideological secretary of the Estonian Communist Party's central committee, Rein Ristlaan, in the magazine *Sirp ja Vasar* ('Hammer and Sickle') in June 1987: 'If you think, don't speak; if you speak, don't write; if you write, don't sign it; if you sign it, then don't wonder!'[1] In briefly surveying the history of Estonia under communism, three periods can be identified: the Stalinist era between 1945 and 1955; the 'Thaw' of 1956–68; and the 'Period of Stagnation' of 1968–86.

From Stalinism to Stagnation, 1945–86

There were four main features of the *Stalinist era*, 1945–55. First, there was the enforced collectivisation of agriculture beginning in 1947, a process accelerated by Stalin's mass deportation of farmers two years later. Those remaining preferred *kolkhozes* (state-controlled collectives) in Estonia to those in Siberia and by 1950 the task of compulsory collectivisation was effectively completed. Second, there was the in-tensive industrialisation of the urban areas and the concomitant im-migration of workers from Russia. This wholesale colonisation pro-cess meant that the proportion of Estonians in Estonia dropped sharply, from 94 per cent to 72 per cent between 1945 and 1953. Third, there was the exodus to the West of a significant proportion of the most highly educated. Literary output in Estonia accordingly dropped to an all-time nadir between 1950 and 1951, when various cultural figures were the targets of the authorities. Finally, beginning in March 1950, there was a massive purge of the Estonian Commu-nist Party (ECP) and its appropriation by Russian Estonians, that is people who had emigrated from Estonia to Russia between 1850 and 1920. In particular, the ECP First Secretary, Nikolai Karatamm, was replaced by the Russian Estonian Ivan (Johannes) Käbin. The Stalinist era was based on terror and, by the dictator's death in March 1953, most Estonians had come to view the Soviet occupation with resig-nation and to accept it as something of a fact of life (rather than merely a temporary arrangement).

  The Thaw years, 1956–68, witnessed Estonia, along with Latvia, becoming one of the wealthiest of the Soviet republics. Deported Estonians began to return and, for the first time since the Second World War, there was a chance to contact relatives and friends who had defected to the West. Moreover, while politics and ideology remained in the exclusive hands of the ECP until 1988, the 'cultural public sphere' developed comparatively autonomously after 1956.[2] A young group of *literati*, including the poets Jaan Kaplinski and Paul-Erik Rummo (whose political contributions will be discussed later) emerged, while a characteristic feature of this period was the appear-ance of satire. Social conditions, especially in the housing area, im-proved and the ECP attempted minimally to legitimise its position by sanctioning nationalist symbols such as a football team and re-publican prizes for arts and science. There were, to be sure, 'night frosts' during the thaw. Immigration, which had virtually stopped by 1953, began to rise again in the 1960s. In a welcome development in 1957, regional economic councils were created in the Soviet Union – these elevated each republic to the status of a separate planning unit – and their introduction represented increased economic indepen-dence in Estonia and the transference of significant industrial manage-ment powers to Tallinn.[3] Khrushchev's replacement by Brezhnev in 1964, however, led the following year to the abolition of the econ-omic councils and a return to centralised direction from Moscow. Yet overall, despite the uneven nature of developments, 1956–68 were years of hope and improved living standards.

  The Soviet invasion of Czechoslovakia, which inaugurated the *Period of Stagnation* of 1968–86, had an enormously dispiriting effect on Estonians. Many sought distraction in the 'never had it so good' materialism of the first half of the 1970s, when consumer durables became much more readily available and a Western lifestyle was visible daily on Finnish television (at least in northern Estonia). A minority, in contrast, sought to protest about, among other things, the absence of human rights and free elections, increased pollution, rising immigration levels, housing shortages and a range of other social problems. Yet, as Rein Taagepera has astutely observed, the widespread solace (escapism) sought in material possession weakened the ideological underpinnings of both the regime *and* dissent.[4] By the second half of the 1970s the mood changed and a sense of deepening despair (coinciding with the return of food shortages) accompanied the appointment of another Russian Estonian, Karl Vaino, as ECP First Secretary in 1978. In that year, Vaino was instrumental in the implementation of a Russification programme set out in a secret Moscow decree of 13 October. This required the use of Russian for half the day in kindergartens, the increased employment of Russian as a teaching medium in first (junior) schools and more Russian in universities and the media. The Soviet invasion of Afghanistan and the draft of Estonians into active military service merely exacerbated matters. The ageing Russian Estonian leadership presided over a growing mood of popular frustration at what was seen as the directionless drift at the top. True, Gorbachev and the belated impact of *perestroika* were to change things, but the historic legacy of the Period of Stagnation was the 'double-think' which once more gained ground. There was a clear distinction, in short, between what people said in public and what they discussed among themselves.[5] Nonetheless, by the early 1980s dissent was on the increase. Indeed, it seems timely at this point briefly to consider the various types of regime resistance during the ESSR. Four categories can be identified, although the boundaries are fluid and demarcation is not without its attendant difficulties.

Patterns of Regime Resistance

Partisan resistance in the form of a pro-independence guerilla force, the Forest Brothers (*metsavennad*) which was concentrated in the countryside, characterised the period up to Stalin's death. At the height of resistance there were between 10 000 and 15 000 brothers in Estonia, although this was barely one-third of the strength of their Lithuanian counterparts. Unlike the latter, they lacked (fearing Soviet infiltration) a unified national command, training courses for officers and an underground press. The guerilla groups, moreover, varied in size from several hundred people to isolated individuals and obviously the longer partisan resistance lasted the smaller the groups became. The first wave of recruits, fired by the terror of the 1940–41 Soviet occupation and its resurgence following Moscow's reacquisition of Estonia in 1944, mostly comprised German collaborators (willing or unwilling), former Estonian members of the Finnish army and, later, Soviet army deserters.[6] The second wave of guerillas stemmed in large measure from the enforced collectivisation of agriculture and associated deportations in 1949. The eight-year 'backwoods' resistance exacted a heavy toll in life. Approximately 1000 collaborators with the Soviet system were murdered, but losses among the Forest Brothers were almost certainly higher.[7] The end of the Korean War, however, denoted the end of any realistic hope of Western action against the Soviet Union and this, coupled with the numerical superiority of the Soviet forces, contributed to weakening the partisan resistance in Estonia. Fighting largely ceased after Stalin's death and the Forest Brothers gradually re-entered civilian life, assisted by a Soviet amnesty in 1955. Remarkably, the last-known of them, August Sabe, drowned in 1978, rather than surrender to the occupying power.

A second type of regime resistance was *dissidence*, which may be defined as organised (usually underground) anti-systemic protest, planned rather than spontaneous, which is illegal in character and often invokes assistance from an outside agency in publicising desired goals. Organised activity of this kind in Estonia dates back at least to the Prague Spring of 1968 and intensified enormously in 1980–81. However, since visibility is a *sine qua non* of effective dissent, its precise extent in the ESSR can never really be known. For example, as early as 1956, a Tartu university biology student, Mart Niklus, was arrested and subsequently sentenced to ten years in prison for sending abroad what were regarded as unflattering photographs of Soviet building and construction work. The absence of records, however, prevents a reliable estimate of the total number of imprisonments for comparable offences.

Before embarking on the briefest overview of dissident activity in Estonia between 1968 and 1988, a number of general points are in order. First, much of the dissidence, especially from the late 1970s, was pan-Baltic in character and conjoined Estonians, Latvians and Lithuanians in demonstrative action against the occupying power. Second, although dissent was largely 'hushed up' by the authorities and consequently did not impinge on the public consciousness, the fate of some dissidents, particularly the death of Jüri Kukk, contributed to a nationalist 'martyrology' which in turn added both rationalisation and legitimation to the independence movements of 1988–91. Third, the human cost of dissent, so to speak, fell as the terror of the Stalinist era was replaced by the less draconian sanctions of the Period of Stagnation. Finally, among the dissidents were several individuals who became notable political leaders during the transition to, and indeed following the achievement of, Estonian independence. In a real sense, a history of dissidence enhanced their status as leaders of the social movements and political parties that emerged from 1988 onwards.

In the last-mentioned context, several subsequent leaders of the Estonian National Independence Party, formed in 1988, were involved in a joint memorandum in October 1972 which was the work of two miniscule groups, the Estonian National Front and the Estonian Democratic Movement. It was addressed to the United Nations General Assembly (with a covering note to the secretary-general, Kurt Waldheim) and demanded the restoration of an independent Estonia and UN-monitored elections. Moreover, although there was no personnel overlap, a letter in May 1977, written by 18 environmentalists, which protested against Soviet phosphorite mining and attendant oil-shale dumping, was in many ways the precursor of the 'Phosphate Spring' of 1987 and the rise of a popular 'green' movement in Estonia.

The regional scale of dissident activity was well illustrated by the so-called 'Baltic Charter' of August 1979. On its fortieth anniversary, four Estonians joined Latvian and Lithuanian dissidents in demanding the cancellation of the secret protocols of the Molotov–Ribbentrop pact. The four were Mart Niklus, who had been imprisoned in 1958 and released after eight years, Endel Ratas and Erik Udam, both of whom had also served jail sentences, and Enn Tarto, who was first arrested during the 1950s for joining an unofficial student organisation. Tarto, incidentally, in 1989 became the leading figure in the foundation of the Conservative People's Party. In January 1980 Estonians were signatories to a petition protesting against the Soviet invasion of Afghanistan. They included Jüri Kukk, an associate professor of chemistry at Tartu university who, together with Niklus, took the document to Moscow to be passed on to Brezhnev and the Western press. In October of the following year, moreover, 13 Estonians signed a Baltic letter demanding that the three states be included in the proposed nuclear-free Nordic zone which the USSR supported. On 27 March 1981 Kukk died en route to detention in the Urals and, although he was weakened by a hunger strike, the circumstances of his death were never fully explained. The case and, in particular, his unmarked grave made the Western press.[8]

One of the last acts of dissent in the ESSR was a letter in December 1984 addressed to those states possessing nuclear weapons which called for disarmament. The advent of Gorbachev, shortly thereafter, however, betokened the beginning of the end of dissidence – though not, of course, the dissident tradition in Estonia. In seeking to generalise by way of summing up, it can be said that Estonian dissidents were often intellectuals; some took their inspiration from Christianity; most, however, were simply fervent patriots or nationalists who remained implacably opposed to communism. Though widely recognised by ordinary people, they remained far removed from them. Indeed, since a brand of hardline communism dominated their thinking over the transition to independence, the former dissidents tended later to be regarded by many as extremists lacking the necessary spirit of compromise. Unlike the partisan resistance, the dissidents had a *samizdat* (underground) press dating back to the early 1970s. Between 1978 and 1987 a total of 25 issues of the magazine *Lisandusi vabade môtete levikule Eestis* ('Addenda to the Free Flow of Ideas and News in Estonia') were published in manuscript form.[9] The circulation was small, although *samizdat* publications were passed on and read by many people.[10]

In contrast to dissidence, *civil disobedience* embraces demonstrations and other forms of public protest action which involve relatively large numbers of people and entail a significant measure of spontaneity. Intermittent activity of this sort in Estonia dates back to the early 1970s. Thus when, in April 1972, less than four years after Soviet tanks crushed Dubcek's 'Prague Spring', a Czechoslovak hockey team defeated the USSR, students from the Tallinn Polytechnic Institute poured on to the streets shouting, 'We won!'[11] In autumn 1985, moreover, hundreds of Estonian and Russian youths confronted one another in Tartu during preparations for Soviet constitution day. As these cases illustrate, civil disobedience usually involved young educated people and was not infrequently associated with events (sports fixtures, pop concerts and so on) at which a mass attendance was permitted.

In December 1976, a thousand students roamed the streets yelling anti-Soviet slogans after a rock event was banned. Understandably, such proscriptions could be the trigger for deeper-seated protest, as in October 1980 when the cancellation of a pop concert sparked extensive youth mobilisation against ECP First Secretary Vaino's Russification programme. Young people, mostly still at school, moved about the streets with banners carrying slogans such as 'A Free Estonia', 'A Free Language', 'Take Russian out of the Schools' and 'Let's have an Estonian-speaking Minister of Education'. Predictably, in a television response, the minister of the interior, Marko Tibar, replying to viewers' letters, gave the students short shrift, referring dismissively to what he described as 'recent acts of hooliganism'.[12]

Civil disobedience of an entirely different kind could perhaps be detected in the January 1979 census returns which revealed that the number of Estonians declaring that they could speak Russian had dropped to 24.2 per cent, compared with 29 per cent in 1970. It has been argued that this falsification of the facts constituted the first act of mass insubordination in the history of the ESSR, being directed against Vaino and his Sovietization policies.[13] However, by 1987 occasional civil disobedience had given way to the routinised mass mobilisation of the population – particularly in support of environmental and nationalist demands – and this bore witness to the renascence of civil society in Estonia. Before sketching the events of 1987, a final form of resistance – attempted 'third-way reformism' – warrants a brief, separate note.

Attempted 'Third-way Reformism'

On 28 October 1980, a five-page letter, signed by 40 established Estonian intellectuals – communist and non-communist – was addressed to *Pravda, Sovjetskaya Estonia* and the ECP organ, *Rahva Hääl*, but was not published in any of them. It criticised, albeit it in relatively moderate terms, the repression of what it saw as Vaino's neo-Stalinist management style, denounced the increase in ethnic tensions in Estonia and made out a powerful case for the protection of the Estonian language and culture. Though it went unreported in the Estonian and Soviet press, the 'Letter of Forty' was mentioned on Radio Free Europe on 8 December 1980, published in the Stockholm-based emigrant newspaper *Eesti Päevaleht* two days later (according to the editor Ülo Ignatsi, the letter reached Sweden in microfilmed form) and almost two weeks thereafter it was discussed on *Voice of America*. The basic premise of the signatories was that the suppression of all criticism had split the Estonian population into two camps, conformists and dissidents, the latter employing illegal means and appealing for outside help. The Letter of Forty, therefore, represented the search for a third way between conformism and dissidence and, by addressing the local ECP hierarchy in expectation of a response, it hoped to instigate a public debate and, by extension, create a legal, reform-minded opposition.[14]

The influence of Solidarity's victory in Poland in August 1980 on the thinking of the '40' was obvious. Translations of newspaper articles on Solidarity's achievement circulated widely and intellectual ammunition was acquired from statements such as the one by Kristof Toepliz in the magazine *Kultura*: 'The basis of political culture is debate, both within the party *and* between the governors and society.'[15] Other background factors in provoking the letter included the secret All-Union Russification edict of October 1978 and its corollary, the youth disturbances in Tallinn and elsewhere in Estonia in October 1980. Interestingly, six of the '40' were Communist Party members; coincidentally, this was about the same ratio of party members to the population as a whole. Two hailed from an older generation of so-called 'June [1940] communists'; one came from a middle-aged group of party members; and the remaining three, Marju Lauristin, Rein Ruutsoo and Jaan Tamm, belonged to the 1960s generation which, while recognising the ESSR's existence as an objective reality, sought, Dubcek-style, to reform it from within.[16] The presence of party members among the '40' was significant, not least because it prevented the document from being written off by the authorities as the mere fabrication of dissidents. This was, indeed, probably the first time rank-and-file party members had manifested themselves as an independent power resource and it unquestionably rankled with the ECP machine.

The seminal figure orchestrating the discussions and preparations which underscored the 'Letter of Forty' was very probably the poet Jaan Kaplinski (nicknamed 'Janka') – precisely whose idea it was remains unclear – and most of his network of associates in turn had been prominent in the resurgence of Estonian culture in the 1960s. Of course, approaches to potential signatories had to be made with the utmost caution, and in several cases they were rebuffed. Among members of the older generation the fear prevailed that the whole project, if not a KGB ruse, would be used by the KGB to expose Estonia's leading cultural figures as potential enemies of the state.[17] Among parents asked, anxiety was invariably expressed about the likely consequences for their children's education. For students there was the understandable concern about the implications for their graduation and career prospects. For example, his imminent doctoral ceremony was one of the reasons cited by the young philosopher Ülo Kaevats for not signing.[18]

Inevitably, the mass distribution of the 'Letter of Forty' proved difficult: private typewriters were rare; the sale of typewriters with the Latin (Estonian) alphabet (as opposed to the Cyrillic Russian) had effectively ceased; the use of office typewriters was a risky business since all of them were registered by the KGB; only authorised persons were permitted to use duplicating facilities; and only authorised material could be copied. Furthermore, there were virtually no photocopy machines in Estonia at the time. However, although the letter was usually copied by hand – some people did as many as ten manual copies – it achieved a remarkably widespread circulation.

Despite this fact, the letter signally failed in its objective of initiating a public debate and, consequently, it fell well short of generating a de facto opposition to the monopolistic Communist Party. Rather, interrogations were set in train. Indeed, if both those who underwent KGB cross-examination and those called to the Prosecutor's Office are counted, almost half the signatories were obliged to give a greater or lesser account of their actions.[19] The sanctions imposed on the '40' were in truth relatively mild and included the withdrawal of foreign travel permits, the prevention of career advancement and, in the case of the six communist members, expulsion from the party. Finally, it might be noted that the Estonian dissidents published the 'Letter of Forty', in their underground press. There was, however, no suggestion of cooperation on their side. The dividing line between nonconformity and the varying shades of systemic acquiescence was too starkly etched for that.[20] As 'third-way reformism' was stifled, dissent, as noted, increased in both scale and scope in the early 1980s.

1987: the Re-emergence of an Embryonic Civil Society in Estonia

Phosphorite mining to produce phosphate fertilisers had a history in Estonia dating back to the earliest years of the First Republic, but the 1960s-style Soviet open-pit mines were both inefficient and constituted a considerable ecological hazard. Poor-quality oil shale above the phosphorite layer was simply dumped and ignited on contact with air. By 1987 about 50 million tons of oil shale lay in dumps, intermittently catching fire and polluting the air and water supplies.[21] Moreover, the deposits contained radioactive waste and it was this risk from gamma ray radiation which had been highlighted in several Estonian studies. Ultimately, sizeable environmental protest was precipitated by plans announced in Moscow for a new mining development at Rakvere, between Tallinn and Narva, which was to begin operations in 1987. It threatened to contaminate water supplies across a vast area (about one-third of Estonia) and would also require large quantities of (what it was feared would be imported) labour.

Although adverse evidence submitted by an anonymous group of Estonian scientists was brushed aside by Moscow, a series of events served to popularise the risk the new mining project posed to the Estonian countryside. First, the phosphate issue was effectively politicised when it was raised at a widely reported meeting of the Estonian Writers' Union in December 1986. Next, it came to the attention of a much larger public following a television interview in February 1987 in which the director of the responsible Soviet mining agency reiterated his view that the whole project must get under way immediately so as to achieve the objective of full working capacity by the year 2000. Finally, the issue was taken up with Gorbachev during his visit to Tallinn on 27 February 1987 by the chairman of the Writers' Union and the latter's speech was later published in the weekly magazine *Sirp ja Vasar*. Throughout the spring and summer of 1987, the phosphorite question became the dominant issue in Estonia, engaging an ever-wider public.

The large-scale environmental protest of the 'Phosphate Spring' represented a direct challenge to the ECP establishment and prompted a retaliatory response from its leading figures. At a press conference on 31 March 1987 a beleaguered prime minister, Bruno Saul, insisted that the ecological risk from phosphorite mining had been wildly exaggerated. His view was vigorously challenged by the attendant reporters, however, although the evening's television coverage omitted these exchanges with the press. It was nonetheless a sign of the widespread popular interest in or concern about the subject that an unabridged video of proceedings enjoyed an extensive circulation.[22] Another local luminary, the ECP central committee's ideological secretary, Rein Ristlaan, railed (unavailingly) against the press, and *Sirp ja Vasar* in particular, for what it was implied was its irresponsible treatment of 'green' questions (Ristlaan was replaced by Indrek Toome in January 1988). The search for information on topical issues stimulated by the Phosphate Spring, incidentally, provoked an enormous growth in the press. In 1987 there were 217 periodicals in Estonia. During 1988–93, however, nearly 500 new publications were launched, the vast majority being small local newspapers and newsletters, although 47 national newspapers and 44 new magazines also appeared.[23]

In the offensive against the Rakvere project, students played a leading role, especially in organising expert debates. For example, on 2 April 1987, at a meeting in the ceremonial hall of Tartu University, to which specialists and cultural figures were invited, the poet Hando Runnel for the first time implicated the ECP in the post-war programme of labour immigration, claiming it had accepted the drafting of large numbers of Russian workers into Estonia. At a similar event in the Tartu Agricultural Academy on 20 April 1987 a leading Estonian geologist, Evald Mustjõgi, was openly accused of being one of the people primarily responsible for backing the phosphorite mine blueprint.[24] On May Day 1987, the Tartu University students forsook their traditional show of fraternal solidarity with the working class; rather, they took to the streets bearing green anti-phosphorite banners with slogans which they often sang. There were similar student demonstrations in Tallinn on 1–2 May. Predictably, on 6 May, the staff of Tartu University were notified that the student activities had been 'childish and provocative' and demeaned the status of the university.[25]

In addition to the student initiatives, it is important to emphasise that, over the course of 1987, ordinary people began to organise 'green' meetings in towns and villages across the country and at these an expert was invariably present. In short, a civil society was beginning to re-emerge in Estonia. Moreover, attitudes were rapidly hardening against the Rakvere development. In an opinion poll (one of the first conducted in the ESSR) it emerged (not surprisingly) that three-quarters of the population in the affected region were against the proposed mining project.[26] The weight of this popular opposition soon began to tell on the authorities. As early as 30 March 1987, there was evidence of governmental equivocation in that a commission headed by Prime Minister Saul announced a proscription on mining projects in Estonia until further investigations had been carried out. Over the summer, moreover, the magazine *Eesti Loodus* ('Estonian Nature') was effective in bringing out just how low the phosphate content of Estonian phosphorite was. Finally, at an ECP central committee meeting on 27 October 1987, Saul announced that Moscow had decided to call a halt to new phosphorite mining projects in Estonia. The 'Phosphate Spring' had borne fruit in an autumn victory which represented a watershed in the history of the ESSR. A number of points are in order.

First, the 'greening of Estonia', the arousal of a mass eco-consciousness and its corollary the rebirth of an embryonic civil society in 1987, were triggered in large measure by the Chernobyl disaster in Ukraine the previous year. Unlike parts of the USSR such as Ukraine or Belorussia, however, Estonia had a civil society tradition dating back to the First Republic and the estrangement of the people under communism (except during the Stalinist era) was never quite as great in Estonia as elsewhere. Nonetheless, the Phosphate Spring represented a classic case of single-issue mobilisation, it expedited the demise of the ECP's 'old guard' and presaged the belated advent of *perestroika* in Estonia.

Second, in amassing and presenting specialist evidence which in the main challenged the wisdom of the proposed mining development at Rakvere, Estonian natural scientists, such as the physicist Endel Lippmaa, inevitably exceeded their technical function and assumed willy-nilly a political role. When marshalled by the Estonian environmentalists – the Estonian Naturalists' Society, the magazine *Eesti Loodus* and so on – these expert findings became central to the campaign against 'further colonialist exploitation' of the Estonian countryside.

Third, the events of the Phosphate Spring 1987 spawned a class of opinion-leaders – scientists (like Lippmaa), journalists (Juhan Aare, Ilmar Rattus), cultural figures (Runnel and others) – which came to comprise a new elite or, rather, counter-elite, implicitly challenging the position of the ECP bureaucracy and leadership. Thus organised public meetings routinely involved an invitation to a leading geologist, biologist or economist, while the press gradually shed its shackles to become an independent disseminator of the facts.

Fourth, the phosphorite crisis stimulated the growth of a mass public opinion in Estonia, mobilised in search of information and influence. Most conspicuously, the students, including Komsomol (young communist) groups, which paraded with anti-mining placards on 1 May 1987, reassumed their (rightful) historical position in the vanguard of change and reform. But evidence of the existence also of a mass public opinion in spring that year can be found in the form of hundreds of letters sent to the television, radio and newspapers, all with multiple signatories, from those seeking to affect the outcome of the phosphate question by expressing their own view.[27] The 'green' issue, in short, galvanised the entire social spectrum.

Finally, the electronic media encouraged and facilitated a dialogue between elite and mass public by devising programmes in which experts were confronted directly by questions from viewers and listeners. The opportunity for feedback enhanced the subjective competence (the individual's sense of being able to exert influence) of ordinary citizens and provided a further catalyst for change.

Lauristin, Vihalemm and Ruutsoo concluded thus:

> The 'phosphate awakening' was not confined to ecological questions. There was suddenly a new mood in the air which amounted to a crisis of confidence. The nation simply did not believe any longer that the party could handle matters in a competent fashion. Quite soon, moreover, there was open talk of a threat not only to Estonia's nature but to its culture and, indeed, people.[28]

This is an important point, since environmentalism became an extended umbrella under which a diverse array of anti-system grievances could be mobilised. Ecological issues, moreover, were not overtly nationalist in character and in the new spirit of *perestroika* the various manifestations of protest could not easily be circumscribed by the authorities.

A second component in the mass mobilisation of 1987, which focused on the Molotov–Ribbentrop pact and culminated in a rally in Hirvepark in August that year, was, however, expressly nationalist. On 23 August 1987 a crowd, variously estimated at between two and five thousand converged on Hirvepark, near the seat of government at Toompea in the Old Town quarter of Tallinn, to demonstrate in favour of the publication of the secret protocols of the 1939 Molotov–Ribbentrop pact. The Hirvepark gathering, unlike the earlier environmental protest action, was clearly anti-systemic in intent, since the secret provisions of the pact (dividing Eastern Europe into spheres of influence and allocating Estonia to Stalin) bore on the very legality of the Soviet regime in Estonia. Moreover, in contrast to the environmental protest, which had been orchestrated by mainstream figures and organisations, Hirvepark was organised by dissidents and formed part of a pan-Baltic initiative. Some of the activists, like Lagle Parek and Tiit Madison, had in fact only recently been released from detention (Parek was later a driving force in the creation of the Estonian National Independence Party). Although implicitly challenging the legality of the ESSR, Hirvepark was not in itself illegal since permission had been sought by the organisers and authorisation given by the city officials to stage the rally, albeit not at the venue originally planned. During the Hirvepark demonstration signatures were collected with the aim of creating an MRP–AEG action group (*Molotov–Ribbentropi Pakti Avalikustamise Eesti Grupp*), discussed later, to press for the publication of the Molotov–Ribbentrop pact. In many ways, Hirvepark marked the formal end of dissidence in Estonia, although participation in the activities of the subsequent MRP–AEG group remained a risky business and its membership assumed none of the proportions of the 'green' protest earlier in the year.

Just over a month after Hirvepark, on 26 September 1987, the Tartu daily *Edasi* published the so-called 'Four-Man Proposal' for the economic autonomy (self-management) of Estonia. The four principal signatories were Edgar Savisaar, Siim Kallas, Tiit Made (all three will be referred to extensively later in the text) and Mikk Titma – later the ECP's ideological secretary – who, although not involved at the drafting stage, was welcomed, not least because of his good contacts in Moscow. Several other originators of the proposal declined to sign out of fear of reprisals.

The Four-Man Proposal canvassed the extensive devolution of economic management powers to Estonia and the transference to national control of, *inter alia*, the railways, navy and those firms that were responsible to All-Union agencies. It also sought the restructuring necessary to ensure the preferential development of those profitable economic sectors based primarily on local resources; the introduction of a convertible rouble and separate taxation system; and an explicit recognition that inter-republic trade be based on the marketplace. The blueprint engendered a lively debate as well as ensuring a further measure of elite mobilisation, since Estonian sociologists and economists formed study groups to examine the central issues. The Four-Man Proposal commanded widespread support. On 26 February 1988, *Edasi* reported that about a hundred supportive pieces had been published in the Estonian press, compared with only five articles opposing the prescription for economic autonomy.[29] During the autumn of 1987, to be sure, there was criticism of the document from the ECP establishment.

There were also some signs of a prospective backlash to the re-emergence of civil society on the part of the authorities and a desire to revert to the status quo ante using tried and trusted methods. Violence was only narrowly avoided in the small town of Võru in southern Estonia in October 1987 when local youths, who had tidied up the graves and wanted to hold a memorial service for those who had fallen in the 1918–19 War of Independence, were confronted by a special brigade of the local police. Common sense ultimately prevailed, but the episode seemed to reflect the view of officials that intimidation would, as a last resort, still work.[30] Indeed, an MRP–AEG demonstration in Tartu on 2 February 1988 (called to commemorate the Estonian–Soviet peace treaty in 1920) was brutally dispersed by the police.

At this stage, a clear divergence over tactics emerged between those radical (ex-dissident) elements who urged large-scale demonstrations on Estonian Independence Day (22 February 1988) and a corresponding body of gradualists who canvassed a more pragmatic approach, fearing that an openly confrontational stance would prove counterproductive. The moderates called on Estonians to mark the seventieth anniversary of their independence with 'scholarly conferences, respectful debate and reflections in the press', that is measures which would avoid the possibility of clashes with the authorities. In the event, neither the MRP–AEG demonstration in Tallinn nor the public lectures that took place simultaneously were restricted or dispersed by the authorities. But the division between hardline nationalists and pragmatic reformists was later to become institutionalised in the two major social movements of this transitional period: the citizens committee movement and the Popular Front, respectively.

By spring 1988 an embryonic civil society had emerged in Estonia, but the state remained controlled by a monopolistic Communist Party and its 'old guard' leadership. Pressure for change, however, was becoming irresistible. Paragraph 19 of the final statement of a joint meeting of the Creative Unions on 1–2 April 1988 made the point:

> It is crucial to underline that the nation expects more initiative and firmness of principle to be displayed by the ESSR leadership in its defence of the republic's constitutional rights … The meeting wishes to express its dissatisfaction with First Secretary Karl Vaino and prime minister Bruno Saul's contribution so far.[31]

In proceeding to consider Vaino's fall from grace, it is also worth attempting briefly to analyse the ECP's contribution to the achievement of Estonian independence in 1988–91. Did the ruling party, whose monopoly of power was soon to be broken and whose popularity had plummeted by 1990, work towards or against national independence?

Notes

1 Cited in Sirje Kiin, Rein Ruutsoo and Andres Tarand, *Neljankymmenen kirje* (Otava: Keuruu, 1990), pp.228–9.
2 Svennik Høyer, Epp Lauk and Peeter Vihalemm (eds), *Towards a Civic Society: The Baltic Media's Long Road to Freedom* (Nota Baltica: Tartu, 1993), p.200.
3 Rein Taagepera, *Estonia. Return to Independence* (Westview: Boulder–San Francisco–Oxford, 1993), p.91.
4 Ibid., p.99.
5 Høyer *et al.*, *Towards a Civic Society*, p.216.
6 Taagepera, *Estonia*, p.79.
7 Ibid., p.80.
8 Ibid., p.115.
9 Høyer *et al.*, *Towards a Civic Society*, p.217.
10 Taagepera, *Estonia*, p.113.
11 Ibid., p.101.
12 Kiin *et al.*, *Neljankymmenen kirje*, p.35.
13 Ibid., p.25.
14 Ibid., p.46.
15 Ibid., p.21.
16 Ibid., p.179.
17 Ibid., p.60.
18 Ibid., p.69.
19 Ibid., pp.150–51.
20 Ibid., p.219.
21 Taagepera, *Estonia*, p.121.
22 Marju Lauristin, Peeter Vihalemm and Rein Ruutsoo, *Viron vapauden tuulet* (Gummerus: Jyväskylä–Helsinki, 1989), p.123.
23 Høyer *et al.*, *Towards a Civic Society*, p.263.
24 Lauristin, *et al.*, *Viron vapauden tuulet*, p.139.
25 Ibid., pp.123–4.
26 Taagepera, *Estonia*, p.122.
27 Lauristin *et al.*, *Viron vapauden tuulet*, pp.138–9.
28 Ibid., p.118.
29 Taagepera, *Estonia*, p.130.
30 Lauristin *et al.*, *Viron vapauden tuulet*, pp.126–8.
31 Taagepera, *Estonia*, pp.133–4.

5 The Estonian Communist Party's Contribution to the Regaining of Independence, 1988–91

There are three ways of getting out of prison. You can dig a tunnel, but it might collapse on you; you can blow the place up, but then you will perish with it; or you can find the keys of the gaol. The Estonian Communist Party leaders knew they had the keys in their pockets. (Interview with Social Affairs Minister Marju Lauristin, 20 September 1994)

After exercising a monopolistic stranglehold on power in the Estonian Soviet Socialist Republic (ESSR) for nearly half a century, the Estonian Communist Party (ECP) became a victim of the exponential social and political change that characterised the period 1988–91. In the space of these few years, Estonia was transformed from an atomised and alienated aggregation of inhabitants into a highly mobilised and highly politicised civil society. The ECP, of course, sought to respond to this 'acceleration of history' and maintain its power base. But it appeared to be overtaken by events – events which for a time it orchestrated and managed, but over which it ultimately lost control. The ECP's 'life cycle' in these dramatic years can be traced in three phases which broadly corresponded to steps in the decline in its standing.

First, despite the advent of a 'nationalist' leadership of the ECP in June 1988 – when Vaino Väljas replaced Vaino as first secretary and in turn cut the ground from under the Russian–Estonian 'old guard' – and the party's enormous popularity during autumn 1988, when it was instrumental in a momentous 'declaration on sovereignty' (*suveräänsus*) – the first in the Soviet Union – the ruling party had largely lost the initiative by 1989. This had passed to the reformist communists, several of them undersignatories of the Letter of Forty, heading the Popular Front (PF) and the dissident-inspired citizens committee movement.

Second, having accepted the PF (initiated in April 1988) as a 'legal formation' in January 1989, and ended its own monopolistic status by deleting article six from the ESSR constitution on 23 February 1990, the ECP lost both its electoral support base and governmental power to the Edgar Savisaar-led PF following the Supreme Soviet elections of 18 March 1990.

According to Väljas, the ECP suffered first and foremost from a type of 'guilt by association' syndrome: its name had a pejorative association in the minds of ordinary people and the creation by leading communists of a group called Free Estonia (*Vaba Eesti*) in January 1990, in the build-up to the Supreme Soviet elections, could be seen as evidence of a desire on the part of the ECP's centrist faction to avoid being tarred with the 'party' brush.[1] The head of the Praesidium of the ESSR, President of Soviet Estonia between 1983 and 1990 and the independent Estonia Republic from 1991 to 1992, Arnold Rüütel, in contrast, has contended that, unlike the PF's re-vised programme of October 1989, which came down clearly in fa-vour of the ultimate goal of independence, the ECP at that time still saw Estonia as part of the USSR. True, exhorted by Väljas (who took over as speaker for the occasion) even the 'diehard' ECP deputies in the Estonian Supreme Soviet – it was elected under an antiquated electoral system – voted in favour of the 'declaration on sovereignty'. But, according to Rüütel, the ECP did not articulate the goal of full independence early enough. There was too much prevarication.[2]

Third, following its twentieth party congress on 25 March 1990, the ECP formally split into two: a majority-based pro-independence party and a pro-Moscow minority party. Unlike what happened to its Bal-tic counterparts, however, there was no change of name on the part of the pro-independence party in the lifetime of the Soviet Union. Neither was there in Estonia the type of economic blockade imposed on Lithuania over the early summer of 1990 or, indeed, the violence of Vilnius in January 1991. Was this pure coincidence, or was it the result of a grand sacrificial gesture on the part of the Independent Communist Party, retaining its name (and thus forfeiting the possi-bility of power) in order to maintain communication lines with the Kremlin?

The present chapter ponders this and the other issues raised above. On 20 September 1992, the ECP (the minority party was earlier pro-scribed) contested the first post-independence parliamentary elec-tions, but it did not win a single seat in the 101-seat *Riigikogu* (par-liament). In the changed climate of post-communist Europe such a result was perhaps inevitable, but what had been the ECP's overall contribution to the achievement of Estonian independence?

In line with the minimalist 'prison warder' view presented in the introductory quotation from Marju Lauristin, the ruling ECP elite possessed the keys – control of the institutional means – to initiate change, but unlocked the gaol doors of society only with the greatest reluctance when it was clear that the prisoners (gathered in the new social movements and particularly the PF) were anyway planning a mass breakout. According to this interpretation, necessity was the mother of ECP reformism and, for Lauristin, Väljas remained the same person who, as the ECP's ideological secretary in 1975, shut down the sociological laboratory in Tartu University.[3] For the pragmatic communists at the helm, moreover, the status quo bestowed privilege and influence, both of which would be lost if the ECP surrendered custody of the reform process. Was this Lauristin line unduly harsh and dismissive? In order to consider the party's role over the transitional years more thoroughly, it is worth considering first the principal functions of the ECP during the heyday of the ESSR.

The ECP's Role in the ESSR

From the time of the Soviet annexation in 1940 and the reannexation in 1944 until (at least) the middle of 1988, Estonia was ruled by the Central Committee of the Estonian Communist Party, *Eestimaa Kommunistlik Partei*, which constituted a regional wing of the Communist Party of the Soviet Union (CPSU). During that time, the ECP performed three principal functions. First, it served as the monopolistic source of power and the instrument of a massive programme of Sovietisation conducted from Moscow. This saw Estonia purged of dissident elements (as noted, the patriotic guerilla movement, the Forest Brotherhood, worked in the 1940s and early 1950s to restore national independence) and become, in turn, something of a transit lobby for an itinerant band emanating from all over the Soviet Union. During 1940–55, Estonia lost in the order of 25–30 per cent of the population of the First Republic, either to purges or to emigration. Indeed, during the period 1941–9 alone, almost 80 000 Estonians were accused of political crimes and arrested by the KGB. Approximately two-fifths of these subsequently died, usually in Siberian prison camps, while the average length of detainment for political prisoners was in the order of 12 years.[4] In the entire post-war period, moreover, 7.5 million people moved into Estonia, of whom seven million ultimately continued on elsewhere. The upshot of this migration activity was a significant alteration in the ethnic balance: by the

1980s, about 60 per cent of the population comprised Estonians and 40 per cent non-Estonians (mainly Russians, Belorussians and Ukrainians).

Second, the ECP provided a career structure for politicians and officials who, in turn, constituted a privileged class or caste, the *nomenklatura*. Initially, there was no indigenous group of communists and the ruling cadre had to be 'imported'. The long-serving ECP leader, Vaino, who moved to Estonia about 1948 and held the first secretary's office during 1978–88, was born in Siberia of Estonian parents and never fully mastered Estonian. His successor, Väljas, in contrast, was Estonian by birth and upbringing and Enn-Arno Sillari, who took over as first secretary in March 1990, was the member of a long-standing Estonian family.[5] The fact that it was necessary to be a party member in order to be active in public life meant, of course, that the ECP incorporated a wide range of views, something which made it potentially unstable from 1987 onwards, when greater tolerance of differing opinions was displayed.

Third, through its fraternal links with the Kremlin, the ECP acted as the voice of Estonia 'in high places'. Thus the ECP's first secretary, albeit he alone, was traditionally a full member of the CPSU central committee. Johannes Käbin, who held that office for over a quarter of a century between 1950 and 1978, acquired a considerable reputation as a skilled mediator between the ECP and the central leadership in Moscow. A Russian Estonian whose command of Estonian improved, he was known in the press in the late 1950s by his Russian forename 'Ivan' (with the derogatory connotations that possessed), but by the mid-1960s had become accepted by his adopted (and Estonian) 'Johannes'. By contrast, lacking Käbin's experience and standing, Vaino's bargaining power with Moscow was weaker.[6] Indeed, during Vaino's time at the helm, there was a deepening mood of pessimism, disenchantment and lethargy among the people of Estonia, which stood in contrast to the up-tempo beat of the Käbin years in the late 1960s and early 1970s. While references to a 'neo-Shakhovskoi era' and comparisons with the Russification of the late nineteenth century were exaggerated, Vaino was associated with a period in which, as a result of an All-Union campaign, Russian had become increasingly important in education and administration, while in the early 1980s non-Estonian immigration began to rise again. Living standards, moreover (at best) levelled out. It will be recalled from Chapter 4 that, the same month as the Savisaar broadcast initiative, speakers at a leadership meeting of the Creative Unions (writers, critics, artists, journalists and so on) openly indicted the ECP bureaucracy and, indeed, Vaino by name.

The significance of dialogue with Moscow grew, of course, when Mikhail Gorbachev became CPSU first secretary in 1985, since the

programme of restructuring (*perestroika*) he set in train released centrifugal forces across much of the Soviet Union. Equally, another of
its effects was to leave the ECP leadership, with weakened backing
from Moscow, to face alone the demands of an increasingly mobilised Estonian public. Indeed, in the changed climate fostered by
Gorbachev's brand of 'liberal communism', reformist communists
(though not Vaino and his entourage) recognised that the ECP would
have to assume a crucial fourth function, namely to provide a genu-
ine channel of communication between state and society and between the historic nation (Estonians) and imperial nation (Russians).
Put another way, *perestroika* in society dictated the need for *perestroika*
in the party. A first step was change at the top.

Väljas' Appointment as ECP Leader

Väljas' appointment as first secretary on 16 June 1988, at the instigation of the ECP's reformist wing, vested the party with substantially
enhanced popular legitimacy. It was no coincidence that, less than
one month after his assumption of office, the full text of the Letter of
Forty was published in Estonia for the first time, appearing in the
July 1988 issue of *Vikerkaar*. This was at the instigation of the editor,
Rein Veidemann, who had wanted to print it in spring 1987. Two
months later, moreover, at the ECP central committee plenary on 9
September 1988, Väljas castigated the previous leadership for ignor-
ing the signals given by the Letter of Forty, banning its publication
and censuring its authors. He acknowledged that the agenda of the
'40' had lost none of its salience and would provide a starting-point
for social reform.[7]

Väljas' appointment reflected the importance attached to bringing
the party into line with the new mood in Estonia and, above all, the
need for it to respond to the challenges of the nascent civil society.
Vaino's demise, in turn, although precipitated by a series of tactical
blunders, reflected more generally the way he largely failed to comprehend the nature and significance of the changes that were taking
place. On the point of strategic errors, Vaino's decision on 31 May
1988 simply to nominate the 32-strong Estonian delegation to the
nineteenth CPSU conference in Moscow that July – rather than organising the multi-candidate elections urged by the CPSU leadership
– along with his exclusion of PF leaders from the delegation, led to
press criticism and widespread unrest in the party. Some ECP organisations called for the election of a new central committee and there
was an abortive attempt to remove Vaino. Moreover, when the PF
leadership called for a mass meeting with the Estonian delegates to
Moscow, which it set for 17 June, Vaino apparently panicked and

(unavailingly) sought Russian military intervention. This would seem to have completed the case for the prosecution, so to speak, as a little earlier the Kremlin had received reports that Vaino had seriously contemplated the use of force to disperse the 60 000 young people who gathered for a rock festival in the Tallinn Old Town on 11–12 June.[8] A week earlier various youth organisations had come together as the Independent Youth Forum. This held its first meeting in Tallinn on 4 June 1988, when it argued that the main reason for the passivity of young people was the totally discredited nature of the government and central administration which, it claimed, were totally out of touch with the people.[9] Lacking fluency in Estonian and increasingly delegating matters to Prime Minister Saul, Vaino had become a liability to Moscow and on 16 June 1988, he was duly dismissed.

Gorbachev, who was kept well informed about Estonian developments by reformist communists like Savisaar and Marju Lauristin, clearly believed that the ECP had forfeited its popular trust and that Väljas, whom he had known since 1956 when both were national Komsomol secretaries, was the man to restore it. Väljas had no inkling of future developments. He had spent eight years outside Estonia, six as Soviet ambassador in Venezuela and the remainder in Nicaragua, where he played a modest role in brokering the US–Soviet peace settlement with the Sandinistas. On 13 June 1988 he left Nicaragua for a vacation in Estonia, only to discover on his arrival at Moscow airport the following day that Gorbachev had requested to see him immediately. In a three-hour conversation it was made clear that his task in Nicaragua had been successfully completed and that it was time to return home. Since on 16 June Väljas was elected ECP first secretary almost unanimously, it is clear that Gorbachev was giving his endorsement to a vigorous lobby of reformist anti-Vaino elements in the ECP. Equally, the long personal acquaintance between Väljas and Gorbachev was important and may well have provided vital insulation at a later stage against the views of reactionary elements in Moscow prevailing in respect of Estonia. Väljas, incidentally, had a second valuable personal contact in Moscow in the form of Eduard Shevardnadze, whom he had known since the time the latter was Georgian Komsomol leader in the late 1950s.

Under Väljas, the ECP's role in the vanguard of events in autumn 1988 warrants emphasis. The first secretary himself likened the transformation in the Estonian political climate in the eight years he had been absent to the difference 'between night and day'.[10] It was in October 1980, as noted, two months after Solidarity's victory in Poland and against the backdrop of the spontaneous demonstrations of young Estonians opposed to the intensified Russian-language programme in schools, that the Letter of Forty was written. Interrogations and reprisals followed, leading Sirje Kiin, Rein Ruutsoo and

Andres Tarand to conclude that 'the basic features of the Stalinist system, the ordering of individuals and their submission to these commands, remained very much in evidence'.[11] By the time Väljas became ECP leader in June 1988, in contrast, the plenary session of the Creative Unions (1–2 April) and the formation of the PF (13 April) had contributed to a wholesale radicalisation of attitudes and the incipient mobilisation of a previously passive citizenry.

Encapsulating something of the heady mood of the so-called 'Singing Revolution' of summer 1988 was the highly-charged ECP central committee plenary on 9 September 1988. It was attended by an exceptionally large number of people (over 600), including representatives of both the PF and Creative Unions. The leader of the embryonic PF, Savisaar, gave a speech and a spokesman of the Creative Unions, Enn Põldroos, was elected onto the ECP's Politburo. In his keynote address, broadcast live on the radio to a mass audience, Väljas showed that he grasped the supreme psychological importance of giving ordinary people hope and belief. Acknowledging the popular aspirations to renewed independence – and even using the Estonian term for independence, *iseseisvus* – Väljas also alluded to the notion of the 'nation-state', as well as referring to the need to elevate the status of the Estonian language.

This new 'nationalist face' of Estonian communism was particularly in evidence over the late autumn and early winter of 1988–9. Most notably, there was the 16 November 1988 'declaration on sovereignty', the first of its kind in the Soviet Union and one which, remarkably, was not ultimately withdrawn.[12] It gave Estonian laws precedence over Soviet legislation and vested the Estonian Supreme Soviet with the right to veto the jurisdiction of All-Union enactments in Estonia. In addition, there were amendments to the ESSR constitution legitimising private property and stipulating that the ESSR had the exclusive ownership of Estonia's natural resources and basic means of production. Predictably, the 'declaration on sovereignty' was rejected in Moscow, but the ECP refused to climb down and in January 1989, moreover, passed a law affirming Estonian as the sole official language and another later restricting the voting rights of recent immigrants. Väljas' message was clear: the ECP was ready to be guided by the prevalent sentiments of the people.

Indeed, in Väljas' effusive view, the principal objective of the 'declaration on sovereignty' was to show that the party in power supported independence. It was important, he believed, to give 'constitutional nuance and form to independence' and, moreover, to design a means of marketing the fact to a wider international community.[13] Agreement was reached with the two other Baltic republics that they would follow suit with their own pronouncements on sovereignty and subsequent visits from senior KGB personnel to all three confirmed that there was an anticipation of events in Moscow. The reluctant acquiescence of the ECP's 'old guard' – the Estonian Supreme Soviet had been elected several years earlier, using the old Soviet electoral system – was ultimately obtained when, breaking with precedent, Väljas himself acted as speaker. The result was that, of 258 delegates present at the vital vote, a mere five abstained and only a single delegate came out against the 'declaration on sovereignty'. Clearly, a show of virtual unanimity was essential to maximise the effect of the step in Moscow.

Gorbachev was in India at the time, but his response to a Reuter journalist, when asked about the Estonian 'declaration on sovereignty', that 'that's *perestroika!*' belied his considerable irritation at developments. Publicly, Moscow pressed without success for the annulment of the declaration; behind the scenes it took all Väljas' resilience to withstand a reaction which he described with massive understatement as 'far from pleasant'.

Before proceeding it must be allowed that the 'declaration on sovereignty' was largely dictated by exogenous events, events which cast the ECP in a reactive role while also underlining its need to respond in a manner consonant with the mood of the nation at large. The point is that the extraordinary session of the Estonian Supreme Soviet on 16 November 1988 was convened in the aftermath of proposed amendments to the Soviet constitution which Gorbachev appeared to be trying to railroad through the Supreme Soviet of the USSR. These amendments threatened to undermine the key article 72 (granting the republics the right to secede from the Union) by vesting the Congress of People's Deputies in Moscow with exclusive decision-making powers on questions relating to the composition of the Soviet Union. In the narrowest sense, then, the 16 November 'declaration' was intended to be a clarification of an Estonian sovereignty already extant in principle under the Soviet constitution. As Taagepera has emphasised, what was novel and audacious was not that the ESSR was proposing to leave the Soviet Union – it was not – but that the Estonian Supreme Soviet had the temerity to 'propose an interpretation of the constitution rather than meekly accepting however Moscow chose to construe it'.[14]

If Taagepera's moderating remarks provide a useful counterpoise to the expansive interpretation of proceedings set out by Väljas above, it is nonetheless crucial to reiterate that, in issuing the 'declaration', the ECP was the first of the parties in the Soviet Union to challenge Moscow on constitutional changes that struck at the heart of the sovereignty of the republics. In doing so, moreover, it endeavoured to respond in the spirit, if not the letter, of public opinion, since it seems that a majority of Estonians favoured invoking article 72 and detaching the republic from the Soviet Union before the proposed constitutional amendments blocked (or complicated) this course of action. Perhaps when the language of the 'declaration' was decoded it was indeed interpreted by the people, as Väljas claimed was the intention, as a pillar in the ECP strategy of working towards independence in gradual stages. Whatever the case, the document also contained a wide-ranging critique of the economic and ecological consequences of nearly five decades of rule from Moscow.

The contrast in the ECP under the leaderships of Vaino and Väljas cannot be understated. Under the nationalist and reformist direction of Väljas, the ECP's popularity soared in the autumn of 1988, when it was widely perceived to be the experienced wheeler-dealer – the seasoned campaigner – and, accordingly, the organisation best equipped to negotiate with Moscow in the national interest. This popularity proved ephemeral, but it is important to record that, for at least half a year following Väljas' accession to the ECP leadership, the ruling party in Estonia had forged a working relationship with the people.

The twin impact of the PF and the citizens committee movement conspired against both the ECP's support and its authority. By February 1990, only 45 per cent of Estonians accepted that the ECP's central committee was acting (either wholly or partly) in the national interest, compared with 81 per cent who thought this was the case in December 1988. By the beginning of 1990, in fact, the ECP faced nothing short of a crisis of legitimacy. Its support was down to 1 per cent; membership, which in the 1970s had been the third highest per thousand persons among the 15 Union republics, had plummeted

Table 5.1   Estonian Communist Party (ECP) membership, 1953–91

Year	Total membership	Ethnic Estonians (%)
1953	22 320	43.6
1956	22 524	44.6
1961	37 848	49.2
1966	59 094	51.9
1971	73 168	52.3
1976	84 250	51.9
1981	97 923	50.8
1990	105 600*	—
1991	47 000	—

Note: * This figure is almost certainly inflated since many people did not actively resign their ECP membership although they ceased in practice to belong to the party.
Source: Toivo U. Raun, *Estonia and the Estonians*, 2nd edn (Hoover: Stanford, California, 1991), pp.190, 223. Reprinted with the permission of the publisher, Hoover Institution Press. Copyright 1987 and 1991 by the Board of Trustees of the Leland Stanford Junion University.

(see Table 5:1); leading communist figures were founding groups of their own; and on 23 February 1990 the ECP 'leading role' was deleted from the constitution.[15] The ECP was now engaged in a search for survival and risked being simply overtaken by events.

The ECP in the Electoral Arena, 1989–90

Initially, the 'ideological distance' between the reformist communists leading the PF and the reformist ECP under Väljas was relatively small. On 28 April 1988 the ECP's central committee sanctioned the PF's formation (although its official registration was delayed until 2 February 1989) and at the Front's inaugural congress on 1–2 October 1988 Väljas spoke in conciliatory terms (the PF leader Savisaar had, as noted earlier, addressed the ECP's central committee plenary on 9 September). There was also in these early months considerable personnel overlap between the PF and ECP. In June 1988 the PF boasted about 40 000 members, of whom perhaps one-third were simultaneously ECP members; moreover, at the PF's launch in October, 22 per cent of more than 3000 delegates present were ECP members.[16] A gulf between their respective leaderships began to develop, however, in December 1988 when the ECP-dominated Estonian Supreme Soviet voted merely to register its Soviet counterpart's rejection of the 'declaration on sovereignty' rather than (as the PF seemed to want) protesting against it. It widened further as the hardline Moscow-minded Intermovement became increasingly vocal in its opposition to social and political reform. Indeed, the ECP was soon to feel the PF's challenge in the electoral arena because at the March 1989 elections to select delegates for the Congress of People's Deputies in Moscow the PF won 29 of the 36 seats.

Far removed from the old-style, one-party, stage-managed elections of the Käbin and Vaino eras, the contest to select the Estonian allocation of seats for the Congress of People's Deputies in Moscow on 26 March 1989 was a notably modern affair. All voters (Estonian and non-Estonian) were permitted a choice: minimally the (entirely novel) decision of whether to vote or not and, thereafter, the option of a wide variety of ideas, programmes, personalities and groupings. There was a clear issue agenda embracing questions such as citizenship, economic autonomy and annulling the Molotov–Ribbentrop pact; extensive media involvement including candidate debates on the television and a Scandinavian-style election night results sequence; and a lively campaign with meetings, posters and the distribution of leaflets. A turnout of 87 per cent (95 per cent among Estonians and 75 per cent among non-Estonians), despite a boycott by the dissident-based Estonian National Independence Party, reflected both the popu-

lar interest in the election and the extent to which Estonia had progressed towards a mobilised society and shed the passivity and disillusion of the pre-Väljas era.

Above all, though, the elections for the Congress of People's Deputies in March 1989 were a pluralistic event, a competitive rather than,
as previously, a 'non-competitive' election, with candidates representing a range of different organisations. This was the first election
since the Second World War in which the ruling ECP encountered
both de facto opposition and open public criticism.[17] For example,
Prime Minister Indrek Toome's rival in the Võru constituency was
the popular Moscow correspondent for Estonian radio, Marika Villa,
who was not an ECP member and built her entire campaign on
criticism of the party. Similarly, in Tartu, the writer, Arvo Lõhmus,
ran as a non-communist candidate against the local ECP secretary. In
the event, both these non-communist candidates were unsuccessful,
suggesting that the ECP fared relatively well at the People's Deputy
elections.

Such an interpretation would be rather misleading, however, since
there were, in all but name, two communist parties contesting the
election. The one was the nationalist, reformist, Väljas-led wing which
worked closely with the PF (the latter backed the vast majority of
winning candidates); the other was the so-called 'internationalist'
Intermovement wing, which adopted a hardline pro-Moscow stance.
At its congress in early March, at a demonstration in Tallinn on 14
March and, exactly a week later, in a vituperative piece in *Pravda*, the
Intermovement strongly criticised the ECP leadership in the run-up
to polling and demanded changes at the helm. In the short term, this
'agitation' appeared to be counter productive because the ECP leadership of Väljas, Rüütel and Toome were elected overwhelmingly on
26 March. In the longer term, however, a perception of the deepening
division in its ranks, accentuated by the Intermovement's anti-lead-
ership campaign, undoubtedly contributed to the ECP's sharp loss of
support during the spring and early summer of 1989. According to a
Mainor poll conducted in April 1989, 16 per cent of all residents
would have voted for the ECP – 'had there been an election tomor-
row' – compared with only 11 per cent who would have done so two
months later. Among Estonians the figures were 7 per cent and 6 per
cent, respectively; among non-Estonians 32 per cent and 19 per cent.[18]

Although the ECP (or at least its Intermovement wing) was easily
the first choice among non-Estonians (mainly Russian inhabitants) in
the above survey, there is evidence from 26 March of non-Estonian
support for reformist candidates too. The defeat of such Inter-backed
candidates as Viktor Vaht and Boris Moronov in highly mixed ethnic
constituencies (where solidary non-Estonian voting would probably
have produced a different result) seems to support this point. Equally,

the Intermovement leader, Evgeni Kogan, was comfortably returned for Tallinn.[19] The best conclusion might be that the 26 March elections to the Congress of People's Deputies drove deeper the wedge between the two wings of the ECP while, with the emergence of a variety of organisations competing for votes, the 'party' label came to be seen as a liability by some reformist communists. For them there were two possibilities: either the ECP could change its name or they could found a surrogate grouping.

The ECP split became still more apparent at the local government elections on 10 December 1989, with Soviet television reporting on the eve of voting that Intermovement's decision to boycott the election – and organise its own ballot in the work collectives – had been condemned by the overwhelming majority of Estonian communists. There was talk, too, that the hardliners were contemplating the creation of a separate Russian-speaking *oblast* in north-east Estonia. Perhaps the ECP's role of providing a bridge between the nationalities was doomed, and division became inevitable, when the majority of reformist communists determined to follow public opinion and chart a gradualist course towards independence. Whatever the case, when a new local government law, intended to disenfranchise Russian soldiers and other itinerant elements, was adopted by the Estonian Supreme Soviet on 8 August 1989, ethnic tensions rose sharply. Weeklong strikes against the measure were organised by Intermovement and these halted production in the All-Union factories and shipyards. A rail stoppage also caused some shortages of goods in Tallinn. True, after the Praesidium of the USSR Supreme Soviet issued a decree on 16 August, insisting that the election law violated the Soviet constitution, the Estonian Supreme Soviet compromised and on 6 October deleted the controversial requirement of a two-year residence qualification for voters, but this was not enough to prevent Intermovement inveighing against the ECP leadership and proceeding with the planned boycott. Only the Väljas wing, therefore, contested the 10 December local elections and, moreover, it did not do so, along party lines. As at the 26 March contest for the Congress of People's Deputies, there was evidence of popular support for leading individual communists, but for the ECP's reformist wing, facing the rapid approach of the 18 March 1990 Supreme Soviet elections, the new year brought with it some stiff challenges.

In view of the dramatic decline both in its membership and its support, the foremost task facing the ECP at the beginning of 1990 was to achieve a heightened measure of legitimacy in an increasingly crowded political market-place. The ECP also needed to be seen to respond to the fact that several of its best-known members, many of whom had also been leading lights in the PF, were proceeding to found their own parties. How then could the ECP, which still exercised a de jure monopoly of power, adapt to the escalation of alternative political organisations? And could an ECP member be simultaneously a member of a competing political party?

The ECP central committee's political statement, issued at its sixteenth plenary on 4 January 1990 (and reported in *Rahva Hääl*), addressed some of these questions. First, it espoused the thoroughly pragmatic approach – in reality making a virtue of necessity – of recognising the existence of a proliferation of groupings and urging practical cooperation between them. There was no reference to those long-serving communists who were now engaged in other political projects, although elsewhere Väljas was adamant that there would be no expulsions. On an Estonian radio phone-in programme on 28 December 1989, the first secretary emphasised that the matter was one of individual conscience, although he expressed the clear hope (if not exactly expectation) that the individuals concerned would remain within the ECP. Using maritime metaphor appropriate to his native Hiiumaa island, Väljas commented: 'Once you have put your hands on the oars, you must hold tight and never let go, even if you get cramp in the middle of a thunderstorm.'[20]

Second, despite its earlier pragmatism, the central committee's statement implied the time was not ripe, given that the supreme task of state-building was incomplete, for proto-parties like Marju Lauristin's Estonian Social Democratic Independence Party and the Estonian Free Democrats (both discussed fully in Chapter 7) to go solo. Their outline programmes had been studied, it was noted, and their content did not diverge so greatly from the mother party (ECP) that there was any need to split off organisationally from the main body of reformist communists.

Finally, the central committee statement emphasised the centrality of the ECP's role in ensuring a peaceful transition to pluralist democracy in Estonia and by extension its commitment to dismantling the apparatus of the 'party state' that had served as its power base for nearly half a century. In addition to the annulment of article 6 of the ESSR constitution, enshrining the party's 'leading role', which it supported (despite hardline opposition), a party law was canvassed with a view to providing a framework for the operation of the new political groupings. In fact, most of the leaders of the breakaway parties had already resigned their ECP membership by early 1990 (including the PF leader, Savisaar); the Free Estonia group which formed to fight the Supreme Soviet elections in March 1990, however, remained very definitely communists, albeit now in a non-party guise.

Free Estonia was officially launched on 20 January 1990 and its nucleus of activists included notable ECP figures such as the prime minister, Indrek Toome, Siim Kallas and Mikk Titma (the last two mentioned signatories of the 'Four-Man Proposal' for economic autonomy in September 1987) and Jaak Allik, a prominent younger member of the central committee. Titma, the ECP's ideological secretary, stated in an interview in the *Financial Times* shortly after Free Estonia's creation that he believed a majority of ECP members would defect to 'a Socialist Party, as you call it in the West'.[21] It may be that Free Estonia was envisaged by some of its architects as a rallying-ground for the emergence of (what it was hoped would be) a dominant Swedish-style Social Democratic movement, occupying the political space to the left of centre and appealing to a type of pragmatic democratic socialist voter. Certainly, this would be consistent with the Free Estonia pioneers' attempt in December 1989 – unsuccessful and acrimonious as it turned out (see Chapter 7) – to incorporate the Lauristin circle of nascent Social Democrats into the fold. Importantly, these abortive joint talks were based on solid reasons of *realpolitik,* since both the Toome and Lauristin cliques shared a growing mistrust of PF leader Savisaar.[22] Although all Free Estonia's founding figures were former communists, they calculated that in a straight fight between the ECP and Savisaar in the Estonian Supreme Soviet elections (the Estonian National Independence Party had again announced it would boycott the poll) the PF would win an absolute majority of seats.

Free Estonia's slogan during a high-profile campaign was 'Competence, Tolerance, Cooperation'.[23] Its leaders stressed their political experience and how this could be deployed to secure the best possible deal from Moscow. At the same time, Free Estonia, as its designation implied, underlined its commitment to building a free and independent Estonia predicated on 'the basic principles' (whatever they were!) of the 1920 Tartu Peace treaty. For the hardliners on the political right, of course, all this was simply evidence of the communists manoeuvring to stay in power. Free Estonia contested the Estonian Supreme Soviet elections on separate lists from the ECP, however (running 30 candidates out of a total of 392) and, ultimately, it succeeded in its objective of denying the PF an absolute majority of seats and, in gaining about one-quarter itself, performed creditably.[24] It did not become a party after the election and, accordingly, was able to accommodate both ECP members, those who left the party (especially after its formal bifurcation at the 25 March 1990 congress) and those whose credentials were less clearly identifiable.[25] It operated as a distinct faction in the Estonian Supreme Soviet in autumn 1990, largely working to oust Savisaar from power.

For the Väljas-led reformist wing of the ECP, Free Estonia added to the exponential fragmentation of the political landscape while also complicating the task of projecting a distinct electoral image. Since independence was by far the most important issue in the Estonian Supreme Soviet campaign, moreover, a final split between the nationalist and federalist (pro-Moscow) wings of the party came to be regarded as inevitable and this meant that the reformist ECP's fortunes became tied ever more closely to popular leaders such as Väljas and Rüütel. In truth, the elections were anyway largely about personalities and at best 'half party political', in the words of the deputy-minister of culture, Jaak Joerüüt.[26]

From an ECP perspective, two main events formed the prologue to the Estonian Supreme Soviet elections. First, the outgoing Estonian Supreme Soviet, on 23 February 1990, voted almost unanimously to amend article 6 of the ESSR constitution so as to abolish the ECP's 'leading role'. There were 215 delegates in favour and only nine against. For many in the ECP's 'old guard' this momentous decision was rendered marginally easier by the fact that the CPSU had abolished the comparable article in the pan-Soviet constitution at the beginning of the same month.[27] Second, at elections to the Congress of Estonia (a 499-seat body elected only by citizens of the inter-war republic and their descendants) on the following day, 24 February, the ECP won 39 seats.[28] Throughout, Väljas had displayed little sympathy towards the citizens committees and their plans to elect a Congress of Estonia, fearing that the hardline legalism of the former dissidents, who sought recognition of the de jure continuity of the Estonian state and illegal nature of the Soviet 'occupation', would prove counterproductive to the goal of achieving renewed statehood.[29] The citizens committee movement, however, had an undoubtedly radicalising impact on the character of the 'independence debate' in Estonia and this probably persuaded pro-independence ECP elements to participate (albeit not as party candidates).[30] No less a figure than President Rüütel became a deputy-member of the Congress of Estonia for Tartu.

Less than a month after the Congress of Estonia elections, the ECP gained 30 seats in the 105-member Estonian Supreme Soviet (a better performance) and all its leading figures were re-elected. Twenty seats went to reformist communists, with Rüütel polling the highest individual vote of any candidate (Lauristin, the Social Democrat, was second and Väljas third); ten went to Russian-speaking activists including Pavel Panfilov from Tallinn, Vladimir Malkovski from Narva and Nikolai Zaharov from Kohtla-Järv.[31] In general, the ECP's performance mirrored those for the Congress of People's Deputies and the municipal elections the previous year: its prominent personalities performed well, but otherwise the popular vote was divided between the PF and the many other organisations competing for representation. The PF in fact emerged as the election winner and could subsequently rely on the backing of between 41 and 45 delegates – the largest bloc, although short of an absolute majority. Significantly, the Intermovement supporters, gathered in the so-called 'Group for

Equal Rights', could not muster the one-third of seats necessary to veto major measures. This in turn facilitated the decision of the new PF-dominated Estonian Supreme Soviet on 30 March 1990 to declare that the Soviet constitution was no longer valid in Estonia and to announce the beginning of the restoration of the legal republic.[32] The decree stopped short of a Lithuanian-style proclamation of independence, but the Russian delegates nonetheless did not take part in the voting. By then, in any event, the ECP had reached the parting of the ways.

The ECP: Sacrificed on the Altar of Independence?

In an increasingly public debate at the beginning of 1990, the communist leaders attached considerable importance to modernising and democratising the party and, in particular, to recognising and harnessing the diversity of views within it. In the forceful words of Väljas: 'If we wish to restructure society, the party must be the first one to restructure – ideologically, organisationally and morally. Self-purging must take place within the party.'[33] Much weight was given to the need to attract and involve young people. Some younger communists felt, however, that the best way to resolve the party's crisis of legitimacy was to change its name. In the run-up to the twentieth ECP congress in March 1990, Jaak Allik, from the small town of Viljandi and a member of Free Estonia, proposed a new name so as to recognise its democratic pretensions.[34] He also insisted that the ECP should acknowledge unequivocally that Estonia had been illegally occupied since 1940.

At the 25–6 March congress itself, however, Allik apparently changed his mind and the question of a new party designation was simply not put to the vote. Far from this representing a tactical mistake, Allik has presented the retention of the party's historic name as an act of self-sacrifice on the part of the reformist communists, based on a conscious recognition that, as long as the CPSU remained in power in Moscow, the ECP would be needed as a buffer. The ECP, he argued, deliberately rejected the Lithuanian strategy – breaking with Moscow so as to retain control – in order to keep communication lines open both to Gorbachev and to the Russian community in Estonia. Accordingly, whereas by the twenty-eighth CPSU congress in Moscow in July 1990 only hardline, federalist–communist parties remained in Lithuania and Latvia, Estonia still possessed a national communist voice and it was no coincidence that it succeeded in getting its nominee, Enn-Arno Sillari, elected onto the CPSU's Politburo.

The contrast with Lithuanian developments is, indeed, striking since on 20 December 1989 the Lithuanian Communist Party (LICP) declared itself independent of the CPSU and provisionally adopted a resolution committing the party to creating 'an independent socialist Lithuanian state and a democratic society'. Shortly afterwards, Moscow denounced the Lithuanian party breakaway as illegal and criticised its leader, Algirdas Brazauskas, in the sternest terms. Lithuania's declaration of national independence on 11 March 1990, moreover, led Gorbachev on 17 April to institute an economic blockade of the country. Before that (in fact, during the ECP's fateful congress on 25 March 1990) and two weeks after the Lithuanian proclamation of independence, Soviet troops, in a small-scale operation avoiding bloodshed, moved into two LICP buildings and mounted guards outside them. After the massive LICP majority in favour of separation from Moscow, the buildings automatically ceased to be Soviet property.[35]

Allik has claimed that, unlike the Brazauskas party which (in its reformist guise) regained power in Lithuania in the post-independence period – an independence gained at the cost of the economic blockade of summer 1990 and the bloodbath in Vilnius in January 1991 – the ECP, eschewing opportunism, spared Estonia the worst reprisals on the road to independence, while in so doing knowingly consigning itself to the pages of history. The ECP, in short, sacrificed itself in the national interest. This view, incidentally, is supported by Väljas, and his successor as first secretary, Sillari, too, has noted that 'the ECP went voluntarily to the stake in the Estonian cause'.[36]

Allik's thesis is as tendentious as it is initially persuasive. The facts appear to be the following. First, throughout the Soviet period there was a rift in the ECP's ranks and this was aggravated by the increasingly nationalist mood of the 'movement society' that was emerging in 1988 (see Chapter 6). Put simply, one wing of the party, largely, though not exclusively Estonian-speaking, used the ECP to promote Estonia's interests (a high proportion of scientists and intellectuals also perceived the party as a means of disseminating their ideas). The Intermovement wing, in contrast, was reactionary and servile to Moscow. Väljas' task as first secretary was enormously complicated by this deepening split. The ECP plenary on 9 September 1988 marked a significant watershed in the formation of an Independent Communist Party in Estonia. Väljas' speech, in which he recognised that the people see the only way out as renewed independence, albeit achieved in a gradualist step-by-step fashion, was simply anathema to hardline elements.

Second, the ECP began openly to fragment by the beginning of 1990. In January that year, as noted earlier, the Free Estonia group was formed by a 15-strong body of leading former communists (some, like Allik, retained their ECP membership) with the manifest goal of full independence and making the transition to a market economy.

Free Estonia never became a registered political party, but during autumn 1990 it functioned as a parliamentary group (faction) in the Estonian Supreme Soviet under the name of Independent Democrats (*Sõltumatud Demokraatid*).

Third, at the ECP's twentieth congress in Tallinn on 25–6 March 1990, a new programme, originally formulated at the beginning of February, which contained a clear commitment to Estonian independence, together with the independence of the ECP from Moscow, was approved by a majority of 432 votes to three with six abstentions (although 228 delegates did not take part in the voting). This split the Estonian communists into two organisations. The minority formed a shadow party, also called the Estonian Communist Party, and most but, importantly, not all the Russian-speaking members, especially those based in Tallinn, joined this new grouping.[37] The pro-Moscow ECP was linked to the hardline, pro-Union Intermovement (although not all sections of the party approved of this connection) and it was ultimately banned following the abortive coup in the Soviet capital in August 1991, after which the Estonian government shut down all the CPSU's premises on its territory.

The majority wing came to be known as the Independent Communist Party. It officially registered as a political party in June 1991, presented itself as an integral component of the emerging multi-party scene in Estonia and favoured, among other things, the privatisation of property and extension of democracy. A proposal to liquidate the Independent ECP after Estonia regained full sovereignty in August 1991 was defeated and several among the losing minority, including Jaak Allik, promptly resigned their membership. The party subsequently proceeded to contest the 1992 general election as part of an electoral alliance called Leftist Alternative (*Vasak Võimalus*), but having failed to win a single Riigikogu seat it transformed itself into the Estonian Democratic Workers' Party (*Eesti Demokraatlik Tööpartei*) on 28 November 1992.[38]

Fourth, it is clear that, in CPSU circles, the split in the Estonian communist movement was viewed with concern because it meant that the Russian-speaking population was divided between two communist parties. It seems that some hardline CPSU elites would have preferred the division to have followed clear lines of nationality as in Latvia and Lithuania. Equally, the Independent ECP, by dint of its 'mixed' Estonian–Russian membership and the preservation of its historic name – here Allik would seem to have a point – was generally perceived as a legitimate instrument of change in Estonia. Indeed, there were those reformists in Moscow, among them Alexander Yakovlev and Eduard Shevardnadze, who, in view of the reactionary and intractable character of the Intermovement wing, saw the necessity of splitting the ECP and privately urged Väljas to bring matters to a head. In any event, it was significant that, despite the Estonian Supreme Soviet's declaration on 30 March 1990 of a transitional period, albeit of unspecified length, 'towards the restoration of the constitutional institutions of the Republic of Estonia', that is *restitutio ad integrum*, Gorbachev's threatened blockade never materialised.[39]

Finally, in conjunction with the twentieth congress vote favouring the independence of the ECP from the CPSU, there was the announcement of a six-month transitional period prior to the implementation of the break with Moscow. Ostensibly, this was to allow individual members to decide whether to jettison the CPSU link or not, but in practice it was designed to allow the ECP to participate in the twenty-eighth CPSU congress, permit extended consultations 'in high places' and appease Gorbachev.[40] It appeared to work, since the pro-independence ECP majority apparently retained Gorbachev's confidence and it was with his express backing that Sillari was elected to the Politburo ahead of the choice of the ECP's hardline minority, Alexander Gussev. Significantly, the Narva party secretary, Vladimir Malkovski, was one of the key Russian-speaking members of the Independent ECP to back Sillari.[41]

Summing up, it appears that, while Allik's interpretation of events does not exactly violate the facts, it does entail a generous measure of rationalisation. In the domestic political arena, in particular, it is clear that the ECP had lost the initiative well before the 1990 congress. True, the ECP reformists were well aware that, in abolishing article 6 of the ESSR constitution encapsulating its leading role, they were signing their own electoral death warrant, so to speak. It is much less clear that this could be regarded as a sacrificial gesture, however, because in many ways it was doing no more than give legal force to the accentuated de facto pluralism already in existence. Some reformists, indeed, Allik included, had, in the shape of Free Estonia, already created their own competing organisation – and one seeking to avoid any odious association with *the* party.

Allik appears on much safer ground in the 'foreign policy field', namely in his interpretation of the ECP's handling of the 'independence question' and relations with Moscow. The comparison with Lithuania is instructive. The ECP broke with the CPSU just over four months after its Lithuanian counterpart, LICP. The majority at the 25 March congress favouring separation from Moscow was smaller than in the ethnically homogeneous Lithuania and, unlike the latter, it did not presage a declaration of national independence. The ECP proceeded with altogether greater caution. True, the ECP leadership did express its general solidarity with Lithuanian aspirations, but it also emphasised that the situation was not analogous.[42] Unlike the LICP, moreover, the ECP instituted a six-month transitional period before going solo (a type of 'velvet divorce') and, again unlike the LICP, the Independent ECP did not change its name before the collapse of the Soviet Union (achievement of independence), although this option was considered. Accordingly, it retained contacts with fraternal parties elsewhere in the USSR and, uniquely among the Baltic states (as Allik claimed), both Estonian communist parties attended the twenty-eighth CPSU congress in July 1990. Finally, in the person of Vaino Väljas, the ECP, both before and after the split with Moscow, boasted a leader who was known and respected by Gorbachev and reformist elements in Moscow. It was significant that the decision taken at the 1990 ECP congress to 'promote' Väljas from first secretary to the chairmanship – largely to enable him to devote more time to relations with Moscow – was taken by an overwhelming majority of both wings of the party. Interestingly, in refusing to run against Väljas for the post of chairman, Allik insisted that any alternative candidate should be a non-Estonian, but a Russian-speaking nominee was simply for forthcoming.

Overall, perhaps the fairest conclusion is that both Väljas and Rüütel were justified in their assessments of the ECP's contribution to independence – assessments which prefaced the present chapter. In line with Väljas, the ECP's reformist wing did indeed seek to follow the mood of a highly mobilised populace, witness the way it became the first party in the Soviet Union to initiate a 'declaration on sovereignty' and, perhaps more remarkably, was able to withstand pressure to rescind it (Väljas' personal contacts and negotiating skills were undoubtedly relevant here). The ECP may also be said to have achieved two other goals frequently laid down by Väljas: it presided over the peaceful transition to democracy in Estonia and acted as an effective mediator between Tallinn and Moscow as the nation became impatient for independence. Yet Rüütel was probably also justified in arguing that, despite the radicalised nationalist mood generated by the citizens committee movement, the ECP majority still saw Estonia as part of the USSR in 1989– or at least it did not articulate the notion of independence forcefully enough. To have done so, of course, would simply have hastened the split that occurred the following year and might have triggered the deleterious ramifications of the LICP's more bullish strategy.

True, the reformist ECP wing under Väljas was hardly unaffected by strategic considerations of its own best interests. But this is not to concur with the thrust of Lauristin's 'prison warder' thesis that the ECP leader opened the door to social change only because he had his arm twisted behind his back, so to speak, by the enormous grassroots popularity of the PF. Thus, for example, Lauristin would view Väljas' recognition at the ECP central committee plenary on 9 September 1988 of the continuing salience of the agenda of the '40' as primarily a

tactical and enforced switch to a new code, namely an acknowledge-
ment of the de facto relevance of the mass language of nationalism in
contradistinction to the official Marxist tongue 'spoken' by the pre-
reformist party elite. Even during the 'Estonian spring' of 1988, she
recalled how the ECP's ideological secretary had asked incredulously
how she could possibly have put her name to the infamous Letter – it
was, he claimed, 'capitalist, not marxist and was even cited on the
BBC!'[43] Yet at least over the second half of 1988 the interests of the
reformist (Estonian-speaking) ECP leadership appeared largely to coincide with the national interest and under Väljas there was an attempt to use the keys (the existing institutional machinery) to move in
small steps towards greater independence (caution appeared the better part of valour) rather than planning to tunnel under the prison (PF)
or to blow the gaol up (hardline nationalists).

When the ECP lost power in April 1990 and Toome was replaced
as prime minister by the PF leader, Savisaar, the establishment of
party *nomenklatura* – officials, industrial managers, *kolkhoz* and *sovkhoz*
bosses and so on – remained, to be sure, largely intact. Equally, the
transitional period saw a growing tolerance by the ECP of a diversity
of views and personnel. As early as autumn 1987, for example, a
non-communist became editor of *Looming* and at the end of 1988 the
first non-communist, the composer Lepo Sumera, was appointed to
the cabinet as deputy-minister of culture.[44] In these, and a variety of
less conspicuous ways, the nascent pluralism of the movement society was tolerated. Typically, although radical publications such as
the student newspaper *Heinakuu* were not legalised, neither were
they suppressed.

It is to an examination of the anatomy of the aforementioned 'movement society' that we must now turn. Just one postscript should first
be added, however, on the role of personal contacts in understanding
the way Estonia avoided Lithuanian-style violence in January 1991.
In his recollection of events Rüütel has argued that the principal aim
of *perestroika* was to legitimise Soviet power in Western eyes and that
under pressure from reactionary elements in the party (Ligachev and
others) Gorbachev was intermittently marginalised and at times became almost a spectator of events rather than the leading actor. In
Rüütel's submission there were in 1991 reactionary figures in the
Kremlin who would have been ready to create the same situation in
Estonia as in Lithuania and whose goal was the elimination of the
president of the Russian Federation, Boris Yeltsin, and the leaders of
all three Baltic states. Yeltsin, whose own position had been tenuous
at the time of Estonia's 'declaration on sovereignty' in November
1988, had nonetheless entered into a mutual assistance deal with
Estonia and three years later the Yeltsin–Rüütel axis may well have
contributed in no small measure to obviating a bloodbath in Tallinn.[45]

Notes

1   Interview with Vaino Väljas, 22 June 1994.
2   Interview with Arnold Rüütel, 20 June 1994.
3   Interview with Marju Lauristin, 20 September 1994. Also Mikk Titma on Estonian television, 4 January 1990.
4   'Oppressed demand retribution for Soviet "genocide"', *The Baltic Independent*, 1–7 April 1994.
5   Jyrki Iivonen, 'Viron kansallisesta itsemääräämisestä', *Politiikka*, 3, 1990, p.189.
6   Toivo U. Raun, *Estonia and the Estonians*, 2nd edn (Hoover: Stanford, California, 1991), p.192.
7   Sirje Kiin, Rein Ruutsoo and Andres Tarand, *Neljankymmenen kirje* (Otava: Keuruu, 1990), pp.231–3.
8   Rein Taagepera, *Estonia. Return to Independence* (Westview: Boulder–San Francisco–Oxford, 1993), pp.135–6.
9   Marju Lauristin, Peeter Vihalemm and Rein Ruutsoo, *Viron vapauden tuulet* (Gummerus: Jyväskylä–Helsinki, 1989), pp.257–66.
10 Interview with Vaino Väljas, 22 June 1994.
11 Kiin *et al.*, *Neljankymmenen kirje*, p.138.
12 'Viron muutosten tase', *Uusi Suomi*, 18 February 1990.
13 Interview with Vaino Väljas, 22 June 1994.
14 Taagepera, *Estonia*, p.145.
15 Rain Rosimannus, 'State-power and public confidence in Estonia 1985–91', *Emor Reports*, 1, (1), 1991, p.18. See also Rain Rosimannus, 'Do the People Trust the Authorities?', *Emor Reports*, 2, (4), 1992, pp.5–10.
16 Taagepera, *Estonia*, p.142.
17 Lauristin *et al.*, *Viron vapauden tuulet*, pp.308–9.
18 Ibid., pp.252–3.
19 Ibid., pp.314–5.
20 Väljas on Estonian television, 28 December 1989.
21 'Party faces demise in Estonia', *The Financial Times*, 16 February 1990.
22 For Free Estonia's critique of Savisaar, see 'Nya politiska strider efter folkomröstningen', *Hufvudstadsbladet*, 16 March 1991.
23 'On election eve, Communists manoeuvring to keep power', *Homeland*, 7 March 1990.
24 'Itsenäisyys tärkein Viron vaaleissa', *Helsingin Sanomat*, 18 March 1990.
25 Taagepera, *Estonia*, p.196. Evidently, Free Estonia projected a pragmatic image – so much so that an active Russian-speaking delegate, Pavel Panfilof, stated on television that its members were potential 'discussion partners': 'Itsenäisyyskysymys voi jakaa Viron kommunistipuolueen', *Helsingin Sanomat*, 23 March 1990.
26 Jari P. Havia, 'Viron liberaaliliike muotoutumassa', *Polttopiste*, 13 February 1990.
27 'Kommunistien valtamonopoli kaatui vihdoin Virossakin', *Helsingin Sanomat*, 24 February 1990.
28 'Viron kongressin vaaleista', *Helsingin Sanomat*, 6 March 1990.
29 'Iseseisvus', *Uusi Suomi*, 18 February 1990.
30 On the impact of the 'independence debate', see, for example, the tenor of Marju Lauristin's comments in 'Itsenäisyys Viron ainoa tavoite', *Helsingin Sanomat*, 22 March 1990.
31 'Rahvarinnen ehdokkaat voittivat Viron vaaleissa', *Helsingin Sanomat*, 20 March 1990.

32 'Viron parlamentti äänestää N-liiton perustuslain kumoamisesta', *Helsingin Sanomat*, 28 March 1990.
33 Estonian radio broadcast, 21 December 1989.
34 Sole Lahtinen, 'Itsenäisyys voi jakaa Viron kommunistipuolueen', *Helsingin Sanomat*, 23 March 1990.
35 'Russian troops occupy party buildings in Vilnius', *The Guardian*, 26 March 1990.
36 Interview with Jaak Allik, 12 September 1993.
37 'Viroon syntyi toinen kommunistipuolue', *Helsingin Sanomat*, 27 March 1990.
38 Eesti Demokraatliku Tööpartei, *Programm ja Põhikiri* (Tallinn, 1993).
39 'Defiant Estonia rejects Soviet sovereignty', *The Guardian*, 31 March 1990.
40 'Viron kommunistipuolue itsenäiseksi', *Helsingin Sanomat*, 26 March 1990; 'Viron seuraa Liettua', *Helsingin Sanomat*, 27 March 1990.
41 'Estonian Communists use Moscow Congress to gain internal victory', *The Estonian Independent*, 25 July 1990.
42 'Väljas selitti Ekp:n tehtävää', *Helsingin Sanomat*, 24 March 1990.
43 Interview with Marju Lauristin, 20 March 1994. Lauristin noted how the language of the 'Letter of 40' was one of its most radical facets. It was, she noted, 'an exercise in cutting through conventional ideological games'. Indeed, when later interrogated about the document, she was continually asked why there were no quotes from Lenin!
44 Lauristin *et al.*, *Viron vapauden tuulet*, p.251.
45 Rüütel's account brings out the high drama of events. News of developments in Vilnius came through at 3 am and, following a call to Vytautas Landsbergis, it was agreed that the two heads of state should exchange information on an hourly basis using the Lithuanian president's wife's telephone. Rüütel recalls a sense of fatalism and inevitability – a feeling that it was only a matter of time before there was parallel conflict in Estonia and Latvia. At 6 am Rüütel tried to call Yeltsin, who was not at home, and Gorbachev, who was not available. Half an hour later he got through to the Soviet minister of defence and at 9 am to the Baltic Military Command headquarters. A message was left for Gorbachev that any military action in Estonia would be strongly resisted. Subsequent contact with Yeltsin led Rüütel to propose that the former visit Estonia to address the army and the Russian population. At noon Yeltsin concurred with this, although by the time he arrived (in the afternoon) the situation in Vilnius had deteriorated. Yeltsin agreed to use the radio and television to address the Russian-speaking population and, although the situation remained confused for some time, nothing untoward happened. (Interview with Arnold Rüütel, 20 June 1994. See also Arnold Rüütel, 'The Baltic States – looking back, looking ahead', paper presented at the 1994 Sietar Europa Symposium, Jyväskylä, Finland, 11–13 March 1994.)

6 From 'Movement Society' to Estonian Statehood Regained

The idea of a Popular Front would probably have surfaced even if it had not been proposed on the *Mõtleme Veel* television programme [on 13 April 1988]. But that is not the important point. What was crucial was that the idea *was* mooted, that it immediately attracted a nucleus of capable and enterprising individuals who worked to give it substance and that public support for it was both overwhelming and uncompromising. Support groups were formed in the workplace, the towns, *kolkhozs* and countryside and within weeks those involved numbered fifty thousand. (Tiit Made, *Mu Isamaa. Viron toivo ja pelko* (Kirjayhtymä: Helsinki, 1988), pp.142–3)

Ultimately, the Estonian Communist Party (ECP) was outflanked by the interaction of four social movements which combined to propel Estonia from totalitarianism to pluralist democracy. First, there was the Green movement. Environmental issues mobilised and politicised the population over the course of the Phosphate Spring 1987 when, it will be recalled, mass protest against Moscow's plans for a new phosphate mining project at Maardu did much to recreate civil society in Estonia. Although this 'ecological phase of national self-assertion' ended in victory (the cancellation of the Maardu pit development plan), the television journalist Juhan Aare, who had helped to popularise environmental issues, founded the Estonian Green Movement (*Eesti Roheline Liikumine*) in May 1988.[1]

Second, there was the Popular Front (*Rahvarinne*) which was mooted by Edgar Savisaar during a brainstorming session on the television programme *Mõtleme Veel* (Let's Think Things Through') on 13 April 1988 and was originally called the 'Popular Front for the Support of Perestroika'. Savisaar, a social philosophy graduate, was the former director of long-term planning for the ESS' Planning Committee and one of the signatories of the 'Four-Man Proposal' for economic self-management in Estonia in September 1987. At the Popular Front

(PF)'s inaugural conference in October 1988, he charted a middle course between what he called the extremes of Stalinism – whose representatives, he claimed, were still in powerful places in Estonia – and the 'unrealistic restorationists' who felt the pre-1940 republic had to be re-established without any compromises.[2]

Third, there was the KGB-inspired Intermovement (*Interdvizhenie*), a hardline, 'counternationalist' organisation based on the Russian community, which appeared first two months after the appearance of the PF, but did not hold its founding congress until 4–5 March 1989. This was followed in short order by a demonstration of 30–40 000 people and included demands for the repeal of the January 1989 language laws (making Estonian the official language and stipulating the knowledge of it necessary as a job requirement); a ban on the use of the Estonian flag; the shelving of plans for economic self-management; the cleansing of 'nationalist' elements from the ECP leadership; and for both north-east Estonia and Tallinn to be incorporated into the Leningrad *oblast* of the Russian Federation.[3]

Finally, there was the unambiguously irredentist movement of citizens committees, which began in earnest in February 1989, led by Trivimi Velliste, the chairman of the National Heritage Society, and a year later elected a Congress of Estonia (*Eesti Congres*) which claimed to be the only legal organ of the state. The dynamic tension between the PF and the citizens committee movement (CCM) was particularly important in wresting power away from the ECP. In Velliste's words, through its extensive grassroots mobilisation the PF gave a 'physical signal' of the need for change; the citizens committees in turn gave a 'moral signal' of the re-emergence of the Estonian nation from its long period of oppression.[4]

Analysing the period 1986–91, Rein Ruutsoo describes Estonia as a 'movement society', characterised by a number of interacting 'political campaigns', and proceeds to identify four phases in the transition to pluralist democracy.[5] The first period from the second half of 1986 to late 1987, under the comparatively belated impact of *glasnost*, witnessed a shift in official attitudes from repression to limited tolerance. It amounted to the practical toleration of public organisations outside the direct control of the party. The political awakening of the bulk of the Estonian population, however, began in spring 1987 with the so-called 'phosphorite crisis'. As noted in Chapter 5, the successful popular opposition to plans to expand phosphorite mining in north-east Estonia was not exclusively concerned with environmental issues. In practice, the question spawned a period of radical change that had been incubating throughout the half-century of 'acculturation' from Moscow.

The second phase in the evolution of the 'movement society' involved the highly-charged mass mobilisation of the so-called 'Singing Revolution' and covered the period between spring 1988 and the end of that year. The third was dominated by radical nationalist elements and saw the creation of the first citizens committees in February 1989. The fourth witnessed the stagnation of the 'movement society' and the advent of liberal democracy based on political parties. An analysis of the formation of political parties follows in Chapter 7, but the remainder of the present chapter concentrates on the second and third phases of Ruutsoo's schema and the organisations that characterised the 'movement society'.

The 'Singing Revolution' and the Popular Front

The 'Singing Revolution' beginning in Spring 1988, gained its name from the cartoonist Heinz Valk when describing his impressions of the Night Song Festival in Tallinn on 11–12 June. Staged in the capital's Old Town, the festival saw an estimated 60 000 young people wave blue, black and white Estonian flags until dawn without the slightest hint of disorder. Thereafter, the long 'hot summer' of 1988 embraced a series of cultural events, rock concerts and so on culminating in a massive outdoor song festival in early September, which served as 'non-political' stages for the choral expression of a solidary and highly-charged desire for political change. The song festival tradition dated back to the mid-nineteenth century when it was closely associated with the birth of nationalism. Revived under Khrushchev, there were six national song festivals between 1955 and 1980 and the one in 1969, the centenary of the first Estonian choral festival in 1869 and consisting predominantly of works by native composers, represented a powerful national demonstration attended by approximately one in four Estonians. However, the Song of Estonia 1988 (*Eestimaa Laul 1988*) event on 11 September 1988, organised by the PF, surpassed even that by attracting an estimated 300 000 people – one third of all Estonians – and was the culmination in many ways of the 'Singing Revolution'. All in all, the 'Singing Revolution' was a time when discussions were initiated about the role of civil society and when a measure of redistribution of power was achieved. It was a period dominated by the PF which became the embodiment of regime opposition.

Savisaar's PF initiative on 13 April 1988 was primarily motivated by a concern that Vaino, the ECP first secretary, and others in his immediate entourage, were conspiring to thwart the implementation of Gorbachev's reforms in Estonia. The proposal should also be viewed against the backcloth of a number of theories of limited ('contained') civil society – '*perestroika* from above', so to speak – that had been circulating in Moscow during 1987 and also calls from the Soviet press for the formation of grassroots popular movements. Prior to the television broadcast, Savisaar discussed the PF notion with the producer of the current affairs programme *Mõtleme Veel* (in turn it had been debated among those close to the autumn 1987 'Four Man' economic self-management programme) but neither anticipated the scale of the reception it would receive.

Mõtleme Veel was an extremely popular, live, two-hour monthly discussion programme in which a studio audience, comprising some of Estonia's best minds and representing a broad cross-section of the population, debated topical social issues. There was also provision for viewers to telephone in with questions. The central theme on 13 April was 'How could *perestroika* be advanced in Estonia?' and there was to be a related analysis of the reasons for the reactionary attitude of the local party bureaucracy when faced with pressure for social change. When, during the programme, one of the chairmen, Feliks Undusk, seized on Savisaar's PF proposal and it was agreed to set up an 'initiative group' to take matters further, the response from the public was overwhelming. During the transmission itself, viewers called the studio to express their support in numbers. The PF may thus be said to have been a product of the 'electronic democracy' age in so far as *Mõtleme Veel* acted as a type of 'invisible college' linking kindred reformist spirits, many of them previous participants on the programme, with a highly responsive mass public.

Matters moved ahead quickly thereafter. In the small hours of the night of (Thursday) 14 April a group of *Mõtleme Veel* participants completed a PF 'declaration' (a relatively brief statement of intent) and the same day this was sent to the ECP central committee and the Estonian Supreme Soviet Speaker's Council with the request that it be cleared for publication in the press. This, however, was vehemently refused and the whole enterprise denounced as the worst form of nationalism. The result was that the PF declaration was not in fact published, in the newspaper *Edasi*, until 30 April. Its principal goals were to mobilise all pro-*perestroika* forces in Estonia, accelerate social change and resist any return to Stalinism – objectives which, it was claimed, were entirely consonant with the CPSU's own strategic programme. Furthermore, the PF was committed to the democratisation of society; aspired to be involved in the preparation of key policy decisions; and sought to take part in elections and election campaigns. In sum, it called upon all reform-minded people, irrespective of nationality and whether they were ECP members or not, to join in realising a PF for the support of *perestroika*. The declaration was signed by 16 individuals (in addition to Savisaar and Undusk, they included Rein Järlik, later a Green MP, Vello Saatpalu, subsequently a founding figure in the Social Democratic Party, and Jaak Tamm, who was active in the creation of the Rural Centre Party) and the Estonian television's telephone number was given so that people could call in with expressions of support.

Within two days of the post-*Mõtleme Veel* declaration, a PF support group had been founded in Tartu. On Saturday 16 April, the National Heritage Society was due to organise a parade at which for the first time the colours making up the blue, black and white of the flag of the Estonian republic were to be on display. In the meantime, however, Professor Viktor Palm, one of the signatories of the PF declaration, had brought a copy with him from Tallinn and he proceeded to join the parade, slowly driving his red car in which, displayed in the back window, was the text of the *Mõtleme Veel* group. Incidentally, the first name on the sheets of Tartu PF supporters pinned on the walls of a room in the university was that of Juri Lotman, who claimed his 'artillery experience' would come in handy! Lotman, a Jewish academic, had been effectively obliged to move to Estonia and in Tartu University he had created a highly distinctive and prestigious school of Russian philology. His insistence on being, not just a supporter, but later an individual PF member was particularly significant because, in a real sense, he embodied the Russian culture in Estonia.

Despite a formal application to be registered, the PF was not immediately sanctioned by the ECP central committee, although by dint of its express (and tactical) support for *perestroika* it could hardly be proscribed either. Instead, the ministerial council (government) stalled for two weeks, during which time literally hundreds of meetings were convened across the country in support of the PF idea. In Tartu alone, where Marju Lauristin, a sociology professor in the university, was a leading light, over 3000 signatures were collected requesting its approval. When the ECP central committee finally took the decision on 28 April to allow the PF it seems likely that it was in large part making a virtue of necessity. The approach of May Day brought with it the possibility of large-scale demonstrations if the PF were not permitted and memories of the anti-phosphorite action on the part of the Tartu University students on 1–2 May 1987 were doubtless still vividly etched in the government's minds.[6] In any event, the PF's outline declaration (policy statement) was published on 30 April 1988. Its primary goal was to gain recognition of the Soviet republics as 'sovereign states' – a rather equivocal term, to be sure, which fell short of independence. The PF document also advocated cooperation with the ECP, albeit as a means of realising its basic objectives. These included the achievement of economic self-management; a minimum wage; improvements in the health-care system; restrictions on the further influx of non-Estonians into Estonia; the right of women to chose between work in and outside the home; and, in the foreign policy sector, the achievement of a nuclear-free Nordic zone incorporating the Baltics.[7]

With its latent rationale opposition to Vaino's reactionary rule, the PF undoubtedly contributed to expediting (indeed, was possibly implicated in moves to bring about) Vaino's dismissal on 16 June 1988. This was achieved after the PF had initiated a mass meeting, set for 17 June, at which the Estonian contingent to the forthcoming Congress of People's Deputies in Moscow was challenged to give a public account of its views. It will be recalled from Chapter 5 that all 32 delegates had been personally nominated by Vaino, so pre-empting an election, despite the fact that the ECP had recruited more candidates than there were seats available and the CPSU was urging competitive selection procedures. At the full ECP central committee meeting on 16 June and, prior to that, among the general public, there was indignation at Vaino's unilateral action in aborting an election. Pressure mounted on the first secretary during the first weeks of the Singing Revolution. The Tallinn Old Town rock festival on 11–12 June 1988 attracted vast numbers of young people (in what Vaino clearly regarded as a menacing development) and at the same time excitement grew as notices of the PF's meeting with the People's Deputies appeared in the press. There was speculation about how many of the Vaino-nominated delegates would turn up; how many would assemble in the Song Stadium; and how both the delegates and the public would conduct themselves. There was also concern among officials about clashes between Estonian and Russian-speaking groups. Ultimately, at the ECP central committee meeting the day before the Song Stadium event, Vaino was replaced as first secretary by Vaino Väljas.[8]

From a PF perspective, the 17 June 'show trial' of People's Deputies (only five arrived) had a dual purpose. While it was principally intended to throw down the public gauntlet to Vaino and a highly unpopular party establishment, it would also serve the secondary purpose of indicating something of the extent of the PF's mass support less than two months after its inception. The end result on both counts was highly satisfying. Vaino lost the ECP leadership after more than a decade and an estimated 150 000 people assembled in the Song Stadium the following day in elated mood, many carrying slogans demanding economic self-management, together with a new language law. Moreover, although the evidence is not conclusive, it is at least possible that Gorbachev both knew of and indeed condoned the 17 June event as a means of levering out of office an increasingly discredited first secretary.

Initially, there was division among its pioneers over whether the PF should be built to a 'party model' or 'social movement' design. Like the ECP, the former would involve creating a highly cohesive, top-down organisation with authority flowing from a central machine to individual members who would be bound by formal institutional rules; the latter would entail a loose-knit, bottom-up structure, permitting individuals the maximum latitude and the option of participating (or not) when matters of vital concern arose. A majority of those in the vanguard of the PF (especially Lauristin) were critical of the 'party model' favoured by Savisaar, in large part because of evidence that many ECP members were exasperated at their inability to exert any influence within the party. The PF, it was argued, must counteract such feelings of low subjective competence and facilitate individual influence, as well as providing a mechanism for bringing capable people into politics, that is mobilising a counter-elite. It should not, however, seek to acquire power itself.

Ultimately, then, the PF was constructed to an anti-party specification, eschewing the hierarchical, bureaucratic structures and individual membership of the ECP blueprint in favour of an open, flexible approach based on the registration of self-standing local 'support groups'. This was intended to encourage grassroots participation while also preserving the anonymity of activists (there was still widespread fear of the KGB). The decentralised character of the original PF movement warrants emphasis. At the outset, partly to circumvent article 6 of the ESSR constitution embodying the ECP's 'leading role', it comprised only local associations – the Tartu Popular Front, Võru Popular Front and so on – and the intention was only later to set up an Estonian Popular Front. True, there was a central 'think-tank', operating in the guise of the PF 'initiative group' and led by Savisaar, which proposed measures to the local groups, although, technically, it had no powers to do so.[9]

At the PF's foundation congress on 1 October 1988, the movemental features of the PF outlined above were given formal confirmation. The basic grassroots components of the movement were 'support groups' or local associations which by the time of the inaugural conference numbered over 1700. Delegates nominated by these support groups would constitute 20 regional Popular Front councils which in turn were to elect regional executive committees. Every regional council was to choose one representative for a 105-member national council. Also sitting on the national council were to be representatives of the bodies affiliated to the PF, among others the Forum of Nationalities and the Town and Country Workers' Association. Finally, the annual congress was directly to elect 57 members of the national council (see Table 6.1) along with the entire seven-member national executive.[10] Incidentally, although the local PFs were registered over the summer of 1988, the Estonian PF, founded in October 1988, was not registered as a national movement until 2 February 1989.

It was a measure of the PF's political 'clout' by the end of 1988 that its national council began to operate as a 'quasi-parliament', issuing

Table 6.1   **The composition of the National Council of the Popular Front**

Representatives of regional councils	20
Representatives of affiliated bodies*	28
Representatives elected by the annual congress	57
Total	**105**

Note: *The moderate Forum of Nationalities, which was created on 24 September 1988 and led by Hagi Šein, embraced representatives of no less than 17 national minorities, ranging from Russians to Armenians. On 18 May 1989, the Forum split from the PF to become the Estonian Union of National Minorities (*Eestimaa Rahvuste Ühendus*).

rulings that enjoyed a high degree of legitimacy among the people.[11] These 'enactments', which effectively challenged the decisions of the ESS, were disseminated through the pages of its newspaper *Vaba Maa*, initially distributed free of charge. The 'legislative' activity of the PF's national council was frenetic. All-day sessions were held every second Sunday and more were convened if necessary; committees prepared detailed reports; experts were prevailed upon; and the government was asked to give evidence at 'hearings' (even the ESSR chairman, Arnold Rüütel, was once called to attend). Above all, the amorphous, vacuous rhetoric of the communist past was abandoned, issues were analysed in depth and tactics worked out. As one participant noted, 'Lack of information was at the outset the real problem for the PF and its national council was accordingly obliged to act like a spy to obtain it.'[12]

Not only did the PF's outline programme on 10 April 1988 advocate cooperation with the ruling ECP, but the personnel overlap between the two – at least until the later part of 1989 – was considerable. Four of the seven-member national executive elected at the PF's inaugural congress on 1 October 1988 were ECP members, while 28 per cent of conference delegates were party members (see Table 6.2). The PF also supported the ECP (and other bodies) during early autumn 1988 in collecting signatures to protest against the planned amendments to the Soviet constitution (see Chapter 5) and to support the proposed 'declaration on sovereignty' on 16 November. It was only the following month, when the ECP-controlled ESS merely noted (rather than objecting to) the USSR Supreme Soviet's rejection of Estonia's 'declaration on sovereignty', that a rift between the PF and the ECP began to develop. It needs emphasis, however, that the ECP did not, as is sometimes suggested, create the PF, only then to lose control of its offspring. Rather, the involvement of ECP leaders like Väljas, who spoke at the PF's launch in October 1988, represented an attempt to be seen to bring the party closer to the mood of the people. In reality, the PF established its independence of the ECP from the outset. Its primary goal was to activate the population and by exerting concerted social pressure to achieve revolutionary change from below. The vigorous articulation of grassroots demands would, it was hoped, transform the state and win control of it from the occupation power. The PF's burgeoning popularity appeared to hold out considerable promise of realising its objectives. In July 1989, 56 per cent of all Estonians would have voted for it had there been a general election and the PF had clearly displaced the ECP as the major political actor.

Table 6.2   The political allegiance of delegates at the PF's founding congress on 1 October 1988 (per cent)

ECP members	28
National Heritage Society members	19
Green movement members	10
Membership of religious organisations	2
Estonian National Independence Party members	0.2
Others	40

Source: Marju Lauristin, Peeter Vihalemm and Rein Ruutsoo, *Viron vapauden tuulet* (Gummerus: Jyväskylä–Helsinki, 1989), p.165.

Like all the social movements in Estonia at the time, the PF was engaged in the total reproduction of the power structures of the state and, accordingly, developed a voluntary defence organisation, members of which were entitled to wear a badge and a special armband. Many of the leading positions in this force went to former policemen (often they had been dismissed from their posts) and Afghanistan war veterans. The aim of the PF's 'Home Guard' was principally to maintain order at its public meetings and to prevent skirmishes provoked by KGB agitators. The maintenance of discipline was important to the PF's reputation and to avoid providing the authorities with ammunition with which to discredit it. In addition to the KGB, the Estonian police was predominantly in Russian hands.

Repossessing the State: the Citizens Committee Movement and the Congress of Estonia

Ruutsoo's third phase in the evolution of the 'movement society' in Estonia was marked by the end of *perestroika*-inspired change and the establishment in February 1989 of the first citizens committees. The radical nationalist citizens committee movement was the dominant force during the aforementioned year. The 'ideological distance' between the reformist ECP and PF, on the one hand, and citizens committee movement (CCM), on the other, was enormous. For the former, the CCM leaders were 'hardline nationalists' (Väljas) or 'unrealistic restorationists' (Savisaar), whose uncompromising stance lacked tactical acumen. It was too draconian in approach: the politics of fantasy rather than hard-headed reality. There was also a sharp gulf in the outlook – a considerable 'psychological distance' – between the rival sets of elites. On the ECP and PF side, the leaders were communists and former communists, whereas the CCM tended to engage former dissidents and those with no record of party membership. The PF elite drew extensively on the (by then) middle-aged generation of the 1960s 'Thaw', whereas the CCM mobilised a disproportionately large number of young people. Moreover, relations between the PF and CCM were often strained and increasingly competitive, with the result that the two main components of the 'movement society', the PF and CCM, were – at least for most of 1989 – agencies of conflict rather than social cohesion. Above all, the CCM's agenda was both radical and non-negotiable.

In contrast to the gradualism of the Väljas-led ECP (that is, its step-by-step approach to achieving greater independence), the CCM propounded the fundamentalism of a strict adherence to Estonia's juridical rights to statehood. In place of the PF's pragmatism (working with the ECP for sociopolitical reform), the CCM posited the principle of condemning unequivocally the Soviet occupation and the agents of communist rule in Estonia. Instead of the PF's demand for 'recognition of the Soviet republics as sovereign states' (set out in its outline programme of October 1988), the CCM pressed for the restoration of the legally existing independence of Estonia as laid down in the 1920 Treaty of Tartu with Soviet Russia. Crucially, the CCM was 'past-directed' in the sense of striving to generate an awareness of Estonia's past as an historic nation and subsequently nation-state (the inter-war republic) – not for its own sake, but as a means of highlighting the injustice and illegality of the present regime.

Under communist authoritarianism for nearly half a century, the Estonian nation had been denied its memory. Under Stalin millions of history, politics, fiction and children's books had been destroyed; documents were shredded; events and personalities became taboo subjects; graves and monuments disappeared. After Stalin the official history of the ESSR involved a wholesale falsification of the past and the perpetuation of lies. It was no coincidence that the CCM brought together those individuals and organisations which, in their various ways, were actively engaged in the task of historical recall and in facilitating the nation's recall of memory. As Mart Laar noted in *Noorte Hääl* on 3 September 1988: 'Nobody can deprive our nation of its memory; nobody can deprive our nation of its memoirs; nobody can deprive our nation of its history'. Two organisations in particular were crucial in the public re-examination of the past and the campaign for the publication of matters that had previously been hushed up. The first was the MRP–AEG, the Estonian 'branch' of a pan-Baltic organisation agitating for the publication of the secret articles of the Molotov–Ribbentrop pact of 23 August 1939 which assigned Estonia (and the other Baltic states) to the Soviet 'sphere of influence'. The MRP–AEG group comprised 16 members, all former dissidents, including Lagle Parek, Tiit Madisson, Heiki Ahonen and Arvo Pesti, and was instrumental in the Hirvepark rally in Tallinn on the forty-eighth anniversary of the Hitler–Stalin pact in 1987.

The second organisation was the National Heritage Society (*Eesti Muinsuskaitse*), officially founded on 12 December 1987 after months of illicit activity. In fact, a forerunner of the National Heritage Society, in the form of the so-called 'Tõru' society, appeared in December 1974 with the aim of promoting Estonian culture and a basic understanding of the nation's history, but in the reactionary Brezhnev era it proved short-lived. Then, in 1982 and 1983, memoranda were addressed (unavailingly) to the ECP leadership making a powerful case for a national heritage organisation. In October 1986, however, 12 underground heritage clubs met in the cemetery of the Jüri church in Tallinn, elected a council and planned the agitation ahead. Several meetings were held and a programme formulated before the National Heritage Society's breakthrough in December 1987 and, in addition to Velliste, one of its pioneering figures was Jüri Kuuskemaa.

Among the wide range of activities, the National Heritage Society (NHS), coordinated the endeavours of various groups working to restore monuments to the victims of Stalinism. Many of these monuments had been buried (to prevent their destruction) during the Stalinist repression and the NHS assumed responsibility for contacting those familiar with the whereabouts of hidden gravestones, statues and so on with a view to unearthing and reinstating them. The NHS was organised into local sections which, significantly, were based on the historic Estonian parishes and not the Soviet administrative districts (indeed, the NHS worked to restore old churches). It boasted approximately 10 000 members by the end of 1988 and on 16 April that year had been the first organisation openly to display the Estonian flag at one of its parades in Tartu (the day Palm flaunted the PF declaration in his car window). The NHS received useful practical and material support – tools and chemicals for restoration work, duplicating machines and so on – from its sister body, the Expatriate Estonian Heritage Society, and much interest was generated by the visit to Estonia at the beginning of 1989 of the expatriate organisation's secretary, Professor Rein Taagepera.[13]

In addition to its restoration work, the NHS was engaged in accumulating the memoirs of 'veterans' of the First Republic. Young people cycled round the countryside recording interviews with the inter-war generation on tapes purchased with expatriate funds and imported from Finland. A number of peripatetic theatre groups also collected and collated the personal reminiscences of elderly people, and their performances – compilations of verbatim diary entries, miscellaneous local anecdotes and rediscovered folk songs – were received enthusiastically by audiences throughout Estonia. In addition, in Tartu, Jüri Luik (foreign minister in the Laar coalition in 1994) and his friends founded a theatre group called *Valhalla* which successfully performed Estonian plays from the 1920s. Luik also breathed new life into the historic Estonian Student Society which the Soviets had suppressed.[14] Above all, the NHS regarded it as supremely important to support the young Estonian family. It sought to influence young people, using the slogan 'Respect the fatherland and the mother tongue'.

Historians also played a central role in the reappraisal of the past; indeed, over the course of 1988 they acquired enhanced status, no longer acting as regime apologists but, as in the case of Evald Laasi, Hannes Valter, Mart Laar and others, working with the new social movements to mould the nation's perception of events. It was indicative of the shift in the cultural climate in Estonia that, in 1988, Christmas (previously banned) was officially celebrated and schoolchildren were given a Christmas holiday. True, in contrast to Poland and Lithuania, where the struggle for national liberation was closely bound up with religion and actively supported by the clergy, the Lutheran church did not reappear in Estonia until well into 1988,[15] but individual Christians had nonetheless been among the architects of the NHS and were active, too, in promoting the CCM.

The founding father of the CCM was Trivimi Velliste, the chairman of the NHS and a keynote speaker at the massive Song of Estonia 1988 gathering. In November 1988, Velliste visited Toronto to address the Expatriate Estonian Heritage Society and, in subsequent discussions, its secretary Rein Taagepera urged the importance of defining the notion of 'legal citizenship' and keeping a register of the 'legal citizens' of Estonia. Shortly afterwards, back in Tallinn, Velliste was approached in the street by an elderly man called Tillemann, who canvassed the idea of convening a national congress, a 'legal parliament' which, it was implied, would be elected on purely ethnic lines and operate in contradistinction to the institutions of the ESSR. Velliste's contribution was then to combine the substance of both 'inputs' – the concept of legal citizenship emphasised by Taagepera and the importance Tillemann attached to forthright political action – into an original synthesis. Legal citizens, and they were not exclusively Estonians since about 100 000 non-Estonians had been citizens of the First Republic, would be entitled to register and form citizens committees which would in turn elect a Congress of Estonia as the representative organ of the 'historic nation'. Velliste recalls how the whole project 'dawned' on him during a restless night in January 1989. The following day, matters having been discussed with Mart Laar and Tunne Kelam, both leading figures in the NHS, in the Moskva cafe in Tallinn, plans were laid to launch the CCM at the earliest possible date.[16]

On 24 February 1989, the seventy-first anniversary of Estonian independence, Velliste delivered two public addresses (in Tallinn Town Hall Square and the Estonian Congress Hall, respectively) and, shortly afterwards, a nine-strong executive committee was set up, comprising three members each from the NHS, the Estonian National Independence Party and the Estonian Christian Democratic Party (both parties are discussed in Chapter 7) and based on the principle of rotational leadership. During the initial phase in the formation of citizens committees, Velliste and his colleagues emphasised that the CCM sought to embrace persons from the left, right and centre – that is, legal citizens across the entire political spectrum – and that the Congress of Estonia would be a genuinely representative parliamentary body. However, recruitment over the spring and early summer of 1989 proved sluggish, for a number of possible reasons. First, although in May 1989 the PF had given the fledgling CCM a guarded welcome, commending the extra option it would provide, rivalries and animosities between the two movements quickly developed. They were mirrored at the grassroots level in the fact that, although there were people who were at once members of both a citizens committee and a local PF association, this was certainly not the norm. At the top, moreover, the PF's attitude became increasingly negative. Indeed, as early as 24 February 1989 (the effective launch of the CCM), the PF, at the last minute, pulled out of a planned rally with the radical nationalists, preferring to join forces with the ECP in replacing the ESSR's red flag with the blue, black and white of the First Republic on the Pikk Hermann tower of Toompea castle.[17]

Second, the CCM ruled that the citizens committees should be formed locally and not by agents from the capital. Yet in the field the initial response was tepid, partly because some citizens regarded the whole CCM enterprise as fanciful, even Utopian, whilst others found it unduly confrontational. The logic of both reactions was that the movement was unlikely to succeed in its objective of electing a Congress of Estonia that would be capable (as was its aim) of engaging the Kremlin in talks on troop withdrawal. It took recruitment drives from the 'centre' really to set things moving.

Third, Väljas and the ECP leadership were, as noted in the previous chapter, intolerant of what they regarded as the bull-headed approach of the restorationists. Their intransigent legalistic stance, it was believed, would prove counterproductive in needlessly antagonising Moscow. The local party bosses consequently sought to ensure that people kept away from the CCM recruitment meetings. Velliste recalled speaking at gatherings of as few as a dozen people. In the build-up to the Congress of Estonia elections in February 1990, moreover, the ECP authorities subjected the CCM both to vigorous criticism and then to something of a news embargo in the official press. Nonetheless, both the ECP and PF ran candidates for the Congress, albeit deciding to do so at the last minute.[18]

The CCM's teething-troubles in mobilising support lasted until about late summer 1989. By September, however, when about 300 000 citizens had registered, and especially by 11 November, when a 50-strong General Committee was elected, the CCM had generated a real head of steam. The NHS network of local branches provided a valuable infrastructure; the Estonian National Independence Party also canvassed support; and the increasingly assertive nationalist mood was beneficial to the CCM – a mood reinforced by the accelerated liberation of the East European states from communism during autumn 1989. Gorbachev, it seemed, was indeed willing to apply the 'Sinatra Doctrine' of letting the Warsaw Pact states 'do it their way'. Obliquely acquiescent comments from such reformist ECP stalwarts as Indrek Toome, the prime minister, suggested (at least) the possibility that the CCM might even have gained cautious approval in Moscow, although this has never been confirmed.[19]

Ironically, although organised by the Popular Fronts of the region, the massive roadside protest known as the Baltic Chain – which stretched from Tallinn to Vilnius on the fiftieth anniversary of the Molotov–Ribbentrop Pact on 23 August 1989 – may indirectly have fed recruitment to the CCM. What is clear is that, despite an estimated participation of between one and two million people across the Baltics, the Estonian PF was at that time losing the initiative as the popular mood hardened and shifted decisively towards independence. True, the ESS had denounced the Molotov–Ribbentrop pact on 18 May 1989 and the PF subsequently requested that it declare the illegal Soviet annexation of Estonia null and void. But the decision on 20 July 1989 of the chairman of a Gorbachev-instigated commission inquiring into the infamous pact not to underwrite the majority view that the secret protocol was authentic merely hardened the Estonian resolve for independence. So, probably, did the Intermovement 'strikes' in Tallinn between 11 and 16 August in protest against the proposed new local government election law. Significantly, moreover, the Baltic Chain, although borrowing from the nationalist repertoire of the MRP–AEG (compare Hirvepark two years earlier) fell short – in the ensuing common statement by the three Popular Fronts – of demanding independence. By the time of the revised PF programme of October 1989 which did support independence, the CCM had taken off and registration was proceeding apace. By February 1990 approximately 600 000 people had registered in the citizens committees. By then 97 per cent of Estonians favoured complete independence.

Since all citizens of the Republic of Estonia or their descendants, irrespective of place of residence, were eligible to register, citizens committees sprang up as far afield as Leningrad (St Petersburg), Moscow, Riga and across the United States.[20] There was division among leaders of the movement about the timing of the Congress of Estonia (COE) elections. Velliste favoured May 1990; he was outflanked, however, by more radical elements who won the case for an earlier date. Accordingly, on 24 February 1990 (Independence Day), all 16-year-old and over citizens and prospective citizens were eligible to vote for a COE (Estonians used blue ballot papers, while applicants for citizenship – mainly, of course, Russians – had green slips). Some 90 per cent of those eligible participated, with 1200 candidates representing 30 political groupings contesting the 464 seats. Thirty-five delegates were elected from the refugee communities abroad. Non-citizens were entitled to attend as observers, but did not possess voting rights. As Taagepera has noted, the COE election in February 1990 was probably the only privately run general election ever staged.[21]

As mentioned, an important by-product of the growth of the CCM was a growing radicalisation in the PF's standpoint. Its new programme in October 1989, written in bold, broad-brush terms by Edgar Savisaar, was intended first and foremost to position the PF between the communists and former communists on the left and the hardline nationalists on the radical right. It represented a turning-point in the history of the PF. Friction was generated at the leadership level between Savisaar and a number of senior colleagues, who began to plan their own organisations; others even saw the possibility of the PF transforming itself into a Scandinavian-style Social Democratic Party.[22] The main point, however, was that the October 1989 programme came out in favour of the ultimate goal of full independence, albeit by a circuitous route. For example, it advocated gaining Gorbachev's approval for a referendum on independence, with participation restricted to legal citizens of the inter-war republic and their descendants – a clear attempt to steal the CCM's thunder – and also favoured concluding a temporary treaty on confederation with the Soviet Union, incorporating a fixed date for independence. The CCM responded by opposing the proposed referendum on independence on the grounds that the legal independence of Estonia already existed.[23]

The contradictory strategies and strains between the PF and CCM – that is, the dynamic tension between the two main Estonian social movements – provided an important vehicle of change and warrants a brief note. The PF gained 43 per cent of the 105 seats in the ESS following the 18 March 1990 election (despite a 10 per cent drop in its standing in the polls since the previous December) and proceeded to form a cabinet under Savisaar. The CCM leaders (particularly those from the Estonian National Independence Party), however, refused as a matter of principle to accept the authority of the ESS, which was viewed as an organ of the imperial power, and boycotted the elections to it. Unlike the PF, the CCM worked via the Congress of Estonia to achieve revolution from above by simply repossessing the occupation state. Its aim was twofold: to mobilise and represent the indigenous nation (it virtually appropriated recent Estonian history) and to repossess the state annexed by the imperial power in 1940. The act of registering as an Estonian citizen would, it was envisaged, generate a moral force. According to a leading CCM figure, Sirje Endre, 'When a person signs and reflects upon the fact that he is truly a citizen of this legally-existing Republic of Estonia, he becomes consciously aware of all his past, his progenitors, his ancient land, his five thousand years spent here on the Baltic coast. So the Congress of Estonia will become an essential turning point. It will elevate our degraded people again into proud citizens.' (There were similar activities in, among other places, Latvia and Georgia.)[24]

Unlike the demonstrative 'movemental' activities of the PF (the song festivals, mass rallies and so on which it eschewed, the Council of Estonia (the executive body of the Congress) sought to integrate the historic nation through its network of citizens committees. Indeed, the PF was possibly rather complacent towards the CCM and the impending COE elections – it only nominated candidates at the eleventh hour – and lost ground to the radical nationalists. By March 1990, the PF's support had fallen to 22 per cent.[25]

Interestingly, while the rhetoric of the fundamentalists (radical nationalists) drove deeper the wedge between the Estonian and non-Estonian populations (Velliste, for example, spoke of 'illegal immigrants' and referred to the 'civil garrison' of the 'occupying power') the reality was that, since those immigrants applying for citizenship could register and vote at the COE elections, the CCM may actually have contributed in modest measure to improving ethnic relations. What is clear in any event is that not all Russians supported the Soviet connection and the status quo ante towards Moscow. When asked the question: 'How would you like to see Estonia in the year 2000 – an integral part of the Soviet Union, a sovereign Soviet repub-

lic [a rather ambivalent term given currency by the ECP first secretary, Väljas] or an independent Estonian republic?', 16 per cent of
non-Estonians in January 1990 favoured full independence, although
another 57 per cent went for the compromise Väljas option.[26] Two
months later, moreover, an opinion poll in *Sovjetskaya Estonija* revealed that 33 per cent of the 96 per cent Russian-speakers in the
north-eastern town of Narva favoured the independence of the ECP
from Moscow, a preference suggesting at least a measure of integration on the part of an element of the ethnic minority in the area of its
densest concentration. To be sure, 61 per cent demanded that the ECP
remain a wing of the Soviet party, and it was upon this majority of
non-integrated Russians that the Intermovement leadership directed
its sights.[27]

Counter nationalism: the Intermovement

Intermovement, or 'The International Movement of Workers in the
ESSR', first appeared in July 1988, just over two months after the
formation of the PF. In the interval between the birth of the two
movements, PF speakers visited Russian-speaking factories to brief
the workforce on the historic background to recent events and to
explain the ESSR's immediate goals and ambitions. There was the
conviction (erroneous as it turned out) that there would be sufficient
Russian supporters of its broad-based democratisation programme
to make the PF a genuinely multi ethnic reformist movement. In
practice, the PF leaders quickly acknowledged their failure to grasp
the fundamental differences in outlook between the 'two nations'
and it was significant that in place of the integrated movement that
had been envisaged a separate Russian section of the PF was set up
in autumn 1988.[28] By then, however, the first signs of Russian
reactionism were apparent with the emergence across the Baltics of
the Intermovement (IM), so called because (despite the vast majority
of its leaders and followers being Russian-speaking monoglots) it
defended the classical Soviet concepts of 'internationalism' and 'working-class solidarity' against what it saw as 'bourgeois nationalist'
movements in the republics. In fact Intermovement is best described
as a 'counternationalist' phenomenon, its 'internationalist' slogans
making a strong emotive appeal to an insecure section of the Russian-speaking population which found itself surrounded by an increasingly self-confident native population whose language it did
not understand.

The first ominous stirrings of the IM took the form of a demonstration in Tallinn on 19 July 1988, led by Evgeni Kogan, a maritime
engineer and the son of a Soviet naval officer, who was noted for his

extremist views and inflammatory rhetoric. It attracted about 2000 people. Concurrently, there were demands for the separation from Estonia of two predominantly Russian-speaking towns in the north-east, Kohtla-Järve and Sillamäe; in a third, Narva, the hardliner Vladimir Chuikin, who rose to prominence following Gorbachev's accession to the CPSU leadership, ensconced himself as a powerful IM leader precisely because he avoided the popular resentment associated with the perks and lifestyle of the old '*nomenklatura* communists', with their dachas and limousines.[29] Founded against the backdrop of the mass mobilisation of the indigenous population – beginning with the Phosphate Spring and reaching a climax during the Singing Revolution of summer 1988 – IM sought to 'counter mobilise' a previously passive Russian population against the accelerated Estonianisation of Estonia (the 'nationalisation' of its language, economy and so on) and, of course, moves towards greater independence. The IM was, in short, federalist: it favoured Estonia's existing membership of the USSR and was led by those who had a strong vested interest in maintaining the Soviet connection. By late 1989 IM claimed between 150 000 and 200 000 supporters and demanded an autonomous republic in north-east Estonia.[30]

Closely linked to Intermovement was the Joint Council of Work Collectives (JCWC) which was founded on 30 November 1988, less than two weeks after the ECP reformist Toome had replaced Saul as prime minister. It was led by Vladimir Yaravoi, the manager of the All-Union military plant, Dvigatel, in Tallinn, who may well have been placed there by Moscow in an attempt to consolidate 'Soviet loyalism' following the PF's formation.[31] Certainly visits to Tallinn, such as the one from the CPSU central committee secretary, Viktor Tshebrikov, on 11–14 November in anticipation of (and to 'advise' the ECP against) the 'declaration on sovereignty' helped (in a variety of ways) to stiffen the resolve of the Russian hardliners. Initially, the JCWC's principal logic was to obstruct any Estonian attempts to remove factories from Moscow control – a corollary of the economic self-management programme – and in these All-Union enterprises communist officials were active on the shop floor galvanising workers in the struggle against independence. Symbolising the Russian hardliners' resistance, red ESSR flags were run up across Tallinn on rooftops, factory chimneys and even cranes.

Counternationalist agitation in autumn 1988 focused on the two proposals in the ESS which excited the greatest support among the Estonian population: the 'declaration on sovereignty' (enacted on 16 November 1988) and the 'language law' (ultimately passed on 18 January 1989), the latter making Estonian the official language and requiring its use by civil servants from top officials and senior medical staff down to waiters.[32] The language legislation, which was very much the work of a leading PF figure, Mati Hint, could not conceivably be described as xenophobic. Ordinary Russians had the right to use their own language in public places and there was state support for a diverse range of national minorities, all of which could receive education in their own tongue. The language law, indeed, followed closely the multilingual, multicultural model of the 1925 Statute on Cultural Autonomy – one of the most liberal in inter-war Europe. All of this was lost on (more probably ignored by) the Intermovement which, on the eve of the 'declaration on sovereignty', between 14 and 16 November 1988, called for meetings in the workplace to support Gorbachev's amendments to the Soviet constitution downgrading the secessionary provisions of article 72. IM's own estimates put the numbers involved in these 'meetings' (political strikes) at 100 000 and, with the composition of the Estonian Supreme Soviet divided along ethnic lines – 65 per cent Estonian, 35 non-Estonian – there was at least the possibility of the Russian hardliners preventing the two-thirds majority necessary for adopting the 'declaration on sovereignty' and other amendments to the Estonian constitution (for instance, permitting privatisation).

As noted, Väljas' intermediation (acting as speaker for the crucial Estonian Supreme Soviet session) served to avert such a development, but when there were calls from Moscow for the cancellation of the 'declaration' the ECP split, manifest all autumn, between the nationalist–reformist wing and the 'Inter' wing, deepened.[33] Ultimately, moreover, almost 50 Estonian Supreme Soviet members voted against the revised language law passed on 18 January 1989 – the first of its kind in the Soviet Union – and the fact that the ECP secretaries from Tallinn and Narva led the opposition indicated both the extent and visibility of the ethnic split in the ruling party.[34] It was clear in connection with the debate on the language legislation that there were powerful hardline elements among the Russian-speaking population (former members of the military's 'political staff', along with the KGB) that would never compromise and saw Estonia as merely a Russian *oblast*.

It is important to stress the way the IM and JCWC leaders succeeded in playing on the anxieties of the Russian population. For example, the IM argued that the implementation of the economic self-management programme (IME), which the ESS approved in spring 1989, would mean the closure of the All-Union factories and a 30 per cent rise in unemployment, mostly affecting the Russian population. Rumours spread in relation to the language law, moreover, that Russian schools would be closed and Russian children no longer able to get an education in their own language.[35] The IM also utilised the pan-Soviet press to promote its allegations of the violation of Russian rights in Estonia. All this added heightened uncertainty to an already insecure Russian population.

Intermovement's official formation, that is, its founding congress, took place on 4–5 March 1989 and was followed on 14 March by a mass demonstration timed to take place within two weeks of the 26 March elections to the Congress of People's Deputies in Moscow. The protest, staged during working hours, saw managers in the All-Union factories 'urge' their employees to take to the streets and this they did on the scale of 30–40 000 people. Significantly, the radical programmatic demands of the inaugural Intermovement congress, which included the repeal of the language law, shelving Estonia's economic self-management plans, the removal of nationalist–reformist elements from the ECP leadership and the incorporation of Tallinn and the whole of north-east Estonia into the Leningrad district of the Russian Federation, were restated in *Pravda* a week later. At the Congress of People's Deputies elections, IM officially supported 21 of the 104 candidates (for 32 seats) and, ultimately, five were elected, including Kogan, who defeated PF national executive member and *Vikerkaar* editor, Rein Veidemann, at the second run-off ballot on 9 April.[36]

The primary target of the industrial action by the Russian-speaking workforce, organised jointly by IM and JCWC in late July and August 1989, was a new local government electoral law reform which included a two-year residence qualification for voting and was designed to disenfranchise Russian soldiers and sailors temporarily stationed in Estonia. There were at least three other important contributory factors, however. First, there was the Soviet Congress of People's Deputies' agreement in principle on 27 July to grant the Baltic states economic autonomy, with the details to be worked out over the following autumn. Next, there was the ECP's further move in a nationalist–reformist direction (albeit stopping well short of independence) reflected in its explicit support of the PF's original demand (October 1988) for a loose confederation agreement between Estonia and the Soviet Union. Finally, there was the need to counter plans, already at an advanced stage, for a massive Baltic Chain demonstration against the Molotov–Ribbentrop pact, a pact which in May 1989 the Estonian Supreme Soviet had itself denounced. The joint IM–JCWC action, billed as a general strike, was more a lockout than a strike – it was backed (almost certainly organised) by Russian factory managers and the workers continued to be paid – and involved a relatively modest 18–30 000 workers. In Tallinn docks and elsewhere, political strikes, staged in the name of equality and justice between nations, condemned the citizens committee movement and demanded its dissolution.

At times the IM, backed by the KGB, seemed to be acting at the direct behest, or at very least in close empathy with the mood, of the Kremlin. For example, at 4 o'clock on the afternoon of 15 May 1990, a body of Russian speakers, variously estimated at between two and five thousand and led by Mikhail Lysenko, a former policeman dismissed on corruption charges, assembled in front of the government and parliament buildings on Toompea hill. The demonstration was in protest against the Estonian declaration of a transition to independence and the reintroduction of state symbols. Thus, on 30 March, only days after the formal split in the ECP and the formation of majority pro-independence and minority pro-Moscow parties, the newly-elected Estonian Supreme Soviet declared Estonia (the terms ESSR and ESS were at the same time abolished) an illegally occupied country in transition to independence. Shortly afterwards, the Supreme Soviet of the USSR enacted a complex law on separation from the Union – ostensibly implementing article 72, but in practice making secession an extremely protracted and therefore problematical process – and Gorbachev demanded the cancellation of the declaration. Despite the start of an economic blockade of Lithuania (18 April 1990) in retaliation against Vilnius' declaration of *restored independence* on 11 March, and similar threats by Gorbachev against Estonia and Latvia, moreover, a law of 8 May 1990 reinstated the state symbols (flags and so on) of the 'Republic of Estonia'. The day after the Soviet leader pronounced that law null and void, the IM mob gathered at Toompea, while at the same time cadets from the Soviet Aviation Academy and soldiers in civilian dress were agitating outside the parliament building in Riga.[37]

At half past six in the evening the crowd, which also demanded the resignation of the head of state, Arnold Rüütel, broke into the inner courtyard of the government building and twice raised the (old) ESSR flag.[38] In response, Prime Minister Savisaar, describing in a dramatic radio broadcast what he saw as an 'attempted coup', appealed (successfully) for help from PF activists. Perhaps as many as 15 000 Estonians quickly arrived on the scene and formed a corridor through which the Russians eventually dispersed. Savisaar then led 'his people' in a chorus of the Estonian national anthem from his position on a balcony in the parliamentary wing of Toompea. It was the only time in the five years leading up to the regaining of independence that large crowds confronted one another in the streets and, in the event, the IM following quickly dispersed. The whole 15 May episode, incidentally, gave Savisaar the opportunity of transforming the PF volunteer force into a fully-fledged Home Guard.

Summing up, although contriving an intermittently high profile, survey evidence suggests that support for the IM and JCWC never exceeded one-third of the Russian-speaking community.[39] Moreover, despite the predominantly working-class character of the non-Estonian population, about 65 per cent of IM's membership comprised white-collar workers and managers of Estonia's large All-Union industries. Their managerial personnel stood to lose most from political and economic reform in Estonia, while the language law similarly threatened the plant managers with loss of control.[40]

The 'Ecological Phase of National Self-Assertion': the Green Movement

In addition to the three main social movements, the PF, CCM and IM, there were other important currents in the 'movement society'. A loose christian democratic movement emerged over the course of 1988 (closely linked to the NHS) although this later split into a political arm – which formed a party – and those activists more concerned to engage in 'social work' such as prison reform. In July 1989 a feminist (women's) movement was founded, initially fired by the inadequate conditions in maternity hospitals.[41] It was also active, along with other organisations, in picketing Soviet military bases to demand that, if Estonian youths had to do military service in the occupation army (which it opposed), they should be allowed to do it in their native country and not in a far-flung corner of the Soviet Union, where tales of harassment, even brutality, were commonplace.

Radical reforms in military service were also high on the agenda of a gathering of young people held in the Kosmos cinema in Tallinn on 4 June 1988, a week after the fourth full sitting of the Komsomol central committee. This Independent Youth Forum embraced a diverse collection of groups, ranging from a PF support group (a majority of young people, however, viewed the PF as a middle-aged project steeped in the thinking of the communist system), pacifists, Greens, the MRP–AEG and the Evangelical Lutheran Church's Theology Institute. The initiative group behind the Kosmos meeting was led by Hans H. Luik and Margus Mets and the session was widely reported on radio and television. The Independent Youth Forum's programme, which was dispatched to the ESS leadership and published in *Noorte Hääl* on 18 June 1988, contained sections on the state, the protection of the environment, cultural life, the young family, rights, military service and the economy. By July 1988, Estonian schoolchildren had founded their own organisation, *Eesti Laste Organisatsioon*, initially seeking to operate outside the party's pioneers, but later opting to function within the framework of the latter. It was open to all school pupils and those adults supporting its aims. Ultimately, on 21 July 1988, an Information Centre to coordinate the work of the various youth groups was set up, representing, among others, the Greens, the Estonian National Independence Party, the Free and Independent Youth Column Number 1, the Võru Scout Troop and the Estonian State Arts Institute's Students' Union. The daily vigil outside the Estonian Supreme Court building in Tallinn over the summer of 1988 to demonstrate for the release of the political prisoners Mart Niklus, Enn Tarto and Sivert Zoldin was in large part the work of the youth organisations.

Above all, however, there was the Green movement, founded by Juhan Aare in May 1988, which was the first of its kind in the Soviet Union. It will be recalled that, as early as the late 1970s, 'green' issues had been the focus of dissent and in 1977 18 natural scientists condemned the pollution resulting from indiscriminate oil shale and phosphate mining in Estonia. A decade later, however, in the marginally more tolerant climate of *perestroika*, environmental protest prompted an unprecedented mass mobilisation of ordinary Estonians, as well as providing an umbrella for diffuse regime opposition. When, on 1 May 1988, for example, the MRP–AEG group, marching with the Greens, displayed flags in the blue, black and white of the national colours, the Greens felt obliged to apologise to the Tallinn authorities.[42] The Greens were extremely critical of Vaino for retarding social change (the latter did nominate Aare as a token reformist on his personally nominated slate of 'candidates' for the Congress of People's Deputies' 'election' in March 1988) and pressed for Prime Minister Saul's resignation during summer 1988. Indeed, though the initial battle against phosphorite mining development appeared (at least temporarily) won, Estonia's environmental problems remained serious and the Greens had a wider agenda, including demands for economic, cultural and political sovereignty, a halt to immigration and the establishment of ESSR citizenship.

The official formation of the Green movement in May 1988 capitalised on the highly-charged and highly politicised mood of the Estonian people during the Singing Revolution and virtually coincided with the emergence of the PF. Initially, the relationship between these two movements was close and at times the Greens appeared to operate as the radical wing of the PF. Of the delegates at the PF's inaugural congress in October 1988, 10 per cent belonged to the Green movement, although the latter nonetheless retained its identity. Interestingly, one of the speakers at the ceremony to mark the raising of the blue, black and white Estonian flag on the Pikk Hermann tower on Independence Day, 24 February 1989 – standing alongside senior ECP and PF leaders – was the Green representative, Andres Tarand.[43] The Greens also ran candidates in conjunction with the PF at the Congress of People's Deputies' elections on 26 March 1989. One of their number, Hans Trass, was even prevailed upon to stand down in order to allow the ECP leader Väljas, whom the PF was backing, a straight fight against a strong IM challenge.[44] The popular Trass, a leading academic and environmentalist, would undoubtedly have split the 'reformist vote' and possibly let IM in by the back door.

Although cooperating closely with it, the Greens came to regard the PF as too moderate by mid-1989 and through its executive body, the Green Forum, it advocated the restoration of full independence. There were solid ecological grounds, as well as reasons of 'high politics', for this since, as a senior Green figure, Eino Väärtnou, observed: 'Only an independent Estonia can resolve our massive environmental problems. As long as Estonia is part of the Soviet Union, we cannot take the decisions which will save our nature.'[45] Apart from an unequivocal espousal of independence (compare the circuitous route mapped out in the PF's revised programme of October 1988), the Green movement developed several distinctive characteristics over the second half of 1989. First, the highly generalised, albeit far from vacuous, demands of its late 1987 programme – including economic, cultural and political sovereignty – although they remained highly salient, gave way to a Green agenda which was more issue-related and acquired a greater degree of ecopolitical specificity. The Green movement had been a member of the international Friends of the Earth organisation since August 1988, but now there was altogether wider cooperation with global environmental bodies as well as growing consultation with Scandinavian officials and experts. Particularly urgent issues were stressed : the overdue modernisation of pollution-control technology (purification systems and so on), for example, and the crucial need for investment on environmental protection equipment. It cited one cellulose factory in Tallinn, whose purification plant no longer functioned, which dated back to czarist times! The Greens also urged the case for a far more responsible attitude from the imperial authorities, noting that, in the form of the All-Union factories, approximately 90 per cent of Estonian industry was directly controlled from Moscow. The Greens shared with its partner nationalist movements, the PF and the rapidly escalating CCM, the goal of independence, but emphasised more than the other two independence *as a means*: a necessary condition of effective environmental policy.

Second, among its active members, the Green movement became more age-specific, largely involving young people (compare the predominantly middle-aged PF elites) who, in the style of West European ecological protest, engaged in a range of demonstrative activities. Thus in June 1989 about 3500 people took part in a 'cycle march' to remonstrate against the wholesale despoliation of the northern coast of Estonia and a level of pollution that was so great that it was acknowledged to be damaging the Swedish and Finnish as well as Estonian environments. The inventory of problems compiled by the protestors was extensive. In the predominantly Russian-speaking north-east, it was claimed that nearly two-fifths of the annual discharge of the coal-based thermal power stations near Narva was sulphur dioxide, while the Sillamäe nuclear plants, it was alleged, were dispatching radioactive waste into the Gulf of Finland.[46] In the Greater Tallinn area, the Maardu mining complex and Kunda cement factory were also fouling large areas of the Gulf of Finland. As for the capital itself, the atmosphere was being contaminated by a fearsome mixture of sulphur, phenol, formaldehyde, nitrogen compounds, dust, ammonia, heavy metals and (accounting for about 60 per cent of overall pollution) car exhaust.

Third, at the end of 1989 the Greens profited from the heightened ecological awareness caused by a disaster which, albeit on nothing like the scale of the Chernobyl reactor leak three years earlier, had a comparable impact on the public consciousness. In December 1989, 150 tons of aircraft fuel leaked into the river Pärnu after fractures developed in the pipes running from the local Soviet military base. Lacking the necessary cleaning chemicals, the local Pärnu authorities set fire to the oil, which sandwiched the ice (above and below) on the river, and this burnt in black clouds as far as the town centre itself.[47] A large demonstration followed, along with complaints about the apparent indifference shown by the Soviet army officials (apparently, teams of conscripts used only a single bucket to extract the oil from the river). All of this highlighted the way the Gulf of Riga (Pärnu stands at its gateway) was becoming as badly polluted as the Gulf of Finland

Although increasingly polarised by personality conflicts among its leaders and a growing split between its Tartu and Tallinn wings, support for the Green movement ranged from 9 to 15 per cent in the polls in 1989. It was also the only social movement during this transitional period to command the backing of a significant section of the non-Estonian population. Following the December 1989 local elections, Greens held eight seats on the Tallinn city council and by early 1990 there were an estimated 4000 active members of the movement. As the first of the Estonian social movements of 1987–91, the Greens understandably appealed to a wide range of regime opponents, several of whom later founded political parties: Tiit Made, the leader of the Entrepreneurs' Party, and Kalle Kulbok, the 'territorial marshal' of the Royalists, are cases in point (see Chapter 7).

In addition to the Greens, the two principal Estonian social movements, the PF and CCM, spawned an alternative political class (counter-elite) which stood in contrast to the 'old guard' of *nomenklatura* politicians in the ruling ECP. The PF attracted a body of essentially middle-aged leaders, a *Komsomol* generation of reform-minded communists, who had been influenced by the 'Thaw' and the events of the 'Prague Spring' of 1968. Marju Lauristin in fact claimed to have been a social democrat since 1968. The CCM, like the Greens, appealed to young people while also providing opportunities for a disparate array of previously 'anti-system' elements – intellectuals, clergy, Second World War veterans, expatriates and former dissidents – to move centre-stage. Deep divisions between the new political elites over strategy and the desired mode of restoring independence led, according to Ruutsoo, to a fourth and final phase – the stagnation of the 'movement society' and the transition to pluralist democracy based on parties. The social movements, he claims, increasingly became captives of the embryonic parties and forfeited their mass support.

The Congress of Estonia Becomes Marginalised: March 1990– August 1991

Ruutsoo has claimed that, between spring 1990 and summer 1991, the PF was the object of an organisational takeover and became the extended arm of the People's Centre Party, led by Savisaar, while the Congress of Estonia came increasingly to be dominated by the Estonian National Independence Party which viewed its sessions largely as a vehicle for promoting the party's interests.[48] This seems a rather exaggerated proposition since the party–movement distinction remained blurred and the same personalities headed both. Nonetheless, the disintegration of the 'movement society' does provide a crucial backdrop to understanding the process of party formation and in this context the marginalisation of the COE between March 1990 and August 1991 warrants a brief note.

According to Taagepera, the COE, which gathered for its inaugural session on 11–12 March 1990, missed a vital strategic opportunity to act to downgrade the ESS to little more than an advisory second chamber. Elections to the latter, it will be recalled, were due on 18 March and, despite its morally weak and undemocratic character, the ESS thus stood to acquire the authority of an elected body, along with the administrative resources and experience to appoint a government that the Kremlin would be obliged to recognise. Accordingly, Taagepera advocated the immediate use of the COE's extensive network of citizens committees to persuade local and district councils to submit themselves to the Congress. This, he contended, would create a chain reaction at the end of which the ESS would feel obliged to seek the COE's permission to remain in office.[49] In Taagepera's judgement, its inaction at this critical juncture meant that the COE's highpoint was its election and, thereafter, a precious window of opportunity was missed. The steps in his blueprint are worth examining.

Crucial to understanding Taagepera's schema was his calculation that, for Gorbachev, granting independence to the ESS would create a dangerous precedent elsewhere in the Soviet Union and that he would be able to work more easily with the COE. By recognising the COE, the Soviet leader could in practice confirm that the Stalinist annexation of Estonia in 1940 had been illegal and tacitly acknowledge the right to secede. Indeed, Gorbachev could make favourable international capital out of treating the Baltics as a special case. The plan, therefore, was that representatives of the COE would negotiate with Gorbachev in Finland on the basis of (only) three conditions: the withdrawal of Soviet troops from Estonian soil; guarantees of Estonian neutrality; and economic cooperation between Estonia and the Soviet Union at world market prices.[50] To facilitate this action plan, Taagepera publicly appealed to the ESS chairman, Rüütel, to resign and urged the real power-holders at the local level to recognize the COE.[51] The ESS elections would then be demoted in status and the members returned would constitute a provisional *Riigikogu* (national assembly) which would function like a type of House of Lords (dual membership with the COE would not be permitted).[52]

Reactions to Taagepera's plan, published in *Eesti Ekspress* in late February and early March 1990, varied from the tepid to the openly hostile. There was a modicum of support from a number of radicals in Tartu, but this evaporated when Taagepera put a written proposal to the COE (he was not himself granted a visa to attend, having earlier addressed an Estonian National Independence Party gathering) in which he advocated allowing non-Estonians voting rights at the Congress and not simply the right of participation. Several in the PF, moreover, felt that, if the COE 'gained power' along Taagepera's lines, Soviet military intervention in Estonia would be inevitable. With the advantage of hindsight, Taagepera has admitted that, from his distant view of proceedings in the United States, he misjudged Gorbachev's readiness to allow the Baltics to secede from the Union. The Soviet leader simply did not regard them as a special case.[53] Indeed, on the one hand Gorbachev consistently underestimated the significance of the nationalities question and never found a workable policy to deal with the issue. On the other, as Toivo Raun states: 'Gorbachev had no desire or incentive to preside over the loss of key territory conquered under the Tsars and recaptured under Stalin, especially since the Western powers continued to base their policy on him and feared the consequences of any weakening of his position.'[54]

If it would be extremely harsh to condemn the COE for missing a golden opportunity of asserting itself as the supreme legislative body during the week 12–18 March 1990, it was nonetheless surprising how rapidly it was outflanked by the PF-dominated ESS and reduced to the ranks of the so-called 'democratic opposition'. True, in the first days of its session, the ESS passed several resolutions imbued with the spirit of cooperation. For example, on 30 March 1990,

it recognised the COE as 'the restorer of the state power of the Republic of Estonia'. More significantly, of course, the same day it
proclaimed the beginning of a transitional period from illegal Soviet
rule which would end only with the creation of 'constitutional organs of state power'.[55] But relations between the PF and COE were
fractious from the earliest post-election days. Perhaps it was because,
as Kalle Müüli wrote in the Tartu daily *Edasi*: 'Some have been communists far too long; others have been dissidents far too long.'[56] In
other words, while some lacked a clean record, others had little or no
political experience.

In any event, it was significant that at its second session on 25 May
1990, the COE decided to set its face firmly against the ESS (Tunne
Kelam, one of its founding figures, claimed that the 70-member Council of Estonia, *Eesti Komitee*, was simply being ignored by the ESS)
and to appropriate to itself the right to pass legislation. Predictably,
many PF delegates in the Council refused to participate in this vote
and the PF soon afterwards adopted a resolution condemning the
existence of parallel legislative bodies.[57] By the time of its third session on 26–7 October 1990, the COE was not alone in believing that
Savisaar, the prime minister, was seeking to introduce 'a dictatorship
and heavy-handed regime in Estonia'.[58] Kelam demanded the resignation of Savisaar's cabinet and its replacement with a coalition of
national unity although, as five months earlier, a majority of PF
delegates in the COE opposed the proposed vote of 'no confidence'
in Savisaar. When, however, in the so-called 'Eight-Person Proposal'
on 4 November Kelam, in association with reformist communists,
sought to install Siim Kallas, the chairman of the Estonian central
trade union organisation, as prime minister, this 'unholy alliance' of
'new left' (Free Estonians) and 'hard right' (fundamentalists close to
the Estonian National Independence Party) – which Savisaar with-
stood – was symptomatic of the extent to which the COE had become
marginalised from the centre-stage of events (the 'Eight-Person Proposal' is discussed again in Chapter 7).[59] Critically, by wheeling and
dealing with representatives of the 'old guard', the COE to a degree
stained its reputation as the moral conscience of the historic nation
and frustration among its members was clearly discernible in the
press.

All in all, there is no evidence to support the conclusion of Diuk
and Karatnycky that 'The Congress of Estonia … established a dual
leadership. The Estonians rendered unto the Kremlin what was supported by the Kremlin – the Supreme Soviet – but continued to look
for leadership to the Congress of Estonia. The dual leadership lasted
until well after the Moscow coup and the final proclamation of independence.'[60] The fact is that the COE's star quickly faded since it
lacked legislative authority and, just as important, was not involved

in day-to-day governance like the ESS.[61] Yet, although the COE became increasingly sidelined after its dramatic first session on 11–12 March 1990, the original citizens committee concept was invaluable in permitting Estonian citizens living abroad and their refugee organisations to join forces with the domestic independence movement in defence of the legal continuity of the Estonian state. The Estonian exiles in turn contributed significantly to promoting the cause of Estonian independence on the wider international stage. Andres Küng, a well-known Swedish–Estonian journalist, for example, was only one of several leading names who fought for Estonian independence from Sweden.

The COE did not go empty-handed. Ultimately, on 20 August 1991, Estonia did not issue a declaration of independence, but rather took a decision to re-establish independence on the basis of the historic continuity of the state. The COE, in short, like the PF and the ECP, contributed to the restoration of independence and, in particular, to creating a mood in which citizens came to expect independence. Many of those actively involved in the 'movement society' went 'into independence' not politics; for others, the social movements became instruments that were too blunt to articulate desired reform programmes. In an increasingly pluralistic political climate, the social movements themselves were affected by internal pluralism and began to split into political parties.

Notes

1   Rein Taagepera, *Estonia. Return to Independence* (Westview: Boulder–San Francisco–Oxford, 1993), p.127; Toivo Raun, *Estonia and the Estonians*, 2nd edn (Hoover: Stanford, California, 1991), p.196.
2   Toivo Raun, 'The Re-establishment of Estonian Independence', *Journal of Baltic Studies*, **XXII**, (3), 1991, pp.251–8, especially p.252.
3   Toomas Hendrik Ilves, 'Reaction: The Intermovement in Estonia', in Jan Arveds Trapans (ed.), *Toward Independence: The Baltic Popular Movements* (Westview: Boulder–San Francisco–Oxford, 1991), pp.71–83, especially p.72.
4   Interview with Trivimi Velliste, 11 January 1994.
5   Rein Ruutsoo, 'Transitional Society and Social Movements in Estonia', *Estonian Academy of Sciences, Humanities and Social Sciences*, **42**, (2), 1993, pp.195–214.
6   Marju Lauristin, Peeter Vihalemm and Rein Ruutsoo, *Viron vapauden tuulet* (Gummerus: Jyväskyla–Helsinki, 1989), p.154.
7   Marjut Kuokkanen, *Puolueiden muotoutuminen Virossa 1988–1992* (Politiikan tutkimuksen laitoksen tutkimuksia 127, 1994: Tampereen yliopisto, 1994), pp.27–31.
8   Lauristin *et al.*, *Viron vapauden tuulet*, pp.159–60.
9   Ibid., pp.155–8.
10 Ibid., pp.164–5.
11 Ruutsoo, 'Transitional Society', p.203.
12 Interview with Rein Ruutsoo, 12 September 1993.

13   Lauristin *et al.*, *Viron vapauden tuulet*, p.217; 'Poliitik Jumala armust. Jüri Luik', *Helsingin Sanomat*, Kuukausiliite 17, 20 August 1994, p.25.
14   Lauristin *et al.*, *Viron vapauden tuulet*, pp. 178–79.
15   Ibid., p.194.
16   Interview with Trivimi Velliste, 11 January 1994.
17   Taagepera, *Estonia*, p.151.
18   Ibid., p.174.
19   Interview with Trivimi Velliste, 11 January 1994.
20   Juhan Talve, 'Viro on itsenäinen mutta miehitetty', *Helsingin Sanomat*, 23 February 1990.
21   Taagepera, *Estonia*, p.174.
22   Rein Taagepera, 'Rahvarinde Sotsiaaldemokraatlikust Platvormist', *Vaba Maa*, 4 December 1989.
23   Taagepera, *Estonia*, p.171.
24   Estonian radio broadcast, 10 January 1990.
25   Ahto Lobjakas, 'Six Years of Political Pluralism in Estonia', *Emor Reports*, **2**, (4), 1992, p.11.
26   'Mitä Viro tahtoo?', *Helsingin Sanomat*, 25 March 1990.
27   Sole Lahtinen, 'Itsenäisyyskysymys voi jakaa Viron kommunistipuolue', *Helsingin Sanomat*, 23 March 1990.
28   Lauristin *et al.*, *Viron vapauden tuulet*, p.288.
29   Anatol Lieven, *The Baltic Revolution: Estonia, Latvia, Lithuania and the Path to Independence* (Yale University: New Haven–London, 1993), p.193.
30   Figures in a report by Raul Mälk on Estonian radio, 14 December 1989.
31   Lieven, *The Baltic Revolution*, p.190.
32   Ibid., p.192.
33   Lauristin *et al.*, *Viron vapauden tuulet*, pp.232–3.
34   Ibid., pp.201–3.
35   Ibid., p.231.
36   Ibid., p.315.
37   Lieven, *The Baltic Revolution*, p.197.
38   'Venäläisten valtausyritys lyötiin takaisin Tallinnassa', *Helsingin Sanomat*, 16 May 1990.
39   Ahto Lobjakas, 'Emerging multi-party system and public opinion in Estonia 1989–1991', *Emor Reports*, **1**, (1), 1989, p.9. See also Ahto Lobjakas, 'The Estonian Party System. An Attempt in Analysis', unpublished paper, Lund University, 1992.
40   Ilves, 'Reaction', p.81.
41   Lauristin *et al.*, *Viron vapauden tuulet*, p.308.
42   Taagepera, *Estonia*, p.133.
43   Lauristin *et al.*, *Viron vapauden tuulet*, p.184.
44   Ibid., p.308.
45   'Viro hukkumassa saastaan', *Helsingin Sanomat*, 27 February 1990.
46   'Radioaktiivisia jätteitä upotettu Virossa Suomenlahteen', *Helsingin Sanomat*, 1 March 1990.
47   Riianlahden mustat ajat', *Helsingin Sanomat*, 11 February 1990.
48   Ruutsoo, 'Transitional Society', pp.208–9.
49   Taagepera, *Estonia*, p.175.
50   'Rein Taagepera kava Eesti ja N. Liidu Läbirääkimisteksi Variant A', *Eesti Ekspress*, 23 February 1990. As early as 1970, in his long-term action plan for Estonia entitled 'Thirty', Taagepera underlined the importance of geopolitical and geoeconomic realities and, accordingly, the need to forge a working relationship with the 'Big Neighbour' even after independence. See Rein Taagepera,

'The History of a Document: A Broad Plan for a Small Nation: "Thirty"', *Journal of Baltic Studies*, **XXIII**, (3), 1992, pp.261–82.

51 'Ülemnõukogu Äralõpetamisest', *Eesti Ekspress*, 9 March 1990.
52 'Ülemnõukogu Äralõpetamisest', *Eesti Ekspress*, 2 March 1990.
53 Interview with Rein Taagepera, 13 September 1993.
54 Raun, 'Re-establishment of Estonian Independence', pp.251–5.
55 Mari-Ann Rikken, 'The Restoration of Estonian Independence', unpublished manuscript, June 1993.
56 Vello Pettai, 'Political cooperation turning sour', *The Estonian Independent*, 18 April 1990.
57 'Congress of Estonia to rival Supreme Soviet for legislative powers', *The Estonian Independent*, 30 May 1990.
58 'Congress of Estonia warns against Estonian dictatorship', *The Estonian Independent*, 1 November 1990.
59 'Dissidents and communists sign deal to oust Savisaar government', *The Estonian Independent*, 8 November 1990. On 11 November 1990, the eight politicians insisted that they would continue their consultations on forming a government around Siim Kallas: 'Savissar opposition standoff continues', *The Estonian Independent*, 15 November 1990.
60 Nadia Diuk and Adrian Karatnycky, *New Nations Rising*, (Wiley: New York, 1993), p.122.
61 Raun, 'Re-establishment of Estonian Independence', p.254.

7 Patterns of Party Formation in Estonia

De facto multipartism in Estonia predated the amendment on 23 February 1990 of article 6 of the ESSR constitution enshrining the ECP's leading role. No less than 31 parties or 'proto-parties' contested the ESS elections on 18 March 1990 and they included three women's parties. Moreover, at the first general election in the 'restored republic', which took place on 20 September 1992 (exceptionally, there were simultaneous presidential elections), 17 parties or electoral alliances contested the 101 seats in the unicameral *Riigikogu*. Nine were ultimately successful in gaining parliamentary representation, although the Greens and Entrepreneurs returned only a single member each. The distribution of parliamentary votes and seats by party/electoral alliance is set out in Table 7.1. The turnout of 67.8 per cent was virtually the same as at the referendum held to approve the new constitution on 28 June 1992. In contrast to Lithuania (see Allik's thesis in Chapter 5), not a single candidate from the ECP (renamed the Democratic Labour Party of Estonia) was elected.

In proceeding to give a thumbnail sketch of the parliamentary parties, it is convenient to distinguish the three groupings – *Isamaa* (the Estonian name is preferred to the translations 'Pro Patria' or 'Fatherland'), the Estonian National Independence Party and the Moderates, which formed a majority coalition after the 1992 general election – from the opposition parties. The three governing groupings clearly profited from the electoral system, gaining a narrow absolute plurality of 51 seats with only 40.4 per cent of the vote. The *Isamaa* alliance, with 29 seats, supplied the prime minister, Mart Laar; the Estonian National Independence Party with 10 seats provided the home affairs minister; and the Moderates with 12 seats were allocated the social affairs and environment portfolios. The three governing parties will be considered in the chronological order of their foundation.

Table 7.1   The distribution of votes and seats by party/electoral
alliance at the *Riigikogu* election of September 1992

Party/electoral alliance	Votes	%	Seats
Isamaa	100 828	22.0	29
Secure Home	62 329	13.6	17
Popular Front	56 124	12.2	15
Moderates	44 577	9.7	12
Estonian National Independence Party	40 260	8.7	10
Independent Royalists	32 638	7.1	8
Estonian Citizens	31 553	6.8	8
Greens	12 009	2.6	1
Entrepreneurs	10 946	2.3	1
Others		14.3	—
		100	101

Turnout 67.8 per cent.

The Roots of the Parties in the 1992–5 Governing Coalition

The Estonian National Independence Party

The Estonian National Independence Party – *Eesti Rahvusliku
Sõltumatuse Partei* (ERSP) – was officially (and illegally) formed on 20
August 1988 and became the first party openly to oppose the ruling
Communist Party, not only in Estonia, but throughout the Soviet
Union.[1] Its active founding figures were virtually all former dissidents, several of them with a long history. At least two ERSP activists, for example, had been involved in 1972 when the first comprehensive programme aimed at toppling the Soviet regime was formulated. It will be recalled from Chapter 4 that this emerged from twin
underground organisations, the Estonian National Front and the Estonian Democratic Movement – the latter inspired by pro-Sakharov
groups and linked to counterparts in Russia – which had partially
overlapping personnel and boasted a combined membership of between 20 and 30. The 1972 programme was smuggled into the West;
a memorandum was also despatched to the United Nations (UN)
requesting it to administer free elections to a constituent assembly
and press for the withdrawal of Soviet troops. Another plea for respect for human rights was sent to the inaugural gathering of the
Conference on Security and Cooperation in Europe (CSCE) in Helsinki in 1975. The illegitimate nature of Soviet rule in Estonia and the

wanton violation of international law were openly condemned, more-over, in other documents sent to the Council of Europe and the European Parliament.[2] Despite a series of arrests in December 1974, the secret house meetings of the early dissidents continued.

By the late 1980s, the dissidents behind the creation of the ERSP were associated with two highly risky organisations, largely involving the same people, that were committed to exposing the illegal and inhuman character of the Soviet regime. The first was the MRP–AEG group for the publication of the secret articles of the Molotov–Ribbentrop pact of 23 August 1939 which assigned Estonia to the Soviet Union. The MRP–AEG group comprised 16 members, all of them dissidents. Best known among them was, perhaps, Lagle Parek, an engineering technician, who was the daughter of an Estonian army captain shot shortly after her birth. Parek was released from prison in January 1987 having learnt, in her own words, 'that it is possible to live anywhere; indeed, that it is interesting to live anywhere'.[3] Other members of the group were Tiit Madisson, Heiki Ahonen and Arvo Pesti. On 23 August 1987, the anniversary of the Hitler–Stalin pact, the MRP–AEG activists, as noted earlier, organised the first open demon-stration against Soviet rule in Estonia. Despite warnings from Mos-cow, the rally, which paralleled similar events in Riga and Vilnius, attracted several thousand people to Hirvepark in Tallinn.

The second organisation was the Movement for the Restoration of the Monuments to the Victims of Stalinism, orchestrated by the Nat-ional Heritage Society (NHS), which was founded in December 1987. Organised into local clubs on the basis of the historic Estonian par-ishes, the NHS boasted about 10 000 members by the end of 1988 and in April of that year was the first organisation openly to display the Estonian flag at one of its meetings in Tartu.

The original initiative to found an ERSP came on 21 January 1988 when 14 Estonians managed to get published a demand for the resto-ration of the Estonian republic. Two of the founding figures simply travelled to Moscow and announced their fundamentalist (and highly dangerous) cause at a conference of foreign journalists. As a result, four of the activists were subsequently forced to leave Estonia, in-cluding Parek's nephew. Parek herself, though harassed, was not rearrested, presumably because the adverse publicity at home and abroad would have been deleterious to the somewhat more open state–society relations (*glasnost*) which Moscow was seeking to en-courage. In any event, the ERSP proposal was at this stage essentially demonstrative and agenda setting: the prospects of such a radical, nationalist and thus anti-system party being allowed freely to oper-ate were remote, while the goal of renewed independence doubtless seemed a further way off still. It had certainly not entered the heads of ordinary Estonians.

It bears emphasis that the proposal for a National Independence Party was an extremely bold and daring development. Indeed, although the ERSP used the softer and slightly ambiguous *sõltumatus* rather than the unequivocal *iseseisvus* – which would have been too provocative – to render the word 'independence' in its title, not all radicals supported it. Tunne Kelam, for example, later a leading ideological figure in the ERSP, was opposed to the January 1988 launch. Earlier Kelam had lost his post as an editor of the *Soviet Estonian Encyclopaedia* and spent a period as nightwatchman on a chicken farm. He was not directly involved in the MRP–AEG group, however, though he maintained contacts with it, and he was not directly involved in the original ERSP proposal in January 1988.

In April 1988, a steering committee was set up to prepare the basic documentation in readiness for the inaugural meeting of the ERSP. Its foundation was facilitated by the slightly more tolerant mood following 25 March 1988 when, according to Parek, the 'reign' of the KGB in Estonia was effectively over. The climate became still more conducive over the early summer of 1988 when a daily picket was organised by the MRP–AEG group in front of the Supreme Court building to demand the release of the well-known political prisoners Mart Niklus and Enn Tarto. A number of well-known intellectuals became involved (at least in signing the petition) at this stage and it may be said that these vigils by MRP–AEG members became a rallying-point in mobilising a more coherent radical opposition. Moreover, the inescapable conclusion to be drawn from the marathon picket was that it was now possible to express open opposition to the Soviet system – for the action embodied a total rejection of Gorbachev's reforms – with relative impunity.

It was against this backdrop that the Estonian National Independence Party was officially founded in the Pilistvere church on 20 August 1988 and immediately recruited 100 members. As one of its first actions, in September 1988, the ERSP composed and transmitted a detailed document which strove to enlist UN assistance in the restoration of Estonian independence. This proved a valuable exercise in publicising and marketing Estonian grievances on the wider international stage. By the end of 1988 a party organisation had developed. Indeed, the ERSP became the first, and the only one, of the nascent parties before the 1992 general election to boast a national organisation. Surprisingly, however, an opinion poll in April 1989 indicated that only 10 per cent of Estonians would have voted for the ERSP had there been an immediate general election (only 1 per cent of non-Estonians would have done so) – five times less than the PF's support and three times less than would have backed the Greens.[4] The party was clearly still associated in the popular mind with risk: the risk of losing one's job, house or some other 'perk' of conformity.

Interestingly, though, by summer 1989, one-quarter of the adult Estonian population claimed (at least) to support the ERSP's activities.[5]

In January 1989, it will be recalled, Kelam and the Christian Democrats, Velliste and Laar, engaged in discussions on the COE plan and this was subsequently approved by the ERSP's governing body. Over the course of 1989, the ERSP in fact played a vital and active part in the local citizens committees, along with the NHS and Christian Democrats. Yet the COE elections in February 1990 proved something of a disappointment. Despite the considerable financial support of émigré groups, who were involved at an early organisational stage in the ERSP, the party claimed only one-fifth of the seats in the Congress. Furthermore, the ERSP was debarred from endorsing candidates at the ESS elections in March 1990. To be sure, it could have sponsored suitable persons through citizens' initiatives, but declined to do so for strategic reasons, preferring not to bestow legitimacy on the structures of the occupation state.[6] With the advantage of hindsight, one or two of its leading figures have viewed the ERSP approach as something of a tactical error.[7]

Between spring 1990 and summer 1991, the COE came to be dominated by the ERSP and their histories became ever more closely intertwined.[8] It was symptomatic of a growing reaction against the party's stranglehold on the Congress that in October 1990 an attempt was made to replace the ERSP leader, Kelam, as COE chair with the former political prisoner Enn Tarto. Tarto was as critical of the ESS as the ERSP, but refused to join the latter. In the event, Kelam retained his position by 60 votes to 40.[9] The following month, as noted in Chapter 6, the reformed communists in Free Estonia and four radical nationalists, including Kelam, joined forces in the 'Eight-Person Proposal' designed to unseat the Savisaar government. Kelam and others signed the joint declaration without consulting the ERSP and COE leaderships. In private, many of their fellow radicals were horrified, realising what a blunder it was. They felt it sacrificed their principal asset, a reputation for eschewing political games and acting as the moral conscience of the nation. Kelam has since insisted, however, that he was 'proud, not ashamed' of the deal with Free Estonia.[10] The aim of the COE was to unite all Estonian citizens behind the goal of renewed independence and, he insisted, there were nearly 30 communists in the Congress. By late 1990, in short, the ERSP was an opposition party which appeared willing to engage in the necessary in-fighting in its attempt to oust the Savisaar government.

After the realisation of its primary goal, the restoration of full independence, the party played an important role in constitution building, supplying 13 of the 30 members allocated to the COE on the 60-member Constitutional Assembly (the other 30 were nominated by the ESS – now the Supreme Council). A draft document adopted as the basis of the Assembly's work was prepared by ERSP members and one of its number, Jüri Adams, was particularly influential in shaping the final form of government.

At the September 1992 general election, running as a separate party rather than as part of an electoral alliance, the ERSP polled 8.7 per cent and won 10 *Riigikogu* seats. This was a respectable result, but still only 1.6 per cent ahead of the 'anti-party' Independent Royalists who campaigned for a monarchical system. The ERSP's presidential candidate, Lagle Parek, fared considerably worse, polling only 4.2 per cent of the vote (see Table 7.2). Her credentials as an outstanding dissident had a much greater appeal to Estonian exiles than to citizens resident in the restored republic. Her support among Estonians abroad – an astonishing 99.3 per cent of whom turned out to vote – rose to 20 per cent

A member of the post-election coalition, along with the parties in the *Isamaa* and Moderates' electoral alliances, the ERSP declined an offer to merge with the *Isamaa* bloc when its constituents united in a single party in January 1993. Kelam and other leaders were not altogether opposed to throwing in their hand with the new party – the name *Isamaa* was retained – but refrained from doing so for two main reasons. First, there was a concern to attract more votes by retaining a separate electoral identity. Second, the majority of grassroots members were opposed to the merger. In May 1993 the ERSP's parliamentary group (*Riigikogu* 'factions' must comprise a minimum of six members) was increased to 12 following two defections from the populist Estonian Citizens movement. However, at an extraordinary party conference in Tallinn on 17–18 July 1993 the ERSP witnessed the first real break with its original leadership. Ants Erm was elected chairman, replacing Parek, the minister of home affairs, who decided not to run.[11]

The ERSP was the first real opposition party in the Soviet Union when it was founded in 1988, but suffered from a degree of life-threatening factionalisation and fragmentation as a governing party

Table 7.2   The popular vote for the presidential candidates,
20 September 1992

Candidate	Party	Votes	Percentage
Lennart Meri	*Isamaa*	138 317	29.5
Arnold Rüütel	Secure Home	195 743	41.8
Lagle Parek	ERSP	19 837	4.2
Rein Taagepera	PF	109 631	23.4

and approached the 1995 election as a broken force. Internal strains and tensions came to a head after the so-called 'Pullapää incident' in July 1993 when a rebel rifle company refused to subordinate itself to the Estonian armed forces. As a consequence, the ERSP defence minister, Hain Rebas, resigned on 4 August 1993.[12] The ERSP, however, failed to secure a replacement minister, the post being 'poached' by the leading governing party, *Isamaa*. This prompted an emergency meeting of the Tallinn and district ERSP organisation at which Kelam and Vardo Rumessen were expelled for 'damaging the party's interests'. Although Kelam was subsequently reinstated, a breakaway group, including Arvo Kiir, a clergyman, *Riigikogu* member and the ERSP executive board's candidate for the post of defence minister, split and on 19 August 1993 founded the Future Party (*Tulevikupartei*).[13]

Centred on the discussion club *Kuppel* (meeting in the National Library) the Future Party boasted two parliamentarians previously in the ERSP faction. In addition to Kiir there was Jaanus Raidal from Otepää, although, ironically the latter was not an ERSP party member as such. Kiir identified two main reasons for leaving the ERSP. First, he claimed the party was not internally democratic in that board decisions in respect of ministerial appointments should be binding (a thinly-veiled reference to the fate of his own candidacy). Second, he noted that the ERSP was something of a spent force: its support was declining and it had missed the opportunity of joining forces with *Isamaa* in January 1993. He was critical of Kelam for not actively supporting the merger.

The architects of the Future Party claimed that it was unique in striving for a fundamental reorientation in the culture (values and attitudes) of both people and politicians. The unity of the revolutionary period, they noted, had been succeeded by conflict and intolerance; fraternity by personal enmity. Consequently, there was a need to look forward – to the future – not back, to reopen old wounds of the communist past. In doing so, it was important to strike the right balance in society between the ethical and material, the spiritual and the secular. Minds should be open(ed), not closed; information should be readily available to fertilise those minds; and Estonia should profit from the power of free thought: 'mental force, not armed force'.[14] Although not explicitly critical of any other party, the Future Party clearly hoped to trade off dissatisfaction with the performance of the more established parties and the discordant tone they had set.

The ERSP lost two more *Riigikogu* faction members when the National Progress Party (*Eesti Rahvuslik Eduerakond* – ERE) was formed on 27 November 1993. Named after Jaan Tõnisson's inter-war party, it was largely the creation of Ants Erm and he was joined by Toivo Uustalo who was originally elected on the Estonian Citizens' list. The two ERE parliamentarians became members of an Independents

Table 7.3 The Independents Faction in the *Riigikogu*, 1994

National Progress Party	*Future Party*	*Others*
Ants Erm	Jaanus Raidal	Mart Niklus
Toivo Uustalo	Arvo Kiir	Kalju Põldvere

Note: Niklus was formerly a member of the Estonian Citizens' faction; Põldvere was formerly in the *Isamaa* faction.

faction, along with the two Future Party MPs and two others (see Table 7.3). The ERE initiative stemmed from September 1993 and involved for the most part former ERSP board members and people who had been active in the Tallinn district organisation. Erm's departure, however, reflected wider divisions in the ERSP.

Originally active in the PF, Erm became a COE representative in February 1990 and joined the ERSP exactly one year later, mainly because of its forceful line on the 'national question'. He became ERSP chairman in July 1993, defeating Jüri Adams in a very close race. Adams, one of the first ERSP members, inclined towards the pragmatic stance that the ERSP could exercise influence through active participation in policy coalitions; Erm, in contrast, adhered to a more 'principled line', eschewing the 'power at all costs' wing of the party. The ERSP, it was inferred, had gone soft on the national question.

Indeed, the ERE programme took a hardline position on the national question. Its goal was an Estonia comprising only Estonian citizens and, in order to achieve this, the vigorous promotion of the Estonian language and culture was viewed as essential. Measures were also to be taken to support Estonian families and to increase their birth rate. While the fledgling ERE did not favour the deportation of Russians, it held that state support should be made available for voluntary repatriation. Moreover, Erm was strenuously opposed to the Laar government's decision to grant retired Soviet officers and their families the right to apply for work and residence permits in Estonia.[15] The ERE opposed Estonian membership of the EU, principally because of the threat of migration that would imply. Standing out against the politics of compromise, the ERE hoped to benefit from a higher electoral turnout at the March 1995 general election than in September 1992 by delineating the way in which the Estonian nation should make progress. In the event, the ERE fought the 1995 *Riigikogu* election as part of the radical rightist 'Better Estonia' alliance (see Chapter 9).

The ERSP received yet another body blow when, following growing criticism of the Estonian government's failure to curb crime,

President Lennart Meri dismissed the minister of the interior, Lagle Parek, on 28 November 1993. The dismissal took place two days after a shooting incident in central Tallinn in which two police investigators were badly injured. Parek was replaced, not by a member of ERSP's *Riigikogu* faction, but by the 28-year-old Heike Arike, a former ECP member and senior civil servant in the Ministry of the Interior. He was nominated by the ERSP on the basis of his practical experience in the relevant department, but the party was divided over backing a man with a clear communist past. At the 1995 general election the ERSP, in contrast to three years earlier, formed an electoral alliance with *Isamaa* and in summer 1995 announced plans to merge with it.

Isamaa

Although the *Isamaa* electoral alliance was formed to fight the 1992 general election, the five proto-parties sheltering beneath its umbrella were considerably older than that and, curiously, they included two Christian parties. One, the Estonian Christian Democratic Party (*Eesti Kristlik Demokraatlik Erakond* – (EKDE) was in fact the first of the re-emergent parties dating back to the Singing Revolution of summer 1988, its creation on 23 July predating the ERSP by a month. Initially, it brought together 16 young Christians, mostly students from the Technical High School and Teacher Training College in Tallinn, none of them, unlike the leadership of its sister party, practising clergymen. The other, the Estonian Christian Democratic Union (*Eesti Kristlik Demokraatlik Liit* – EKDL) was founded on 17 December 1988 (originally as the Estonian Christian Union – *Eesti Kristlik Liit*) and was grounded in NHS networks. Mart Laar, Illar Hallaste and Trivimi Velliste (who joined the party at the end of 1989) were all members of the National Heritage Society's governing body. The initial preparations began in May 1988 and brought together representatives of the Lutheran, Catholic, Orthodox, Methodist and Baptist churches at a time of relative tolerance of the church by the state authorities.

Between the wars, an overwhelming majority of the Estonian population was Lutheran; a separation of church and state was instituted from the outset; and in the four general elections between 1920 and 1929, as noted in Chapter 3, a Christian Democratic Party (*Eesti Kristlik Rahvaerakond*) won between four and eight *Riigikogu* seats before merging in 1931 into the newly formed Centre Party. EKDL indeed subsequently claimed to have inherited the ideological mantle of this inter-war Christian party. Stalinism, of course, imposed strict penalties on religious observance, including giving religious instruction to children. It abolished the traditional parish administration, destroyed churches and in various other ways systematically suppressed the 'counter-ideology' of Christianity. Yet from the late 1980s onwards, there was something of a religious revival in Estonia. Large numbers of Bibles were donated from abroad (mainly Finland); in 1988 Christmas was officially celebrated again; in that same year there were over seven times more baptisms and nearly six times as many confirmations as 10 years earlier; and in March 1990, the weekly organ of the Lutheran Church, *Eesti Kirik* ('Estonian Church') resumed publication after half a century.

Nonetheless, much of the old restrictive legislation remained on the statute book and it was against this background of heightened de facto tolerance of, but continuing legal restrictions on, the church that in May 1988 a proposal for the creation of a Christian grouping in support of *perestroika* appeared in the newspaper *Edasi*. As in the case of the PF (with which, incidentally, it had absolutely nothing to do) the explicit backing for Gorbachev's goal of restructuring was largely tactical and designed to bestow a modicum of legitimacy at a time when religious organisations were not officially permitted. In any event, the architects of EKDL hoped that christian democracy, a leading political ideology in Western Europe, would take firm root, elevate the Estonian nation to independence – as the German CDU (Christian Democrats) had revived a demoralised people after 1945 – and provide the catch-all base with which to embrace all religious creeds. Yet when planning was well advanced, the other denominations opted out and the EKDL emerged as a predominantly Lutheran political organ. According to its leader, Hallaste, its principal objective was 'to influence the decision-making process so as to give the church a pre-eminent position in society'.[16]

In addition, EKDL's programme stressed the need for a minimum wage/income, supported marginal groups such as students, pensioners and young families and, while propounding the cause of the social market economy and a firm and expeditious line on the restitution question, recognised that there would be casualties of the transition who would need protection. The programmes of the two Christian parties in fact differed relatively little, although there was the conviction in some EKDL circles that EKDE was too far removed from the church. EKDL's desire to exert influence in the political arena was quickly evident, since at its inaugural meeting, in December 1988, there was virtual unanimity in favour of nominating candidates for the elections to the Congress of People's Deputies in Moscow on 26 March 1989. EKDL, moreover, was active over the course of 1989 in promoting the formation of citizens committees in readiness for the COE elections.

In June that year, however, a split developed in its ranks over whether the party should concentrate mainly on social work (prisons, orphanages and so on) or political activities. This division was institutionalised with the creation of separate groups: the Estonian Christian Democratic Association (*Eesti Kristlik Ühendus*) focused on social work whereas the EKDL continued as a political party (indeed, it changed its name from Estonian Christian Union to Estonian Christian Democratic Party at this stage).[17] By gaining observer status in the Christian Democratic International in September 1989 and full membership the following year, EKDL became perhaps the first internationally known Estonian party during the transition to renewed independence. In 1990 it set up a Youth Organisation, with Tõnu Koiv as chairman, and at the ESS elections on 18 March that year the EKDL elected six delegates. The party's initial membership derived principally from southern Estonia and the western part of Virumaa.

The other three members of the *Isamaa* electoral alliance in September 1992 were all founded in 1990. The Conservative People's Party (*Eesti Konservatiivne Rahvaerakond* – EKRE) was founded on 6 January 1990 with Enn Tarto, one of the most prominent dissidents and later rector of the Estonian Institute of Human Rights, as its leading figure. Tarto was arrested during the 1950s 'Thaw' for joining an unofficial student organisation, spent nine years in prison and then stoked coal into boilers in apartment houses. In 1983 he was rearrested, this time for drafting an open letter supporting a Baltic nuclear weapon-free zone. He returned home in October 1988, the last of the political prisoners to be released. Indeed, the EKRE was, above all, a party based on dissidents and political prisoners and claimed to be the only one to have no former communists in its midst (even the ERSP had some).

Preparations for the party began during June and July 1989. They attracted at most about 80 activists, all of them united in their commitment to see the restoration of independence in their own lifetime. A sizeable proportion of the party's pioneers – perhaps one-third – were former NHS activists who rejected the clericalism of the EKDL and wanted the strict separation of church and state, together with protection for religious minorities. They themselves were Orthodox and Catholic church members and also included believers in the Estonian god, Taara. Other founding figures had been involved in the intellectual conservative society *Res Publica*.

First and foremost, the EKRE was wedded to the legal continuity of the Estonian state. The party's name, which was finalised only at its founding congress in June 1990, was intended precisely to denote the need to 'conserve' the legality of the inter-war republic and to promote it as the basis for international recognition of the restoration of Estonian independence. EKRE fought (albeit unsuccessfully) in the COE for a resolution in favour of the ultimate reinstatement of all Estonia's pre-existing laws and, significantly, it maintained contacts with the (as it saw it, legitimate) Estonian government-in-exile in Sweden. Plainly, in the light of these fundamental objectives, the EKRE had much in common with the ERSP, although relations became strained by what was seen as the latter's attempt to dominate the COE.

Rebuilding the Estonian state, EKRE held, would require a series of urgent measures and the party was extremely critical of Prime Minister Savisaar for retarding the restitution of property process, aggravating an economic crisis and, crucially, failing to set up a national army. In this last respect, EKRE's programme appeared the most radical of all in being the only one publicly to canvass a series of military demands. These included the restoration of the Defence League (*Kaitse Liit*), the revival of the Border Guard and, ultimately, the recreation of the Estonian army. The restoration of the Defence League possessed symbolic as well as military importance, since it was originally founded in 1918 to maintain law and order during the two-year War of Independence. The Defence League resumed its activities after the abortive communist coup in 1924 and eight years later had 32 117 members. During the 1940s and 1950s, many of its former members were 'Siberianised'. Revived by the EKRE on 17 February 1990 – it was not, according to Tarto, under the control of the COE, as was sometimes suggested – the Defence League's remit was to protect the 'legal' citizens of Estonia.[18] Indeed, in safeguarding their private property, the Defence League was perceived by the EKRE as a necessary adjunct of renascent Estonian democracy against attacks upon it from the civil garrison of Russians. For a time, the revived Defence League had no parallel. Admittedly, the PF had its volunteer force (complete with badges and armbands), largely to protect its meetings from falling prey to KGB-inspired provocation. But it was 15 May 1990 before the IM's attempted seizure of Toompea castle gave Savisaar the opportunity of transforming the PF corps into a full-blown Home Guard (*Kodukaitse*). When the restoration of independence allowed the role of the Estonian defence structures to assume rather less overriding importance, the EKRE was able to consider joining forces with other small right-wing groups.

In some ways, EKRE appeared imbued with the negative isolationist spirit of inter-war nationalism. Thus, while foreign economic investment was encouraged, foreign ownership was not deemed permissible. The party, moreover, eschewed a single economic market in the Baltic and did not envisage a special cooperative relationship with the Nordic states. Not surprisingly, perhaps, the EKRE, unlike most of the other nascent parties, never received any financial or 'technical assistance' from abroad. Its model seemed to be a Swiss-style neutral Estonia which would remain outside military alliances.

The Estonian Liberal Democratic Party (*Eesti Liberaaldemokraatlik Partei* – EDLP), which was founded on 9 March 1990 and gained four seats in the ESS shortly afterwards, was a merger of two groups. One stemmed from November 1989, when a number of PF activists worked to found a Liberal People's Party. They responded to the Social Democrats' call to leave an increasingly Savisaar-dominated PF and shared with the Social Democrats under Marju Lauristin, who mooted that party marginally earlier, the sense that the sands of time were running out for the 'movement society'. Privatisation was in the air and the time seemed ripe for a broadly-based liberal party. About 20 activists were involved in the Liberal People's Party initiative.

The second group, which sought simultaneously to create a Free Democratic Party, emanated from cultural circles and a manifesto underwritten by 18 leading cultural figures (who resigned their ECP membership), including the artist Enn Põldroos, publications committee chairman, Jaak Joerüüt and writers Viivi Luik and Paul-Erik Rummo. Rummo, who was prolific as a poet in the late 1960s (when his output inevitably assumed political significance), was an active figure in the Cultural Council of the Creative Unions in the late 1980s and became minister of culture and education in September 1992. For two years the Cultural Council had its own radio broadcast and the Free Democrats may therefore be said to have possessed both political experience and a good understanding of the mood of ordinary people. Their manifesto lacked much of the 'nationalist embellishment' of the other right-of-centre parties.[19]

The merger of the Liberal People's Party and Free Democrats was facilitated by the extensive personnel overlap between the two. In a small country, each group was well aware of the state of play in the other. Accordingly, only two joint meetings were needed to prepare for a pooling of resources. Although representatives of the Estonian émigré liberal organisation *Eesti Liberaal–Demokraatlik koondis eksiilis*, which was founded in 1945, attended the foundation congress of the EDLP in March 1990, these elderly exiles in Sweden had not played an active part in the creation of the party. The first EDLP programme was extremely broad-brush in character. Later versions, however, stressed the need for cultural and educational reforms which were viewed as a *sine qua non* of economic progress. 'Soviet education' was simply regarded as having been a contradiction in terms. In general, the Liberals posited a series of humanistic values as a counterweight to the unbridled entrepreneurialism of the free marketeers.

Initially, the cohesion of the EDLP was relatively low, with internal disagreement focusing in particular on the question of cooperation with the Savisaar-led PF. The party rode out the storm, however, and was granted observer status at the Liberal International's congress in October 1990, so becoming the first East European party to be admitted to that organisation. The Estonian Liberal Democrats also played host to an executive committee meeting of the Liberal International in Tallinn in July 1993.[20]

Finally, the Republican Coalition Party (*Eesti Vabariiklaste koonderakond – EVKE*), which emerged in September 1990, brought together three groups. First, there was the *Res Publica* group of young intellectuals, especially notable among whom was Jüri Luik, who became minister without portfolio in 1992, minister of defence and then foreign minister a year later. Next, there was the Union of Work Collectives (*Eesti Töökollektiivide Liit*), founded in November 1988 as a counterpoise to the Russian JCWC and headed by industrialist Ülo Nugis and physicist Endel Lippmaa. It consisted in the main of the managing directors of those large firms that remained independent of Moscow. Finally, there was a group known as the Independent Right. On the party's left wing, in short, there were former communists, whereas its right-wingers, largely emanating from the *Res Publica* club, tended to gather around the person of (the future president) Lennart Meri. Among their number, incidentally, was the grandson of inter-war president and authoritarian leader, Konstantin Päts.

The EVKE's right wing in particular espoused much of the thinking of Thatcherite conservatism. Property rights were to be secured by law as the foundation for an economy organised on as free a basis as possible. Taxes were to be fixed as low as possible to encourage enterprise and entrepreneurialism and progressive taxation was opposed because it was held to penalise initiative. Foreign investment, indeed, was to be attracted by creating a conducive taxation climate. In the social policy sector, welfare provision was to be provided, not by the state, but by a range of private funds, trusts and charities which would in turn be supported by favourable tax allowances from the state. In terms of foreign policy, the EVKE attached considerable importance to the withdrawal of Russian troops. Otherwise, it was feared they might exploit the unsettled conditions to intervene in domestic Estonian affairs. There was even talk of ultimate Estonian membership of NATO.

The technical electoral cooperation between this assortment of christian democrats, conservatives, liberals, neoliberals and nationalists led to an amalgamation of four of the small right-of-centre groupings which, as mentioned, fused on 21 November 1992. A functional alliance was thus transformed into what was hoped would be a cohesive political party using the same name, *Isamaa*. The ERSP, it has been seen, declined to join and the EDLP also maintained its separate identity. Tensions within the merged party have tended to follow generational as well as ideological lines. The Pullapää incident is a case in point. Tarto, the former EKRE leader, wanted the reasons for the episode fully investigated, whereas the young leaders from the former EVKE wanted to hush things up. As a result, Tarto was sacked from the *Riigikogu*'s Defence Committee in September 1993 and 'exiled' to the Committee on the Environment. In policy terms, moreover, the principal influences on the *Isamaa* programme clearly came from the 'free marketeers' in the EVKE.

By summer 1994 both the *Isamaa*-led coalition and the *Isamaa* Party showed clear signs of fragmentation. Criticism of Prime Minister Mart Laar's leadership style and, more particularly, his role in an Estonian–Israeli arms deal, spawned a bewildering sequence of events, including the dismissal of the defence minister, Indrek Kannik (for reasons that were not made wholly clear) and the attempted resignation of the head of the Estonian armed forces, Aleksander Einseln (refused by President Meri) – events which culminated in an extraordinary *Isamaa* party conference on 11 June 1994 (see Table 7.4). Laar's leadership was confirmed, albeit relatively narrowly, against challenges from Kaido Kama, former minister of justice, and Ülo Nugis, the *Riigikogu* speaker (who, as one ERSP parliamentarian cryptically put it, 'suspended his suspended *Isamaa* membership'). Promptly

Table 7.4 **Fragmentation in the *Isamaa* party over the summer of 1994**

---

26 May 1994   Dismissal of Indrek Kannik as minister of defence.

3 June 1994   Attempted resignation of Major-General Aleksander Einseln, head of the Estonian Armed Forces, refused by President Meri.

11 June 1994   Extraordinary *Isamaa* party conference called following an internal mutiny against the prime minister, Mart Laar, and against the backdrop of the calamitous collapse in *Isamaa*'s popularity. Laar survived, polling 191 votes against 86 for Kaido Kama (previously minister of justice) and *Riigikogu* Speaker Ülo Nugis' 56 votes.

12 June 1994   Two EDLP ministers, Heiki Kranich (finance) and Paul-Erik Rummo (culture and education) resigned.

27 June 1994   EKRE extraordinary party conference at which it was decided to split from *Isamaa*. It was claimed, *inter alia*, that the ethical crisis in *Isamaa* persisted and that MPs did not receive sufficient information about government policies.

29 June 1994   EVKE also decided to break with *Isamaa*.

30 June 1994   EKRE, EVKE and two Christian Democrats combined to form a new *Riigikogu* faction, the Right-Wingers.

---

thereafter, however, the two EDLP ministers resigned their cabinet seats, while at the end of June 1994 the EVKE and EKRE delegates (together with two Christian Democrats) left *Isamaa* to found a nine-strong *Riigikogu* faction called the 'Right-wingers' which committed itself (by no means uniquely) to promoting Estonian national values and a free-market economy. Both the two right-wing groupings in the government, in short, the ERSP and *Isamaa*, were in a state of considerable disarray by summer 1994.

The Moderates

The third arm of the 1992–5 governing coalition comprised the Moderates (*Mõõdukad*), an electoral alliance which brought together two parliamentary groups in the ESS – the Social Democrats and the Rural Centre Party – both initially supporting Savisaar, both headed by former PF leaders and both ultimately alienated by the Savisaar style of leadership. Hence the call for a moderate approach. Their cooperation dated from January 1992 when they united in opposing the Savisaar government on the restitution issue and they fought the September general election that year with the slogan 'Estonia is One' (*Eesti on üks*). At the simultaneous presidential election, the Moderates backed Lennart Meri.[21]

The Estonian Social Democratic Party (*Eesti Sotsiaaldemokraatlik Partei* – ESDP) was formed following the merger of three groups on 19 September 1990. The first was the Estonian Democratic Labour Party (*Eesti Demokraatlik Tööerakond* – EDTE) which was founded on 27 April 1989 by a group of 18 activists, only three of whom had previously been communists. Andres Mandre, a moving force in the party (and subsequently secretary of the merged party), to be sure, left the ECP only two months after the EDTE's inception, but he was retroactively incorporated into the latter's inaugural membership. The EDTE's primary instigator was Vello Saatpalu who mooted the idea at the PF's foundation congress in October 1988. A graduate electrician and middle manager, Saatpalu was never an ECP member; he became a member of the PF's national executive and later a COE deputy.[22]

The EDTE may be said to have grown out of the PF and involved those who heeded Saatpalu's call for a new party, passed on by word of mouth at the PF's founding congress. Preparations for the launch began in secret over September and October 1988. By January 1989, an informal four-member 'inner circle' emerged and over the course of three meetings wide-ranging discussions further laid the ground. In addition to Saatpalu and Mandre, this steering group comprised Tiit Made, an Estonian delegate at the Congress of People's Deputies in Moscow, who subsequently left to found the Entrepreneurs' Party, and Siim Kallas, deputy-editor of the newspaper *Rahva Hääl* and chairman of the central trade union organisation, who later became Governor of the Bank of Estonia and whose contribution as an economics expert was vital. At the end of February 1989, preceded by only a small notice in the press, Saatpalu and Mandre organised an open meeting at the Tallinn Technological Institute at which the concept and principles of social democracy were presented and interest was gauged. The response was encouraging: attendance was around 200 and a sizeable proportion of the students seemed keen to join the embryonic party. Nonetheless, as Mandre has observed, knowledge of social democracy in the audience was very limited, the atmosphere was not quite right and it was decided to postpone matters.[23]

Preparations continued, however (the EDTE's first statutes were printed in the offices of the central committee of the ECP!) and the Estonian Democratic Labour Party was officially founded in April 1989. Its first statue maintained, in accordance with the Lima Mandate adopted at the Seventeenth Congress of the Socialist International in 1986, that the EDTE would not identify itself with any particular philosophical interpretation of socialism, but rather would chart its own Estonian course in the years ahead. Symptomatically, the Estonian '*erakond*' was used so as to avoid the cosmopolitan and rather pejorative term 'party' in the organisation's designation and there was concern, too, to avoid duplicating the name 'Labour Party', one of the groups in the inter-war republic. The EDTE developed local branch organisations, usually comprising less than 10 members, and also incorporated Russian-speakers, many of them former students at the Tallinn Technological Institute. Ironically, the EDTE's name was appropriated, quite unethically according to Saatpalu, by the redesignated communists who in autumn 1991 became, as noted earlier, the Democratic Labour Party of Estonia (Saatpalu's letter of complaint on the subject received no reply).[24] Before its merger with the other two social democratic groups, the EDTE forged contacts with the Social Democrats in Sweden and Finland and three of its number were guests of the Swedish party at the Socialist International in Stockholm in August 1989, although for tactical reasons they attended as PF delegates.[25]

The second arm of the nascent social democrats comprised the Russian Social Democratic Party of Estonia led by the businessman Josif Jurovski. Concentrated in Tallinn, the party was a breakaway from the Intermovement. Its total membership probably never exceeded 30 people and several were simultaneously members of Saatpalu's EDTE. In short, it was scarcely a party, even by Estonian standards.

The largest of the social democratic groups was the Estonian Social Democratic Independence Party (*Eesti Sotsiaaldemokraatlik Iseseisvuspartei*

– ESDIP) which was based in Tartu and formed on 11–12 January 1990 under the leadership of Marju Lauristin. A sociologist at Tartu University, Lauristin was the daughter of the first post-annexation premier of the ESSR and one of the signatories of the 'Letter of Forty'.[26] Three factors may be said to have accounted for the decision to found the Social Democratic Independence Party, along with the timing of its creation as a separate group in January 1990. First, there was the growing personal rivalry between 'the father and mother of the Popular Front' – Edgar Savisaar and Marju Lauristin. Like the EDTE, in short, the ESDIP grew out of the PF, though, unlike Saatpalu's party, it stemmed from conflict within the leadership of the Front. Put simply, there was growing concern at Savisaar's increased domination of the PF, as evidenced in the movement's new programme in October 1989, which Savisaar wrote personally and which Lauristin, among others, sought to moderate. Around Lauristin there formed a group of predominantly middle-aged people active in the Tartu PF, including Rein Ruutsoo, Rein Veidemann and Ülo Kaevats.

Second, the Lauristin group's arm was twisted, so to speak, by the formal launch in January 1990 of the reformist communists' Free Estonia group, since the latter sought to stake out the ground on the non-communist Left prior to the ESS elections in March. Initially, there had been no intention of rushing a new party into existence and in November 1989 the Lauristin group set up a preparatory debating club which, it was envisaged, would run for between six and 12 months and act as an important agency in diffusing the ideas of social democracy. Ironically, the leading figures in the ESDIP themselves confessed to wholesale ignorance of the fundamental precepts of Western social democracy. However, in response to plans for Free Estonia, an ESDIP programme outline was published in the press on 15 December 1989. According to Veidemann, 'aside from intellectuals', the new party planned 'to stand up for the interests of retired people' who, it was argued, would become especially vulnerable in the transition to a market economy.[27] The same month, Lauristin rejected a deal proposed by the Free Estonia activists at a meeting in Siim Kallas' house.[28]

Finally, two international socialist gatherings held in Estonia in January 1990 created propitious conditions and favourable publicity for the launch of the ESDIP which, according to an Eke Ariko opinion poll that month, was supported by 22 per cent of the electorate. The Estonian Social Democratic Forum, held in Tartu on 11–12 January, brought together social democrats from 14 countries, including representatives of the Swedish Social Democrats and British Labour Party, as well as the two existing Estonian social democratic parties. A provisional board of the ESDIP was formed on the final evening of the Forum. As a follow-up to the Forum, Tallinn played host to the founding congress of the Social Democratic Association of the Soviet Union, whose aim was to prepare the ground for creating social democratic parties in Russia and the other Soviet republics.[29]

The initiative towards the merging of the three social democratic parties was taken by the Lauristin group, which twice over the winter–spring of 1989–90 proposed that the EDTE join forces with it. However, it was June before it was agreed that negotiations could take place on the basis of parity between the parties. Thereafter matters progressed speedily and on 8 July 1990 the chairmen of the three Estonian social democratic parties and the Exile Association of the Estonian Socialist Party (*Eesti Sotsialistlik Partei Välismaa Koondis*) issued a public appeal for the pooling of resources in a single party. In a joint statement it was asserted that 'the social transition to self-regulation and free enterprise demands greater attention to social protection against assaults from both the extreme left and right'. When the merger took place on 8 September 1990 it constituted the first union of fraternal parties from both the Estonian and Russian-speaking communities.

There were several reasons for the fusion of social democratic groups. None was registered as a political party, whereas together they could muster the minimum of 200 members necessary for registration; there was pressure to unite from the exiled Socialists in Sweden; their programmes were broadly similar; the Socialist International admitted only one socialist party per country; and, not least, strength lay in numbers in the preparations for the *Riigikogu* elections, which it was (mistakenly) expected would take place over the winter of 1991. Significantly, two days after the founding congress of the Estonian Social Democratic Party, a delegation from the Socialist International arrived in Estonia to meet leaders of the new ESDP. At its inception, 244 members were enrolled, about half deriving from the Lauristin group and one-fifth from the Russian Social Democratic Party of Estonia. However, there had been significant opposition to the merger at the EDTE conference in Pärnu and many members of the Estonian Democratic Labour Party did not in fact join the new party.

The Rural Centre Party (*Eesti Maa-Keskerakond* – EMKE) was founded on 7 April 1990. The two leading figures in the germination of the idea during autumn 1989 were Ivar Raig, who held a doctorate from the Institute of Economics, and Jan Leetsaar, who was prominent at the Land Reclamation Institute and subsequently became minister of agriculture.[30] Also active at a slightly later stage were Uku and Liia Hänni, the latter a minister in the Laar coalition after September 1992. Raig was unique at this crucial juncture in the formation of parties, in that he was concurrently a member of three legislative or quasi-legislative bodies, as well as belonging to the Council of Estonia. He was secretary to the Agricultural Committee of the Congress of People's Deputies in Moscow; chairman of the Rural Section of the Popular Front and one of its founders in Tartu; and a member of the ESS. Raig, moreover, was one of the architects of a new property law which the ESS adopted on 13 June 1990, providing a legal basis for private property ownership through buying and selling.[31]

EMKE was not an *externally created party* in Duverger's sense of resting on a pre-existing base outside the national assembly, though it was grounded in the active support of the first private farmers and it did have an institutional foundation in the form of the Private Farmers' Union, which was set up in 1989. Many of the small body of private farmers which emerged from spring 1988 onwards (see Table 7.5) were mobilised by Raig's speaking tours and the newspaper articles he wrote from the first *perestroika* years of 1985–6 onwards, attacking both the state farm (*sovkhoz*) and collective farm (*kolkhoz*) systems.[32] The Private Farmers' Union was created by Raig and Aldo Tamm, director of Saku Agricultural College near Tallinn, and its immediate goal was to work to ensure the implementation of the private farm legislation, especially the Farm Act of 6 December 1989.

The formal initiative towards EMKE's creation was published in *Maaleht* on 25 January 1990. Originally an ECP organ, *Maaleht* developed into a weekly of the progressive Left and with sales of 220 000 (compared with a circulation in 1993 of only 50 000) was the most widely-read newspaper over the transitional period. The party itself was officially founded on 7 April 1990. However, of the 70 people present at the initial gathering, only 40 proceeded to join the new EMKE, a reminder that affiliation to explicitly non-communist organisations was still regarded as a rather risky business. EKME was born in Türi in central Estonia, a region of traditionally wealthy farmers, which was chosen so as to symbolise the party's desire to reconstruct a system of prosperous agriculture. Indeed, one of the main planks in EMKE's first programme was the restoration of private ownership and private farming, which were viewed as the key to the economic and ecological survival of Estonia.[33] Despite the emphasis on the growing stratum of medium-sized family farms, the EMKE eschewed the label 'class party', emphasising instead its commitment to the economic and cultural regeneration of the whole countryside. Nonetheless, in September 1993, 39 per cent of its 456 members comprised private farmers and another 15 per cent were former *sovkhoz* and *kolkhoz* farmers.[34]

A member of the strongly free-market Laar coalition formed in September 1992, the EMKE ran against the grain in working to secure necessary measures of protection for Estonian agriculture against

Table 7.5   **The growth in the number of private family-sized farms registered in Estonia, 1990–92**

Year	Number
1990	1 000
1991	4 000
1992 (January)	8 611
1992 (July)	8 127

Note: The farms comprised an average 26.5 hectares, of which 11 were made up of cultivatable land. In 1992 family farms accounted for 40 per cent of the total agricultural output.
Source: Ivar Raig, 'Agrarian Reform in Estonia', unpublished paper, kindly made available by the author.

the import of cheap Eastern poultry and dairy products and the dumping of Russian wheat and rye flour. The decision taken in late August 1993 to impose a 70 per cent import duty on Russian flour, however, was opposed by the minister of finance and the minister of economics. The latter, Toomas Sildmäe, indeed, noted that Russian wheat could be imported duty-free via Latvia and held that the domestic market could have been protected (if this was deemed absolutely essential) by fixing quotas.[35]

Opposition Parties, 1992–5

The (People's) Centre Party

The principal opposition parties after the 1992 general election had been grouped into two electoral alliances, the Popular Front (*Rahvarinne*) and Secure Home (*Kindel Kodu*). In the first half of 1991, the PF core, the residue of senior personnel following the exodus of leading figures to found Social Democratic, Liberal Democratic and Rural Centre parties, formed a distinct People's Centre faction in the ESS. Talks about setting up a separate party, mooted by, among others, Peet Kask and Ignar Fjuk, made little headway, however. This was in large part because Savisaar, the prime minister, was concerned about losing support from allied parties if he created his own.[36] According to Taagepera, the restoration of independence nonetheless forced the PF's hand – by then its support had dwindled to 16 per cent – and the People's Centre Party (*Rahva Keskerakond* – RKE) was founded by a number of leading PF figures on 4 September 1991. There is some evidence, to be sure, that 'Savisaar agreed to form a party' *before* the achievement of independence, namely in early

August 1991; that an 'initiative group' was formed shortly afterwards; and that the press announcement of the proposed new party (with a telephone number for prospective new members to call) did not appear until early September.[37] In any event, RKE's aim was to chart a pragmatic central course between reformist communism and hardline nationalism.

In addition to Savisaar, the RKE's leaders included Mati Hint, a docent at the Pedagogical High School in Tallinn, who was one of the seven members of the PF's original governing body and had been the primary architect of the 18 January 1989 language law. While confirming Estonian as the state language, this also afforded greater guarantees to Russia and consequently aroused protest among sections of the Estonian population. Hint also acted as the chair at a well publicised meeting of the executives of the PFs of Estonia and Latvia and the Lithuanian *Sajûdis* held in Tallinn on 13–14 May 1989. Other founding-figures included the poet and essayist Jaan Kaplinski ('Janka'), who was the driving force behind the 'Letter of Forty'; Peet Kask, a physicist and also a signatory of the aforementioned letter; Olav Anton and Krista Kilvet; and, shortly after its launch, Rein Taagepera joined the party. At its inception, therefore, RKE could undoubtedly boast experienced leaders but, stripped of its social democratic, liberal democratic and agrarian elements, it lacked a clearly defined ideological focus.

The RKE was not an opposition party at birth since the Savisaar premiership did not end until January 1992. By then, however, he had become extremely unpopular, not only with other politicians but among the public at large. Savisaar had been a consistent advocate of compromise with the Russian-speaking population and before August 1991 was regularly attacked, even by cabinet colleagues such as Endel Lippmaa, the minister with responsibility for relations with Moscow, for his conciliatory approach towards the Kremlin.[38] Indeed, Savisaar communicated regularly with the Soviet commanders in Estonia and, accordingly, secured Soviet acquiescence in the Estonian reform programme. His popular image was seriously tarnished in June–July 1991, however, when, faced by Soviet pressure to concede local demands for a Russian-speaking province in north-east Estonia, Savisaar offered Narva the status of a free-trade zone. Although this move was overtaken by events – the restoration of full independence – Savisaar again came under fire in autumn 1991 for his refusal to implement a voucher scheme which would have given citizens the wherewithal to participate in the privatisation programme.

His position was further undermined, as the nationalist mood hardened, by his covert endeavours to build a moderate Russian political formation (the Russian Democratic Movement) in Estonia and his commitment to the so-called 'Zero Option' stance on the citizenship question (in fact on 6 November 1991 the ESS – now the Supreme Council – adopted the 1938 legislation which involved stripping the Russian population of its existing citizenship). The final blow came in January 1992 amid a serious energy shortage prompted by cuts in fuel supplies from Moscow. Emergency plans to evacuate large numbers from Tallinn to the countryside were avoided only by Western aid, but Savisaar resigned in the face of accusations that he had failed to anticipate the cuts by seeking alternative supplies on the open market.

More generally, Savisaar's loss of popularity was inextricably linked to his authoritarian Soviet-era style of addressing the nation. Thus, at press conferences, Savisaar fixed both the number of questions and the number of journalists who could put them and demanded to speak on the radio at peak listening times. As Lauristin (who, of course, broke with Savisaar) and Vihalemm noted: 'Against all expectations, such steps backfired. Instead of earning respect and obedience, this politician [Savisaar] laid himself open to ridicule'. They added that many journalists recorded how Savisaar's domineering style was instrumental in forcing his cabinet to resign in January 1992.[39]

In view of the former prime minister's unpopularity, it was not surprising that it was Taagepera and not Savisaar who, in July 1992, was adopted as the PF's presidential candidate in a (successful) attempt to prevent the incumbent head of state, Arnold Rüütel, from obtaining the absolute majority of popular votes necessary for outright election at the first ballot. In contrast to the RKE's disappointing 12.2 per cent poll at the September 1992 general election (it was widely regarded as too conciliatory towards the Russian-speaking minority) Taagepera gained 23.4 per cent in the simultaneous presidential contest.[40] This compared with 41.8 per cent for Rüütel, the chairman of the ESSR between 1983 and 1990 and president of the Estonian republic thereafter. His popularity surpassed that of any other public figure among the Estonian and non-Estonian populations.[41]

In 1993, the RKE sought to strengthen its identity and ideological moorings by reducing its name to 'Centre Party' along Nordic lines. As early as 16 June 1989 Savisaar, representing the PF, had signed a cooperation agreement with Swedish Centre secretary, Åke Pettersson – it dealt with economic, political and cultural matters – and the close links with the Swedish Centre were doubtless influential in the decision to simplify the RKE's name.[42] Electoral considerations also played a part, since by early 1993 RKE's support had sunk to 5 per cent in the polls. Following the change in name, plans were set in train to wind up the Popular Front organisation and the PF was finally disbanded at its fifth congress on 5 November 1993. The 'movement society' was formally over. Like its Scandinavian fraternal parties, the RKE has emphasised decentralisation and the importance of developing and activating local decision-making structures. It has attached much importance to social policy, not least the need for legislation on equal rights for women. Above all, however, it has taken a pragmatic rather than doctrinal approach to the complex question of the restitution of property.

By summer 1994 the RKE's *Riigikogu* strength had plummeted from 15 to five members – below the minimum of six necessary for the status of independent 'faction' – and on returning from a year in an American university, Peet Kask indicated his intention of leaving the party. Crucially, in March 1994, four of the RKE's parliamentary number – Hint, Kaplinski, Fjuk and Ants-Enno Lõhmus – defected to form the mainstay of a new Free Democrats faction in the *Riigikogu*. These PF veterans complained bitterly about the very strict discipline in the RKE faction and in particular about Savisaar's highly confrontational style which effectively amounted in their view to 'opposition for its own sake'. Accordingly, the manifest objective of the RKE renegades was to work constructively with the government to improve the overall quality of the legislative process, that is to consider proposals on their merits.

Significantly, several of the RKE's turncoats (notably Lõhmus and Fjuk, along with the Social Democrats Valve Kirsipuu and Eiki Nestor) were involved in October 1993 in the formation of a cross-party deliberative forum, the Association of Free Parliamentarians (*Vaba Parlamentaarne Ühendus*). Approximately 20-strong at its inception and drawing support from members of five parliamentary parties (both government and opposition) – the Centre, Rural Centre, Liberal Democrat, Social Democrat and Coalition parties – the AFP, which had very similar aims to those of the RKE rebels, was predicated on two main premises. First, there was the belief that the rather rudimentary programmes of the embryonic parties did not diverge all that significantly and that the common denominators could and should be explored. Second, it was felt that the parliamentary parties were still at a formative stage of development and that the consequences of the conflict between their leading figures were damaging the entire legislative process. In a highly fragmented parliamentary party system, in short, opposition should be cohesive and constructive and based on policy rather than personality.

Although those attending meetings of the AFP (initially these were held in informal surroundings outside parliament) remained members of their respective parliamentary groups, its participants immediately came to hold the balance of power in the *Riigikogu*. If the AFP had transformed itself into a political party it would have become at a stroke easily the largest parliamentary party in Estonia. In any event, the AFP and subsequent Free Democrats – along with ERSP

and *Isamaa* renegades – were a reminder that three years after renewed independence Estonian parties were even less developed in
the parliamentary than in the electoral arena: parliamentary groups
('fraktions'), bearing party names, were largely labels of convenience
and not all members of the party groups were members of the party!

The Kindel Kodu Parties

The second grouping of opposition parties after September 1992, the
Secure Home (*Kindel Kodu*) alliance, may be said to have profited
from something of a 'Rüütel effect'. The name 'Secure Home' attempted to capitalise on Estonian concern about rising crime rates. It
embraced three groupings. The Estonian Rural Union (*Eesti maaliit* –
EML), according to Taagepera, was registered on 24 October 1991,
although he notes that its origins date back to 1989, when it was
created by *kolkhoz* and *sovkhoz* bosses as the rural ally of the Estonian
wing of the ECP.[43] Arvo Sirendi, the party leader's version of events
differs somewhat. According to him, EML originated in 1988 against
the backdrop of the high rural mobilisation around the nationalist
issue and a meeting of the Union of Kolkhoz bosses which he claims
took place even before the momentous plenary session of the Creative Union on 1–2 April 1988. On 7 May 1989, a sociopolitical association was formed in Tartu ('association' was a euphemism since
parties were still not allowed) and EML was registered as a political
party on 23 March 1991.[44] Moreover, the party, Sirendi noted, initially
comprised both communists *and* former members of the original
Rural Union in the First Republic. EML's leadership consisted in the
main of educated rural people, while the typical member was on the
elderly side.[45] The principal architect of the revivified EML was Ernst
Kirs from Mulgimaa.
    Although the party claimed to base itself on the peasantist think-
ing of Santeri Alkio – the leading ideologue of the early Finnish
Agrarian Party (*maalaisliitto*) who stressed the spiritual and cultural
values of the rural way of life – it emerged as something of a *single-
issue party* demanding local free choice and self-determination (that
is, referenda) on the landholding question.[46] In other words, EML
opposed paying for the legacy of Stalinist collectivisation (the costs
of reacquiring private land that had been forcibly acquired by the
state) but also set its face against restitution by what it saw as legislative diktat, that is state-driven privatisation. Self-determination, it
believed, would have seen part of the *kolkhoz* land returned to its
original owners and the remainder continue to be deployed on a
cooperative basis. Sirendi claimed that at the local level people were
ready for change, but they wanted to determine the nature of change
themselves, rather than having it imposed upon them.

EML's advocacy of a slow track to agricultural privatisation involving a 10-year transitional period may be explained in part by the fact that some of the *kolkhozs* and *sovkhozs* in Estonia were relatively productive compared with those elsewhere in the former Soviet Union and in consequence not all those employed in the agricultural sector were interested in farm privatisation. In any event, EML was in principle in favour of the restitution of land to its former owners, albeit with the proviso that agricultural workers should also have the opportunity to obtain holdings. EML, moreover, envisaged a role for the state, in buying, selling and renting land to those who worked it and in supporting Estonian farming which, it claimed, was obliged to operate in difficult natural conditions. EML urged the need for a comprehensive state-backed social security system and protection for the elderly. Like several of the embryonic parties, it was vehemently anti-Savisaar.

Distinctively, EML did not forge fraternal links with parties in Scandinavia or elsewhere in Western Europe, claiming this to be against its principles. At the 1992 general election it spent only the 9000 crowns needed to cover the costs of the candidates' deposits, relying heavily on cooperation with the Coalition Party (considered shortly) to promote its ideas on television. All four of EML's *Riigikogu* representatives between 1992 and 1995 were agronomists and agriculturalists aged over 50. The fact that the party's roots are to be found in the rural past, a past of state-owned plants and collective farms, together with the existence of personality conflicts between their respective leaderships, have ruled out any prospect of cooperation between the Rural Union and the other parliamentary agrarian party, Raig's Rural Centre Party. Thus overtures from Raig in summer 1994 were firmly rebuffed and there was bitterness in the way EML leaders recalled how Raig had stood (unsuccessfully) for the board of the nascent EML and had wanted to take the new party over.

The Estonian Democratic Justice Union (*Eesti Demokraatlik Õiglusliit*) was founded in December 1991 to act as a pressure group to protect and promote the interests of marginal groups such as pensioners and invalids.[47] It did not, in short, view itself as a political party, at least in the Western sense of the term. Its two *Riigikogu* representatives, Professor Raoul Üksvärav, a former chair of the ESS, and Edgar Spriit, a journalist, were 64 and 72 years old, respectively, on their election in 1992. A separate Pensioners' Union (*Eesti Pensionäride Liit*), incidentally, polled 3.7 per cent of the vote and the Union of Handicapped Societies (*Eesti Invaühingute Liit*) 0.4 per cent in September 1992, but neither managed to elect any members of parliament. In order to make its objectives more explicit, the Democratic Justice Union in 1994 changed its name to the Association of Pensioners and Families (*Eesti Pensionäride ja Perede Liit*). It has perhaps the clearest profile of all the political parties, with the result that the Pensioners performed well at the October 1993 local elections.

The Estonian Coalition Party (*Eesti Koonderakond – EKE*), which was founded on 9 December 1991 in the Trade Union House in Tallinn, was named after the main conservative party in Finland, *Kokoomus*. Indeed, in a real sense its architect was Tiit Nuudi, Rüütel's personal advisor, who was commissioned to undertake a special trip to Finland to study the Kokoomus party. Rüütel, for his part, was in touch with the German Christian Democrats (CDU) and it may be deduced from these external exemplars that the aim was to create a modern, pragmatic party of the Right with a cohesive programme and set of objectives – a party, it might reasonably be implied, not dependent for its identity on its leading personalities. Rüütel, however (who has subsequently allowed that it might have been better if he had joined), remained detached from the whole enterprise, being convinced (at that stage) that parties were essentially vehicles for realising personal ambitions.[48]

The EKE initially consisted of two core groups: those former managers of small- and medium-sized state enterprises who sought to retain their privileged position, albeit within the new market system and, consequently, were committed to the cause of economic reconstruction; and the lion's share of the reformist communists in Free Estonia, a group whose manifest political goal was attained when Estonia regained her independence.[49] Former communists, in short, joined forces in an explicitly right-wing, pro-capitalist party. The two wings of the party warrant closer inspection.

Free Estonia itself was officially launched on 20 January 1990 in time to compete in the ESS elections in March that year. Its nucleus of activists, Toome, Kallas, Allik, Titma and Kahma, as discussed earlier, tried unsuccessfully to incorporate the Lauristin circle of nascent social democrats into the fold in December 1989, but shared with the latter a growing mistrust of the PF leader, Savisaar. Interestingly, the involvement of representatives of Free Estonia in the 'Eight-Person Proposal' to install Kallas as prime minister in November 1990 was motivated by the same fundamental anti-Savisaar logic that in large part had propelled the group into existence. Savisaar, it was held, was conducting negotiations with Moscow in secret, was developing his own secret service and had established control of the press. Moreover, his growing domination, it was argued, was anchored in a style of crisis management that would render genuinely democratic elections impossible. As part of the deal with Kelam and his COE associates, consideration was even given to the appointment of a Russian-speaking representative – a manager, not an active politician – as deputy premier. Although the eight-person manoeuvre failed in its primary purpose, it may have achieved its secondary aim of educating public opinion in the belief that Savisaar was not irreplaceable.[50]

Most of the Free Estonia group joined the EKE at its foundation in December 1991. They were not, however, the prime movers in the party. Rather, the idea (although developed by Nuudi) originated in two ministers in the Savisaar government – Tiit Vähi (transport) and, above all, Jaak Tamm (industry) – both of whom were highly critical of the prime minister's viscose and outdated approach to economic management. The old command economy style of issuing central directives was no longer appropriate. Savisaar, it was argued, 'talked about the economy, but he was a command economy man. He tried to control prices and even visited enterprises personally to determine what they had in their store rooms'.[51] It was Savisaar's reluctance to deregulate prices, opposed by nearly half the cabinet, which led to Tamm's resignation in autumn 1991 and he, in turn, initiated the preparations leading to the creation of the EKE. Some 200 people applied to join the party before its formal inception, about one-third of them state managers, and Tamm was elected chairman unopposed.

Ultimately, the fuel crisis (prices rose between 200 and 300 per cent) and the attendant introduction of rationing in January 1992 precipitated the fall of the Savisaar cabinet and the advent of an EKE government under Vähi. Vähi was formerly an automotive engineer from Valga who had been one of the Estonian delegates at the nineteenth CPSU congress in Moscow in August 1988. He and his ministers immediately resigned their party membership (so as to have free hands in dealing with the *Riigikogu*), leaving Tamm to hold the party fort, so to speak. In power EKE sought to lay the foundations of a 'social market economy': prices were liberalised, export controls were effectively abolished, and Estonian *kroon* was introduced, a visa system with Russia was brought in and measures of privatisation were undertaken. A prior commitment from the government not to take part in the forthcoming general election (public reference was made to the need to avoid the worst excrescences of careerism found elsewhere in Eastern Europe) meant in practice that the EKE could not campaign in its own name: hence the importance of the *Kindel Kodu* umbrella. True, the *Kindel Kodu* programme did not entirely coincide with that of the EKE.

After the September 1992 general election, the EKE emerged as the most effective opposition party. It modernised its programme in March 1993 and performed well at the October 1993 local elections, especially in the capital, subsequently claiming the leading position in Tallinn. Vähi became the new chairman of Tallinn City Council and his EKE colleague, Jaak Tamm, was re-elected mayor for a second term. According to an Emor poll in November 1993, 21 per cent of

Estonian citizens would have voted for the EKE if there had been an election then – three times more than for any other party. Significantly, for EKE, too, another EMOR survey in August 1994 indicated that 61 per cent of respondents held that the government's policies did not correspond to their best interests.[52] EKE's performance in the March 1995 general election is discussed in Chapter 9.

Of the four remaining parliamentary opposition groups between 1992 and 1995, the one-man Entrepreneurs' Party (*Eesti Ettevõtjate Erakond* – EEE) had in common with the larger opposition parties that it was founded and led by a well-known reformist communist. Tiit Made, who left the ECP on 7 November 1989, was one of the signatories of the 'Four-Man Proposal' for the economic self-management (autonomy) of Estonia on 26 September 1987. He was also a former Green and had flirted with both Estonian Social Democratic parties – the Saatpalu and Lauristin groups – as well as Free Estonia before directing the creation of the Entrepreneurs' Party on 2 March 1990. Made, in short, represented the classic case of a *political entrepreneur*.

The party itself may be said to have been built on twin organisational pillars. First, there was the Union of Private Enterprises and Cooperatives (*Eesti Kooperatiivide ja Eraettevõtete Assosiatsiooni Liit*) which was founded in June 1988 (again with Made pulling the strings) and developed contacts both within the Soviet Union and further afield. At the end of November 1989, the union began to run weekly discussion sessions for a membership which at its peak numbered about 300. It drew principally on the so-called 'cooperatives' facilitated by *perestroika*, that is, the private restaurants, coffee shops, small transport firms and so on that had a licence to produce and/or sell goods and services. Second, there was the Small Business Association (*Eesti Väikeettevõtete Assosiatsioon* – EVEA), several of whose members were involved in the EEE's foundation. The employer-based Union of Work Collectives, which was later involved in the creation of the EKE, was also supportive of the Entrepreneurs' Party. One of the specific reasons for the timing of the EEE's foundation, however, was the desire to oppose the Indrek Toome government's proposal to raise taxes on the new (private) 'cooperative' enterprises.

Unlike Raig's EMKE, which has drawn extensively on the class of private farmers, but has not sought narrowly to concentrate upon this social stratum, the Entrepreneurs' Party aspired to precisely the status of *class party*. Its 1992 general election slogan, 'Hard Work, Entrepreneurship and Determination Produces Results', reflected this fact although, ironically, the following year, only about one-third (30 per cent) of its membership comprised entrepreneurs. Made, a populist figure with a broad appeal, also attracted a significant proportion of males between 15 and 37 and, indeed, retired women. In the

opinion polls, the EEE's support stood at 11 per cent among Estonians (3 per cent among non-Estonians) in February 1991, but it
managed only 2.3 per cent at the general election in September 1992.
By Made's own admission, the party erred when, for tactical and
cost-cutting reasons, it ran only one candidate per constituency.[53] On
at least two occasions (at the 1991 party congress and after the 1992
general election) there was discussion of changing the party's name
more accurately to reflect the breadth of its support base (at its inaugural gathering, the discussion focused only on whether to include
'private' in the party's title). The EEE developed international links
only with New Democracy in Sweden and it shared with the latter
an overriding concern to lower taxation and eliminate VAT from
certain items. Before the 1995 general election, Made threw his hand
in with Savisaar's Centre Party and in this way secured his parliamentary future.

A second one-man parliamentary band after the 1992 general election was the Green delegate. The Greens, it will be recalled, were
initially one of the major social movements and in fact the only one
to attract support in roughly equal measure from both Estonians and
non-Estonians. During summer 1989, however, the movement was
debilitated by the cumulative effect of internal power struggles and
Left–Right splits and by the following year two separate Green parties were created, both, ironically, called Estonian Green Party. The
first, the ERP (*Eesti Roheline Partei*), was founded on 10 August 1989
and immediately disowned by the 'mother movement' ERL. It comprised essentially those right-wing elements in ERL that were critical
of what was seen as the PF's 'appeasement policy' towards the
Kremlin and its refusal clearly to demand independence. Indeed,
ERP activists supported the alternative CCM and the election of a
COE. In truth, ERP was at best a 'pale green' affair and its programme did not really deal with environmental questions as such.

The second was the EERE (*Eesti Roheline Erakond*) which was
founded in May 1990 under the leadership of Vello Pohlaa with the
intention of coordinating ERL's political activity. In practice it acted
as something of a subsidiary of the Green Movement. A decline in
overall support for the latter – the result of both its internal bifurcation and the formation of new political parties – may well have been
the primary motivating factor in the decision to set up the ERE.
Ultimately, in December 1991, after two years of fragmentation, a
new party, the Estonian Greens (*Eesti Rohelised* – ER), emerged, based
on the ERP and EKE, as the unified political arm of the Green Movement.[54] In September 1992, only a single Green, Rein Järlik, was
elected to the *Riigikogu*, although by April 1993 support in the opinion polls had risen to 5 per cent. Interestingly, it appears that, since
the achievement of independence, the Green movement, unlike its

'new middle-class' (post-materialist) support base in Western Europe, has been strongest among the less well educated industrial workers.

Two protest groups in the 1992 general election are left to be considered: one 'softline', the Royalists; the other 'hardline', the Estonian Citizens. The Independent Royalists (*Sõltumatud Kuningriiklased*) were founded in September 1989 by Kalle Kulbok (formerly a well-known Green) and seven other enthusiasts in a classroom in the University of Tartu. It was in Tartu, indeed, in late autumn 1980 that Kulbok, then the Komsomol secretary of a building firm, had organised a public debate in an attempt to 'legalise' and mobilise support for the 'Letter of Forty'.[55] The Independent Royalists started out as something of a joke and came to the public's attention by using time on Ralf Parve's satirical television programmes. There is an obvious parallel here with the later and sensational progress of New Democracy in Sweden since, over the winter of 1990–91, Bert Karlsson and Ian Wachtmeister got support for their 'joint venture' from Siewert Öholm in his TV programme *Svar direkt* ('Direct Reply'). The Independent Royalists will be considered again later, but since their foundation they have sought systematically to ridicule the rules of the political game – rules which the other 'serious' parties have tried conscientiously to implement. The Royalists' much-publicised and (to opponents) outrageous opposition to the introduction of a religious service in the *Riigikogu* at the beginning of each week is a case in point. The service was abandoned in late autumn 1993.

The Estonian Citizens (*Eesti Kodanik*), which polled 6.8 per cent in September 1992, were the creation of US army veteran Jüri Toomepuu, who registered his motley collection of independents on the last date for registration and began a campaign costing a mere 500 American dollars only 10 days before the election. Toomepuu embodied a vehemently anti-communist, anti-establishment, personality-oriented populism. The Citizens' slogan in September 1992 summed up their intractable opposition to the Soviet past: 'Ei uhtegi tegelinskit tagasi Toompeale' – 'Not a single one of the old notables back to Toompea [parliament]'. They were backed by a small armed volunteer force which rejected the authority of the Estonian government in favour of the self-appointed 'government in exile' (based in Sweden) in which Toomepuu was the defence minister.[56]

Patterns of Origination in Party Formation

Several of the fledgling parties of the 1988–92 period originated in the personal networks built up around the leading individuals in the Popular Front, figures such as Savisaar, Lauristin and Raig. The PF ultimately spawned five parties: the Greens, Social Democrats, Rural Centre Party, (at least part of) the Liberal Democrats and (People's) Centre Party. While personal rivalries, ambitions and differences in outlook, intensified by the approach of the Estonian Supreme Soviet elections in March 1990, undoubtedly played a part, an important structural factor in the PF's fragmentation was its elevation from social movement to governing bloc. Thus, when the PF formed a cabinet under Savisaar in April 1990, it was placed in the virtually impossible position of being at once the government *and* part of the opposition to Moscow. It was then that a tendency towards bureaucratisation and elitism developed and secessionist pressures grew stronger at the leadership level.[57]

An important source of the original PF networks, incidentally, was the 'Letter of Forty' in October 1980. As noted earlier, the letter became household property and had an explosive effect: the ECP and the KGB claimed that the CIA was behind it, but its popularity among party members created a sense of impotence among the leadership.[58] At least 10 of the 40 later became active figures in the PF.[59]

A second 'resource bank' for the embryonic parties was to be found in the cultural networks of painters, writers and musicians which, from the early 1980s onwards, used 'the arts' as a medium of creative opposition. Particularly important during the second half of the decade was the Cultural Council, comprising four representatives each from the unions of writers, artists, musicians, architects, journalists and film and theatrical staff. Increasingly, contemporary political questions were debated and the Council's opinions published in the weekly *Sirp ja Vasar* ('Hammer and Sickle'). In February 1988, the Cultural Council was given a weekly hour on Estonian radio. A direct transmission, permitting listeners to telephone in questions, this performed important agenda-setting and opinion-building functions.[60] Several leading cultural figures, including the publications committee director, Jaak Joerüüt, writers Teet Kallas and Viivi Luik and artist Enn Põldroos, were instrumental in March 1989 in forming a Free Democratic Party which, as mentioned, quickly merged with another liberal initiative, based on a group of PF activists, to produce the EDLP.[61]

Third, behind the parties of the 'fundamentalist Right' and the ERSP in particular were networks of active nationalists generated by membership of the NHS, the MRP–AEG group and subsequently the CCM. They often identified with one or more of the leading dissidents. Lagle Parek is a case in point. Her family was deported to Novosibirsk in 1949, but she returned to Estonia in 1955 (at the age of 14) and by 1980 much of the informal organisation of dissent emanated from her office at the Tartu branch of the Institute of Cultural Monuments. In 1987, of course, Parek was one of the leading figures in the Hirvepark demonstration which called for the publication of the secret protocols of the Molotov–Ribbentrop pact.

Also active on the radical Right (and elsewhere on the political spectrum) were various émigré networks, especially the contacts maintained by Estonians living in Sweden, Canada and the United States. Thirty-five of the 499 COE seats were reserved for expatriots (some of whom later became members of parliament) and the ERSP quickly developed branch organisations for Estonians living abroad. Significantly, the Laar cabinet, formed after the September 1992 general election, included three Estonian émigrés.

Next, underpinning several of the proto-parties that worked together within the *Isamaa* electoral alliance were entrenched networks of highly educated people linked to university-level institutions. The twin pillars of the nascent Christian Democratic Party (EKDE) were discussion groups, extant since the early 1980s, based on graduates of the Technical University of Tallinn, on the one hand, and humanities graduates in various teacher-training colleges in Estonia, on the other. Ironically, clerical involvement in the EKDE was limited, although the presence of pastors at the mass song festivals in summer 1988 served to raise the profile of the church and the meaning of religion in national life. The young intellectuals in the *Res Publica* group, influenced by New Right ideas in Western Europe, were also the driving force behind the Republican Coalition Party (EVKE), although there was corporate-sector participation, too, especially from the managing directors of those large firms that had been independent of Moscow. Yet despite the role of young intellectuals – several of whom, like Mart Laar and Jüri Luik, went on to ministerial appointments – in the formation of right-wing parties and, to a lesser extent, the Greens, young people in general remained alienated and passive. Significantly, the PF failed to establish a Youth Organisation and a general suspicion towards the 'old guard' was widespread.

A final source in the initiation of political parties in the transition to independence comprised former communist networks based on privilege (and grouped in the Secure Home electoral alliance) which sought to protect the position of old elites in changing times. The Estonian Coalition Party (EKE), in particular, mobilised the *nomenklatura* – former party officials, collective farm managers, planners and so on – often with an advanced training in economics, agronomy or the management sciences. They stood to lose from the shift to a competitive polity, with the attendant elite renewal, and sought to profit from the shift to a competitive economy, with the associated privatisation.

Summing up on the origination of the political parties in Estonia during 1988–92, a number of general points can be made. First, the formation of the parties owed much to the initiative of a nucleus of *political entrepreneurs,* many of whom acquired experience in the business of politics in the late communist (*perestroika*) period and/or the social movements that characterised the transition to independence. However, while many of the active leaders in the movement society went into independence and not politics and subsequently took a back seat, a knot of entrepreneurs went into independence *and* politics and founded their own parties. Hallaste, the Christian Democrat, who by his own account put politics before his work as a cleric; Made, who had a finger in several party 'projects' before going solo; and Lauristin, the 'mother' of the PF and creator of her own social democratic party (when one was already in existence) are clear cases of political entrepreneurs.

Second, the process of party formation was indebted in some measure to a diffusional effect. The emergence of proto-parties bred more embryonic (atomistic) parties, often based on little more than personality conflicts. The anti-Savisaar factor was, as noted, a powerful contributory element in the birth of several nascent groupings, *inter alia* the Social Democratic Independence Party, Liberal Democrats and Free Estonia. The concept of 'party', however, was weakly understood and the Western ideologies upon which several of them were based were largely taken 'on trust'. There was the general elite perception that parties constituted a necessary condition of stable democracy – a view reinforced by Western 'sponsors' – although they inherited from the inter-war years the reputation of being 'hagglers out of touch with the people'.[62]

Third, the Estonian parties were *internally created parties* in the terms of Duverger's classic typology. True, the newly-formed unions of private farmers and private 'cooperative' businesses played a role in the emergence of the Rural Centre and Entrepreneurs' parties. But they defined the active constituencies (membership) of these parties, rather than providing the motor force in their creation. Parties were not the products of organisational ventures: for example, as the political arm of a trade union. Indeed, the level of interest-based associationalism was low and, though Siim Kallas, the chairman of the central trade union organisation, was active in politics, the latter organisation distanced itself from the nascent parties. The Estonian parties, in short, were mooted in private houses and not trade union rooms.

Fourth, in terms of the wider genealogy of the parties and the personal networks of the political entrepreneurs, three 'resource banks' were important. The reformist communists in and around the Free Estonia group staffed the parties to the left of centre: that is, those grouped in the *Kindel Kodu* alliance, especially the Coalition Party (it must readily be allowed that the spatial positioning of the Estonian parties at the time constituted highly treacherous ground and the

EKE undoubtedly saw itself as a right-wing group). The PF provided the active personnel of the centre-based parties: the Centre Party, Rural Centre Party, Social Democrats and Liberal Democrats. The CCM/COE in turn furnished the *Isamaa* bloc and the ERSP. At the individual level, of course, the route map of elite recruitment was far more complicated to draw. Hence, while dissidents and political prisoners instigated the ERSP, not all dissidents (witness Enn Tarto) joined the last-mentioned party. There were former communists, moreover, in the ERSP as well as in *Kindel Kodu*.

Finally, two groups were relatively inactive in the initiation of the political parties: young people and Russian speakers. 'The relative quiescence of the young generation,' it has been observed, 'robbed the social movements of potential sources of energy and dynamism.'[63] The same could be said of the fledgling political parties, with the exception of the young Christians behind the Christian Democratic Party, the young intellectuals involved in the EVKE and a number of university students engaged in the two social democratic parties. The parties of the centre and centre-right in particular attracted essentially middle-aged leaders, many of them 'liberal (young) communists' influenced by Dubcek and the 'Thaw' in the late 1960s. The involvement of Russian-speaking activists in the Estonian parties was effectively confined to the social democratic movement. Otherwise, party formation was an exclusively Estonian occupation.

Notes

1   Marjut Kuokkanen, 'Puolueiden muodostaminen Virossa', *Ulkopolitiikka*, **4**, 1991, p.53.
2   Interview with Tunne Kelam, 19 September 1993.
3   Interview with Lagle Parek, 14 September 1993.
4   Erik Andersen, 'Hvis der var valg i Estland', *Nordisk Østforum*, **4**, 1989, pp.71–6. See also Erik Andersen, 'Estland: På vej mod selstændighed?', *Nordisk Østforum*, 3, 1989, pp.35–40.
5   Marju Lauristin, Peeter Vihalemm and Rein Ruutsoo, *Viron vapauden tuulet* (Gummerus: Jyväskylä–Helsinki, 1989), pp.156–7.
6   Rein Taagepera, 'The Baltic States', in a special issue on 'Elections in Eastern Europe', *Electoral Studies*, **9**, (4), 1990.
7   Interview with ERSP *Riigikogu* member K. Jaak Roosare, 26 May 1993.
8   Rein Ruutsoo, 'Transitional Society and Social Movements in Estonia', *Estonian Academy of Science, Humanities and Social Sciences*, **42**, (2), 1993, pp.208–9.
9   Rein Taagepera, *Estonia. Return to Independence* (Westview: Boulder–San Francisco–Oxford, 1993), pp.184–5.
10   Interview with Tunne Kelam, 19 September 1993.
11   'New head to coalition party', *The Baltic Independent*, 23–9 July 1993.
12   'Estniskt förband gjorde myteri', *Svenska Dagbladet*, 5 August 1993.
13   Among the founding figures was Eve Pärnaste, although she was not a mem-

ber of the *Riigikogu*. The Future Party claimed to have 300 members and to be aiming at 1000.

14   The party would appear to have financial backers since it has been able to run television commercials. One showed a young boy getting out of bed and holding a globe at his open window. Presumably this was intended to symbolise the need to build a society full of open, inquiring minds. To invert the axiom, 'in corporo sano: 'healthy in mind, healthy in body'.

15   'Estonia grants residence rights to ex-Soviet officers' *The Baltic Independent*, 26 November–2 December 1993.

16   Interview with Illar Hallaste, 14 September 1993. Hallaste studied law at Tartu University, but left in his third year in 1979 for 'religious and political reasons'. He later studied theology in Tallinn and trained as a priest. Conditions for Christians were extremely oppressive and Hallaste's experience was not uncommon. Indeed, an employee was frequently handed his or her last pay packet or fired out of the university for 'religious reasons'. In order to hold religious services, moreover, each minister had to obtain a licence which was confiscated whenever the KGB believed that he had been 'disloyal' See Mare Kukk, 'Political Oppression in Soviet Estonia 1940–1987', *Journal of Baltic Studies*, **XXIV**, (4), 1993, pp.369–82, especially p.380.

17   Kuokkanen, 'Puolueiden muodostaminen Virossa', p.52. Also Marjut Kuokkanen, *Puolueiden muotoutuminen Virossa 1988–1992* (Politiikan tutkimuksen laitoksen tutkimuksia, 127, 1994: Tampereen yliopisto, 1994), pp.53–8, 89–92.

18   Interview with Enn Tarto. Paradoxically, *Kaitse Liit*, although founded by the Conservative People's Party, also lost support to it, at least in so far as its members were not permitted to become actively involved in party politics.

19   Interview with Paul-Erik Rummo, 14 September 1993.

20   'Liberaaliperhe kasvaa ja kukoistaa', *Polttopiste*, 10 September 1993.

21   Tõnu Vare, 'Miksi just Lennart Meri?', *Mõõdukad Valimisleht*, September 1992, p.4.

22   *Uus Valik Mõõdukad* (ESDP kirjastus: Tallinn, 1992), p.18.

23   Interview with Andres Mandre, 14 September 1993.

24   Interview with Vello Saatpalu, 13 September 1993.

25   The EDTE was not registered for the Supreme Soviet elections in March 1990. Saatpalu personally requested registration from Rüütel, without success. Saatpalu was, however, represented as an individual in both the Supreme Soviet and the Congress of Estonia.

26   Taagepera, *Estonia*, p.115.

27   'Social democracy to fill in for Communism', *Homeland*, 10 January 1990.

28   The meeting at Kallas' house involved Kallas, Allik, Titma and Kahma for the nascent Free Estonia group and Ruutsoo, Lauristin, Veidemann and Kaevats for the Social Democrats. It lasted four hours and, according to one of the participants, broke up when Lauristin peremptorily declared that Titma, the ECP's former ideological secretary, 'had never been a left-wing politician'!

29   'Social democracy returns to Estonia', *Homeland*, 24 January 1990.

30   It was an academic contact, discussing Leetsaar's paper at the Institute of Economics, that brought the two leading figures together.

31   'Private property legalized', *The Estonian Independent*, 27 June 1990.

32   On 8 April 1993 the constitutions of state farms and collective farms became invalid under new privatisation laws.

33   Eesti Maa-Keskerakond: *Põhikiri, Põhiprogramm*, pp.10–12.

34   Information provided by the party secretary of the Rural Centre Party, Uku Hänni.

35   'Tariffs on Russian flour', *The Baltic Independent*, 27 August–2 September 1993.

36   Taagepera, *Estonia*, p.196; interview with Peet Kask, 21 June 1994.

37 Interview with Kullo Arjakas, 21 June 1994; see also, 'Miks ma R-is olen', *Eesti Aeg*, 17 September 1991.
38 Anatole Lieven, *The Baltic Revolution: Estonia, Latvia, Lithuania and the Path to Independence* (Yale University: New Haven–London, 1993), p.279.
39 Svennik Høyer, Epp Lauk and Peeter Vihalemm, *Towards a Civic Society: The Baltic Media's Long Road to Freedom* (Nota Baltica: Tartu, 1993), pp.279–83.
40 Rein Taagepera, 'Running for President of Estonia: A Political Scientist in Politics', *Political Science and Politics*, June 1993, pp.302–4.
41 Taagepera, *Estonia*, p.198.
42 Lauristin *et al.*, *Viron vapauden tuulet*, p.218.
43 Taagepera, *Estonia*, p.150.
44 Lauristin *et al.*, *Viron vapauden tuulet*, p.246.
45 Interview with Arvo Sirendi, 22 June 1994.
46 David Arter, *Bumpkin against Bigwig*: The Emergence of a Green Movement in Finnish Politics (Tampereen yliopiston politiikan tutkimuksen laitoksen tutkimuksia, 47, 1978), pp.17–90.
47 Interview with the Estonian Democratic Justice Union MP, Professor Raoul Üksvärav, 27 May 1993.
48 Interview with Arnold Rüütel, 20 June 1994.
49 For *Vaba Eesti*'s critique of Savisaar, see 'Nya politiska strider efter folkomröstningen', *Hufvudstadsbladet*, 16 March 1991.
50 Interview with Jaak Allik, 12 September 1993.
51 Interview with Tiit Vähi, 11 January 1994.
52 'Reasonable politicians merge', *The Baltic Independent*, 1–7 April 1994.
53 Interview with Tiit Made, 15 September 1993.
54 Kuokkanen, 'Puolueiden muotoutuminen', pp.77–83; see also Tor Bjørklund, 'The Green Orientation among Estonians compared with Scandinavians', paper presented at WAPOR Regional Seminar, Tallinn, 11–12 June 1993.
55 'Royalists tilt at Kingdoms', *The Baltic Independent*, 12–18 November 1993, see also, Sirje Kiin, Rein Ruutsoo and Andres Tarand, *Neljankymmenen kirje* (Otava: Keuruu, 1990), p.111.
56 Lieven, *The Baltic Revolution*, p.73.
57 Ruutsoo, 'Transitional Society', p.208.
58 Lauristin *et al.*, *Viron vapauden tuulet*, pp.103–13.
59 Ibid., p.112.
60 Ibid., pp.141–2.
61 Enn Põldroos, 'Oh seda vaest demokraatiat ehk legend rahvussühtsusest', *Päevaleht* 28 May 1993.
62 Rain Rosimannus, 'Parteistunud Eesti on vaid kukujtelm V', *Hommikuleht*, 30 July 1993.
63 Ruutsoo, 'Transitional Society', p.211; Kuokkanen, 'Puolueiden muotoutuminen', p.30. The typical PF supporter, for example was aged between 35 and 64 years and had a working-class job in Tallinn, while only 25 per cent of its followers possessed an academic education.

8 Estonia: The Challenges of Party-building in an Anti-party System

> I am sure that great changes will take place in the Estonian political landscape in the near future and in a few years' time there will be only two or three large and influential parties in Estonia. (Aleksei Semyonov: speech at the Annual Meeting of the Russian Assembly, May 1994)

It was significant that by no means all the groupings vying for *Riigikogu* seats in September 1992 called themselves political parties in the sense of using the international loan word *partei*. The word 'party' possessed a pejorative connotation resulting from, among other things, its association with the former ruling ECP and, consequently, the somewhat dated term *erakond* was preferred, especially by right-wing groups, to denote a break with the communist past and a new beginning. Nonetheless, the mass political culture was largely antipathetic to the new parties. Survey data before the 1992 general election revealed that only one in 10 Estonians and one in 20 non-Estonians 'believed in' parties. The only institution Estonians trusted less than parties was in fact the Russian army stationed in Estonia! The police, courts and trade unions all rated more highly than the political parties.[1] The transition to pluralist democracy, in short, saw Estonia display the three primary features of an *anti-party system* set out earlier in this study.

Estonia as an Anti-party System

Relatively Low Levels of Partisan Voting

First, in striking contrast to the situation in Western Europe, where MPs are, in practice, elected as members of a party, the significance of the partisanship of candidates in determining Estonian voter choice at the polls in September 1992 was relatively low when compared with the role of their personality and past history. So much is borne out in a survey of 1000 citizens conducted in October 1992 which revealed that only 31 per cent of respondents regarded the party orientation of candidates as important, compared with over half who viewed the personality and/or 'pedigree' (past record and so on) of the candidate as decisive in their electoral choice (see Table 8.1). 'Personality voting' was particularly strong, it seems, among candidates of *Kindel Kodu*, the Moderates and Independent Royalists. A week after the September election, moreover, one-quarter of voters could not even remember the party coalition their candidate belonged to.[2]

Table 8.1   The basis of candidate choice at the 1992 Estonian general election (per cent)

Non-Soviet background or strong personality	52
Party orientation	31
Circumstantial factors	8

Note: N = 1000.

A year after the general election partisanship in Estonia remained relatively weak when viewed in a wider European context. When, in 1993, Estonian voters were asked the question 'Do you feel close to a party?', only 13 per cent replied in the affirmative, in contrast to a European Union (EU) average of 30 per cent. The proportion of strong identifiers among Estonian respondents was 17 per cent whereas it was a mere 5 per cent among non-Estonians. Furthermore, when this small minority of strong partisans is examined more closely, it transpires that almost half (44 per cent) were 'merely sympathetic' to a party; 34 per cent stated they were 'fairly close' and only 17 per cent were 'very close'.

Estonia fared no better when levels of partisan identification were compared with the situation in post-communist Eastern Europe. As Table 8.2 demonstrates, Estonian levels were on a par with Poland, but were little more than one-third of the number of Czechs identifying with a political party and only just over half of the number of Hungarians doing so. Volatility has also been high in Estonia. In a poll conducted five months after the 1992 parliamentary elections it transpired that only 44 per cent of voters had persevered with their party preference at the election.

Table 8.2   Party identification in Eastern Europe, 1992–3

Country	Year	Partisan identifiers (%)
Czech Republic	1993	36
Slovakia	1993	31
Hungary	1992	23
Poland	1992	13
Estonia	1993	13
Estonians in Estonia	1993	17
Non-Estonians	1993	7

Source: Rain Rosimannus, 'Full-Fledged Multi-Party System in Estonia is a Mere Imagin-ation', transcript of material appearing in *Hommikuuleht*, 26 July–3 August 1993, p.3, kindly made available by the author.

During the Soviet era, of course, elections were essentially focused on individuals, and a 'personality element' was perpetuated in the new electoral system adopted in April 1992. True, the single transfer-able voting system (STV), used for the December 1989 local govern-ment elections and the ESS elections in March 1990, was abandoned and a PR list voting system adopted, precisely because, it was claimed, STV was suited to 'multi-candidate elections', but not to a *multi-party* poll. But in the new PR system the personality factor was retained, in three ways. First, as with the Finnish system, voters cast an indi-vidual preference vote – writing the unique code number of the candidate on the ballot paper – and did not simply opt for a party list. Second, unlike the practice in Finland, independent candidates were permitted to stand. Third, if a candidate received sufficient personal votes to achieve the district electoral quota (that is, the total valid vote divided by the number of seats to be filled), he or she was automatically elected. Only personal votes, in short, were relevant at this first stage in the allocation of seats. Because of the high district quota, however, only a relatively small minority of 17 per cent of candidates were elected on the strength of their personal ballot alone (see Table 8.3).

Importantly, after the initial allocation of seats on the basis of personal votes, the distribution arrangements were designed to favour the parties. Thus, at the second stage of counting, seats were allocated on the basis of the total party list: the total party list was divided by the electoral quota. If seats still remained to be filled (there were 60 altogether in September 1992) they were to be trans-ferred to a national pool for allocation in proportion to the national votes of those parties exceeding a 5 per cent threshold of the total

Table 8.3   **The allocation of seats by personal preference, party list and compensation mandates in the September 1992** *Riigikogu* **election**

Party/Electoral Alliance	PP	PL	CM	Total
Isamaa	7	10	12	29
Secure Home	2	5	10	17
Popular Front	1	3	11	15
Moderates	1	1	10	12
ENIP	1	2	7	10
Royalists	2	1	5	8
Estonian Citizens	1	2	5	8
Greens	1	0	0	1
Entrepreneurs'	1	0	0	1
	17	24	60	101

Notes:
PP = Personal preference (the first stage).
PL = Party list (the second stage).
CM = National compensation (mandates) – the third stage of seat allocation.

vote. A modified d'Hondt divisor was then deployed in respect of the national lists of party candidates.

Although no Independent candidates were elected in September 1992, they often polled far more than the 200 or less votes which sufficed to elect the lowest-placed deputies on the party lists, a fact tending to confirm the importance of candidate-based, compared with partisan, voting. The most extreme case was that of Toivo Uustalo who was elected for the Estonian Citizens' list in Põlva, Valga and Võru with only 51 votes. He climbed into parliament on the back of the extraordinary popularity of Jüri Toomepuu, whose individual poll of nearly 17 000 was comfortably the highest in the country.

Indeed, despite the complexities of the electoral system (little understood by voters) and its attempt to elevate 'party' above 'personality', it is clear that far more salient for the majority of voters than a candidate's partisan affiliation was the importance attached to a 'clean' past and the absence of a history of (close) association with the previous regime. This preference for 'new blood appointments' was well illustrated by the case of an Estonian expatriate, working as an attorney at law in the United States, who travelled back to Estonia only a week before polling, ran a vigorous media campaign – which hammered home his candidate number with a variety of jingles – and was duly elected for the ERSP in the Tartu district. It was also reflected in the success rate of candidates connected with the COE, a counter-elite which had eschewed any dealings with the occupation state.

The Drop in Electoral Turnout after Regaining Independence

A second feature of the Estonian anti-party system was the extent of electoral abstentionism: that is, popular 'support' for what the Finns call the 'sleeping party' or what the German Andreas Dimpfel dubbed his 'Party of Non-Voters'.[3] The contrast between the mass mobilisation of the revolutionary period – in particular between the high turnout at the March 1991 referendum on restoring national independence – and the demobilisation which followed the achievement of independence was striking. Indeed, the scale of political mobilisation during 1988–91 is worth recalling briefly.

Following the ECP central committee plenary on 9 September 1988, which was broadcast live and engendered massive popular interest, 21 480 letters were addressed to the ESS supporting the proposed amendments to the ESSR constitution, and this correspondence was underwritten by no fewer than 861 987 signatures. After the momentous 'declaration on sovereignty' on 16 November the same year, moreover, crowds jammed the entire route from Liberty Square to Toompea. As Väljas has recalled, the walk from his home to parliament, which normally took 15 minutes, took him over one and a half hours that day.

There was an extremely high level of popular involvement – an estimated 87 per cent turnout overall and as much as 95 per cent among Estonians – at the March 1989 elections to the Congress of People's Deputies in Moscow, despite uncertainties about the electoral system and a boycott by the ERSP.[4] It was a similar story of an extremely high turnout at the COE elections on 24 February 1990. According to final figures published in *Helsingin Sanomat*, 591 508 citizens voted, out of about 700 000 registered (other estimates put the numbers registered at 630–650 000) making a turnout of between 84.2 per cent and 93.7 per cent.[5]

A creditable 78.3 per cent of *all* residents voted at the ESS elections on 18 March 1990, notwithstanding the fact that the newly constituted COE called the legitimacy of the ESS into question, it was the second election within a month for 'citizens', and the ERSP canvassed a boycott of the poll. The ESS ballot, moreover, was held under a new election law. This enfranchised all 18-year-old residents, reserved four of the 105 ESS seats for representatives of the Soviet military stationed in Estonia, but removed such flagrant anomalies as the right of Russian tourists to vote in a special ballot box in the railway station. Candidates (there were 392 altogether) were required to have lived in Estonia for 10 years and be at least 21 years of age. In general, turnout was somewhat higher in the rural areas than in the towns.[6]

Table 8.4 documents the sharp decline in turnout in Estonia at the three popular votes held from 3 March 1991 to 20 September 1992. From a notable 83 per cent of *all* Estonian residents who voted at the 3 March 1991 referendum on restoring the national independence and sovereignty of Estonia (mobilisation topped 90 per cent in strong Estonian-speaking areas such as Hiidenmaa) turnout declined to 66.3 per cent by the constitutional referendum on 28 June 1992. Estonian citizens were then asked to vote on the question of approving a new form of government and whether those (approximately 5000 people) who had applied for citizenship before 1 June 1992 should be allowed to participate in the forthcoming parliamentary and presidential elections. Indeed, concerned about the negative impact on the mood of voters of the recent currency shift from the rouble to the kroon and the general inertia bound up with the summer holiday period, Mart Rask, the minister of justice, made a specific appeal to voters via the media to turn out at the referendum. This was in order

Table 8.4   The decline in electoral turnout in Estonia between the 26 March 1990 Congress of People's Deputies' elections and the general election of September 1992

26 March 1989   Elections to the Congress of People's Deputies in Moscow. Turnout 87 per cent.

24 February 1990   Congress of Estonia elections. Turnout among 'citizens' estimated at between 84.2 per cent and 93.7 per cent.

18 March 1990   Elections to the Estonian Supreme Soviet. Turnout 78.3 per cent.

3 March 1991   Consultative referendum on the question: 'Are you in favour of restoring the national independence and sovereignty of Estonia?' Turnout 83 per cent; 78 per cent in favour.

28 June 1992   Consultative referendum on two questions: (1) approving the draft of a new constitution; (2) whether those who had applied for citizenship before 1 June 1992 should be allowed to vote in the forthcoming parliamentary and presidential elections.

(1)   Turnout 66.3 per cent; approved by 92.2 per cent.

(2)   Turnout 66.3 per cent; rejected by 52.0 per cent.

20 September 1992   Simultaneous presidential and parliamentary (*Riigikogu*) elections. Turnout 66.9 per cent.

to achieve the threshold of one-half of the eligible electorate necessary to validate the result.[7]

A small episode may be noted, moreover, in so far as it symptomised wider elite fears that, after (what emerged as) a dull campaign, turnout at the parliamentary and presidential elections on 20 September 1992 would fall still further.[8] Arrangements were made for bussing into the country those Estonians living in Petserimaa on the Russian side of Estonia's south-eastern border (an area allocated to Estonia by the 1920 Treaty of Tartu, but conjoined to the Russian Federation by Stalin in 1940) in order that they could go to the polls.[9] By the time of the local government elections in October 1993, turnout among the Estonian-speaking population had dropped further. Whereas 83 per cent of Tartu voters used their ballots at the 3 March 1991 referendum, only 34 per cent did so in October 1993.

The growing disengagement of the electorate from politics over the 18-month period between spring 1991 and early autumn 1992 warrants emphasis. The 3 March 1991 referendum focused on the paramount question of renewed independence (a contemporaneous referendum was held on the same issue in Latvia) and it was intended as a demonstrative riposte to the pan-Soviet vote which Gorbachev had called for 17 March (that is, two weeks later) on approving a new All-Union Treaty. The Estonian authorities had determined to boycott the latter. The 3 March vote was also staged at a time when there were increased trappings of independence – for example, two days before the ballot, and following an agreement with the Soviet Ministry of the Interior (in contrast to Lithuania and Moldova where the step was taken unilaterally), the Estonian militia was transformed into a national police force – but the real thing was proving elusive. Both Estonians and Russians were entitled to vote and the referendum question was formulated in both languages. Significantly, too, social movements representing both ethnic communities canvassed voters. The executive organ, the Council of Estonia, which initially opposed the referendum, insisting that the 24 February 1918 declaration of independence remained legally binding, ultimately exhorted voters to favour independence; the Intermovement, in contrast, urged its supporters to vote 'no'. In Narva, moreover, it appears that a counterreferendum was mooted on whether a 'sovereign Estonia' should continue to form part of the Soviet Union.[10]

In the event, there was a marked contrast both in turnout and in popular support for the restoration of independence. In the Estonian-speaking areas, especially in the countryside, levels of mobilisation were high. In Pärnu in the south-west, for example, 85 per cent voted and 86 per cent of these favoured the restoration of independence. In the predominantly Russian-speaking areas in the north-east, turnout was lower, and so was support for independence. In Sillamäe only 27 per cent voted, of whom 40 per cent backed independence; in Narva the figures were 70 per cent and 25 per cent respectively, and in Kohtla-Järv 70 per cent and 46 per cent. Since over nine-tenths of the Narva population was Russian-speaking, it is clear that, despite Intermovement agitation, a proportion of the national ethnic minority preferred an independent Estonia.[11]

Incidentally, the hardline communist-controlled town councils in Narva, Sillamäe and Kohtla-Järv opted to defy the Estonian boycott and participate in the All-Union referendum on 17 March, while in Tallinn the ECP and Soviet army urged the Russian-speaking population to do likewise. According to *Tass* the turnout in Estonia on 17 March was 25 per cent, although there were, it seems, irregularities in electoral practice and several notable cases of multiple voting. One Erik Kutmetsov was reported to have voted in seven voting districts in Tallinn in the space of a mere three hours.[12] Crucially, though, the Estonian-speaking population did not vote.

The much-reduced turnout of 66.9 per cent at the general election 18 months later may be regarded in some measure as a product of electoral fatigue. This was the third occasion on which Estonians had been asked to vote in relatively short order and, with independence achieved, there were no electoral issues of remotely comparable magnitude. Equally, the parties, which had emerged in numbers, largely failed to differentiate themselves by projecting clear electoral alternatives. They clustered around the national question and deployed a resonant but essentially passé nationalist rhetoric. The electorate, moreover, was primarily interested in the simultaneous presidential contest. The presidential candidates were generally familiar to voters – whereas many standing for the *Riigikogu* were not – and in turn tended to give an identity to the electoral lists.[13] It is a reasonable surmise that turnout at the parliamentary election would have been still lower had it not been for the concurrent vote for a head of state.

Turnout was notably low among people below the age of 24 years. A generally poor response among young voters also characterised the first post-communist local election in Estonia in October 1993. Indeed, in the university town of Tartu at least it appeared that, the greater the extent of economic marginalisation, the higher the level of voter activity. Pensioners (who also campaigned on behalf of low-income groups in general) secured 19 of the 49 seats on Tartu town council, prompting *The Baltic Independent* to lead with the story, 'Pensioners to govern the city of youth'.[14]

In a wider post-communist perspective, it might be argued that the level of electoral participation in Estonia since the regaining of independence has been comparatively good. At the Polish general election of September 1993, turnout was only 53 per cent, broadly the same level as voted to approve Yeltsin's constitution in the Russian Federation on 12 December the same year. In Lithuania, moreover, the 2 November 1993 by-election in the Kaišindorys region had to be staged again because only 36 per cent of the electorate turned out to vote.[15] Nonetheless, the contrast between the present downward electoral trend and the popular activism of the 'Singing Revolution' is striking.

Tied in with the accentuated demobilisation went a marked decline in interest in politics: *depoliticisation*. The number of Estonians claiming to be 'very interested' or 'fairly interested' in politics almost halved between 1989 and 1993 (see Table 8.5) and fell to levels comparable to those of the 1970s and early 1980s when the number who regarded politics and public affairs as important never exceeded 40 per cent.[16] To an extent, the press must bear responsibility for this, at least at the time of the September 1992 elections. Journalists did not in general comment on the progress of the campaign, what the parties stood for and even what the presidential candidates said during the television debates.[17]

Indeed, it may be said that after Estonia regained its independence, the media both reflected and reinforced the prevalent anti-party attitudes. Leading politicians have in practice been unable to publish newspaper pieces which present party policy; rather, the contribution has had to appear as a personal view signed by the author him or herself. Equally, if an article has attempted to be too political and didactic in content it has proved self-defeating (it has been skipped by the ordinary public) and to gain a readership the content has had to be suitably diluted and 'livened up'. In practice, only information from the *Riigikogu* parliamentary factions (groups) has escaped the tight editing (self-imposed or otherwise) which has been the fate of other political contributions.

Table 8.5 The percentage of Estonians 'very interested' or 'fairly interested' in politics, 1989–93

June 1989	91
March 1991	78
September 1992	52
May 1993	50

The Existence of 'Anti-Parties'

The third characteristic of the Estonian anti-party system has been the existence of numerically significant 'anti-parties', diametrically opposed to the agenda and/or style of other political groupings. In the hardline category, there has been the Estonian Citizens, an anti-party political movement, at odds with the new constitution, which sought the restoration of the 1938 form of government. By contrast, the Independent Royalists have been 'softline', marked more by the irreverence of their approach than any root-and-branch opposition to the rules of the political game.

When a US Information Agency Poll, conducted shortly before the September 1992 general election, revealed only 14 per cent support for the political parties, the 62-year-old American Estonian, Jüri Toomepuu, a systems analyst by training, drew the obvious conclusion that in order to be successful it was imperative not to set up a political party! Accordingly, a month before polling, he pulled a group of independent candidates 'off the streets' and set up the Estonian Citizens as an anti-party umbrella organisation. In the space of a mere four weeks, moreover, a vigorous campaign transformed Toomepuu into the best-supported politician in Estonia. Local newspapers were 'blitzed'; local radio stations rang out with his personal jingle, based on a well-known Estonian nursery rhyme about the 'Toomepuu' or Bird-Cherry Tree which blooms in the spring; and a battered mini-bus was commandeered to take Toomepuu on a whistle-stop tour of the Polva, Valga and Voru constituency. In countless speeches, the US army veteran conjured up a series of military images designed to communicate to ordinary people a judicious mix of strength and compassion. 'Officers', he told them, 'never eat before their soldiers are fed' and 'officers always care for the sick and wounded'. The demagogic Toomepuu made no concrete election promises, preferring, when encountering people in shops and at bus shelters, to contrast the position of the (few) 'haves' and the (overwhelming majority of) 'have-nots'. In particular, he compared the pensions of ordinary people with those of politicians in the ESS. Toomepuu's sensational success sent shock-waves through the political classes and it became commonplace to hear him described as 'the most dangerous politician in Estonia'.

The Estonian Citizens were anti-systemic in the sense that they were working for two radical constitutional changes. First, they argued for thoroughgoing electoral reform and attacked the inequity of the situation which arose in September 1992 when unsuccessful Independents polled substantially more votes than successful lower-placed candidates on the party lists. Toomepuu expressed a strong preference for the introduction of a US- or UK-style single-member, simple plurality system. Second, so as to enhance the political influence of ordinary people, the Estonian Citizens advocated upgrading the status of the popular initiative so that the ensuing referendum vote would become binding on parliament. The result of a popular initiative could be overruled by a two-thirds majority in the *Riigikogu*. Before forming the Estonian Citizens, Toomepuu had some involvement in the 'Movement to Restore the 1938 Constitution' led by Endel Lippmaa (he described it as 'inept') and was highly critical of the 28 June 1992 constitutional referendum which, he insisted, only offered citizens a choice between the old Soviet document and the new proposal (that is, it excluded the 1938 option).[18] Constitutional reform, in short, has been an important *raison d'être*.

In addition to wanting to revise the basic system groundrules so as to enhance the political rights of Estonian citizens, Toomepuu, fearful of ultimate Russian control of Estonia, controversially argued the need for a well-financed programme of repatriation and decolonisation carried out under the auspices of the United Nations. Lacking the '100 000 dollars that could wipe out the government', the Estonian Citizens' propaganda for the October 1993 local government elections simply juxtaposed a list of the *Isamaa*-dominated government's promises in 1992 with their track record of failing to keep any of them! Above all, the Estonian Citizens maintained throughout a strong line in conspiracy theory. The government was said to have passed into the hands of the former enemies of Estonia because all the senior ministers had a communist past (simply untrue). Indeed, Toomepuu claimed that the documentary evidence he had amassed proved that the president himself, Lennart Meri, was a KGB agent. In all this, one thing was clear, namely, in the words of its architect, 'No Jüri Toomepuu, no Estonian Citizens'.

The distinctive feature of the Independent Royalists has been their ribald rhetoric and generally irreverent style. The venom and vitriol of Toomepuu's tone have stood in sharp contrast to the levity and jocularity of the Royalists' behaviour. In the 1992 election campaign their leaders appeared in public wearing everything from shamanistic head-dresses to dustbin-liners.[19] They also offered voters nothing but fairy-stories, their leader, the self-styled Territorial Marshal (*maamarssal*) Kalle Kulbok, subsequently comparing their light-hearted style to Wachtmeister and Karlsson's New Democracy in Sweden.

Initially, the Independent Royalists had no particular pretender to the throne in mind, although they indicated that the Swedish Crown-Prince Karl Philip was the type of person who would be well-suited to become King of Estonia. In June 1994, however, Kulbok surprised Buckingham Palace (and almost everybody else!) by writing to the Queen to request that her younger son, Prince Edward, become the first King of Estonia. The letter insisted: 'Your background as an actor and television producer would be ideal to create the majesty which a new king would require in order to combine ancient culture with modern political reality.' According to Kulbok, Prince Edward was young, royal, artistic and talented![20] In any event, rejecting orthodox Left–Right politics, the Royalists have viewed monarchy as in no small measure a magnet with which to attract business investment and tourism into Estonia.[21]

From the very outset, the Independent Royalists systematically ridiculed both the old and new class of Estonian politicians and the rules they sought diligently to apply. Nonetheless, they counted several competent economists among their parliamentary number and contributed in a generally responsible way to the process of policy making. In 1992, the Independent Royalists were clearly able to trade off the widespread disillusion with the party system. In this context, *The Times* correspondent, Anatole Lieven, recorded how in September 1992 he asked a Royalist voter if she really wanted a king. 'Oh no,' she replied. 'I am a very moderate Royalist!' He added that few Royalist supporters seemed to have heard the widespread rumours that they were not a joke after all, but a group deliberately and secretly created by Savisaar to split the right–wing vote.[22]

In any event, the joking continued. Typically, in response to a referendum organised by the local councils in the Russian-dominated towns of Narva and Sillamäe on 16–17 July 1993, in which residents were asked if they wanted regional autonomy, the Independent Royalists organised their own 'counterreferendum' elsewhere in Estonia. The question put was: 'Is it your wish that Vladimir Chuikin (the communist hardliner) be granted the title of President of Narva and bestowed with rights equal to those of other presidents?' The Royalists requested everyone living in Estonia to mail their answer and, if it was in the affirmative, to supply autobiographical details of how long they had been an ECP member and what perks they had received![23]

The grounds for the existence of a mass anti-party culture are not difficult to divine. Above all, the concept of party was tarred with the brush of *the* party – the ruling ECP – and, accordingly, associated in the minds of ordinary people with an authoritarian and repressive past they preferred to put behind them. The ECP under Vaino and his predecessors had effectively crushed civil society, leaving its prospective members to ponder an inhuman and unethical choice. As portrayed by Marju Lauristin at the PF's inaugural congress in 1988, this choice lay between 'party membership and integrity; party membership and compassion; party membership and the freedom of the Estonian nation'.[24] First and foremost, then, popular anti-partism constituted a powerful statement of anti-communism.

For many electors, moreover, the sheer multiplicity of parties was confusing and disorienting and the presence of so many competing groupings appeared to symbolise the destruction of the unity and fraternity of the revolutionary period. The 'Singing Revolution' was a cathartic experience – a collective purging of the lies and fears of the past and the generation of a new solidarity, conviction and set of aspirations for the future. On 11 September 1988, it will be recalled, no less than 300 000 people (one-third of the entire Estonian population) gathered in the Song Stadium in Tallinn. Mass mobilisation on this scale betokened the incipient collapse of the hierarchical Soviet system and the recreation of civil society. Only four years later, however, the emergence of a plethora of parties substituted a picture of conflict for the previous show of unity. Ironically, at an election meeting in September 1992, an elderly lady, bemoaning the state of things, inquired why it was not possible to have just one party. On being politely advised by the candidate that this was exactly the situation Estonians had sung out in protest against, she relented somewhat and declared: 'All right, then, three or four parties, but not more!'

Finally, the emergence of the embryonic parties also coincided with an economic downturn and the inevitable hardships, especially the rise in the cost of living, involved in the shift to a market economy. The parties could offer no panaceas for the teething troubles of privatisation and also suffered to a degree from the perceived inability of democracy to deliver the economic goods.[25] Significantly, in this context, the trade union movement, concerned about the likely drop in its membership, distanced itself from the political parties, including perhaps its most natural ally, the Social Democrats. Clearly, therefore, despite the emergence of an entrepreneurial class and some signs of improved economic times to come, the challenge for the Estonian parties in a predominantly anti-party system was to create a political culture in which parties were accepted as legitimate (or at least efficient) instruments of representation and interest articulation.

The ingrained culture and tradition of voting for individuals, however, may prove difficult to eradicate, especially in a country where the Estonian population (compared with the predominantly Russian-speaking non-citizens) numbers little more than that of Greater Manchester. The assessment of the *Riigikogu* election of September 1992, undertaken by the International Foundation for Electoral Systems, concluded that, in the future, 'those candidates who adopt a more personalised campaign should have an advantage … The framers of the electoral law who hoped it would consolidate "parties" over "personalities" may well be disappointed to find that their intentions are somewhat frustrated by the combined actions of the candidates and voters.'[26]

The Challenges of Party-building

In an anti-party system, the challenges facing the political parties are particularly demanding and involve a paramount commitment to the socialisation, mobilisation and organisation of citizens, that is to the process of society-building. It was recognised by the aforementioned team of international election observers that, in order to counteract the twin maladies of depoliticisation and demobilisation, the parties will need to contribute to a programme of civic education, focusing on the rights and responsibilities of individuals in a democratic society.[27] Indeed, against the backdrop of the high levels of abstentionism among young people and the confusion which exists about the political and electoral systems, notably among the elderly and those resident in outlying rural areas, a rudimentary attempt can now be made to consider the more specific challenges of party building in Estonia. This will be done by reference to the three stages in the cycle, from inception to institutionalisation set out in Chapter 1.

Depersonalisation

At the time of the September 1992 general election, the parties, with the possible exception of the ERSP, had only a relatively weak popular identity; instead, public recognition tended to be conferred on the 'notables' leading them. Toomepuu, Made, Lauristin and Savisaar were obvious examples. So, too, was Ivar Raig, whose popularity dated back to 1985–6, when he spoke out publicly against the 'Red Barons' and the 'small empires' which, as *kolkhoz* and *solkhoz* leaders, they controlled. During the 18 March 1990 ESS election campaign, Raig worked the Viljandi mulgimaa district extremely hard, addressing two or three meetings daily, bedecked in a traditional Viljandi coat which he wore to symbolise the pre-communist past. Indeed, since there was no residence requirement, Raig selected the Viljandi area precisely because it was the home of the dominant inter-war Estonian politician and head of state, Konstantin Päts. Confident of election, Raig held only two meetings before the 1992 general election (he was abroad for most of the campaign) and was still comfortably returned to parliament.

   If the 'personality factor' was paramount, this is not to suggest that 'notable' and party could be correctly associated by ordinary people. The vast majority of the electorate could doubtless have cited one or other of the leading politicians in their region, but it is highly questionable whether they would have been able to connect these leaders with the parties they led (in Raig's case, for example, the Rural Centre Party). Interestingly, a local journalist speculated that probably about three-quarters of the voters in the Tartu district constituency would have come up with the name of Enn Tarto – the prominent dissident and the last political prisoner to be released – if asked to quote one of their 13 *Riigikogu* members. However, he added, they would probably also have thought he was an ERSP delegate, rather than an *Isamaa* MP, because of his uncompromising nationalist stance (he was, of course, a founder of the Conservative People's Party, EKRE). True, both the last two parties mentioned played the nationalist issue as their strong card at the 1992 general election. The ERSP's main slogan was 'Estonia will make a comeback' (*Eesti tuleb tagasi*) while the chief campaign poster of *Isamaa* depicted a man with a broom declaring 'Make Room!', implying the need to sweep away the faces and institutions that had dominated the past.

In the past, of course, politics was at best about personalities rather than issues. Under one-party rule, choice, where it existed, was between individuals and not policies. Reinforcing the tendency of citizens to view the conduct of public affairs in terms of the interaction of the main players went the fact that several of the embryonic parties were created as flags of convenience, supporting and legitimising the election campaigns of those leading figures disaffected with the 'elite congestion' within the PF. In the short term, the personalisation of parties should not be regarded as exceptional – witness the role of the founder/leader of the entrepreneurial issue parties in Western Europe – or particularly problematical, affording a means of differentiation at a time when all the parties espoused the virtues of the nation, liberal democracy and the market. But in the middle term, a measure of depersonalisation appears essential if parties are to achieve an identity of their own.

Built around a notable and his or her personal network, the embryonic parties initially travelled light, carrying little by way of ideological baggage. Subsequently, a number of them, the Social Democrats, Rural Centre and *Isamaa*, for instance, became the protégés of the mainstream West European and especially Scandinavian party families, who assisted with the preparation of their programmes and 'adopted' them in other ways. But these programmes were largely unconvincing, they were not widely read, and they did little to bestow an independent identity on the parties.

There is evidence that the parties have become well aware of the need to depersonalise themselves. There is, of course, a potential electoral risk in doing this in a predominantly anti-party culture, but, in principle, it could be achieved, in at least three ways. First, there is the option of alternating the leadership, with the founding figure withdrawing one remove from the spotlight, while not dissociating him or herself from the party. In fact, the tendency during 1993–4, typical of atomised party systems, was for personality conflicts and related strains to escalate the formation of new parties whose identity then rested almost entirely on their founding figures. The parties emerging from the disintegration of the ERSP and *Isamaa* and the fragmentation of the Centre Party are cases in point although, ironically, in several cases their manifest logic was opposition to a Savisaar-style or Laar-style 'personality cult'.

Second, there is the possibility of refurbishing the party's name with the aim of heightening its electoral identity. While West European party titles such as Social Democrats and Liberal Democrats may provide a reasonable middle-term basis for identity building, the existence of groupings with very similar names – two Christian parties, a People's Centre Party, Rural Centre Party, Rural Union, Republican Coalition Party, Coalition Party and so on – at the September 1992 general election (albeit as part of broad electoral alliances) doubtless added to the perplexity of voters.

Finally, there is scope for strengthening the profile of the parties by engaging in a degree of programmatic modernisation and by creating relevant policies. Identity building, of course, takes time and public perceptions of parties rarely correspond exactly to partisan self-images. Promoting policies and de-emphasising personalities nonetheless appear an essential step especially as, under the impact of economic reform, the social structure becomes diversified; that is, the party system begins to rest on cleavage structures.

Organisation

A clear assumption of the centrality of parties as channels of communication between the people and their politicians was made, on Western advice, when parties were enshrined in the new electoral law. Parties, however, in order to act as effective links between state and society, need to develop as voluntary membership organisations. So far, although most of the Estonian parties boast democratic constitutions prescribing rules and structures based on the voluntary membership model, they lack a grassroots base and, accordingly, have made relatively little progress down the road of this second stage of party-building (the three stages of party building are, of course, analytical rather than chronological concepts).

Analysing the situation after the 1992 election, Mikk Titma, the ECP's former ideological secretary, commented: 'There is really only one party in Estonian politics worthy of the name and that is the ERSP, which has the highest membership and the best network of local organisations of any Estonian political organisation.'[28] When the ERSP's own estimate of 1100 members (distributed between 13 branch organisations) is compared with the party's aggregate poll in September 1992, an impressive voter–member ratio in the order of 1:36 is obtained. However, there is no doubt that this deteriorated appreciably thereafter, despite the regular supply of Information Letters to members produced by a small secretariat in the ERSP's parliamentary group headquarters in the *Riigikogu* building.

Indeed, symptomatic of the increasing depoliticisation of the citizenry, there has been a general decline in party membership. Although the figures produced by the parties themselves may be regarded as highly impressionistic, it is almost certainly correct to state that membership in the period 1992–95 ranged from at most 500–600, in the cases of the ERSP, ESDP and RKE, to under 100 in groups like the EKE and Democratic Justice Union. Active membership was, of course, significantly lower. There were no more than 200 participants at the Social Democratic Party conference in 1993, while the number of active Royalists was then in the region of 20. The network of branch organisations, moreover, remained patchy. Thus EMKE claimed 456 members organised in 10–15 districts in September 1993, but admitted it lacked an infrastructure of any kind in the western region of Haapsalu and Hiiumaa. The ESDP, moreover, was the only party to embrace non-Estonians, about 20 per cent of its members being Russian-speaking.

An alternative perspective on the organisational resources of the parties can be gained from their ability to mobilise candidates at the 1992 election. As Table 8.6 indicates, there were only three parties/ electoral alliances, the ERSP, *Isamaa* and PF, which were able to run a full or virtually full slate of candidates; there was one medium-sized group, the Secure Home alliance, and the rest were essentially small fry. The Estonian parties, then, lacked members and struggled to attract sufficient candidates to fill the public posts available for election. It might be objected that, if a party cannot be considered fully institutionalised before it possesses a mass base, most West European parties would have some considerable way to go. Referring to Italy in the early 1990s, Ruzza and Schmidtke observed: 'Most parties in government have almost completely lost their activist base and are obtaining the resources they need directly from the state through subsidies, or from the economy in the form of bribes.'[29] Significantly, on 11 May 1994 the *Riigikogu* enacted a law on party funding. It contained two main stipulations: one, that to register parties need a minimum membership of 1000 (effective from after the 1995 general election); two, that parliamentary parties will be eligible for state support on a *pro rata* basis. Parties that fail to win *Riigikogu* seats in successive elections will be stricken from the party register. Estonia has thus fallen into line with standard Western practice. However, the point is that, whereas many West European parties have lost a mass base, the parties in postcommunist Estonia have yet to attract one. It remains to be seen if the new party law provides the desired stimulus to the development of parties as mass organisations.

Table 8.6   **The number of candidates at the September 1992 election, by party/electoral alliance**

Party/electoral alliance	Candidates	Seats	Efficiency (%)
PF	104	15	14
Isamaa	101	29	29
ERSP	97	10	10
Secure Home	73	17	23
Moderates	49	12	29
Independent Royalists	30	8	27
Estonian Citizens	26	8	31
Farmers' Union	25	0	0
Entrepreneurs	14	1	7
Pensioners' Union	14	0	0
Left Alternative	14	0	0
Greens	14	1	7
Independents	25	0	0
Total	586		

Note: The efficiency percentage is calculated by dividing the number of candidates nominated by the number of *Riigikogu* seats won.

Stabilisation

The final stage in the party-building process, that is the cycle from inception to institutionalisation, is the stabilisation phase. This involves the parties forging stable and cohesive support bases among the electorate. Curiously, in both liberal–democratic Western and post-communist Eastern Europe a measure of *partisan dealignment* may be said to have occurred. In the West, a growing body of anti-party sentiment has contributed to an erosion of the traditional bases of partisan support. There is a need for the older parties in particular to be adaptive and to reinvigorate the democratic process by creating new support bases that reflect the evolving social structures of advanced technological states. Their challenge, in short, is to achieve a sufficient measure of partisan realignment. In Eastern Europe, in contrast, the task of the embryonic parties in anti-party systems (marked by a variable aversion to the concept of party) is to develop stable patterns of partisan alignment. It was significant that in the newly independent Belarus, for example, there were at least 20 proto-parties by the beginning of 1992, but 56 per cent of inhabitants did not incline towards any of them.[30] In such a situation, the creation of stable party–social group linkages may be regarded as a useful indicator of the progression from the period of democratic transition to that of democratic consolidation. A particularly relevant yardstick is the incidence of sectional parties representing distinct socioeconomic clienteles, since they measure the distance travelled from a party system grounded in the nationalist question and issues connected with regime building.

Because there have only been two general elections since Estonia regained its independence, it is plainly premature to look for the existence of stable voter–party alignments. Regularised voter–party linkages take time to evolve. However, the fact that partisan identification appears relatively weak in Estonia, when compared with West European and indeed most East European levels, suggests that the task of stabilisation facing the political parties will be a stern challenge. It might reasonably be suggested that an important prerequisite for the parties in striving to raise the levels of partisan allegiance is the need to define and concentrate upon particular electoral clienteles. Thus far, though, the parties themselves have appeared unsure who their voters are and, more importantly, which type of catchment they are seeking to attract in the future.

The rudimentary electoral profiles of the parties that follow rely on three sources. First, they draw on an *Emor* survey conducted at the time of the September 1992 general election in which 882 people were interviewed, 855 of them Estonian citizens. Second, they reflect the parties' own impressions of their support bases, impressions usually lacking any systematic empirical base. Third, use is made of ad hoc material, including a breakdown of EMKE's membership by occupation in September 1993. Several important limitations associated with the Emor data should be noted. Tabulations are by electoral alliance rather than by individual party (where parties formed common lists); there is no breakdown of party support by occupation; and there is a high number of people (25 per cent overall) not responding to questions on party preference. Nonetheless, the *Emor* survey at least provides us with systematic information about party support in 1992.

Four key variables are employed. *Place of residence*: the country is subdivided into five regions – the capital city, Tallinn; the old university city of Tartu; other (provincial) towns; small market towns; and villages. *Education*: the data are tabulated in accordance with four levels – elementary school only; secondary schooling; professional/vocational training; and higher education. *Age*: the popularity of the parties is calculated for seven age cohorts – 18–24 years; 25–9; 30–39; 40–49; 50–59; 60–69; and 70 years and over. *Income*: five income brackets are used – 200 kroons (about £10) a month or less; 201–400 kr; 401–600 kr; 601–1000 kr; and over 1000 kroons a month. A general picture of the support for the groupings at the time of the September 1992 general election and afterwards follows.

The Moderates   The electoral alliance of the ESDP and EMKE drew twice its average level of support from Tallinn and slightly more than its average from Tartu. It was significantly weaker elsewhere, especially in the other provincial towns and the villages. The electoral strength of the Tallinn–Tartu axis was particularly notable in the case of the ESDP (the two Estonian wings, led by Saatpalu in Tallinn and Lauristin in Tartu, of course originated in these historic cities), but the party also attracted support in the predominantly Russian-speaking towns of Narva and Sillamäe in north-east Estonia. The rural support for EMKE showed up less clearly in the *Emor* data. Support for the Moderates was very low in the villages, albeit higher in the small market towns where, doubtless, EMKE had support. It would be wrong, however, to regard the latter as exclusively a party of the countryside – at least on the basis of its 1993 membership. Some 15 per cent of EMKE members were based in the towns, 11 per cent comprising urban intellectuals and 4 per cent urban employees.

The Moderates attracted a disproportionate amount of support in 1992 from those with qualifications in higher education. The second largest group of highly-educated persons (13 per cent) supported the Moderates (surpassed only by the 21 per cent supporting *Isamaa*) whereas those possessing only an elementary schooling and those who proceeded no further than secondary school were significantly underrepresented. Interestingly, EMKE did not lack support among the educated, at least judged by its membership: 39 per cent of its members (28 per cent in the countryside and 11 per cent in the towns) possessed higher educational training and there were 3 per cent students among the membership. The electoral alliance recruited its strongest backing from middle-aged people between 30 and 49 years, but there was below-average support from cohorts under 30 and over 60 years. Finally, the Moderates drew their greatest support from those on higher incomes and the weakest response from the lowest paid. It attracted its strongest support of any group from those earning between 601 and 1000 kroons a month.

All in all, the typical Moderate voter was a relatively well-paid middle-aged man or woman (there was no gender differential in its support base) with a training in higher education based either in the capital city or the old university town of Tartu. This corresponded fairly closely to the ESDP's own perception of the urban 'middle class' nature of its support. The EMKE's profile and the presumed urban–rural axis of the Moderates' support did not emerge so clearly and EMKE's backing from the new private farmers (admittedly still a small group) did not show through at all.

Isamaa   The geographical distribution of support for the *Isamaa* electoral alliance was not dissimilar to the Moderates'. *Isamaa* commanded the backing of over one-fifth of respondents (21 per cent) from Tallinn – the highest for any political grouping and rivalled only by the 16 per cent support for the Moderates – and over one-quarter in Tartu. The Tartu figure was three times higher than that of the moderates who were in turn the next best supported group there. In contrast, *Isamaa* was significantly weaker in the small market towns and particularly weak in the villages where it managed less than half its average support and precisely half the support of the *Kindel Kodu* alliance, the best-backed grouping in the villages. *Isamaa* attracted some support from non-Estonians, but because their number in the sample as a whole was very small (only 27 out of 882) this was not enough to substantiate the claim that it was the best-supported bloc among 25–35-year-old Russians (citizens or non-citizens) as a result of its vigorous free-market policies.

Paradoxically, the *Isamaa* bloc attracted more support (21 per cent) from the most highly educated and more support from the least educated (14 per cent) than any other electoral grouping. Support among the most educated exceeded *Isamaa*'s average by 6 per cent. However, although it was the most popular bloc among the least educated, *Isamaa*'s backing among the latter was still slightly below its average level of support.

In terms of the age composition of its electorate, *Isamaa* recruited more than its average support from among the 30–60-year-olds and its lowest proportion of backing from the youngest cohort of voters. Nonetheless, the 10 per cent it gained from the 18–24-year-olds was equalled only by the ERSP and surpassed only by the Independent Royalists. Finally, *Isamaa* witnessed a fairly even and average distribution of support among low- and middle-income earners, but boasted the highest support of all from the best paid. One-fifth of those earning 1000 kroons or more a month supported the *Isamaa* bloc.

All in all, the typical *Isamaa* voter was an urban resident in his or her middle years, probably based in Tartu or Tallinn. Curiously, he or she would either have a university education and earn relatively well or possess no more than elementary schooling and earn very little. On the basis of the *Emor* data, *Isamaa* clearly had the potential to become a *catch-all party* boasting support across the socioeconomic spectrum. It was relatively weak among young voters and in the outlying small towns and villages. As with the Moderates, it was too much a 'tale of two cities'.

Kindel Kodu   The *Kindel Kodu* electoral alliance in September 1992 proved to be an essentially 'up-country' bloc which attracted the highest support of any grouping in the small market towns and villages. This would appear to vindicate the picture of EML, depicted by its political opponents as a party of the rural proletariat: that is, the agricultural workers on the former collectives and state farms. Indeed, *Kindel Kodu* possessed the clearest rural profile of all the parties and electoral alliances.

In terms of the educational background of its supporters, *Kindel Kodu* did not possess strongly distinguishing features. It derived slightly greater than average support from those with only elementary schooling and slightly below average from those with secondary and/or professional qualifications. However, there was not enough evidence in the figures to bear out EKE's self-image of a male-dominated party of highly-trained managers and engineers (opponents would say former *solkhov* and *kolkhov* bosses and other members of the *nomenklatura*).

Kindel Kodu fared very badly among the youngest voters in 1992. It attracted only 3 per cent support among the 18–24-year cohort, barely one-quarter of its average following among the entire sample, but this rose markedly among the 25–29 age group. Significantly, *Kindel Kodu* was the most popular electoral alliance among the 60–69-year category, presumably attracting the pensioners that were behind the foundation of the Democratic Justice Union. It maintained average levels of support across the income spectrum up to, but excluding, the best-off group. Indeed, it contrived only 3 per cent support from those voters earning over 1000 kroons a month.

In summary, the typical voter for one of the *Kindel Kodu* parties appears to have been an elderly rural resident with an average or below-average income and probably no more than basic elementary schooling. Moreover, *Kindel Kodu* was the least 'middle-class' of all the electoral groupings, notwithstanding the management element in its midst.

Popular Front   The attempt to transform the PF from a leading social movement into a major electoral force was not an unbridled success. The political ecology of its support revealed striking lacunae in the villages, where its backing was under one-third of its average, and Tartu, where only 4 per cent of the overall sample favoured the PF. It failed to achieve its average (10 per cent) level of support in Tallinn, too. However, the PF boasted the highest support of all the electoral groupings in 'small-town Estonia': that is, the urban areas outside Tallinn and Tartu. Over one-quarter (26 per cent) of the very small number of non-Estonians, moreover, backed the PF, a figure exceeded only by the 30 per cent in this category who failed to express an electoral preference.

The PF's profile was not sharply delineated in respect of the three other principal variables, making it virtually impossible to define a typical PF voter. It derived slightly below its average support from those with only elementary schooling and fared less well still among those with higher educational qualifications. While the PF's support did not plummet like *Kindel Kodu* among the youngest section of voters (although it was slightly below its average), it shared with the latter the fact that it gained its highest level of support from the 60–69-year-olds. There were no outstanding features with regard to the income of its supporters. The PF drew slightly above its average level of support from the lowest paid and significantly above average from the best paid.

The ERSP The ERSP's support was distributed very evenly across the national territory. In the villages, small market towns and other provincial towns, it attracted precisely the 7 per cent support it gained among the sample as a whole. This figure rose marginally in Tallinn and dipped fractionally in Tartu. The ERSP's following was also very evenly dispersed by education, albeit with a slight bias towards the most highly educated. The ERSP attracted the third best support among people under 30 and the lowest among the 60–69 years age group. In income terms, the party's best support has come from below average earners, that is those with salaries of between 201 and 400 kroons a month.

Anti-parties As anti-parties, support for the Independent Royalists and Estonian Citizens is of interest. The *Independent Royalists*, with 6 per cent support in the *Emor* sample as a whole, boasted their strongest support in the small towns and villages, among those possessing at least a secondary education and, above all, among young people. The Independent Royalists were the best-supported party among the under-24 years category and, indeed, all those under 29. Interestingly, 14 per cent of all 18–24 year-olds supported the Independent Royalists, precisely the same proportion of first voters that backed New Democracy at the Swedish general election of September 1991.[31] The *Estonian Citizens*, in contrast, lacked distinguishing features. They attracted above-average support in Tartu, the provincial towns and the villages; from those with secondary (but not higher education); from men in all the age groups up to 49 years; and from those in the middle-income brackets.

In almost all the parties much lip-service has been paid to the desire to appeal to middle-class voters when the very notion of middle-class remains anything but precise. In their defence, not only is the party system evolving at a rapid pace, but there is certain to be a contemporaneous diversification of the social structure as the economic reforms begin to bite. Estonian society has thus far been relatively egalitarian, characterised by the absence of deep-seated class conflict. It is doubtful if it can remain so much longer.[32] Indeed, it is ironic that, whereas in recent decades there has been an evident blurring of the traditional class contours of Western political societies, class differentiation in Estonia is likely to become more pronounced. This means that in the middle term parties will need to take strategic decisions in anticipation of social structural change. In this context, the Entrepreneurs' Party, for instance, expressly stated its wish to become a sectional party drawing on the expanding class of privatised small and medium-sized businesses. Other parties will doubtless concentrate on the newly independent farmers and those employed in the (as yet modest) tertiary sector.

The surfeit of groups at present vying for the hand of voters in either the towns or the countryside (the urban–rural divide is a prominent territorial cleavage in Estonian politics) will doubtless expedite the process of rationalisation and amalgamation among the parties. Equally, the impact of economic reform should in time facilitate the stabilisation of sectional parties anchored in distinct socioeconomic clienteles. Another crucial territorial cleavage, the division of society into an indigenous nation (Estonia) and an imperial nation (Russians and Ukrainians), the latter with its regional stronghold in the northeast of the country, is bound to prove more of a problem. In its widest sense, the process of stabilisation will entail the political parties in seeking to integrate the 'two nations' by working to mobilise support from among Russian-speaking citizens.

Conclusions

Summing up the challenges of party-building in an anti-party system, the following main points are in order. Half a century of state-led communism suffocated the Estonian citizenry and after the national unity and solidarity of 1988–91 the dual processes of demobilisation and depoliticisation eroded much of the ground gained, so to speak. At the time the new political groundrules were adopted at a popular referendum in June 1992, Estonia was a weak political society. After the 'heroic period' when the nation pulled together to regain independence, an independence which held out the promise of a better future, disillusion increased and interest in politics dropped sharply.[33] True, it is important to set developments in a time frame. Thus Michael Waller, writing on groups, interests and political aggregation in Eastern Europe, noted in 1990: 'the hectic years have not receded far enough for political pressure to replace mobilisation and for stable relations to emerge between clearly-defined constituencies and elites'.[34] The same could be said of Estonia nearly six years after Waller's statement. Indeed, state–society linkages are relatively tenuous and there can be no doubt that the widespread political apathy and passivity of the population as a whole will enormously complicate the task of building stable voter–group alignments.

While Estonia is a party democracy in the sense that the position of parties is ensconced by law (particularly the May 1994 legislation on party funding), parties do not yet control or dominate political society and the mobilisation, socialisation and organisation (input) functions are but imperfectly performed. Partisanship is weak and turnout relatively low or, to put it another way, non-party voting is comparatively high. At the local government election on 17 October 1993 turnout in the overwhelmingly Estonian university town of Tartu was only a fraction over a third of eligible voters. Thus far, to be sure, there has been no reformist communist backlash at the polls. In contrast to Poland, where the Democratic Left Alliance (SLD) became the largest party following the September 1993 general election, with over one-fifth of the vote, or the Czech Republic, where the former communists are the second largest parliamentary party, the Party of Democratic Labour in Estonia polled less than 1 per cent of the vote at the September 1992 general election. But with two anti-parties, the 'hardline' Estonian Citizens and 'softline' Independent Royalists claiming a combined 14 per cent of the vote in September 1992, Estonia appeared a case of an anti-party system.

Notes

1 Rain Rosimannus, 'Parteistunud Eesti on vaid kujutelm V', *Hommikuleht*, 30 July 1993.
2 Juhan Kivirahk, Rain Rosimannus and Indrek Pajumaa, 'The Premises for Democracy: A Study of Political Values in Post-Independent Estonia', *Journal of Baltic Studies*, **XXIV**, (2), 1993, pp.149–60.
3 Andreas Dimpfel founded his German Party of Non-Voters (PDN) in July 1993. Non-voters, disenchanted with mainstream politics, then formed the biggest bloc in Germany. 'Unadulterated party woos votes of Germany's non-voting voters', *The Guardian*, 14 July 1993.
4 Marju Lauristin, Peeter Vihalemm and Rein Ruutsoo, *Viron vapauden tuulet* (Gummerus: Jyväskylä–Helsinki, 1989), pp.304–16; Rein Taagepera, 'A Note on the March 1989 Election in Estonia', *Soviet Studies*, **42**, (2), 1990, pp.329–39.
5 'Virolaiset kongressivaaleihin', *Helsingin Sanomat*, 24 February 1990; 'Viron kongressin vaaleista lopulliset tulokset', *Helsingin Sanomat*, 6 March 1990.
6 'Rahvarinnen ehdokkaat voittivat Viron vaaleissa', *Helsingin Sanomat*, 20 March 1990.
7 'Epätietoisuus äänioikeuden laajuudesta aiheutti hämmennystä', *Helsingin Sanomat*, 29 June 1992; 'Ylivoimainen enemmistö Viron perustuslain taakse', *Helsingin Sanomat*, 30 June 1992.
8 'Lennart Merellä hillitty vaalijuhla Tallinnan torilla; *Helsingin Sanomat*, 19 September 1992.
9 'Eurooppa tarkkailee Viron vaaleja', *Helsingin Sanomat*, 20 September 1992.

10   'Viro toivoo äänestyksestä tukea itsenäisyyshaaveille', *Helsingin Sanomat*, 3 March 1991; 'Virolaiset kävivät innokkaasti äänestämässä itsenäisyydestä', *Helsingin Sanomat*, 4 March 1991.

11   'Viro ja Latvia äänestivät selvästi tasavaltojen itsenäisyyden puolesta', *Helsingin Sanomat*, 5 March 1991; 'Baltian kansanäänestysten jälkeen', *Helsingin Sanomat*, 6 March 1991.

12   'Koillis-Viro äänestää liittosopimuksesta', *Helsingin Sanomat* 7 March 1991; 'Ahkera äänestäjä Tallinnassa', *Helsingin Sanomat*, 18 March 1991; 'Gorbachev näyttää saaneen selvän enemmistön taakseen', *Helsingin Sanomat*, 20 March 1991; 'Virossa kerrotaan helposta vaalivilpistä', *Helsingin Sanomat*, 21 March 1991.

13   'Rüütelillä on hyvä räätäli mutta Meri on maailmanmies', *Helsingin Sanomat*, 20 September 1992.

14   'Pensioners to govern the city of youth', *The Baltic Independent*, 28 October–4 November 1993.

15   'Low turn-out voids Lithuanian election', *The Baltic Independent*, 26 November–2 December 1993.

16   Lauristin *et al.*, *Viron vapauden tuulet*, p.138.

17   Svennik Høyer, Epp Lauk and Peeter Vihalemm (eds), *Towards a Civic Society: The Baltic Media's Long Road to Freedom* (Nota Baltica: Tartu, 1993), p.271.

18   Interview with Jüri Toomepuu, 17 September 1993; 'Eesti Kodanike Liitarvab, et aitab pettusest!'

19   Anatol Lieven, *The Baltic Revolution: Estonia, Latvia, Lithuania and the Path to Independence*, (Yale University: New Haven–London, 1993), p.286.

20   'Palace refuses to let Prince Edward act as saviour king of Estonia', *The Guardian*, 11 July 1994.

21   Interview with Kalle Kulbok, 26 May 1993.

22   Lieven, *The Baltic Revolution*, p.284.

23   'Let's play along', *The Baltic Independent*, 23–9 July 1993.

24   Lauristin *et al.*, *Viron vapauden tuulet*, p.98.

25   Lieven, *The Baltic Revolution*, p.357; Siim Kallas, 'Estonia: Monetary Reform Hard Style', *The Baltic Review*, 1, (1), 1992, pp.40–41. The success of the new Estonian currency, the kroon, introduced in June 1992, affords grounds for cautious economic optimism although, ironically, when Savisaar promised the introduction of the kroon by the end of 1990, necessity was in large part the mother of the new money. The (re-) introduction of an indigenous currency, in short, was effectively imposed on the Estonians by an acute shortage of roubles. As inflation spiralled, the Russian government and State Bank in Moscow came under intense pressure to restrict the printing of money and the resulting cuts in the supply of cash were passed on to the other republics in the rouble zone.

26   International Foundation for Electoral Systems, 'Republic of Estonia. An Assessment of the Election to the Riigikogu and the Presidency', 16–24 September 1992.

27   Ibid., pp.21–7.

28   Mikk Titma, 'Estonia: Right Turn?', *East European Reporter*, 5/6, 1992, p.81.

29   Carlo E. Ruzza and Oliver Schmidtke, 'Roots of Success of the Lega Lombarda: Mobilisation Dynamics and the Media', *West European Politics*, **16**, (2), 1993, p.13.

30   Jan Zaprudnik, *Belarus: At a Crossroads in History*, (Westview: Boulder–San Francisco–Oxford, 1993), pp.155–6.

31   'De började i Hänt i Veckan', *Dagens Nyheter*, 7 November 1993.

32   Ahto Lobjakas, 'The Estonian Party System. An Attempt in Analysis', unpublished paper, Lund University, 1992, p.12.

33 On the popular indifference and ignorance of the representative structures and processes in Estonia today, see Mare Kukk, 'Estnisk publik åser maktkupp och lokalval', *Nordisk Kontakt*, **10**, 1993, pp.11–12.
34 Michael Waller, 'Groups, Interests and Political Aggregation in East Central Europe', *The Journal of Communist Studies*, **8**, (3), pp.128–147.

9 Estonia after the March 1995 *Riigikogu* election: Still an Anti-party System?

The economic situation has taken a turn for the better. Estonia is now on a reformist course and there is no possibility of turning back. Estonia is probably the most European and democratic country of the old East European bloc. (Young Reform Party supporter at the Institute of Humanities, author's survey, March 1995)

A basic assumption in delineating the model in Chapter 1 was that the 'anti-party system' is a transitional phase en route to a more stable form of multipartism, that it will characterise some post-communist systems more than others and that the further the progress along the road to democratic consolidation the more institutionalised the role of political parties will be. Following two general elections and a local government election in the four years since the restoration of independence, how far can Estonia still be described as an anti-party system? Following a brief look at economic developments and ethnic relations in Estonia, the present chapter focuses on the *Riigikogu* election of 1995. Though the Estonian party system continues to display high levels of instability and the process of party formation remains incomplete, the notion of 'party' seems more internalised and support for 'anti-parties' appears in decline.

Socioeconomic Developments in Estonia, 1991–5

Although in June 1992 Estonia was the first of the post-Soviet republics to break out of the rouble zone – when it reintroduced the *kroon* – currency reform was almost inevitably followed by high inflation and falling production. Bread queues formed and milk and meat were rationed. Only a year later, however, Prime Minister Laar was able to express his belief that Estonia would be close to Finnish living standards by the year 2000.[1] Moreover, by autumn 1994, the minister of economics, Toivo Jürgenson, was prompted to liken the 8.4 per cent increase in productivity in the first half of that year to 'the growth rates in Japan in the 1960s' and he pointed to more effective production and changes in property relations as the principal reasons for this highly encouraging scenario. The biggest production increases, incidentally, occurred in the timber industry (158 per cent) and the machine-building industry (162 per cent). The Estonian economy, in short, had reached the stage of economic growth and predictions of 4 per cent growth for 1994 as a whole appeared in order.[2]

Since Estonia regained her independence, the bulk of her foreign trade has been oriented towards Western markets. In comparison to 1991, when 95 per cent of her total trade was with the Soviet/CIS states, this figure had dropped to only 29 per cent in mid-1993. Since then, trade with Russia at least has recovered somewhat, based on Estonian exports of agricultural manufactured products, machine equipment and consumer goods in return for imported gas and petrol, although relations between the two countries have been strained by the high protective tariffs Russia has imposed on foreign agricultural goods.

The search for Western markets has had an underlying political as well as economic logic, that is, to avoid an undue dependency on the former imperial power, and, in the first instance, the Nordic states provided the most obvious and accessible outlet for Estonian goods. By 1993 Finland had become Estonia's leading commercial partner (accounting for nearly one-quarter of her total trade), while between 1992 and 1993 bilateral free-trade agreements (excluding agriculture) were reached with the European Free Trade Association (EFTA) states of Finland, Sweden, Norway and Switzerland. Next came the neighbouring southern Baltic states. In September 1993 a free-trade agreement (covering tariffs and quotas, but again excluding agriculture) was reached between Estonia, Latvia and Lithuania and came into force on 1 April 1994. In the second half of that year, about 8 per cent of Estonia's trade was with the two other Baltic republics. Significantly, on 18 July 1994, Estonia underwrote a free-trade agreement with the EU – previously it had been granted the Generalised System of Preferences (GSP) – and, at the end of that year, approximately 30 per cent of Estonia's trade was with the EU states. Finally, on 1 August 1995, the *Riigikogu* unanimously ratified an 'associate agreement' with the EU, along the lines of those with the Visegrad states, which, distinctively, did not involve the transitional period required of other states.

Table 9.1 sets out the shift in the balance of Estonia's foreign trade between 1992 and 1993. Estonian imports from the CIS states halved, whereas those from the EU/EFTA rose by nearly 16 per cent. Exports to Western Europe, in contrast, increased only modestly and nearly one-third still went to the states of the former Soviet Union. Indeed, despite a marginal growth in exports, some increase in domestic demand and an improvement in the investment climate in Estonia during 1994, several crucial economic challenges remain.

Table 9.1   Estonia's foreign trade, 1992–3

	Percentage of Estonian imports		*Percentage of Estonian exports*	
Year	1992	1993	1992	1993
EFTA	30.3	38.1	30.3	31.5
EU	15.3	23.3	13.7	17.8
CIS	40.1	21.6	34.7	30.3

Source: Ministry of Economic Affairs, *Estonian Economic Survey 1993–94* (Ilo: Tallinn, 1994), p.45.

First and foremost, much more foreign investment is needed (an estimated 100–200 million US dollars annually) if the Estonian economy is to progress rapidly.[3] A secure and comprehensive legislative framework, to generate confidence in prospective foreign investors, is also important. True, there have been signs of improvement. Thus, in the first quarter of 1994, foreign investment exceeded domestic investment in accounting for more than half (57 per cent) of the registered share capital in the Estonian economy. Significantly, there was growing interest in Estonia from Russian investors. But foreign investors, attracted by a cheap and skilled labour force and the easy repatriation of profits, have been deterred to a degree by a dilapidated transport infrastructure and pollution levels well above acceptable EU norms.

Another main economic challenge is the regeneration of the decaying rural regions, especially in the south-east and north-east of Estonia, when the state clearly lacks both the will (at least under the 1992–5 *Isamaa*-dominated governments) and the resources to promote an active regional policy. Official statistics have put the unemployment level in southern Estonia at 7 per cent, though according to the National Labour Market Board the actual figures at the beginning of 1994 were about three times as high.[4] Poor soil conditions, the distance from Tallinn, inadequate information flows, the loss of local markets in Latvia and Russia and the effect of property reforms have all contributed to creating rural poverty in many areas of southern Estonia. In the north-east of the country the problems have arisen primarily from the attempt to restructure the (previously All-Union) military–industrial complex which remains predominantly state-owned. High levels of pollution, particularly the contamination of water supplies, have also quickened rural depopulation in the northeast. In general, measures seeking to encourage the redeployment of people into agriculture-related industries, especially enterprises directed solely to local markets, by providing ready capitalisation (that is, favourable loans) have merely scratched the surface of rural decay.

Estonia possesses a primary sector which is three times as large as the West European norm, in that between 10 and 15 per cent of the economically active population is still engaged in agricultural production. Four-fifths of Estonian farm production is consumed domestically and the average household spends 35–40 per cent of its income on agricultural goods. Yet the *Estonian Economic Survey 1993–1994* paints a bleak picture: 'The small and medium-sized farms are economically questionable and thus threatened. The major problem in the agricultural economy is not production, but the fate of non-urban people … the country way of life in general is under threat due to the fact that development is happening in urban areas, not in the country.'[5]

The case for the economic non-viability of the newly privatised farms – and organised farm protest has become increasingly vocal – rests on the fact that, unlike counterparts elsewhere in Europe, Estonian agriculture receives no subsidies and finds it increasingly difficult to compete in an Estonian market flooded by subsidised Western and Russian products. The tacit government response under *Isamaa* was that, although in a comparative perspective the high numbers engaged in it made farming in Estonia relatively inefficient, agriculture was in fact competitive in terms of unit costs of production. The fact that Estonian farm goods were breaking into the Latvian and Lithuanian markets, where the proportions engaged in agriculture were much larger than in Estonia and the sector was highly protected, was, it was argued, evidence of this fact. Interestingly, the new Vähi coalition, despite its election rhetoric, has not acted to subsidise farming, with the result that *The Baltic Independent*, reviewing its first 100 days in office commented: 'The most neglected area is the Estonian countryside, which offers a desolate picture – unemployed men who start their day drinking; their wives still looking for jobs but also giving up; decaying farmhouses …'[6]

Under Soviet rule there were 360 collective farms, each employing hundreds of people, but by 1994 these had been replaced by 4300 private farms, more than 1200 stock companies and 1300 shareholding companies. However, as the *Estonian Economic Survey 1993–1994* observed, there has been a particular problem in relation to privatising farm product-based enterprises, especially the collectives, since prospective owners have generally lacked investment capital, and this had made the possibility of a 'twin-track' (two-speed) privatisation process a real one.[7] Most of the collectives (producing meat, milk dairy products and so on) have in fact remained state-owned, despite (indeed largely because of) the fact that preference has been given to Estonians, who must find only a 10 per cent purchase deposit, compared with potential foreign buyers who must find the entire sales price. Overall, the collectives have not been very successful, facing strong competition from the Finns in a very limited domestic market.[8]

A final economic challenge is the need to diversify Estonia's foreign trade. True, enormous advantages have accrued from the free-trade agreements with the EFTA states to which Estonia has exported mainly labour-intensive commodities such as clothes and knitwear and resource-intensive products such as timber goods and furniture. Even so, the country of origin rules have limited the benefits of the bilateral agreements since Estonia uses imported inputs in a large proportion of its goods production.[9] Goods manufactured in Estonia which use raw materials originating in Sweden, for example, will not qualify as of Estonian origin when exported to Finland. Equally, there is the risk of overspecialisation in certain goods and an overconcentration on Nordic markets, with the attendant danger of structural dependency. In general, Estonia will need to develop niche markets outside Europe and be ready to respond to demand generated by chance business contacts.[10]

Even though, in a comparative perspective, the transition to a market economy is proceeding relatively smoothly and private enterprises account for 30–40 per cent of the turnover of the Estonian economy, a host of teething troubles have been experienced. A study by the Small Business Association (EVEA), for instance, indicated that start-up loans under the EU's PHARE programme have been restricted by the problems that smaller firms have had in putting together suitable business plans. There have, moreover, been social costs associated with the shift to the market. While private clinics are mushrooming, the state health-care system stands in urgent need of a fundamental overhaul. Crime has risen.[11] Indeed, Estonia has the highest crime rate in Europe and the increase in mafia-related murders (often in broad daylight) is alarming. So, too, is the incidence of Perm- and Chechenya-related smuggling. Ironically, it was a measure of the success of the *kroon* and the increased sums deposited (often by foreigners) that there was a sharp increase in the number of bank robberies in 1993. In 1992 there were none at all! Policing is a problem. The average age of policemen is only 26 and their average experience a mere two and a half years (earlier the police was predominantly Russian). Moreover, relations between the police and the voluntary Defence League (which was revived in 1990) have been strained and several criminal elements joined the Defence League after independence in order to gain possession of firearms.

Relations with the Russian Minority in Estonia

As early as 18 January 1989, Estonian was confirmed as the state language and the law stipulated the level of proficiency required for 'public sector' employment. Then, on 26 February 1992, the 1938 Law on Citizenship was reintroduced, according to which the Estonian citizenry comprises all those who had citizenship on 16 June 1940 and their descendants. This denied automatic citizenship and voting rights to those Russians who had moved to Estonia after its forcible incorporation into the Soviet Union. A proposal in the 28 June 1992 constitutional referendum to extend citizenship automatically to over 5000 non-citizens who had applied for it was defeated by 53 per cent to 46 per cent and the new constitution prevented non-citizens from joining political parties. True, there is evidence that the so-called 'second question' of enfranchising those who had already applied for citizenship was badly understood and little discussed. For some it was evidently seen as a question of whether to give the vote to the entire Russian-speaking population. In any event, the 1992 citizen legislation required all prospective citizens (except those exempted by inter-marriage and those receiving citizenship on the grounds of valuable service to the national defence of Estonia) to meet a two-year residence requirement, pass a language test, demonstrate visible means of support and sign a statement that they have read the constitution and respect the laws of the land.

Among the Russian-speaking political elite, two distinct tendencies may be observed. First, diehard elements – 'irreconcilables' – do still exist and have not lacked support. In the October 1993 local government (municipal) elections, where a residence requirement enabled the bulk of the Russian population to vote and where turnout among Russian 'residents' was significantly higher than among Estonian citizens, a Russian list *Reval*, containing a number of former Interfront communists, came third in Tallinn. Second, 'integrationists' have nonetheless made headway. Thus Vladimir Chuikin and the diehard communists who organised the 16–17 July 1993 referendum in Narva and Sillamäe on regional autonomy have been replaced, while in Tallinn the pro-integration Russian Democratic Movement

(RDM), founded in August 1991, emerged as the second largest bloc in the capital, with 17 of the 65 council seats.

Initially, the RDM was largely based on Popular Front activists and was 'sponsored' by Savisaar, who was instrumental in promoting cooperation between the PF and the Russian faction in the Supreme Soviet on a pro-integration platform. Savisaar in fact attended and spoke at the RDM's inaugural congress at which 150 delegates represented between 1500 and 2000 members. Opposed to the February 1992 citizenship law, the RDM became part of the so-called Representative Assembly, along with Russian Business and the Slavonic Society, with a view to bringing the Russian voice to bear in the policy process. At the annual meeting of the Russian Representative Assembly in May 1994, the RDM leader, Aleksei Semyonov, proposed that a separate Russian party be set up at least as a short-term measure (it might later, he argued, merge with an Estonian party) and he envisaged it occupying a position to the left of centre on the political spectrum.[12] As we shall shortly see, a Russian alliance did contest the general election in March 1995.[13]

Precisely as its political elite, the Russian-speaking population as a whole has not constituted a monolithic bloc. Three groupings may be identified. First, there are the existing citizens (who are generally well integrated), along with those Russian-speakers applying to become Estonian citizens. Together they comprise 3–4 per cent of the total citizenry. At the time of the September 1992 general election, CSCE staff visiting Estonia commented that: 'Russian concerns about the language requirements of the Estonian citizenship law – knowledge of 1500 words – may seem unwarranted and unjustified. But for older people and those not gifted at languages, learning even one and a half thousand words can seem daunting.'[14] Yet there is a section of the older generation of Russian-speakers (the test is somewhat simplified for persons over 60) which is clearly trying to get a working knowledge of the language (however difficult). A friend of the author related how an elderly Russian lady had inquired in the bus queue 'Are you Estonian?' and, on receiving an affirmative response, had asked if her vocabulary could be tested during the journey! For some Russian-speaking citizens, in truth, knowledge of Estonian is more a statement of good intent than having much practical value since in areas like Narva there is little occasion to use it. Indeed, there are cases of conversation groups organised by Russians just to keep up their Estonian.

Second, there are those Russian-speakers who want to remain in Estonia without seeking citizenship. Several reasons can be adduced for this. A number of successful and economically well integrated businessmen view citizenship as unnecessary. There is some evidence that, if they had been enfranchised, they would have backed

Isamaa in September 1992 on the basis of its marketisation programme. Some Estonian-speaking Russians, moreover, reject the idea of citizenship because they view the 'oath of allegiance' as humiliating. There are, of course, also those who see the language examination as too demanding (hence the RDM's insistence on distinguishing the concept of citizenship and language and its view that language should not be a precondition of citizenship). Among a younger generation of Russian-speakers there is a clear preference for English rather than Estonian as their 'foreign language'.

Finally, there are those Russian-speakers who would want to return to Russia if all other things were equal. For these people, politicoeconomic developments in Russia are, of course, of crucial importance since any failure to create an effective market economy would mean that they would be worse off than if they had remained in Estonia. However, the collapse of the All-Union industries hit the blue-collar Russian-speaking workforce particularly hard and, with unemployment in the Russian-speaking towns like Narva remaining extremely high, there is an incentive to leave. Many have already crossed the river to work in Ivangorod where, ironically, unemployment among native Russians has been the result

The survey evidence of a growing convergence in the values and attitudes of the Estonian and non-Estonian population looks cautiously promising. So, too, is the limited evidence of an improvement in ethnic relations in Estonia. The proportion of Estonians who viewed ethnic relations as 'average', 'good' or 'very good' stood at only 45 per cent in December 1988, but this had risen to 89 per cent by autumn 1993. In the same period, the number of Estonians regarding ethnic relations as 'poor' or 'very poor' fell from 55 per cent to 12 per cent and among non-Estonians from 39 per cent to 9 per cent.[15] A growing minority of non-Estonians, it seems, have come to accept the authority of the post-communist state. According to a poll conducted by the Academy of Sciences Institute for International and Social Sciences in the first half of 1994, nearly one in three (30 per cent) of Russians were loyal to the Estonian state and under 10 per cent had totally negative attitudes towards Estonia.[16]

Political Developments, 1992–5

Recapitulating on developments in the political sphere, Estonia was governed by two right-wing coalitions between September 1992 and March 1995. The first under Mart Laar of *Isamaa* held office until October 1994; the second under Andres Tarand of the Moderates saw out the rest of the electoral term. The partisan composition of the cabinet was stable until June 1994, comprising, in addition to *Isamaa*, the two parties in the Moderates' alliance, the Social Democrats and Rural Centre Party, along with the National Independence Party (ERSP). In June, however, the government became a four-party combination when the Right-Wingers split away from *Isamaa*. Tarand's coalition also brought together these four groupings.

At the 1992 *Riigikogu* election, *Isamaa*, itself an electoral alliance of five proto-parties, four of which subsequently joined forces in a unified party, emerged as the largest grouping with 22.8 per cent of the popular vote and 29 *Riigikogu* seats. Differences between the younger generation of Thacherite economic liberals dominating the cabinet and older nationalist elements in the parliamentary group, coupled with mounting opposition to Laar's leadership style, it will be recalled, split *Isamaa* and led to the formation of the Right-Wingers. For its part, the ERSP, the only party to possess a national organisation, polled a rather disappointing 8.7 per cent of the vote and became a junior partner in the two coalitions during 1992–5. The leading dissidents and expatriots at its helm did not generally make good ministers, splits developed and, in contrast to three years earlier, ERSP contested the 1995 election in alliance with *Isamaa*.

Electoral alliances have been a precondition of survival, given the German-style 5 per cent electoral threshold, yet of several such alliances in September 1992, the only one to survive three years later was the Moderates, which polled 9.7 per cent. Their biggest name was Tarand, the (compromise) prime minister following Laar's enforced departure, and he amply compensated for the resignation as leaders of the two pioneering figures in the Social Democrats and Rural Centre, Marju Lauristin and Ivar Raig, respectively, in the nine months before the general election. The weak trade union movement also formed part of the Moderates' electoral alliance in 1995.

Among the best-supported opposition parties in the run-up to the 1995 *Riigikogu* election two, the Coalition and Centre parties, were created and led by prime ministers of the transitional period (Vähi and Savisaar), while a third, the Rural People's Party (*Maarahva Erakond*) was the brainchild of the former ESSR president Arnold Rüütel. All three served in large part as flags of convenience – career vehicles – for the 'notables' of the late communist period. Vähi's Coalition Party was the dominant element in the so-called 'Secure Home alliance' which polled 13.6 per cent in September 1992 and led in the opinion polls for much of the 1992–5 period. The formation of the Rural People's Party, in contrast, was announced in the newspaper *Rahva Hääl* as late as 19 September 1994. The Coalition and Rural People's parties entered an electoral alliance for the 1995 *Riigikogu* election.

The People's Centre Party, later simply Centre Party, had been the main component of the Popular Front alliance which polled 12.2 per cent in September 1992. Although Savisaar's authoritarian management style prompted mid-term splits in the Centre Party's parliamentary ranks, it absorbed Tiit Made's Entrepreneurs' Party and shortly thereafter Made became Centre Party chairman. Savisaar, moreover, enjoyed considerable residual support among such formerly loyalist Popular Front groups as the voluntary Home Guard.

A fourth opposition group to register significant support in the opinion polls, the Reform Party (*Eesti Reformierakond*) dated back only to November 1994. The name was devised by Ignar Fjuk and denoted the need to continue on the course of market reforms. The new party was founded 'Rüütel-style' by Siim Kallas, former head of the puppet trade union movement, a leading figure in the nationalist-minded Communist faction 'Free Estonia' in 1990, the architect of Estonia's break with the rouble zone and return to the *kroon* in June 1992, and the governor of the Bank of Estonia between 1992 and 1995 (he resigned shortly after the election). Although tainted with the same 'roubles sale' scandal that had finally deposed Laar, he sought unsuccessfully to become prime minister in October 1994 and then proceeded to create the new-rightist Reform Party which ultimately incorporated the small Liberal Democratic Party (part of the *Isamaa* alliance in 1992). Backed by big business and a group of economists and financiers who had met informally for over a year (using the curious title of Taxpayers' Union) the Reform Party ran by far the most visible election campaign and its support increased by no less than 6 per cent between January and February 1995 (see Table 9.2).

The smaller political groupings were a motley crew. Two anti-party radical nationalist movements, Better Estonia and the Estonian Citizens, both electoral alliances in their own right, joined forces for the 1995 election. Led by expatriot Estonians, they championed the cause of the indigenous Estonian nation against the Russian colonists and urged people to 'go out and vote or let the Russians into the Riigikogu'. Both worked for repatriation in one form or another. Jüri Estam, the Better Estonia leader, went on a 'partial hunger strike' (!) against the tighter 1995 citizenship law (compare the 1992 legislation discussed earlier in this chapter), with its five-year residence requirement, which he regarded as too liberal.[17] Jüri Toomepuu, the most popular individual candidate of all in September 1992, but following defections the only parliamentary survivor of the Estonian Citizens by 1995, ran much the same populist, anti-communist campaign that had been so successful three years earlier.

On the subject of communists, the Estonian Communist Party, which took the name Democratic Labour Party in autumn 1991, failed to gain a parliamentary toehold a year later. However, under the leadership of Vaino Väljas, it formed an electoral alliance called Justice

Table 9.2   The popularity of electoral alliances and individual
parties, 25 January–27 February 1995 (per cent)

Party	25 Jan.	27 Feb.
Coalition/Rural People's	28.0	30.0
Social Democrats/Rural Centre	13.6	7.0
Centre	11.6	13.0
Reform Party	9.4	15.0
Isamaa/ERSP	6.1	6.0
Right-Wingers	5.8	6.0
Future Party	3.8	2.0
Better Estonia/Estonian Citizens	3.5	2.0
Justice	2.9	3.0
Ind. Royalists/Greens	2.6	2.0
Farmers' Party	2.6	2.0
'Our Home is Estonia'	2.6	3.0
Blue Party	0.9	1.0
Foresters' Party	0.7	1.0
Democratic Union	0.4	0.0
Others	0.9	1.0

Source: Juhan Kivirahk, 'Kuus valimisnimekirja on praegu lävepakust üle', *Eesti Sõnumid*, 25
January 1995; 'Viron puoluekirjo hämmentää', *Helsingin Sanomat*, 1 March 1995.

(*Õiglus*) with the Party for Legal Justice (*Õigusliku Tasakaalu Erakond*)
for the 1995 general election.

Giving some immediacy to the radical nationalist groups was the
emergence of an alliance of Russian parties – the Estonian United
People's Party, the Russian Party and individual members of the
unregistered Russian People's Party – seeking to appeal to those
Russians with Estonian citizenship. It constituted an uneasy accommodation between previously hardline Interfront elements and moderate Russian-speakers which, pronouncing its integrationist intent
and demand for equality of treatment, fought under the slogan 'Our
Home is Estonia' (*Meie kodu on Eestimaa*).

Electoral Issues and Issue Cleavages

Although detailed party platforms appeared in *Eesti Sõnumid* over
the course of February 1995, the electoral agenda was to a real extent
set by a series of 13 questions put to the parties/electoral alliances by
the newspaper *Hommikuu* in the run-up to polling. What emerged

was a relatively low, but, compared with the Finnish general election two weeks later, not unusually low, level of issue differentiation between the main parties.[18] Most significantly, in contrast to 1992, the economy replaced the nationalist question as the main electoral issue. In this respect, the election was about the government and particularly *Isamaa*'s record between 1992 and 95.

Among the several valence issues, there was broad cross-party support for a reduction in business income (corporation) tax from its existing level of 26 per cent in order to encourage entrepreneurship. Backing for this ranged from Justice to the Reform Party, which aimed in stages to abolish income tax altogether. There was also a general commitment to the goal of ultimate Estonian membership of the EU and, again, this encompassed the unequivocal support of the Reform Party (the alternative, it held, was political and economic dependence on Russia) and the somewhat more ambivalent stance of Justice. Only Better Estonia was clearly opposed to the EU. There was also inter-party agreement on the need to improve police salaries and to implement measures to combat crime (there were, of course, differences on the small print).

There were nonetheless differences of emphasis between the parties on many issues. Indeed, three cross-cutting issue cleavages can be identified and may be used to order the parties on a multidimensional political spectrum (see Figure 9.1). The primary political cleavage aligned those forces backing the *market against the state*. Broadly speaking, the moderate rightist parties, anchored in economic liberalism, sought to continue along the reformist course of the Laar and Tarand coalitions and represented perforce the beneficiaries of marketisation. Typical of this group was the Reform Party's position on two central socioeconomic questions: property reform and particularly the privatisation of flats, on the one hand, and pensions, on the other. On the former, it conceded that the property reform legislation had aroused strong social tensions, but held that turning back was simply not an option; on the latter, the Reform Party held that short-term handouts were simply not feasible and that only sustained long-term economic growth would facilitate an increase in pensions. In contrast, the parties of the centre-left, although not challenging the rectitude of the market route *per se*, promised to deploy the state to protect the casualties of capitalism and those groups marginalised by marketisation. The Centre, Coalition and Rural People's parties all committed themselves in different ways to reduce unemployment, raise pensions and protect agriculture. The Centre also posed as the champion of the small entrepreneurs who, it was implied, would suffer at the hands of an influx of big foreign companies into Estonia. Although the Justice alliance was the only one to favour replacing the flat-rate proportional income tax with a system

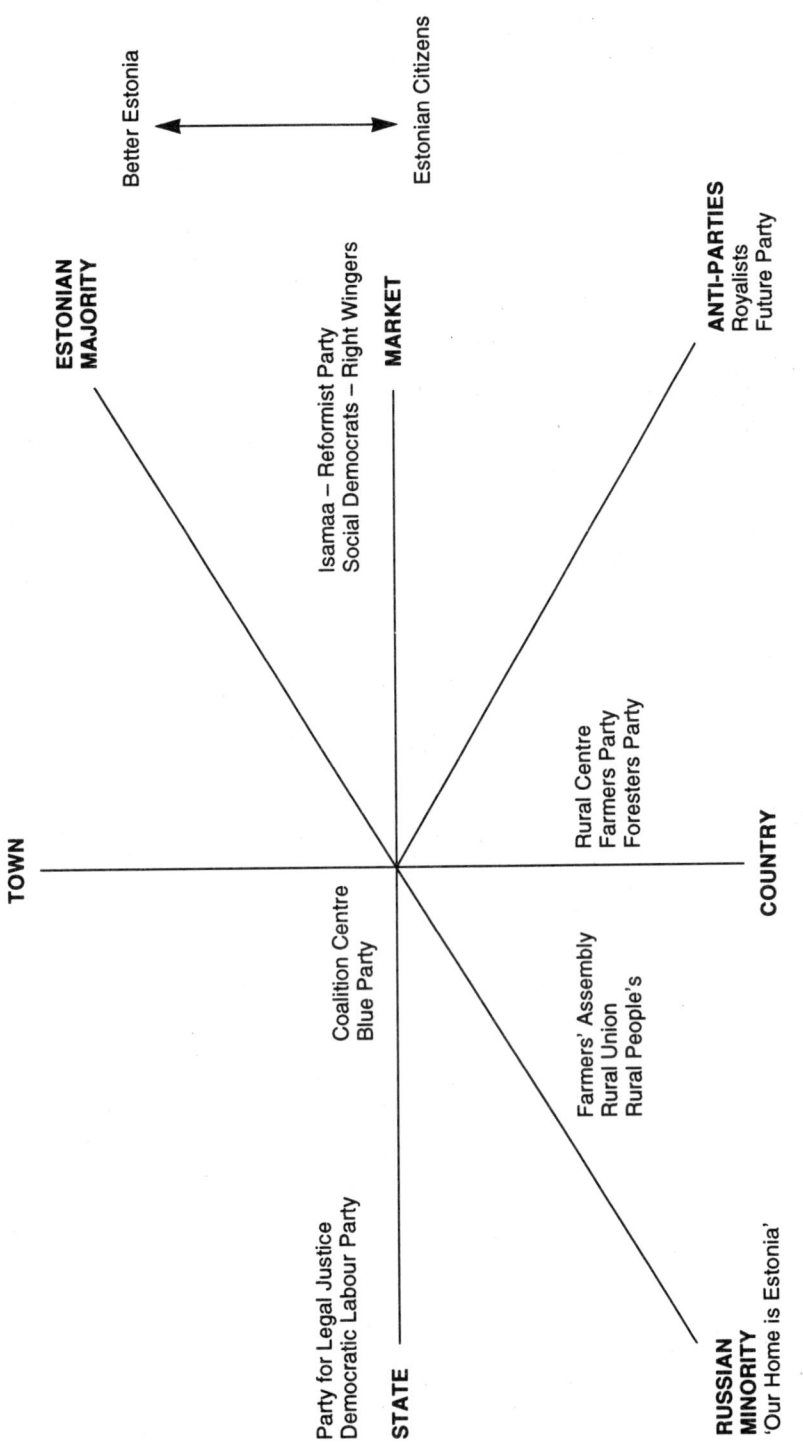

Figure 9.1   The Estonian party system in March 1995

of progressive taxation, the Centre leader Savisaar favoured applying the progressive principle only to those on low incomes.

Closely linked to the Left–Right, state–market conflict, a second cleavage dimension pitted the interests of the *countryside against the towns*. Thus the groupings of the centre-left, along with two small sectional parties – the Foresters' Party (*Metsaerakond*) and Farmers' Party (*Eesti Talurahva Erakond*) – canvassed measures to protect farming and develop regional infrastructures, whereas *Isamaa* and the Reform Party in particular represented the urban centres and their numerous consumers. No less than six rural parties in fact contested the 1995 *Riigikogu* election and two electoral alliances, the Moderates and the Coalition–Rural People's Party alliance, contained conflicting rural–urban elements.

A third cleavage was ethnic in character and aligned *the Russian-speaking against the Estonian-speaking population*. The radical Right took an intransigent line on the national question, Better Estonia arguing that there was a terminal imbalance in the ethnic mix and that decolonisation was a prerequisite of Estonia's survival. As mentioned, the Russian parties, who tended to represent the better-off members of the ethnic minority, were integrationists.

In the event, the second *Riigikogu* election since Estonia regained her independence witnessed a victory for the three main centre-left parties (see Table 9.3). The Rural People's, Coalition and Centre parties polled a combined 46.8 per cent of the vote and in the countryside, where it appears the election was decided, their success was even greater. Excluding the East and West Virumaa constituencies, the three parties managed 53.7 per cent of the poll. The Rural People's Party in particular made extensive inroads in the countryside and its leader, Rüütel, with 17 149 votes, recorded the highest-ever individual ballot, bettering the Estonian Citizen Toomepuu's total in 1992 (the latter managed less than 4000 votes three years later). Conditions were undoubtedly conducive to a shift in support to the former ESSR president whose roots and home were in rural Estonia. Thus, when the old Soviet *kolkhozs* were abolished, the majority of agricultural workers, instead of setting up as private farmers, joined forces in producer cooperatives. Lacking the necessary managerial skills to compete effectively, however, many of these farm cooperatives subsequently went bankrupt and were sold by auction. Not only did their personnel lose their jobs but, to rub salt into the wound, they had no legal claim on the land they cultivated.

The election signified a return to favour (and power) of the 'old guard' of former communist figureheads, albeit in the case of Vähi, the Coalition leader, now professing the virtues of a Ludwig Erhard-style social market economy and a continued Western orientation in defence (pro-NATO membership) and foreign trade policy (ultimate

Table 9.3   The performance of the parties and electoral alliances
at the *Riigikogu* election on 5 March 1995

Party	Electoral alliance	%	Seats
Coalition Rural Union Pensioners & Family Party Farmers' Assembly Rural People's	*Coalition & Rural People's Association*	32.6	41
Centre		14.2	16
Rural Centre Social Democrats Central Trade Union Organisation	*Moderates*	6.0	6
Royalists/Greens	*Fourth Power*	0.8	0
Estonian United People's Russian Party in Estonia	*Our Home is Estonia*	5.9	6
Democratic Labour Party for Legal Justice	*Justice*	1.7	0
Southern Estonian Citizens' Movement Northern Estonian Citizens Progress Party[1] Nationalist Party Jäger Party Estonian Home	*Estonian Citizens/ Better Estonia*	3.6	0
Right-Wingers		5.0	0
Future Party[2]		2.6	0
Blue Party		0.3	0
Reform Party		16.4	19
Foresters		0.6	0
Others		0.6	0
Plus 13 individual candidates		100.0	101

Notes:
1   Founded as a splinter group of the ERSP on 20 November 1993 and led by Ants Erm.
2   Founded on 29 August 1993.
Source: 'Valimiste võitjad väljendavad koostöösoovi', *Eesti Sõnumid*, 6 March 1995.

EU membership). Vähi insisted, in fact, that the Coalition was a centre-right party and its new parliamentary group certainly contained disparate elements, from economic liberals to more traditional conservatives. However, in common with the other leading opposition parties, the Coalition envisaged a role for the state in protecting the disprivileged and, above all, the pensioners, the value of whose rouble savings had dropped when the Soviet Union collapsed. Indeed, it bears restatement that, with a pro-market consensus in Estonia greater than in most East European countries, there was little or no basis for fundamentalist economic opposition, that is for unambiguously anti-system (anti-capitalist) parties. Rather, the centre-left effectively exploited the dissatisfaction with the fall-out from marketisation and resentment of those responsible for managing the post-independence period: the parties of the *Isamaa*-led coalition. For the centre-left voters, the personalities of the transitional period appeared reliable, seasoned campaigners. In the words of the Centre chairman, Made, it was a 'victory for experience'.

For the governing parties, the result represented a bad defeat. They lost well over half their vote and two-thirds of their seats. *Isamaa*, debilitated by the Right-Wingers' split and the loss of the popular Kaido Kama and Ülo Nugis, never recovered from Laar's fall from grace. It lost support in the rural areas to the Rural People's Party and in its stronghold urban areas to the Reform Party, for whom Kallas' involvement in the same roubles sale scandal as Laar apparently proved little if any handicap. With 16.8 per cent of the vote and one-fifth of the *Riigikogu* seats, the Reform Party gained at a stroke more than all the other moderate rightist groups put together. As to the smaller governing parties, the ERSP appeared increasingly overtaken by events and, with the national question receding in electoral importance, struggled to project a distinct identity in economic policy (in May 1995, *Isamaa* and the ERSP announced a merger with a view to running a single list of candidates at the 1996 local government elections). The Moderates for their part sought to promote themselves as a force for stability – a responsible core element in government – but, despite the bonus of the popularity of Tarand, the outgoing prime minister, they fell short of the votes and seats they obtained in 1992.

Confounding the discouraging poll forecasts, the Russian electoral alliance 'Our Home is Estonia' cleared the 5 per cent threshold and, in gaining 5.7 per cent of the overall vote, only narrowly failed to achieve its target of 7–10 *Riigikogu* seats. This was, of course, the first time Russian parties had run slates of candidates (average age 48) at a general election since the reacquisition of independence, although there were Russian-speakers in the Estonian Supreme Soviet during 1990–92 and the retiring *Riigikogu* contained a solitary Russian, Sergei

Zonov, who came in as a substitute member representing the Moderates. The Russian alliance had emphasised the contribution it would make to the integration of the ethnic minority and in facilitating contacts with the Russian Federation. Leaders such as Viktor Andrejev, however, were at pains to dismiss any parallels with the Swedish People's Party in Finland. The Russian bloc, he argued, did not seek to promote and protect a distinctive cultural identity; rather, it conjoined sectional parties working to articulate the broad spectrum of Russian interests. This was also the first time Russian-speaking citizens had voted at a post-1991 general election although, as mentioned, there was a notably higher turnout among Russians than Estonians at the October 1993 local government elections. The party political cohesion of the ethnic minority remains relatively low. Only about one-third of the 18 per cent of Russian-speakers among the total electorate favoured 'Estonia is our Home', many of the others preferring the Centre and Coalition parties.

For the rest, the leftist Justice alliance, including the former communists in the Democratic Labour Party, failed to make a significant impact. The fact that the latter, with the third largest membership, failed to win a single *Riigikogu* seat, made a telling comment on the way Estonian parties are essentially electoral organisations (Väljas, the DLP leader, resigned shortly after the election). The radical rightist Better Estonia/Estonian Citizens also fell well short of the 5 per cent barrier, while Jaanus Raidal's Future Party was clearly too futuristic, and possessed too few concrete answers to the present problems of Estonia to appeal to many voters. The Greens and Royalists in the alliance Fourth Power (*Neljas Jõud*) forfeited their parliamentary seats and, following problems concerning the registration of their candidates, left the *Riigikogu*, embittered. Finally, the Blue Party (*Sinine Erakond*) went empty-handed. Founded on 29 November 1994 and including a number of well-known comedians and actors on its lists, the Blue Party called for greater state support for the performing arts, insisted that a higher priority be given to cultural policy and pointed to the alarming drain of talent out of Estonia. While pro-EU (the party's name was coined because blue is the colour of the European Union and the dominant colour in the national flag), the Blue Party asserted the importance of preserving the identity and individuality of small nation-states in an integrating Europe.

Still an Anti-party System?

Even before the election result was officially known, the former prime minister, Mart Laar, predicted that it would take two more elections in Estonia before a more stable pattern of voter–party alignments emerged. The party system, it was implied, was still in transition and so, too, it might have been added, was the social structure under the impact of marketisation. Yet how much had changed in the 1992–5 parliamentary term, and could Estonia any longer be described as an anti-Party system? In returning to this central question, it is worth reminding ourselves of the three conditions of the model posited in Chapter 1: (a) that for a majority of voters the partisan allegiance of candidates is of secondary importance in determining their voting behaviour; (b) that a substantial proportion of the citizenry (at least one-third) abstains from voting; (c) that one or more anti-parties gain numerically significant support. It is proposed briefly to review some of the evidence in relation to each of these conditions before proceeding to some tentative conclusions.

It will be recalled that survey data before the 1992 general election revealed that only one in 10 Estonians and one in 20 non-Estonians 'believed in' parties and that, in striking contrast to Western Europe, where MPs are in practice elected as members of a party, the significance of the partisanship of candidates in determining Estonian voter choice in September 1992 was relatively low when compared with the role of their personality and past history. Two years later, the situation had changed remarkably little. A poll of 2677 voters in November 1994 revealed that only 4 per cent of respondents would have voted purely for a party if an election had been staged at that time; 12 per cent would have opted for a combination of candidate and party, whereas 67 per cent would have favoured an individual candidate (see Table 9.4).

A corollary of the strength of personality voting has been a relatively low, but stable, level of partisan identification in Estonia since 1992. In the period 1992–5 an average of four out of five Estonians did not consider themselves supporters of any political party. The figure

Table 9.4   What influences your electoral choice?

	%	n
A particular individual	67	1789
Party allegiance	4	119
Personality and party equally	12	330
Don't know	2	64
Neither individual nor party	14	375
Total	100	2677

Source: Data provided by Andrus Saar of the Saar polling agency.

for party identifiers was steady at 20 per cent throughout 1994 and of these, one-third (7 per cent of the electorate as a whole) claimed to be strong identifiers (mostly with *Isamaa* and the Centre Party). The evidence suggests, however, that partisanship rises in the run-up to, and immediate aftermath of, an election. After the local government elections in October 1993, 25 per cent of Estonians said they supported a party, and the figure for January 1995 rose 1 per cent on the 1994 average. It cannot be doubted that, in the two months before the March general election, the repeated exposition of party programmes and policies in the media served in some measure to reinforce a sense of partisanship and distinguish party and leaders.

Equally, it needs emphasis that levels of partisanship have been higher among high-status, well-educated groups and personality voting strongest among low-status (especially elderly and rural) groups. Put another way, personality voting is greatest among the centre-left Coalition and Rural People's parties and weakest among supporters of the parties of the moderate Right. In a survey of students at the Estonian Institute of Humanities in Tallinn conducted by the author in the week before polling on 5 March 1995, it emerged that those voting for a personality alone numbered only 6.5 per cent, compared with 38.7 per cent going for a combination of personality and party and no less than 41.9 per cent voting solely for a party – far beyond the 4 per cent of the Saar poll in November 1994 (12.9 per cent of respondents either had no intention of voting or did not express a clear preference). The most popular parties among the students were those on the moderate Right: 55 per cent adjudged the Reform Party or the *Isamaa*–ERSP alliance to be closest to their interests or thinking and, asked to list the three parties closest to their interests and/or way of thinking, nearly one in five (19.4 per cent) listed a full moderate rightist slate, that is a combination of *Isamaa*–ERSP, Reform Party and Right-Wingers (see Table 9.5).

In considering the second condition of the anti-party system model, relating to the extent of non-voting, it needs to be emphasised that the accentuated mobilisation of the revolutionary period was followed by a sharp decline in interest and the perceived salience of politics (depoliticisation) and a concomitant drop in the levels of popular engagement in politics (demobilisation). From a notable 83 per cent of all Estonian residents who voted at the 3 March 1991 referendum on restoring the national independence and sovereignty of Estonia, turnout declined to 66.3 per cent by the referendum on the new constitution on 28 June 1992. At the simultaneous presidential and parliamentary elections on 20 September 1992, the level of popular participation was 66.9 per cent. By the time of the local government elections in October 1993, turnout among the Estonia-speaking population had dropped further. Whereas 83 per cent of

Table 9.5   Support for the parties among the student population, March 1995

Which party do you think is closest to your interests or way of thinking?

Party	Percentage
Reform Party	32.3*
Isamaa/ERSP	22.6
Royalists	9.7
Future Party	6.5
Others	9.7
No preference	19.4
n = 31	

Note: *Three-quarters of the students were aged under 24 and nearly half (45%) were first-time voters.
Source: Author's own field work.

voters in the university town of Tartu had used their ballots at the 3 March 1991 referendum, only 34 per cent did so in October 1993. Non-voting, it appeared, had become endemic.

The following year, however, marked an apparent turning of the tide. By November 1994, as Table 9.6 demonstrates, 78 per cent of eligible voters stated that they would vote in the event of an imminent election (among those aged over 35, the prospective turnout was 15 per cent higher than in September 1992, and by February 1995 the figure had risen to 81 per cent. Moreover, 16 per cent of the electorate cast their votes during the three postal ballot days prior to 5 March. One Reform Party supporter (previously *Isamaa*) did so because of her strong association of Sundays and elections in the Soviet period. She recalled how, wishing to abstain in principle, she always attended two days beforehand to cross her name off the electoral register, using the pretext that she would be out of Tallinn. It was also to spare the electoral officials paying repeated visits on Sunday afternoon (when virtually everybody else had voted!) to get her down to the polling station.

In the event, there was a marginal decline in turnout to 66.4 per cent at the 5 March *Riigikogu* election. Abstentionism at parliamentary elections, in short, appears to have stabilised just above the level required by the anti-party system criteria.

Turning to the final issue, the existence of numerically significant anti-parties, the 1992 general election saw two anti-parties claim nearly

Table 9.6   Intended participation levels in an imminent *Riigikogu* election by age, November 1994

Age	Yes	No	Don't know	%	N
18–24	69	13	18	100	373
25–34	76	8	17	100	521
35–49	82	6	12	100	708
50–64	82	6	11	100	611
65+	81	8	11	100	463

Source: Data from Andrus Saar of the Saar polling agency.

14 per cent of the active electorate. The Estonian Citizens polled 6.8 per cent of the vote and Toomepuu became the single most popular politician. The Independent Royalists, who offered voters nothing but fairy-stories, polled 7.1 per cent. In the 1995 *Riigikogu* campaign, the Royalists continued their line of eschewing detailed electoral promises. Their programme contained only five points: to prove that the Royalists exist; to prove that the Royalists take things seriously; to prove that a monarchy in Estonia is possible; to find a pretender to the throne; and to declare the Kingdom of Estonia. The programme, it was stated, would be implemented in the order of priority set out above. It was added (though with absolutely no elaboration) that the party had a stance on all current social matters, but preferred to remain above the hurly-burly of Left–Right politics.

This was broadly true, also, of a third and new anti-party, the Future Party, which strove for a fundamental reorientation in the culture of both people and politicians. Based on a young, charismatic leader, Raidal, and 'sponsored' by an investment group which financed two radio stations, the 'New Age' quality of the Future Party was encapsulated in the first two sentences of its election programme. 'Put your mind in order, then you can organise the people and country. Put the people and country in order, then you can organise the world!.'

Meanwhile, Toomepuu, the lone Estonian Citizen in parliament by the 1995 election, deployed the tactics that had served him so well three years earlier. His main poster was two-sided: on the left, there was a picture of the former ESSR president Arnold Rüütel receiving a medal of honour from the CPSU central committee; on the right, he himself was displayed receiving a distinguished services decoration for Vietnam veterans from the US General Westmoreland. It read: 'The Choice is Yours'. In fact, in the southernmost constituency of Võru, Valga and Põlva, which had easily the highest unemployment rate of anywhere in Estonia, nearly five times as many voters chose

Rüütel as chose Toomepuu, whose Estonian Citizens' vote (together with Better Estonia) of 3.6 per cent was only just over half of their 1992 total. The Royalists in the Fourth Power alliance (with the Greens) managed only a meagre 0.8 per cent of the active electorate and the Future Party 2.6 per cent – in the latter case, far less than looked possible some months before polling. All in all, the anti-party vote in 1995 was 50 per cent down on three years earlier.

The electoral mood had undoubtedly changed since the 1992 election. In the towns in particular, from taxi-drivers and shopkeepers to larger entrepreneurs, there was not a little satisfaction with the *Isamaa* government's performance and the progress made over three years. A young Reform Party supporter at the Institute of Humanities commented: 'The economic situation has taken a turn for the better. Estonia is now on a reformist course and there is no possibility of turning back. Estonia is probably the most European and democratic country of the old East European bloc'.[19] The Independent Royalists, it will be recalled, were the best-supported (anti-) party among the under-24 years category in 1992 and, indeed, among all those aged under 29; 14 per cent of all 18–24-year-olds supported the Royalists. In the author's survey of students in March 1995, however, Royalist support had dropped to 9.7 per cent (still well above their national support level) and this compared with 32.3 per cent for the Reform Party and 22.6 per cent for the *Isamaa*–ERSP alliance. In the countryside, too, the electoral climate was different. In 1992 Toomepuu had exploited a diffuse anti-communist mood. Three years later, Rüütel's success was based on his commitment to attend to specific socioeconomic grievances. The conflict line was rural versus urban, not nationalism versus communism.

Conclusions

The post-communist Estonian party system continues to display high levels of fragmentation and instability and the process of party formation remains incomplete. The onset of the 1995 *Riigikogu* election precipitated the emergence of several new and electorally significant parties, as well as other minor groupings (Blue Party, Foresters and so on). About two in five voters backed two parties – the Rural People's Party and Reform Party – which had not existed six months before the election. The growing proximity of polling also prompted the Russian business community belatedly to engage themselves in the political arena, with the resultant creation of the two ethnic minority parties in the 'Estonia is our Home' alliance.

The Estonian party system has already acquired distinctive features of its own and there has been a striking failure of those parties belonging by name to the main Western family types to make much headway. True, several parties claim fraternal links across the Baltic and have received 'technical assistance' (computers, photocopiers and so on) and policy advice. But the christian democratic proto-parties were quickly absorbed into *Isamaa* and, while the Liberal Democrats resisted joining the unified *Isamaa* party in 1993, they threw their hand in with Kallas' Reform Party before the 1995 general election. The Social Democrats, moreover, are far from the status of largest single party they enjoy across the Nordic region. Two of the larger parties, to be sure, do bear the name and claim an ideological affinity with mainstream Scandinavian parties: Savisaar's Centre Party is modelled on its Swedish counterpart and Vähi's Coalition on the Finnish party of the same name.

Economic cleavages have largely displaced the national question as the pivot of the party system, although in 1995 the level of issue differentiation between the parties was relatively small. However, *externally created* (bottom-up) parties *à la* Duverger, those deriving from a pre-existing organisational base outside the political elite or from a popular initiative – especially sectional parties like the Farmers and Foresters – remain small and failed to gain seats in the 1995–99 *Riigikogu*.

Relatively few, if any, of the Estonian parties can be described as mass parties in the sense of being voluntary membership organisations. The only parties with a grassroots membership, albeit rarely exceeding 500, are the Democratic Labour Party, Centre, Coalition, *Isamaa*, ERSP and the Social Democrats. Indeed, three basic challenges may be said still to face the parties in seeking to institutionalise themselves: *depersonalisation* and the generation of an identity distinct from the founding notable (s); *organisation* and the promotion of the party as a voluntary membership structure (compare a governing organisation); and *stabilisation*: the development of a stable and cohesive social support base.

Estonia continues to display features of an anti-party system. Personality voting is dominant and the personalisation of parties widespread. Indeed, the 1995 election turned out to be a victory for the personalities and leaders of the transitional period. Thus, although trading off a mood of rural protest, the Rural People's Party success was based first and foremost on Rüütel's persona. Trust in parties and politicians remains low and the strength of partisan identification weak. *Prima facie* evidence of the latter can be gained from the volatility of voters (one-third were undecided on the eve of polling and about half ultimately voted for entirely new parties) and the steady level of abstentionism. Turnout in March 1995 was no higher than three years earlier and was significantly lower than the numbers indicating their intention to vote. Moreover, the provisional data suggest that, as in 1992, participation levels were lowest among the youngest age cohorts.

On two counts, however, there are signs that Estonia is progressing from an anti-party system to a more stable form of multipartism. First, opinion polls have indicated a rise in the number of people voting for a party or at least for a 'party and personality equally' and the notion of party seems somewhat more internalised. It is, in short, losing the pejorative connotation it had in 1992, when it was widely associated with *the* party – the ruling Communist Party. Second, support for anti-parties has dropped: the Estonian Citizens, Royalists and Future Party all failed to make the *Riigikogu* and a period of consolidation and party building is in prospect.

Finally, society-building and the task of constructing a democratic society lies ahead. Popular involvement in the parties and embryonic interest groups is low and politics has lost the relevance it possessed (as a means to independence) over the revolutionary period. Democracy in Estonia is on firm ground and the integration of the ethnic minority into the decision-making process following the electoral success of the Russian parties represented a significant step forward. A democratic culture, however, in the sense of a decision-making system anchored in sustained levels of popular participation, political knowledge and civic interest, remains still some way off. In this, of course, Estonia is by no means unique.

Notes

1 'Reclaiming its place', *Newsweek*, 30 August 1993.
2 '1994 Year of Growth', *The Baltic Independent*, 9–15 September 1994.
3 Ministry of Economic Affairs, *Estonian Economic Survey 1993–1994* (Ilo: Tallinn, 1994), p.59.
4 'Property reform leaves rural jobless', *The Baltic Independent*, 14–20 January 1994.
5 *Estonian Economic Survey 1993–1994*, p.9.
6 'More character, please', *The Baltic Independent*, 4–10 July 1995.
7 *Estonian Economic Survey 1993–1994*, p.10.
8 An interesting insight into the problems of rural displacement caused by farm privatisation can be gained from the personal experience of Ene Padrik, the senior official responsible for regional planning matters in the Ministry of Agriculture. Prior to renewed independence Padrik was a state-employed breeding consultant in the small town of Rapla. Her salary dropped progressively, however, when the private farmers could no longer afford to pay her and she subsequently moved to the Ministry of Agriculture. (Interview with Ene Padrik, 20 September 1994.
9 *Estonian Economic Survey 1993–1994*, p.46.
10 For example, when in 1994 the Saudis were ready to order 40 000 Estonian sheep, the Estonians could only supply 14 000.
11 At the beginning of 1994 there were approximately 5000 prisoners in Estonian

gaols in conditions which were poor and where tuberculosis was common. (Figures quoted in Finnish television, 9 January 1994.

12   The RDM leader, Aleksei Semyonov, viewed the referendum in the Russian-speaking towns of north-east Estonia in July 1993 as essentially a protest outlet against the first draft of an aliens law which was widely regarded in Russian minority circles as too strict. Semyonov's question to the hardline Communist leaders, however, was: 'What will you do after the referendum?' Ultimately, there was tacit agreement that the government would do nothing to prevent it, but the Narva leaders would accept that it was not constitutional. (Interview with Aleksei Semyonov, 10 January 1994.

13   'Russians to form their own party', *The Baltic Independent*, 10 January 1994.

14   Commission on Security and Co-operation in Europe, *Russians in Estonia: Problems and Prospects* (Washington: September 1992), p.10.

15   Toivo U Raun, 'Post-Soviet Estonia 1991–1993', *Journal of Baltic Studies*, **XXV**, (1), 1994, p.78.

16   'Loyalty of local Russians has increased', *The Baltic Independent*, 15–21 July 1994.

17   Interview with Jüri Estam, 9 February 1995.

18   David Arter, 'The Finnish Social Democrats Storm Back', *West European Politics*, **18**, (4), 1995, pp.194–204.

19   Author's own survey work, March 1995.

10 Conclusion: The Two Europes – Converging Party Systems?

As a rule people in the countryside do not wish to join any party and leave this hobby to townsfolk. (Tiit Kubri, *Rahva Hääl*)

A fundamental supposition of this volume has been that parties have a central role to play in the process of *democratic consolidation* in the states of the former Soviet Union (and throughout post-communist Europe), not only in providing for regular accountability in the management of power, but also in stimulating structured patterns of collective participation among citizens and in socialising them in the modes and precepts of democracy. Party-building, in short, will necessarily entail society-building in the sense of strengthening political society in relation to decisions of the state and developing a democratic political culture at the grassroots.

A further supposition has been that the emergence and/or consolidation of sectional parties may well serve as a useful indicator of progress along the road to democratic consolidation. The significance of sectional parties is twofold: they demonstrate the existence of stabilised (or at least stabilising) party–voter alignments in which the party articulates particular economic interests; they also denote a degree of economic differentiation in society – a convergence between the extent of political and economic pluralism – which is the inevitable corollary of the present programmes of privatisation and marketisation.

A final supposition in relation to party building has been that the 'anti-party system' model is likely to prove a transitional phenomenon. Anti-party sentiment, however, trades off diffuse protest: economic *and* political. With the party systems of the former Soviet Union exhibiting relatively high levels of instability (factionalisation leading to fragmentation) and the number of miniscule parties showing few signs of declining, personalities continue to dominate and

247

both anti-party sentiment and weak partisanship remain prominent. Anti-parties, of course, are by no means peculiar to the former communist states. In Western Europe anti-parties have claimed support in large part as a reaction against the elitist and cartellised character of the established parties and the 'democratic deficit' which has developed between their leaders and rank-and-file members. West European parties have to varying degrees atrophied as voluntary membership organisations. Richard Katz has suggested two principal reasons for this: television has become the pre-eminent source of political information and the dominant channel of communication for elites; and state support to parties has allowed these elites to insulate themselves financially from members. As Katz concludes: 'Party becomes a label by which a group of leaders is known and an organisation for co-ordinating elite activity.'[1] Indeed, the irony would appear to be that (put crudely) whereas in Western Europe 'party' is a label which gives identity to elites and legitimises and coordinates their activity, in Eastern Europe elites give (at least some) identity to parties and the label in turn is designed to authorise and legitimise the actions of their founding figures.

A further irony may be noted in that several former Soviet republics invested in a Western 'party democracy' model at precisely the time its central premises were being challenged by a *partisan dealignment* model. According to this, parties are performing fewer functions and, as a result, partisan identification has become less necessary for voters. Many of the traditional input functions of parties, the argument goes, have been taken over by other institutions. In simplified form, the case for partisan dealignment rests on three basic propositions. First, it is argued that the interest articulation function of parties has been substantially undermined by a proliferation of group demands and the sheer range of new issues that form part of the contemporary political agenda. Parties, it is asserted, have to an extent been superseded by a plethora of special interest groups able to employ the means of modern technology both to identify and educate a sympathetic public constituency. Second, it is held that the socialisation function of parties has largely been usurped by the media which are generally perceived as unbiased and, in the cases of television and radio, constitute more accessible and pervasive delivery systems. Accordingly, there is a reduced need for a party press, a mass party organisation and canvassing to inform voters.[2] Third, it is contended that the programmatic function of parties has been variously weakened by the introduction, among other things, of open primaries, while, in any event, television has transformed elections more into personality contests than party-based contests.

It is not hard to find *prima facie* evidence of partisan dealignment in Western Europe today. Initial corroboration can be found in the *decline in the large-party share of the vote* and, by inference, a growing electoral rejection of 'old politics'. Germany will serve to illustrate the point. Thus the Christian Democratic (CDU–CSU) – Social Democratic (SPD) share of the electorate fell from a high point of 91.2 per cent in the 1976 (West German) Bundestag election to only 74 per cent in a poll conducted for *Der Spiegel* in January–February 1994.[3] Moreover, whereas the third 'old' party, the Free Democrats (FDP) sank below the 5 per cent threshold in the *Land* elections in Lower Saxony and Schleswig-Holstein the following month, backing for the Greens climbed sharply and other small non-parliamentary parties also performed well.

Another strand of support for the partisan dealignment model may be found in the evidence of *a rise in non-party support*, that is backing for the so-called 'sleeping' or 'sofa' parties and, accordingly, increased levels of electoral abstentionism. Confirming that turnout decline may be a short-term phenomenon associated with partisan dealignment, Flickinger and Studlar have demonstrated that in the 18 West European countries whose parliamentary elections were analysed between 1979 and 1989, 10 reported the lowest turnout at the last election.[4] Germany will again serve to illustrate the wider point. In summer 1993, Andreas Dimpfel created his German Party of Non-Voters (PDN), while recent survey evidence points to two trends affecting levels of voter participation.[5] On the one hand, turnout at the October 1994 *Bundestag* election was appreciably lower among citizens in former East Germany than those in West Germany; on the other, the younger the voter, the less likely he or she was to vote (see Table 10.1).

Table 10.1 **The number of non-voters by age and region in Germany, February 1994**

Age group	%
18–24	25
25–29	21
30–44	18
45–59	15
60/over	15
Region	
West Germany	17
East Germany	23

Source: 'Schlamm und Tränen', *Der Spiegel* 10, 1994, p.46.

A third fibre in the fabric of the dealignment thesis comprises evidence of *weakened partisan alignment* (attachment) among voters and a corresponding increase in electoral volatility. It appears that, over the last quarter of a century, the number of West European voters identifying with a political party has fallen. In 1989 Hermann Schmitt observed that the proportion of EU citizens more or less attached to a party dropped from under 70 per cent in the mid-1970s to under 60 per cent in the late 1980s.[6] Put another way, non-partisans number about two-fifths of the voting public within the Community. The picture was much the same in the EFTA states (before Austria, Finland and Sweden joined the EU on 1 January, 1995). It was significant that at the time of the launch of Sweden's first real protest party, New Democracy, early in 1991, the Sifo and Temo polls indicated that 21.2 per cent and 20.5 per cent of Swedes, respectively, lacked any partisan allegiance. Electoral volatility can be measured in a variety of ways including, most obviously, evidence of shifts in support between existing parties and/or backing for a new party; fluctuations in turnout, that is shifts from voting to non-voting and vice versa; and 'eleventh-hour voting decisions' made in the final day(s) of the campaign. In any event, electorates seem less stable and the partisan dealignment view would see volatility as a more or less permanent feature of modern democratic systems.

Further evidence of partisan dealignment could be sought in the marked and widespread decline in party membership. Indeed, in posing the question, 'Is there a future for the mass membership party?', Katz has argued that members are less necessary and an organisation more marginal as a linkage between elites and mass publics.[7] Television has become the dominant source of political information and the dominant channel of communication for elites, while state funding of parties has allowed them to insulate themselves financially from members. From a leadership perspective, the potential costs of members – *inter alia* their accommodation to desired party decisions – may well outweigh their benefits. The incipient collapse of the mass membership party model has been extensively remarked upon. As noted earlier, Carlo E. Ruzza and Oliver Schmidtke, writing about Italy in the early 1990s, observed: 'Most parties in government have almost completely lost their activist base and are obtaining the resources they need directly from the state through subsidies or from the economy in the form of bribes.'[8] According to Peter Mair, 'parties today are capital-intensive not labour-intensive.'[9]

A final and crucial prop in the partisan dealignment construct is evidence of a growing body of anti-party sentiment, reflected not only in non-voting, as evidenced by Dimpfel's Party of Non-voters, but also in support for one or more 'anti-parties'. Thus in Hamburg a so-called 'Instead-of-a-Party' (*eine Stattpartei*), led by Markus Wegner and run by Christian Democratic dissidents, managed 5.6 per cent in the 1993 State election, although in Lower Saxony in March 1994 it gained only 1.5 per cent of the poll.[10] Wegner clearly sought to exploit the *politikverdrossenheit*, the prevalent mood of diffuse disillusion and disenchantment with parties and politicians.

As in post-communist Europe, it is difficult to give a precise definition of an anti-party, but there are (at least) three features in the anti-party syndrome:

1 an anti-party presents itself as diametrically different from and expressly opposed to all the other parties (though not necessarily the system itself) and may well avoid the term 'party' in its title;
2 an anti-party is opposed to the elite culture (the values and orientations) of the old parties and one of its principal resources is often ridicule and the adoption of an irreverent approach to the stylised tone of the 'old guard';
3 an explicit or implicit element in the anti-party thesis is that existing parties have lost touch with political society, no longer perform their 'input' functions and contribute to a 'democratic deficit'.

Anti-parties, in short, challenge the concept, culture and contribution of the established parties. In turn, they trade off anti-party sentiment: alienated voters (young and old) who display mistrust, cynicism and a lack of confidence in parties and politicians and may well also experience low levels of subjective political competence. These *antipartisans* are not to be confused with Russell Dalton's 'apartisans', a younger generation of sophisticated and active post-materialists who, while remaining unattached to any political party, incline towards unconventional political participation.

A couple of anti-parties can be identified *en passant*. During the Swedish general election campaign of September 1991, the twin leaders of New Democracy (*Ny Demokrati*), Bert Karlsson and Ian Wachtmeister, attracted support by referring to the 'crocodile politicians' in the established parties: 'all mouth and no ears'! Indeed, over half of New Democracy's voters expressed the desire for a 'new approach' and for both the Moderates (Conservatives), who made up one-fifth of New Democracy's electorate and the Social Democrats (24 per cent) who changed party, mistrust of politicians (as well as dissatisfaction with immigration policy) were cited as important reasons.[11] As Paul Taggart and Anders Widfeldt have noted, a major component in its success appears to have been precisely New Democracy's image as an anti-party. It strove to establish itself as an *enfant terrible*, poking fun at the existing parties and carving out a niche as a 'fun-loving, establishment-baiting, populist party'; in its ideology (though not in practice) New Democracy deliberately rejected the traditional organisational forms of political parties; and the word 'New' in its title was intended to denote that the 'old parties' were played out.[12]

In Italy, the *Lega Lombarda*, subsequently called the Northern League, *Lega Nord*, was founded in 1982 by Umberto Bossi who in turn was inspired by the leader of the small Northern Italian independence movement *Union Valdotaine*. It has been anti-mafia, pro-federal and anti-*partitocrazia*: 'the suffocating control exercised by the political parties over all aspects of government and policy making.'[13] Mannheimer has assembled abundant survey evidence to show that it was the articulation of anti-state and anti-party feelings (rather than regionalist or racist sentiments) which enhanced the Lombardy League's appeal between the 1987 and 1992 general elections.[14] Opinion polls in summer 1993 put the *national* support for the Northern League at no less than 17 per cent.

In addition to the rise of the *Lega Nord*, two other developments have mirrored the extent of anti-party sentiment in Italy. First, popular rejection of the system, widespread across Western Europe, of giving public subsidies to political parties. Thus, on 18 April 1993, 90.3 per cent voted in a referendum to end state funding. It was far from self-evident to ordinary Italians, it seems, that democracy was benefiting or that the public was getting 'value for money' from the subsidies paid to parties out of taxpayers' pockets.[15] Second, there was the collapse of the Christian Democrats (DCI) – they assumed their former name, *Popolari* – who had been the dominant force in post-war Italian politics and had symbolised the notion of the party state based on patronage *clientelismo*. Having exercised an effective hegemony of power since the late 1940s and, in the process, created a para-state based on partisan appointments, the DCI ultimately came to epitomise the endemic corruption and decay of the Italian political system.

The demise of the *ancien régime* threw up, in addition to the redesignated Christian Democrats, the stridently anti-communist *Forza Italia* ('Go Italy') led by Silvio Berlusconi, head of the Fininvest media empire, and the Democratic Left Party (PDS) – the renamed communists – led by Achille Occhetto, which gained 16.5 per cent at the April 1992 general election. All in all, it may not be far-fetched to suggest that between 1991 and 1993 Italy shifted from a one-party dominant system to an anti-party system in which the old parties collapsed and even the parties themselves rejected *partitocrazia*.

A curious paradox in fact emerges when comparing the state of the parties in Western Europe with those in the new post-communist democracies which this volume has studied. In Western Europe, Sartori-style *anti-system parties*, at least of the communist variety, have virtually disappeared, although the term has remained in use, almost as a residual category, to refer to a variety of protest groups. However, taking the evidence sketched above as a whole, the West European countries, especially Italy, minus the traditional anti-system parties, appear to be inclining some way towards the *anti-party systems* to be found in Eastern Europe.[16] It will doubtless be countered that citizens in the West European democracies have not rejected the concept of party in sufficient numbers, but simply adopt a more instrumental approach to voting and what the parties have to offer. It is nonetheless significant that survey data reveal that only 30 per cent of respondents in the European Union countries replied in the affirmative to the question: 'Do you feel close to a party?' The number of anti-partisans may be much greater than is popularly imagined.

Notes

1   Richard S. Katz, 'Party as linkage: A vestigial function?', *European Journal of Political Research*, **18**, (1), 1990, pp.143–63.
2   Scott C. Flanagan and Russell J. Dalton, 'Parties Under Stress: Realignment and Dealignment in Advanced Industrial Democracies', *West European Politics*, **7**, (1), 1984, pp.7–23.
3   'Schlamm und Tränen', *Der Spiegel*, **10**, 1994, pp.41–5.
4   Richard S. Flickinger and Donley T. Studlar, 'The Disappearing Voters? Exploring Declining Turn-out in West European Elections', *West European Politics*, **15**, (2), 1993, p.13.
5   'Unadulterated party woos votes of Germany's non-voting voters', *The Guardian*, 14 July 1993.
6   Hermann Schmitt, 'On Party Attachment in Western Europe and the Utility of Eurobarometer Data', *West European Politics*, **12**, (2), 1989, pp.122–39.
7   Katz, 'Party as linkage', pp.150–57.
8   Carlo E. Ruzza and Oliver Schmidtke, 'Roots of Success of the Lega Lombarda: Mobilisation Dynamics and the Media', *West European Politics*, **16**, (2), 1993, pp.1–23.
9   Sarah Benton, 'Private profit and public loss of honour', *The Guardian*, 3 July 1993.
10 'Shattered Christian Democrats woo the Greens in Germany, *The Guardian*, 29 September 1993; 'Hamburg leaders woo anti-party', *The Independent*, 12 November 1993.
11 'Det började i Hänt i Veckan', *Dagens Nyheter*, 7 November 1993.
12 However, although 'party' did not appear in its title, New Democracy was expressly formed as a political party. As early as February 1991, barely three months after Wachtmeister and Karlsson set out a new agenda for Swedish politics in an article in the daily newspaper *Dagens Nyheter*, a decision was taken in Karlsson's home town of Skara to found a party (Paul Taggart and Anders Widfeldt, '1990s Flash Party Organisation: The Case of New Democracy in Sweden', paper given at the annual conference of the Political Studies Association of the United Kingdom, University of Leicester 20–22 April 1993).

See also David Arter, 'Black Faces in the Blond Crowd: Populist Racialism in Scandinavia', *Parliamentary Affairs*, **45**, (3), 1992.

13   James L. Newall and Martin J. Bull, 'The Italian referendum of April 1993: Real Change at Last?', *West European Politics*, **16**, (4), 1993, pp.607–15.

14   Tom Gallagher, 'Regional Nationalism and Party System Change: Italy's Northern League', *West European Politics*, **16**, (4), 1993, pp.616–21.

15   Ironically, in a mood of apparent resignation, none of the parties opposed the abolition of state funding.

16   In contrast to Russell Dalton, Howard L. Reiter has argued that those most sympathetic to the 'new agenda' were more likely than other people to be strong partisans: Howard L. Reiter, 'The Rise of the "New Agenda" and the Decline of Partisanship', *Western European Politics*, **16**, (2), 1993.

A Chronology of Events

Spring 1987 'Phosphate Spring'. A successful popular campaign against plans to expand phosphorite mining in the Kabala and Toolse areas of north-east Estonia draws the world's attention to events in Estonia.

23 August 1987 First rally in Hirvepark in Tallinn of the MRP–AEG movement: the Estonian Group for the Publication of the secret protocols of the Molotov–Ribbentrop pact. One of its principal organisers, Tiit Madisson, is subsequently exiled.

26 September 1987 'Four-Man Proposal' by Siim Kallas, Mikk Titma, Tiit Made and Edgar Savisaar for the economic self-management (autonomy) of Estonia.

October 1987 The 'Free and Independent Youth Column No. 1' restores the memorials of heroes of the Estonian War of Independence and flies the national flag.

12 December 1987 Foundation in Tallinn of the National Heritage Society (NHS).

16 December 1987 Establishment of the student organisation EÜS, Sodalicium.

24 February 1988 Anniversary of the (First) Republic of Estonia celebrated in Tallinn and elsewhere for the first time since 1940.

1–2 April 1988 A joint meeting of the Creative Unions (writers, artists, journalists, composers) in Estonia demands more political rights within the framework of the USSR. There is also an insistence on greater economic and cultural autonomy, less immigration and the rehabilitation of the victims of Stalinism.

13 April 1988 Edgar Savisaar's proposal on *Mõtleme Veel* to set up an Estonian Popular Front for the Support of Perestroika (PF).

14–17 April 1988 At the Heritage Days in Tartu, the Estonian blue, black and white national flag is displayed for the first time since 1940. Previously, any use of the colour combination had been banned. Professor Viktor Palm joined the parade, displaying the PF's initial 'declaration' in the window of his car.

April 1988 Estonian Greens officially formed.

16 June 1988 The hardline Estonian Communist Party (ECP) leader,

Karl Vaino, is removed and replaced as first secretary by the Estonian-born Vaino Väljas.

June 1988   The emergence of the 'counternationalist' Intermovement, protecting the rights of the 40 per cent Russian-speaking population.

10 August 1988   For the first time in the USSR, the *Rahva Hääl* newspaper publishes the secret protocol of the Molotov–Ribbentrop pact, under which Estonia was incorporated into the Soviet Union.

21 August 1988   Foundation of the Estonian National Independence Party (ERSP) headed by leading dissidents, Tunne Kelam and Lagle Parek.

9 September 1988   At the eleventh ECP plenary, support is declared for the popular reformist demands.

11 September 1988   High point of the 'Singing Revolution': 300 000 people gather in the Song Festival Stadium in Tallinn to give voice for the first time in public to the case for the restoration of Estonian independence.

October 1988   The release of the last political prisoner, Enn Tarto.

16 November 1988   The Estonian Supreme Soviet (ESS) adopts a 'Declaration on Sovereignty' in which the ESS is declared the supreme legislative body in Estonia.

January 1989   The PF is accepted as a legal formation.

18 January 1989   The communist-dominated ESS enacts a law reinstating Estonian as the state language.

24 February 1989 (Independence Day)   The NHS, Christian League and ERSP urge the formation of Citizens' Committees of the Estonian Republic, which are to supervise the registration of Estonian citizens, who will then elect an Estonian Congress. The ECP and PF initially condemn the initiative.[1]

26 March 1989   PF-backed candidates win a majority in elections to the Congress of People's Deputies of the USSR, the first multi-candidate elections in Estonia since the Second World War.

May 1989   The creation of the Baltic Assembly as a coordinating body of the Popular Fronts in the region.

27 July 1989   The Supreme Soviet in Moscow approves the shift to economic self-management (IME) in Estonia to take effect from 1 January 1990. Ultimately, this is blocked by the Kremlin.

August 1989   The Intermovement steps up its campaign and many Russian-manned factories stop work in protest against new Estonian laws setting residence requirements for voting in local elections. The latter are ultimately rescinded.

23 August 1989   To mark the fiftieth anniversary of the Molotov–Ribbentrop pact, a 600-kilometre human chain is formed, stretching from Tallinn to Vilnius.

12 November 1989   The ESS declares null and void Estonia's incorporation into the Soviet Union in 1940.

24 December 1989   The Soviet Union admits the existence of the secret Molotov–Ribbentrop protocols and declares them null and void from the moment of signing.

23 February 1990   The monopolistic status of the ECP is removed from the constitution of the ESSR.

24 February 1990   The 499-member Estonian Congress, inspired by Trivimi Velliste, is elected by Estonian citizens of the First Republic and their descendants (35 seats are reserved for expatriots). Independents win 109 seats; the PF 107; the NHS 104; the ERSP 70; and the ECP 39.[2]

March 1990   Foundation of an Estonian Entrepreneurs' Party by Tiit Made, one of the architects of IME.

18 March 1990   Multi-candidate elections to the 105-seat ESS. The elections are contested by 31 proto-parties, including three womens' groups (although there are only 24 female candidates out of a total of 390).[3] According to the Deputy Minister of Culture Jaak Joerüüt, the elections are still essentially for individuals and are at most 'half party political'.[4] The elections produce a pro-independence majority of about two-thirds. The PF wins 43 seats; independence-minded communists 20; Moscow-minded communists 20; and the remainder go to representatives of the Russian-speaking minority. Four seats are reserved for representatives of the Soviet army. The Citizens Committee movement (CCM) boycotts the elections.

25 March 1990   The ECP, divided over the independence question, resolves to split from the Soviet party after six months. There are 432 in favour, three against and six abstentions, but 228 delegates (mainly ethnic Russians) do not take part in the vote.

30 March 1990   The ESS declares that its absorption into the Soviet Union had been illegal and that it was beginning a 'transitional period towards independence'. This is rebuffed by Gorbachev in a presidential decree two months later.

3 April 1990   Edgar Savisaar, the PF leader, becomes prime minister.

8 May 1990   The ESS votes to readopt the name 'Estonian Republic' (*Eesti vabariik*).

15 May 1990   Intermovement mob attempts to seize the government and parliament buildings at Toompea, but is dispersed by the countermobilisation of PF supporters.

26 May 1990   Pro-Moscow deputies in the ESS, backed by the Soviet army, meet in Kohtla-Järve to create a bicameral Interregional Soviet of Deputies and Workers – 'to guarantee normal life for the citizens of the USSR residing in Estonia' – together with a National Economic Council, chaired by Vladimir Yaravoi, the director of a major defence plant in Tallinn.[5]

August 1990   ESS declares that the Soviet constitution 'ceased to regulate state and social relations in Estonia'.

3 March 1991   In a referendum, 78 per cent respond 'yes' to the question: 'Are you in favour of restoring the national independence and sovereignty of Estonia?' Two weeks later there is a boycott of Gorbachev's All-Union referendum on the preservation of the integrity of the Soviet Union.

20 August 1991   The ESS declares Estonia independent the day after the attempted hardline coup in Moscow. The latter collapses on 21 August.

22 August 1991   Iceland becomes the first country to recognise Estonia, followed by Russia (24 August) and the United States (22 September).

10 September 1991   Estonia is admitted to the Conference on Security and Co-operation in Europe (CSCE) – and to the United Nations (UN) on 17 September.

9 October 1991   Estonia and the Soviet Union restore diplomatic relations.

January 1992   Tiit Vähi becomes prime minister.

20 June 1992   Estonia becomes the first post-Soviet state to break out of the rouble zone and reintroduces its own currency, the *kroon*, tied to the *Deutschmark*.

28 June 1992   Estonia's new constitution is approved at a popular referendum.

20 September 1992   First presidential and parliamentary election since the reacquisition of independence. No presidential candidate gains an absolute popular majority and Lennart Meri, the *Isamaa* candidate, is subsequently elected by parliament. The *Isamaa* electoral alliance becomes the largest parliamentary faction and Mart Laar leads a three-way coalition of *Isamaa*, ERSP and Moderates.

May 1993   Estonia is admitted to the Council of Europe.

July 1993   Vladimir Chuikin and hardliners on the city councils of the predominantly Russian-speaking Narva and Sillamäe organise referenda on territorial autonomy. Overwhelming support for it, although there is evidence that the voters are not clear what they are voting for.

17 October 1993   Local government elections. Only Estonians can run for office, but Estonians, plus all those resident in the constituency for five years, are entitled to vote. This is the first post-independence election in which non-citizens can participate. Most of the Russian groups boycotted the previous local election in 1989, claiming that it violated the Soviet constitution that was still in force. The Coalition Party becomes the largest party on the Tallinn City Council. In addition to Arnold Rüütel, Tiit Vähi, the former prime minister, is among the successful Coalition Party

candidates in the capital. The governing *Isamaa* fares only very moderately and in Tallinn wins only five of the 64 city council seats. Turnout is much higher in the Russian-speaking towns (Narva 66 per cent and Sillamäe 71 per cent) than in the Estonian. In Tartu only 34 per cent bother to vote. Russian lists do well. The Russian Assembly wins the second highest number of seats (17) in Tallinn and another Russian list, Reval, which contains former Interfront communists, comes in third, with 10 seats.[6]

January 1994 Estonia joins NATO's 'Partnership for Peace' initiative.

18 July 1994 Estonia signs a Free Trade Agreement with the European Union (EU).

31 August 1994 Withdrawal of Russian troops from Estonia.

19 September 1994 Former ESSR President Arnold Rüütel announces the formation of a new party, the Rural People's Party, in the newspaper *Rahva Hääl*.

26 September 1994 Mart Laar resigns after losing a vote of no confidence following the 'sale of roubles' scandal. He is replaced as a 'caretaker' prime minister by Andres Tarand (elected in 1992 on the Moderates' list).

28 September 1994 The joint Estonian–Swedish-owned ferry *Estonia* sinks at Utö off south-west Finland. Extensive loss of life.

November 1994 The new Reform Party is founded 'Rüütel-style' by Siim Kallas, former head of the puppet trade union movement, a leading figure in the nationalist-minded communist faction 'Free Estonia' and, from 1992–1995, governor of the Bank of Estonia.

5 March 1995 The second *Riigikogu* election since the reacquisition of independence. Victory for the three main centre-left parties, the Rural People's, Coalition and Centre parties, which polled a combined 46.8 per cent of the vote.

April 1995 Formation of a new centre-left coalition government under Coalition Party leader Tiit Vähi (prime minister in 1992).

May 1995 *Isamaa* and the Estonian National Independence Party (ERSP) announce a merger with a view to running a single list of candidates at the 1996 local government elections.

June 1995 Vaino Väljas resigns as chairman of the Democratic Labour Party.

August 1995 The *Riigikogu* unanimously ratifies an 'associate agreement' with the EU.

Notes

1 Juhan Talve, 'Viro on itsenäinen mutta miehitetty', *Helsingin Sanomat*, 23 February 1990.

2 'Viron kongressin vaaleista lopulliset tulokset', *Helsingin Sanomat*, 6 March 1990.
3 Helena Kinnunen, 'Itsenäisyys tärkein Viron vaaleissa', *Helsingin Sanomat*, 18 March 1990.
4 Jari P. Havia, 'Viron liberaaliliike muotoutumassa', *Polttopiste*.
5 Ruutsoo 'Transitional Society', op. cit., p.209.
6 'Rysktalande fram i Estlands lokala val', *Dagens Nyheter*, 19 October 1993; 'Ruling Fatherland suffers election setback', *The Baltic Independent*, 22–8 October 1993.

Newspapers and Journals

Aamulehti
Dagens Nyheter
Der Spiegel
East European Reporter
Eesti Aeg
Eesti Sōnumid
Eesti Ekspress
Helsingin Sanomat
Homeland
Hommikuuleht
Hufvudstadsbladet
Independent on Sunday
Newsweek
Nordisk Kontakt
Polttopiste
Postimees
Päevaleht
Rahva Hääl
Svenska Dagbladet
The Baltic Independent
The Baltic Review
The Estonian Independent
The Financial Times
The Guardian
The Independent
Turun Sanomat
Uusi Suomi
Vaba Maa
Via Baltica News

Bibliography

Ágh, Attila, 'The Transition to Democracy in Central Europe: A Comparative View', *Journal of Public Policy*, **11**, (2), 1991, pp.131–51.

Andersen, Erik, 'Estland: På vej mod selstændighed?', *Nordisk Østforum*, **3**, 1989, pp.35–40.

Andersen, Erik, 'Hvis der var valg i Estland', *Nordisk Østforum*, **4**, 1989, pp.71–6.

Arter, David, *Bumpkin Against Bigwig: The Emergence of a Green Movement in Finnish Politics* (Tampereen yliopiston politiikan tutkimuksen laitoksen tutkimuksia, 47, 1978), pp.17–90.

Arter, David, 'Black Faces in the Blond Crowd: Populist Racialism in Scandinavia', *Parliamentary Affairs*, **45**, (3), 1992, pp.357–72.

Arter, David, *The Politics of European Integration in the Twentieth Century* (Dartmouth: Aldershot, 1993).

Arter, David, 'Estonia: the Case of an Anti-Party System?', in Patrick Dunleavy and Jeffrey Stanyer (eds), *Contemporary Political Studies*, Volume 1 (PSA: Exeter, 1994), pp.299–313.

Arter, David, 'Suomen Eurooppa-politiikka – unionistista steppiä vai kansallista tangoa?', *Ulkopolitiikka*, **1**, 1994, pp.18–26.

Arter, David, 'Estonia after the March 1995 Riigikogu Election: Still an Anti-Party System?', *The Journal of Communist Studies and Transition Politics*, **11**, (3), September 1995, pp.249–271.

Arter, David, 'Beetham's 1, 9, 18, 27 and 30 or Will Finland be a "net democratic contributor" to the European Union?', in Lovenduski, Joni and Stanyer Jeffrey (eds), *Contemporary Political Studies 1995*, Volume Two (Political Studies Association of the United Kingdom: Exeter, 1995), pp.799–807.

Arter, David, 'The Finnish Social Democrats Storm Back', *West European Politics*, **18**, (4), 1995, pp.194–204.

Beetham, David, 'Liberal Democracy and the Limits of Democratisation', in David Held (ed.), *Prospects for Democracy*, Special Issue of *Political Studies*, **XL**, 1992, pp.40–53.

Beetham, David (ed.), *Defining and Measuring Democracy* (Sage: London–Thousand Oaks–New Delhi, 1994).

Bennett, A.G.G., 'The Operation of the Estonian Currency Board', *IMF Staff Papers*, **40**, (2), 1993, pp.451–70.

Bjorklund, Tor, 'The Green Orientation among Estonians compared with Scandinavians', paper presented at the WAPOR Regional Seminar, Tallinn 11–12 June 1993.

Birch, Sarah, 'The Ukrainian Parliamentary and Presidential Elections of 1994', *Electoral Studies*, **14**, (1), 1995, pp.93–9.

Bremmer, Ian and Ray Taras (eds), *Nations and Politics in the Soviet Successor States* (Cambridge University Press: New York, 1994).

Bruszt, László, '1989: The Negotiated Revolution in Hungary', *Social Research*, **7**, (2), 1990, pp.365–87.

Clark, Terry D., 'The Lithuanian Political Party System: A Case Study of Democratic Consolidation', *East European Politics and Societies*, **9**, (1), 1995, pp.41–61.

Commission on Security and Co-operation in Europe, *Russians in Estonia: Problems and Prospects* (Washington: September 1992).

Council of Europe, 'Report on the Application of the Republic of Estonia for Membership of the Council of Europe', 14 April 1993 (mimeo).

Davies, Philip John and Andrejs Valdis Ozolins, 'The Latvian Parliamentary Election of 1993', *Electoral Studies*, **13**, (1), 1994, pp.83–6.

Deletant, Dennis, 'The Romanian Elections of May 1990', *Representation*, **29**, (108), 1990, pp.23–6.

Diuk, Nadia and Adrian Karatnycky, *New Nations Rising* (Wiley: New York, 1993).

Eesti Konjunktuuriinstitut, *Market of Baltic States* (Tallinn: 1994) no publisher given.

Fane, Daria, 'Moldova: breaking loose from Moscow', in Ian Bremmer and Ray Taras (eds), *Nations and Politics in the Soviet Successor States*, (Cambridge University Press: New York, 1994), pp.121–53.

Fink-Hafner, Danica, 'Political Modernization in Slovenia in the 1980s and the early 1990s', *The Journal of Communist Studies*, **8**, (4), 1992, pp.210–26.

Fink-Hafner, Danica, 'Anti-Party Sentiment in a Context of Democratic Transition. Slovenia in Comparison to other Post-Socialist Countries', European Consortium of Political Research, Madrid 17–22 April 1994.

Flanagan, Scott C. and Russell J. Dalton, 'Parties Under Stress: Realignment and Dealignment in Advanced Industrial Democracies', *West European Politics*, **7**, (1), 1984, pp.7–23.

Flickinger, Richard S. and Donley T. Studlar, 'The Disappearing Voters? Exploring Declining Turn-out in West European Elections', *West European Politics*, **15**, (2), 1992, pp.1–16.

Gaidys, Vladas and Danute Tureikyte, 'Political Preferences in Lithuania, 1989–1992', *Emor*, **3**, (3), 1992, pp.19–22.

Gallagher, Tom, 'Regional Nationalism and Party System Change:

Italy's Northern League', *West European Politics*, **16**, (4), 1993, pp.616–21.

Gerlach, P. *et al.* (eds), *Regimewechsel, Demokratisierung und Politische Kultur in Ost-Mitteleuropa* (Böhlau: Vienna, 1992).

Griffiths, Stephen Iwan, *Nationalism and Ethnic Conflict* (Oxford University Press: Oxford, 1993).

Harmel, Robert and Lars Svåsand, 'Party Leadership and Party Institutionalisation: Three Phases of Development', *West European Politics*, **16**, (2), 1993, pp.67–88.

Henderson, Karen, 'Divisive Political Agendas: the Case of Czechoslovakia', in Dunleavy and Stanyer (eds), *Contemporary Political Studies* (1994), op. cit., pp.407–419.

Høyer, Svennik, Epp Lauk and Peeter Vihalemm (eds), *Towards a Civic Society: The Baltic Media's Long Road to Freedom* (Nota Baltica: Tartu, 1993).

Iivonen, Jyrki, 'Viron kansallisesta itsemääräämisestä', *Politiikka*, **3**, 1990, pp.188–93.

Ilves, Toomas Hendrik, 'Reaction: The Intermovement in Estonia', in Jan Arveds Trapans (ed.), *Toward Independence: The Baltic Popular Movements* (Westview: Boulder–San Francisco–Oxford, 1991), pp.71–83.

Information Department of the Royal Institute of International Affairs, *The Baltic States: A Survey of the Political and Economic Structure and the Foreign Relations of Estonia, Latvia and Lithuania* (Greenwood: Westport, Connecticut, 1970).

International Foundation for Electoral Systems, 'Republic of Estonia. An Assessment of the Election to the Riigikogu and the Presidency', unpublished report on a visit between 16 and 24 September 1992.

Jänes, Kärt (ed.), *Tundmatu Eesti Vabariik* (Jaan Tônissoni Institut: Tallinn, 1993).

Kallas, Siim, 'Pros and Cons of the Reintroduction of the Estonian Kroon', in *Conference on the Reintroduction of the Estonian Kroon June 18, 1993* (Eesti Pank: 1993), pp.8–20.

Karasimeonov, Georgi, 'The Parliamentary Elections of 1994 and the Development of the Bulgarian Party System', paper given at a conference on 'Party Politics in the Year 2000', University of Manchester, 13–15 January 1995.

Kasekamp, Andres, 'The Estonian Veterans' League: A Fascist Movement?', *Journal of Baltic Studies*, **XXIV**, (3), 1993, pp. 259–65.

Katz, Richard S., 'Party as linkage: A vestigial function?', *European Journal of Political Research*, **18**, (1), 1990, pp.143–63.

Katz, Richard S. and Peter Mair, 'The Cross-National Study of Party Organizations', in Katz and Mair (eds), *Party Organizations: A Data*

Handbook on Party Organizations in Western Democracies 1960–1990 (Sage: London–Newbury Park–New Delhi, 1992), pp.4–6.

Kiin Sirje, Rein Ruutsoo and Andres Tarand, *Neljankymmenen kirje* (Otava: Keuruu, 1990).

Kirby, David, *The Baltic World 1772–1993 Europe's Northern Periphery in an Age of Change* (Longman: London and New York, 1995).

Kitschelt, Herbert, 'The Formation of Party Systems in East Central Europe', *Politics and Society*, **20**, (1), 1992, pp.7–50.

Kivirahk Juhan, Rain Rosimannus and Indrek Pajumaa, 'The Premises for Democracy: A Study of Political Values in Post-Independent Estonia', *Journal of Baltic Studies*, **XXI**, (2), 1993, pp.149–60.

Klíma, Michel, 'The Emergence of a Czech Party System', paper given at a conference on 'Party Politics in the Year 2000', University of Manchester, 13–15 January 1995.

Krawchenko, Bohdan, 'Ukraine: the politics of independence', in Ian Bremmer and Ray Taras (eds), *Nations and Politics in the Soviet Successor States* (Cambridge University Press: New York, 1994).

Krikus, Richard, 'Lithuania: nationalism in the modern era', in Ian Bremmer and Ray Taras (eds), *Nations and Politics in the Soviet Successor States* (Cambridge University Press: New York, 1994), pp.157–81.

Kukk, Mare, 'Political Oppression in Soviet Estonia 1940–1987', *Journal of Baltic Studies*, **XXIV**, (4), 1993, pp.369–82.

Kuokkanen, Marjut, 'Puolueiden muodostaminen Virossa', *Ulkopolitiikka*, **4**, 1991, pp.47–56.

Kuokkanen, Marjut, *Puolueiden muotoutuminen Virossa 1988–1992* (Politiikan tutkimuksen laitoksen tutkimuksia (Research Report 127: Tampereen yliopisto, 1994).

Kuzio, Taras, 'The Multi-Party System in Ukraine on the Eve of Elections: Identity Problems, Conflicts and Solutions', *Government and Opposition*, **29**, (1), 1994, pp.109–27.

Laaman, Eduard, *Erakonnad Eestis. Sissejuhatus Poliitikasse IV* (Eesti Kirjanduse Seltsi kirjastus: Tartu, 1934).

Lauristin Marju, Peeter Vihalemm and Rein Ruutsoo, *Viron vapauden tuulet* (Gummerus: Jyväskylä–Helsinki, 1989).

Lawson, Kay, 'When Linkage Fails', in Kay Lawson and Peter H. Merkl, *When Parties Fail: Emerging Alternative Organisations* (Princeton University: Princeton, 1988).

Lentini, Peter, 'Political Parties and Movements in the Commonwealth of Independent States', *Lorton Paper 7* (Lorton House, 1992).

Lewis, Paul G., 'Democratisation in Eastern Europe', *Coexistence*, **27**, 1990, pp.245–67.

Lewis, Paul, 'Democracy and its Future in Eastern Europe', in David Held (ed.), *Prospects for Democracy* (Polity: Oxford, 1992).

Lieven, Anatol, *The Baltic Revolution: Estonia, Latvia, Lithuania and the Path to Independence* (Yale University: New Haven–London, 1993).

Lobjakas, Ahto, 'Emerging multi-party system and public opinion in Estonia 1989–1991', *Emor Reports*, 1, (1), 1989, pp.7–11.

Lobjakas, Ahto, 'Six Years of Political Pluralism in Estonia', *Emor Reports*, 2, (4), 1992, pp.10–13.

Lomax, Bill, 'Impediments to Democratization in East-Central Europe', in Gordon Wightman (ed.), *Party Formation in East-Central Europe* (Edward Elgar: Aldershot, 1995).

Made, Tiit, *Mu Isamaa*, Viron toivo ja pelko (Kirjayhtymä: Helsinki, 1988).

Mägi, Artur, *Das Staatsleben Estlands während seiner Selbständigkeit* (Almqvist & Wiksell: Uppsala, 1967).

McHale, Vincent E., 'Historical Estonia, 1917–1940', in Vincent E. McHale and Sharon Skowronski (eds), *Political Parties of Europe* (Greenwood: Westport, Connecticut–London, 1973).

McSweeney, Dean and Clive Tempest, 'The Political Science of Democratic Transition in Eastern Europe', *Political Studies*, XLI, 1993, pp.408–19.

Melliss, C.L. and M. Cornelius, *New Currencies in the Former Soviet Union: a Recipe for Hyperinflation or the Path to Price Stability?* (Bank of England, Working Paper Series 26, 1994).

Millard, Frances, *Poland: A Party System in Transition*, Lorton Paper 6, (Lorton House, 1991).

Millard, Frances, 'Nationalism in Poland, 1989–93', paper presented at a conference on 'Integration and Disintegration in Contemporary Europe', Gregynog Conference Centre, Central Wales, 28 October 1993.

Miller, Bill, Stephen White, Paul Heywood and Matthew Wyman, 'Democratic, Market and Nationalist Values in Russia and East Europe: December 1993', paper presented at the Political Studies Association Annual Conference, Swansea, 29–31 March 1994.

Motyl, Alexander J., *Dilemma of Independence: Ukraine after Totalitarianism* (Council on Foreign Relations: New York, 1993).

Muizneks, Nils, 'Latvia: origins, evolution and triumph', in Ian Bremmer and Ray Taras (eds), *Nations and Politics in the Soviet Successor States* (Cambridge University Press: New York, 1994, pp.192–94).

Müller-Rommel, Ferdinand and Geoffrey Pridham (eds), *Small Parties in Western Europe: Comparative and National Perspectives* (Sage: London–New Delhi, 1991).

Newall, James L. and Martin J. Bull, 'The Italian Referendum of April 1993: Real Change at Last?', *West European Politics*, 16, (4), 1993, pp.607–15.

Olljum, Alar and Mare Kukk, 'Regional Co-operation in the Baltic

Sea Area: The Council of the Baltic Sea States', in *Council of the Baltic Sea States* (Multipress: Tallinn, 1994), pp.14–18.

Parming, Tönu, *The Collapse of Liberal Democracy and the Rise of Authoritarianism in Estonia* (Sage: London–Beverly Hills, 1975).

Poznanski, Kazimierz, 'An Interpretation of Communist Decay: The Role of Evolutionary Mechanisms', *Communist and Post-Communist Studies*, **26**, (1), 1993, pp.3–24.

Pridham, Geoffrey, 'Politial Actors, Linkages and Interactions: Democratic Consolidation in Southern Europe', *West European Politics*, **13**, (4), 1990, pp.103–17.

Rauch, Georg von, *The Baltic States: Estonia, Latvia, Lithuania: The Years of Independence 1917–1940* (Hurst: London, 1974).

Raun, Toivo U., *Estonia and the Estonians* (Hoover: Stanford California, 1991).

Raun, Toivo U., 'The Re-establishment of Estonian Independence', *Journal of Baltic Studies*, **XXII**, (3), 1991, pp.251–8.

Raun, Toivo U., 'Post-Soviet Estonia 1991–1993', *Journal of Baltic Studies*, **XXV**, (1), 1994, pp.72–9.

Reiter, Howard L., 'The Rise of the "New Agenda" and the Decline of Partisanship', *West European Politics*, **16**, (2), 1993.

Rodin, Michael, 'Political Trust in Baltic States', paper presented at the Political Studies Association Annual Conference, Swansea, 29–31 March 1994.

Rose, Richard, Mobilizing Demobilized Voters in Post-Communist Societies', *Party Politics*, **1**, 4, pp.549–563.

Rosimannus, Rain, 'State-power and public confidence in Estonia 1985–91', *Emor Reports*, **1**, (1), 1991, pp.14–18.

Rosimannus, Rain, Do the People Trust the Authorities?', *Emor Reports*, **2**, (4), 1992, pp.5–10.

Ruutsoo, Rein, 'Transitional Society and Social Movements in Estonia', *Estonian Academy of Sciences, Humanities and Social Sciences*, **42**, (2), 1993.

Ruzza, Carlo E. and Oliver Schmidtke, 'Roots of Success of the Lega Lombarda: Mobilisation Dynamics and the Media', *West European Politics*, **16**, (2), 1993.

Schmitt, Hermann, 'On Party Attachment in Western Europe and the Utility of Eurobarometer Data', *West European Politics*, **12**, (2), 1989, pp.122–39.

Seton-Watson, Hugh, *Eastern Europe Between the Wars 1918–1941*, (Westview: Boulder–London, 1986).

Silva, Stephen J., 'The SDP in Eastern Germany after Unification', *West European Politics*, **16**, (2), 1993, pp.24–48.

Smith, Graham (ed.), *The Baltic States The National Self-Determination of Estonia, Latvia and Lithuania* (Macmillan: London, 1994).

Swain, Nigel, 'Hungary's New Political Parties', *Lorton Paper 5* (Lorton House: 1991).

Sztompka, Piotr, 'The Intangibles and Imponderables of the Transition to Democracy', *Studies in Comparative Communism*, **XXIV**, (3), 1991, pp.245–311.

Taagepera, Rein, 'A Note on the March 1989 Election in Estonia', *Soviet Studies*, **42**, (2), 1990, pp.329–39.

Taagepera, Rein, 'The Baltic States', in a special issue on 'Elections in Eastern Europe', *Electoral Studies*, **9**, (4), 1990.

Taagepera, Rein, 'The History of a Document: A Broad Plan for a Small Nation: "Thirty"', *Journal of Baltic Studies*, **XXIII**, (3), 1992, pp.261–82.

Taagepera, Rein, *Estonia. Return to Independence* (Westview: Boulder–San Francisco–Oxford, 1993).

Taagepera, Rein, 'Running for President of Estonia: A Political Scientist in Politics', *Political Science and Politics*, June 1993, pp.302–4.

Taggart, Paul and Anders Widfeldt, '1990s Flash Party Organisation: The Case of New Democracy in Sweden', paper given at the Political Studies Association annual conference, University of Leicester 20–22 April 1993.

Unwin, Tim, 'Agrarian change and integrated rural development in a policy vacuum: the case of Estonia', *European Urban and Regional Studies*, **1**, (2), 1994, pp.180–85.

Urban, Michael and Zaprudnik Jan, 'Belarus: a long road to nationhood', in Ian Bremmer and Ray Taras (eds), *Nations and Politics in the Soviet Successor States*, (Cambridge University Press: New York, 1994).

Vardys, V. Stanley, 'Democracy in the Baltic States 1918–1934: The Stage and the Actors', *Journal of Baltic Studies*, **X**, (4), 1979, pp.320–36.

Von Beyme, Klaus, *Transition to Democracy in Eastern Europe* (Macmillan: London, 1996).

Waller, Michael, 'From Mobilising Dissent to Aggregating Interests in Eastern Europe',*The Journal of Communist Studies*, **8**, (1), 1992.

Waller, Michael, 'Groups, Interests and Political Aggregation in East Central Europe', *The Journal of Communist Studies*, pp. 128–47.

Wightman, Gordon, 'The June 1990 Elections in Czechoslovakia: A Plebiscite for Democracy', *Representation*, **29**, (108), 1990, pp.18–22.

Wightman, Gordon (ed.), *Party Formation in East-Central Europe* (Edward Elgar: Aldershot, 1995).

Wilson and Bilous, 'Political parties in Ukraine', *Soviet Studies*, **4**, 1993, pp.693.

Zaprudnik, Jan, *Belarus: At a Crossroads in History* (Westview: Boulder–San Francisco–Oxford, 1993).

Zboril, Zdenek, 'Impediments to the Development of Democratic Politics: a Czech Perspective', in Gordon Wightman (ed.), *Party Formation in East-Central Europe*, Edward Elgar: Aldershot, 1995, pp.202–16.

Index